A Textual History of the Coptic Wedding Rite

Meena Abdou

A Textual History of the Coptic Wedding Rite

Copyright © 2026 by Agora University Press
All rights reserved. Printed in the United States of America. No part of this book may be used or reproduced in any manner whatsoever without written permission except in the case of brief quotations embodied in critical articles or reviews.
For information contact: aupress@agora.edu
Agora University Press: press.agora.edu
ISBN 978-1-950831-49-4
Printed in the United States of America

HIS HOLINESS POPE TAWADROS II
118th Pope and Patriarch of the great city of Alexandria and the See of St. Mark

HIS HOLINESS PATRIARCH IGNATIUS APHREM II
Patriarch of Antioch and All the East

Table of Contents

Introduction v

Chapter 1: The 14th Century – Ibn Kabar 1

Chapter 2: The 15th Century – Pope Gabriel V 13

Chapter 3: The 19th Century – Hegumen Philotheos Ibrahim 33

Chapter 4: The 20th Century 51

Chapter 5: Reconstructing the Rite 67

Chapter 6: The Fully Restored Rite 77

Chapter 7: Conclusion 183

Bibliography 185

Appendix A: Translation of Ibn Kabar 187

Appendix B: Translation of Pope Gabriel 191

Appendix C: Translation of the Holy Synod's Decree 199

Appendix D: A Comparison Table of all the Versions of the Rite 201

Appendix E: A Wedding Sermon by Hegumen Philotheos Ibrahim ... 215

Introduction

The Coptic Orthodox Church is one of the ancient churches in the world. One rite that has changed dramatically over time is that of the wedding. Perhaps no other rite has been so affected by environmental and sociocultural factors. This is an interesting topic to examine the evolution of rites that have a high degree of participation from laity. This book is about the history of the wedding rite in the Coptic Orthodox Church from the earliest documented sources to current times.

First, it is important to review why this rite in particular is so subject to change. Historically, most people only got one chance at a wedding. Virginity prior to marriage was the norm and men and women did not spend time with each other, as in modern day dating, outside of marriage. Therefore, when someone was approaching marriage, they would spend a lot of time preparing for their new life by learning how to live with the opposite sex. Not a lot of time was spent teaching them about the wedding ceremony itself. Furthermore, separation was rare. The Coptic Orthodox Church forbids divorce except in the case of adultery, so for most people, the wedding was a unique unrepeatable life event. It was the one time in a person's life in which they got to spend lavish amounts of money on a big party. Even then, only the wealthy were able to afford opulent festivities. Most people had simple post-nuptial celebrations in their homes that might or might not have continued for multiple days. Over time, as people moved into the middle class, and the wedding industry took shape, certain practices were adopted across the board. Many things were commoditized, and it became possible for everyone to conduct their wedding however they wanted.

In current times there is a lot of customization that goes into a wedding. It is not always done in a Coptic church. This could be due to capacity limitations, location requirements, or aesthetic preferences. Some people like the look of a specific building, which may or may not be built according to the Coptic style or may not be a church at all. Weddings are no longer community or neighborhood oriented. Not everyone in the parish is automatically invited. The prayers themselves are said inconsistently. It is now common for couples to print their own booklets for the ceremony. Even with those booklets in hand, a lot of parts are skipped due to various reasons such as saving time, the familiarity of the available deacons with the hymns, and the preferences of the bride and groom. Everybody wants their wedding to be special. Popular belief is that the bride and groom have full control over who says what and when during the ceremony. There is even confusion caused by the many different versions of the rite available in print. It is easier to control what is said by omitting something than by including it with a note saying it should be skipped. This has led to each bride and groom printing their own booklets with only those prayers they want said, and in many cases even those prayers are only printed in the desired language. A couple will typically borrow the booklet from their friend's wedding instead of starting with an official base edition. The central authority tasked with defining the official text of any rite within the Coptic Church is the Coptic Holy Synod's Subcommittee for Rituals and Hymns. However, anyone anywhere can publish their own book and call it official. The subcommittee can only review what is published and give or deny a stamp of approval, provided the publisher even asks for the subcommittee's review. It cannot prevent the publication from happening. Furthermore, the subcommittee does not meet very frequently as its members consist of bishops who have other duties. A wedding officiated with some of the prayers skipped is certainly not invalid. Therefore, there is nothing to disincentivize publication and use without the subcommittee's approval. The white wedding is the de facto standard now even though historically that was not true. This has led to adopting other practices like flower girls, ring bearers, paired bridesmaids and groomsmen, the father giving the bride away, revealing dresses, tuxedos, as well as reception traditions like the first dance, father/daughter dance, mother/son dance, etc. As people conform to standards projected by mass media and industry conventions, the spirituality of the rite gets lost and practices are adopted without understanding.

The main challenge for a wedding from a sacramental theological perspective is that people want to celebrate and have fun, but the Church also wants to maintain spiritual decorum that is consistent with her beliefs. Marriage is both a sacrament and a rite of passage in which people finally become adults through the marital union. There is always tension between those who want to celebrate in a worldly way and those who want to keep it holy. How can the Church balance correct ritual practice with popular devotions? How can the Church maintain control over the practice of her rituals in an environment in which people like doing things their own way?

The changes that occurred to the wedding rite were never well defined or explained. As is always the case with ritual change, and as this study further proves, changes were made in practice by the people first before becoming official canon. The changes were not made for any theological reason. The tension between official church order and popular practice is evident throughout the literature. People will always follow the dominant culture, especially when a given rite is not practiced very frequently per person. The fact that most people will ever only have one wedding means that they would rather do it their way then the Church's way absent a true understanding of the spirituality of the rite. Rites should help clarify theology and understanding and be engaging for most people.

Structure of this Book

In this book, I go through the different versions of the rite through the historical and contemporary sources. The historical sources I examine are *The Lamp that Enlightens the Darkness in Clarifying the Service* by the priest Shams al-Ri'āsah Ibn al-Shaykh al-As'ad Abū al-Barakāt Ibn Kabar, *The Ritual Ordo* of Pope Gabriel V, and *The Dignified Rank of Crowning* by Hegumen Philotheos Ibrahim. The contemporary sources are *The Coptic Offices for the Coptic Orthodox Church Part II* by Fr. Markos Hanna and *The Essentials in the Deacon's Service* by Albair Gamal Mikhail. I did not use *al-Majmū' al-Ṣafawī* by al-Ṣafī Ibn al-'Assāl because it does not talk about the rite itself, just the rules about marriage eligibility. Normally such a study would be indexed by the parts of the rite. But I found that there are incompatible changes that occurred in this rite that make such a layout undesirable. Therefore, I present each author's version separately. In each version, I compare the actors involved in the rite, where they stand, what they wear, what is said by whom, and with what tune. When presenting hymns, I include the languages that appear in the source. If the source included Coptic only, then I only present the Coptic. If the source included Coptic and an Arabic translation, then I include both Coptic and Arabic. In all cases, I provide my own English translation. If the text is the same from one source to another, I do not repeat the Coptic or Arabic text. I refer to the hymn by the first few words of its English translation. At the end of the book, I present the full text of all prayers and hymns in Coptic, Arabic, and English in a reconstruction of the full original rite with all spelling and grammatical errors corrected.

This book is focused on the rite of first marriage in the Coptic Orthodox Church as seen through the published texts. It does not cover related topics such as rules for who can marry whom, engagement, dowry practices, loosening of the girdle, removal of the crowns, second marriage, grounds for divorce or annulment, or a comparison with the wedding rite in other Churches. I acknowledge that there are many variables to examine in studying the place of matrimony in Christian tradition, theology, and history. The focus of this study is to determine what the full text of the rite should be. A more complete picture may be created by doing a deeper historical analysis of how that text came to be, by comparing practices in various regions within Egypt as well as comparing those with the rite in other Churches, along with a theological analysis. However, those topics are best fit for their own studies.

Definitions of Musical Tunes

The Coptic Church is distinguished by the fact that it does not have a standard notation scheme for its music. Instead, musical tunes are categorized in various ways. The most common category is the liturgical season. But there are some hymns whose tune never changes throughout the year. Other hymns do not align to a particular season but borrow the tune of another hymn. It is common in the literature to encounter a direction to say a hymn "in its known tune" without specifying what that tune is. To avoid confusion throughout the book, I define all the tunes in this section first along with links to examples that demonstrate them. I will refer to each tune by the naming convention presented here instead of how it appeared in the source material. This list is reflective of contemporary musical parlance found in the Coptic Church today.

The first category of tune is that which is aligned to the season. There are five seasonal tunes: Annual, Advent, Lenten, Palm Sunday, and Festal. These tunes are used for antiphonal singing and some liturgical responses. The Palm Sunday tune was originally used during the Feast of the Cross, and it was originally named the Tune of the Cross. But recently it is more popularly known as the Palm Sunday tune so I will refer to it as such throughout this book. For an example of the Palm Sunday tune, see http://tasbeha.org/hymn_library/view/1462?mid=10235. For a longer version of it, see http://tasbeha.org/hymn_library/view/1452?mid=10239. The Festal tune is used in all Lordly feasts and weddings. For an example of this tune, see http://tasbeha.org/hymn_library/view/1043?mid=9349.

The second category is that of readings. There is a different tune for each kind of reading: Pauline Epistle, Catholic Epistle, Acts, Psalm, and Gospel. The Pauline Epistle has annual, paschal, and festal tunes. The Catholic Epistle only has one tune. The Acts has annual and paschal tunes. The Psalm has the following tunes: annual, advent, paschal, festal. The Gospel has annual and paschal tunes. Nowadays, the only readings that are sung at weddings are the Psalm and Gospel. Obviously, neither of them would be sung in their paschal tunes during a wedding. For an example of the Psalm annual tune, see http://tasbeha.org/hymn_library/view/460?mid=9134. For an example of the Psalm festal tune, see http://tasbeha.org/hymn_library/view/239?mid=9446. For an example of the Gospel annual tune, see http://tasbeha.org/hymn_library/view/464?mid=9145.

A Textual History of the Coptic Wedding Rite

Finally, there are tunes that do not change with the season. These may be said at any time and with any text. The first is called the Morning Doxology tune. This is used for the Morning Doxology during Matins Praise as well as during glorification services for saints. For an example of the Morning Doxology tune, see http://tasbeha.org/hymn_library/view/485?mid=10812. The second does not have an official name and usually goes by the name Axios tune because the hymn that uses this tune the most is that of Axios. It is used when making proclamations of worthiness such as during ordinations, glorifications of saints (tamjīd [تمجيد]), or other sacramental prayers. For an example of the Axios tune, see http://tasbeha.org/hymn_library/view/700?mid=10180. The last tune is called muḥayyar [محير]. This is an Arabic word that means confounded or bewildered. This tune was called so by the literature because it appears to have no common identifier. It is said throughout the liturgical year and with a variety of texts. So it is not tied to any one season or any one hymn in particular. It is a general tune that can be used whenever desired. For an example of the muḥayyar tune, see http://tasbeha.org/hymn_library/view/697?mid=10186.

CHAPTER 1

The 14th Century – Ibn Kabar

Biography

The first source comes from al-Shaykh al-Mu'taman Shams al-Ri'āsah Ibn al-Shaykh al-As'ad Abū al-Barakāt Ibn Kabar. He was born into a wealthy family and mastered Coptic and Arabic. He became a secretary to the Mamluk minister Baybars al-Manṣūrī and helped edit the latter's work *Quintessence of Thought in Muslim History [Zubdat al-fikrah fī Tārīkh al-Hijrah]*. Despite his high position, he decided to retire in 1293 during a wave of persecution against the Copts. At that time, Sultan al-Ashraf Khalīl (1290-1292) issued a decree ordering the dismissal of all Coptic officials from public service unless they converted to Islam. After leaving the government, Ibn Kabar devoted all his time to studies and literary production in the fields of theology, history, and linguistics. Around the year 1300, his fame as a man of religion spread among the Coptic community, and he was nominated to be the priest of the historic church of the Virgin Mary known as The Hanging Church (al-Mu'allaqah) in Old Cairo, which was the seat of the patriarchate and the most important religious center in Egypt at that time. In the year 1321, another wave of Islamic persecution swept the Copts. The Muslim mob sought after Ibn Kabar but he was able to successfully evade them. It is said that Baybars al-Manṣūrī, his old sponsor, extended his protection to the great scholar and kept him hidden until his death on May 10, 1324.[1]

---

[1] Aziz Atiya, *Claremont Coptic Encyclopedia*, s.v. "Ibn Kabar," https://ccdl.claremont.edu/digital/collection/cce/id/1049

It is assumed that in the seclusion of these last three or four years of his life, he was able to edit and finalize his monumental works.

Description of His Work

His most important work is *The Lamp that Enlightens the Darkness in Clarifying the Service [Miṣbāḥ al-ẓulmah fī Īḍāḥ al-khidmah]*. It is preserved in multiple manuscripts dating from the 1330s to the 1340s.[2] It was written as an encyclopedic observation of the contemporary practices and not as an instructional manual for clergy. So it does not include everything that could possibly go on during a service. It only includes what is said or sung. In many cases, it does not mention the tune. It does not include things that were so common as to not need documentation. Its oldest manuscript is BnF Arabe 203. The rite of the wedding is described in chapter 20. I used this manuscript along with another version published in Egypt[3] to translate the relevant pieces of that chapter in Appendix A.

Description of the Rite

Ibn Kabar refers to the wedding rite as the contract of properties or 'aqd al-amlāk [عقد الاملاك]. The first word, 'aqd, means contract or covenant. The second word, amlāk, means properties or possessions. The whole term reveals that the nature of the wedding rite was centered around the signing of the marital contract. The word amlāk probably referred to the possessions or gifts that would be transferred to the new couple by the families. Ibn Kabar calls the full name of the wedding rite al-iklīl al-shar'ī wa al-'Aqd al-kanasī [أالاكليل الشرعي و العقد الكنسي].[4] This translates in

---

[2] Ibid.
[3] Salama Salama, ed. *Miṣbāḥ al-ẓulmah fī Īḍāḥ al-khidmah: by Shams al-Ri'āsah Abū al-Barakāt Ibn Kabar [The Lamp That Enlightens the Darkness in Clarifying the Service]* (Cairo: Maktabat al-Karūz, 1971), 237.
[4] Appendix A, Section 1.

English to "the legal crowning and the ecclesiastical contract." He uses the words contract, properties, and crowning interchangeably to refer to the whole rite. However, the first part of the rite, prayed only over the groom, is referred to only as the 'aqd al-amlāk [عقد الاملاك], which translates to the "contract of properties", and is often abbreviated to just the "contract." The crowning is the second part and is prayed over both the groom and the bride. Nowadays, the term crowning is used to refer to the whole rite. The crowning is done only if either the bride or the groom is a virgin. If neither of them are virgins, then neither of them receive crowns. In this case, a different ceremony called the second marriage is used. It is similar in structure to the crowning, but the readings and prayers are different, and they are not crowned.

The first thing Ibn Kabar mentions regarding the wedding ceremony is that it should take place in a church. However, this does not seem to have been the norm. It was common to hold the wedding in the house of the groom, immediately followed by the reception in the same place. However, this was never officially allowed by the Church. Ibn Kabar specifically remarks concerning this practice that "the weddings that take place in houses are merely agreements not weddings; therefore, they are considered void."[5] This same injunction against conducting weddings in personal houses would repeat itself throughout the historical literature until the 20th century. It is not hard to see why this practice was so difficult to stop. Homes were the original churches. Church buildings were not built with cafeterias or side buildings like today so there was no place to have a reception or even greet guests. Having the ceremony at the house allowed more people to attend. Most churches were small and inconspicuous due to laws preventing renovation. There was no industry that catered to large festive events like wedding receptions. Any celebration would have to take place in someone's house. The wealthier the family, the bigger house they had and the bigger their party would be. The reception was a local community event in which people in the neighborhood could stop by for a while, congratulate the couple, and

---

[5] Ibid.

leave. It is likely that only the wealthy, urban elite would have lavish receptions while most people just had the wedding at the church with no party afterward.

The next thing Ibn Kabar mentions is that it be done publicly and not in secret. It should be officiated by a priest and a liturgy should be offered at the same time as the wedding. The liturgy is a requirement for a valid marriage as it is what unites the bride and groom into one body.[6] He starts with the groom standing in front of the sanctuary. There is no mention of entrance or procession but that does not mean none took place. The godparents of the groom prepare a tray containing oblation bread (qurbān [قربان]), a cross, the rings, some sugar, and two crowns made of either silver, gold, or green jewels. The priest begins with the Thanksgiving Prayer [Ⲙⲁⲣⲉⲛϣⲉⲡϩⲙⲟⲧ ⲛⲧⲟⲧϥ]. Then the priest raises incense while the people say Psalm 50. The Pauline Epistle is read, first in Coptic, then in Arabic. The Gospel is read from John. Ibn Kabar does not provide a reference for most of the readings. The three great litanies are said, followed by the Creed. Then the priest says four more prayers. The first prayer begins with "O Master and Philanthropic One [Ⲫⲛⲏⲃ ⲡⲓⲙⲁⲓⲣⲱⲙⲓ]." The second prayer begins with "O God who created [Ⲫϯ Ⲫⲏⲉⲧⲁϥⲉⲣⲡⲗⲁⲍⲓⲛ]." The third prayer begins with "O Master Lord [Ⲫⲛⲏⲃ Ⲡⲟⲥ ⲡⲉⲛ]." The fourth prayer begins with "We thank You [Ⲧⲉⲛϣⲉⲡϩⲙⲟⲧ ⲛⲧⲟⲧⲕ]." Then Our Father is said. The priest recites the Absolution of the Son[7] with the cross placed over the groom's head. This is followed by Lord Have Mercy. Then the wedding vestment is brought. Ibn Kabar calls this vestment "the wedding outfit."[8] In Arabic the term is badlat al-'urs [بدلة العرس]. The word badlah means outfit and nowadays it is used to refer to men's suits. However, in this context, it refers to a priestly liturgical vestment. In the Coptic Church's Arabic literature, this vestment is called

---

[6] Ibid.

[7] The Absolution of the Son is the last of three absolution prayers said by the priest at the end of most services. Their full text is included at the end of this book.

[8] Appendix A, Section 2.

burnus [برنس] and in Byzantine terms it is called phelonion. Ibn Kabar mentions that it is better for it to be white.[9] The priest recites over it a prayer beginning with "O Lord Jesus Christ our God [Ⲡⲟⲥ Ⲓⲏⲥ Ⲡⲭⲥ ⲡⲉⲛⲛⲟⲩϯ]." At the end of this prayer, the priest dresses the groom in the vestment and puts his cap ('amāmah [عمامة]) on the groom's head and tightens the girdle (zinār [زنار]) around the groom's waist. During this, the people sing the hymn, "Come see this bride" in the Palm Sunday tune. Ibn Kabar includes these verses for this hymn:

ⲁⲙⲟⲩ ⲧⲉⲕⲛⲁⲩ ⲉⲧⲁⲓϣⲉⲗⲉⲧ ⲉⲧⲁⲩⲥⲉⲗⲥⲟⲗ ⲙⲡⲓϩⲓⲏⲃ ⲁⲥⲉⲣⲫⲟⲣⲓⲛ ⲛⲟⲩⲛⲓϣϯ ⲛⲱⲟⲩ ⲡⲉⲝⲁϥ ⲛϫⲉ ⲡϣⲏⲣⲓ ⲛϯϧⲁⲣⲁⲃⲁⲓ	تعال أنظر هذه العروسة التي زينت للحمل اشتملت بمجد عظيم كقول ابن الرعد	Come see this bride who is adorned for the lamb. She is engulfed in great glory according to the saying of the son of thunder.
Ⲓⲱⲁⲛⲛⲏⲥ ⲡϣⲏⲣⲓ ⲛⲍⲉⲃⲉⲇⲉⲟⲥ ⲉϥⲱϣ ⲉⲃⲟⲗ ⲉϥϫⲱ ⲙⲙⲟⲥ ϫⲉ ⲥⲉⲣⲟⲩⲱⲟⲓⲛⲓ ⲛϫⲉ ⲧⲁⲓϣⲉⲗⲉⲧ ⲡⲁⲣⲁ ⲡⲓⲥⲓⲟⲩ ⲛⲧⲉ ϩⲁⲛⲁⲧⲟⲟⲩⲓ	يوحنا بن زبدي يصرخ و يقول هذه العروسة مضيئة أكثر من كوكب الصباح	John the son of Zebedee cries out and says, "This bride shines more brightly than the stars of the morning.
ⲉⲧⲉ ⲑⲁⲓ ⲧⲉ ⲥⲓⲱⲛ ⲙⲃⲉⲣⲓ ⲧⲡⲟⲗⲓⲥ ⲙⲡⲉⲛⲛⲟⲩϯ ⲧⲉ ⲉⲣⲉ ⲡⲟⲩⲛⲟϥ ⲛⲧⲉ ⲛⲏⲉⲑⲟⲩⲁⲃ ⲧⲏⲣⲟⲩ ϣⲱⲡⲓ ⲛϧⲣⲏⲓ ⲛϧⲏⲧⲥ	هذه صهيون الجديدة مدينة الهنا و فرح جميع القديسين حال فيها	This is the new Zion, the city of our God. The joy of all the saints dwells within her."

The origins of this hymn are explained by Ibn Kabar as follows, "This psali [song] to the Lady [the Virgin Mary] was prepared by a father among the monks of the Monastery of St. Macarius from the cell of Kidrān

---

[9] Other common colors include gold, red, or blue.

[كدران]. The letters of his name are the first letters of its verses."[10] He goes on to say that it is sung with candles and a procession. They process the groom to just outside the sanctuary to where the crowning will happen. In Coptic architecture, the solea[11] extends much farther out from the iconostasis than in Byzantine churches and includes enough room for the lectern and two choirs on each side. Coptic literature calls it the First Chorus or the Chorus of the Deacons. It is also usually fenced off from the congregation, making it most like a Western chancel. This is where weddings and ordinations take place. They sing the concluding canon[12] of the first part. But he does not include the text of the concluding canon. At this point, the groom is dressed like a priest. He is wearing all priestly vestments except the tunic. He even dons the officiating priest's own cap. Clearly the groom is meant to symbolize a priest, which would mean that, just as a priest is wedded to his church, the groom is the priest of his household. Together with his wife and potential future children, they form their own branch of the Church.

Ibn Kabar calls the second part "the prayer of the wedding and crowning after the contract [صلاة الزواج و الاكليل بعد العقد]."[13] It starts with bride and groom already standing in front of the sanctuary with a broad white cloth covering both their heads. Again, there is no mention of processions, hymns, or how the bride got there. The priest starts with the Thanksgiving Prayer. The people say Psalm 50. Then the Pauline Epistle is read from Ephesians. The Psalm is read from Psalm 18 and the Gospel from Matthew 40 beginning with "And after Jesus completed these sayings." After the readings, the Supplications beginning with "O Lord

---

[10] Ibid.
[11] Solea, or soleas, a Greek word meaning bottom, as in the sole of a shoe, refers to the floor of the sanctuary.
[12] In the Coptic Church, a concluding canon is a hymn consisting of a set of verses that summarize the occasion of the day. It is said just before the priest gives the final benediction and dismissal. There are various concluding canons for each liturgical occasion (fasts, feasts, regular days, funerals, weddings, etc). Its Byzantine equivalent is the Apolytikon Troparion.
[13] Appendix A, Section 3.

God the Pantocrator the Being [Ⲡⲟⲥ Ⲫϯ ⲡⲓⲡⲁⲛⲧⲟⲕⲣⲁⲧⲱⲣ ⲫⲏⲉⲧϣⲟⲡ]" are said facing West toward the couple. At the end of every supplication, the people say Amen. Presumably they were said in Coptic because after this, Ibn Kabar says the supplications may then be translated. "It is better to say them in Arabic, with only three or four of them in Coptic."[14] This was probably an effort to make the ceremony reflect the vernacular. Then they pray the three great litanies followed by the Creed. This is followed by another four prayers. They are said facing the groom. If he was standing directly in front of the sanctuary, then this would be due West. But if he was standing to the side of the sanctuary then it would be either North or South. Since this part of the rite only involved the groom, it is likely he would stand directly in front of the sanctuary and directly behind the priest, like a priest's ordination. The first prayer begins with "O God who exists before all ages [Ⲫϯ ⲫⲏⲉⲧϣⲟⲡ ⲫⲏⲉⲑⲙⲏⲛ ⲉⲃⲟⲗ ϣⲁ ⲉⲛⲉϩ]." The second prayer begins with "O Lord our God the Creator [Ⲡⲟⲥ ⲡⲉⲛⲛⲟⲩϯ ⲫⲣⲉϥⲥⲱⲛⲧ]." The third prayer begins with "O Lord our God the Great [Ⲡⲟⲥ ⲡⲉⲛⲛⲟⲩϯ ⲡⲓⲛⲓϣϯ]." The fourth prayer is labeled a prayer of submission and begins with "Lend your ear [Ⲣⲉⲕ ⲙⲉⲕⲙⲁϣϫ]." It is said facing East.

Then the priest says the Prayer of the Oil beginning with "O Master Lord God the Pantocrator [Ⲫⲛⲏⲃ Ⲡⲟⲥ Ⲫϯ ⲡⲓⲡⲁⲛⲧⲟⲕⲣⲁⲧⲱⲣ]." The priest anoints couple on the forehead and both sides of the hands while saying "O Lord God of powers [Ⲡⲟⲥ Ⲫϯ ⲛⲧⲉ ⲛⲓϫⲟⲙ]." During the anointing, the people chant the following verses. Ibn Kabar provides all but the last verse in Coptic along with an Arabic translation. The verses come from various bible verses. The tune is not specified. Once again, all the text shown here and throughout is exactly what is in the original source. All spelling and grammatical errors are corrected in the last section of this book.

---

[14] Appendix A, Section 4.

ⲁⲕⲑⲟϩⲥ ⲛⲧⲁ ⲁⲫⲉ ⲛⲟⲩⲛⲉϩ ⲡⲉⲕϫⲱ ⲁϥⲧⲁϩⲉ ⲛⲑⲉⲛⲧⲉ ⲡⲉⲧⲁⲙⲁϩⲧ	دهنت رأسي بالزيت وكأسك اسكرني كالصرف	You have anointed my head with oil and your cup intoxicated me (Ps. 23:5)
ⲉⲣⲉⲡⲉⲕⲛⲁⲓ ⲛⲁⲫⲟⲧ ⲛⲥⲟⲓ ⲛⲛⲓⲉϩⲟⲟⲩ ⲧⲏⲣⲟⲩ ⲛⲧⲉ ⲡⲁⲱⲛϧ	رحمتك يطلباني كل ايام حياتي	Your mercy shall seek me all the days of my life (Ps. 23:6)
ϩⲁⲛⲉⲑⲛⲟⲥ ⲧⲏⲣⲟⲩ ⲙⲡⲕⲁϩⲓ ⲛⲁⲉⲣⲙⲁⲕⲁⲣⲓⲍⲓⲛ ⲙⲙⲟⲓ	كل أمم الارض يغبطوني	All the nations of the earth bless me (Lk. 1:48)
ⲡⲁⲗⲁⲟⲥ ⲧⲏⲣϥ ⲛⲁϫⲟⲥ ϫⲉ ⲉⲥⲉϣⲱⲡⲓ ⲉⲥⲉϣⲱⲡⲓ	و الشعب كانوا يقولوا يكون يكون	All my people say may it be may it be
ⲁⲕϭⲓⲥⲓ ⲛⲟⲩⲥⲱⲧⲡ ϩⲓ ⲡⲁⲗⲁⲟⲥ	ارتفعت مختارا في شعبي	You have increased in choice among my people (Ps. 89:19)
ⲁⲓϫⲓⲙⲓ ⲛⲇⲁⲩⲓⲇ ⲡⲓϩⲙϩⲁⲗ ⲁⲓⲑⲟϩⲥ ⲙⲟϥ ϩⲓ ⲡⲁⲛⲉϩ ⲉϥⲟⲩⲁⲃ ⲧⲁϫⲓϫ ⲁⲩⲱ ⲡⲁϫⲫⲟ ⲛⲁϯϫⲟⲙ ⲛⲁϥ	وجدت داود عبدي فدهنته بالدهن المقدس و ان يدي تساعده و ذراعي تعضده	I found David my servant so I anointed him with the holy oil. My hand and my arm shall strengthen him. (Ps. 89:20,21)
ⲁ ⲡⲟⲥ ϫⲱ ⲙⲡⲉϥⲁⲅⲅⲉⲗⲟⲥ ⲁϥⲟⲗⲧ ⲉⲃⲟⲗ ϧⲉⲛ ⲉⲥⲱⲟⲩ ⲙⲡⲁⲓⲱⲧ ⲁϥⲑⲁϩⲥⲧ ⲙⲙⲟⲓ ϧⲉⲛ ⲫⲛⲉϩ ⲛⲧⲉ ⲡⲉϥⲑⲱϩⲥ	قال الرب للملائكة فاخذني من غنم أبي و دهني بدهن مسحته	The Lord said to His angel so he lifted me from my father's sheep and anointed me with the oil of his anointing. (Ps. 151:4)
ⲛⲁⲥⲛⲏⲟⲩ ⲛⲁⲛⲉⲩ ⲟⲩⲟϩⲁⲛⲛⲁϣϯ ⲛⲉ	و اخوتي حسان و هم الكبار	My brothers are handsome and great. (Ps. 151:5)
ϫⲉ ϥⲉ	مبارك الرب	N/A – this is the beginning of a common conclusory verse

Although not present, the conclusory verse is known and is the following:

| Ϫⲉ ϥⲥⲙⲁⲣⲱⲟⲩⲧ ⲛϫⲉ Ⲫⲓⲱⲧ ⲛⲉⲙ ⲡϣⲏⲣⲓ ⲛⲉⲙ ⲡⲓⲡⲛⲉⲩⲙⲁ ⲉⲑⲟⲩⲁⲃ ϯⲧⲣⲓⲁⲥ ⲉⲧϫⲏⲕ ⲉⲃⲟⲗ ⲧⲉⲛⲟⲩⲱϣⲧ ⲙⲙⲟⲥ ⲧⲉⲛϯⲱⲟⲩ ⲛⲁⲥ | مبارك الآب و الابن و الروح القدس الثالوث الكامل نسبحه و نمجده | Blessed is the Father and the Son and the Holy Spirit the perfect Trinity. We worship him and glorify him. |

Then the priest says the Prayer of the Crowns beginning with "O God the Holy [Ⲫϯ ⲫⲏⲉⲑⲟⲩⲁⲃ]." At the end of it, the priest cries out with a loud voice with his hand on the groom's head:

Ⲇⲟⲝⲁ ⲕⲉ ⲧⲓⲙⲏ ⲕⲉ ⲥⲧⲉⲫⲁⲛⲟⲥ ⲁⲩⲧⲟⲩ	المجد و الكرامة للذي يتتوج	Glory and honor to he who is crowned
ⲱ ⲡⲁⲧⲏⲣ ⲉⲩⲗⲟⲅⲓ	الآب يبارك	The Father blesses
ⲟ ⲩⲟⲥ ⲥⲧⲉⲫⲁⲛⲓ	الابن يتوج	The Son crowns
ⲧⲱ ⲡⲛⲁⲧⲓ ⲁⲅⲓⲱ ⲡⲁⲣⲁⲅⲉⲑⲓⲛⲉ ⲕⲉ ⲧⲉⲗⲓⲟⲥ	و الروح القدس يشمله و يملاه	The Holy Spirit surrounds him and fills him

This text is Greek and has some errors indicating that it is very old. The words for 'glory' and 'he' are in the wrong grammatical case and the word for 'son' is misspelled. The Arabic translation provided is not an exact interpretation. The English is my translation of the Arabic. When translating the Greek directly, the first line should say, "With glory, honor, and a crown" but the Arabic says, "Glory and honor to he who is to be crowned." Although, the word crown [ⲥⲧⲉⲫⲁⲛⲟⲥ] appears as a noun, the Arabic treats it as if it were a verb. This could be a mistranslation, or it could be that it was originally intended to be a verb but was conjugated incorrectly. Finally, the third line contains a word [ⲡⲁⲣⲁⲅⲉⲑⲓⲛⲉ] that does not make sense in Greek. The Arabic translates this word as surround [يشمله]. The closest Greek word that could share the same meaning as the Arabic is ⲡⲁⲣⲁⲅⲓⲅⲛⲟⲙⲁⲓ which means to appear beside. The third person singular conjugation of this verb is ⲡⲁⲣⲁⲅⲓⲅⲛⲉⲧⲁⲓ. An alternative form of this verb drops the second gamma, leaving us with ⲡⲁⲣⲁⲅⲓⲛⲉⲧⲁⲓ. If we assume that the tau was replaced with a theta, since it was common for Coptic scribes to use tau and theta interchangeably, and perhaps a spelling error misplaced the penultimate and ultimate syllables, then it is possible to see how ⲡⲁⲣⲁⲅⲉⲑⲓⲛⲉ came about.

The people say Axios [ⲁⲍⲓⲟⲥ] three times followed by Lord Have Mercy three times. Then the priest says several verses of blessing that recall the well-known married couples of the Bible. The first verse starts with "He who blessed our father Adam and Noah [ⲫⲏⲉⲧⲁϥⲥⲙⲟⲩ ⲉⲙⲡⲉⲛⲓⲱⲧ ⲁⲇⲁⲙ ⲛⲉⲙ ⲛⲟⲉ]" and that is all Ibn Kabar includes. These verses are one of the most varied parts of the rite and subsequent sources provide several alternatives. The people then say this doxology "in its entirety" in the Morning Doxology tune:

ϩⲁⲛⲭⲗⲟⲙ ⲛⲁⲧⲗⲱⲙ ⲁϥⲧⲏⲓⲧⲟⲩ ⲛϫⲉ ⲡⲟⲥ ⲉϫⲉⲛ ⲡⲓⲡⲁⲧϣⲉⲗⲏⲧ ⲛⲧⲉ ⲓⲏⲥ ⲡⲭⲥ	أكاليل لا نبلا منحمها الرب لهذا العريس الذي ليسوع المسيح	Unfading crowns the Lord has placed upon the bridegroom of Jesus Christ
ϭⲓⲟⲩⲱⲓⲛⲓ ϭⲓⲟⲩⲱⲓⲛⲓ ⲱ ⲡⲓⲡⲁⲧϣⲉⲗⲏⲧ ⲙⲙⲏⲓ ⲉⲧϧⲉⲛ ⲡⲓⲙⲁ ⲉⲧⲥⲉⲃⲧⲱⲧ ⲙⲙⲏⲓ	استضئ التضئ أيها العريس الحقيقي أنت في مكانك المستعد الحقيقي	Illuminate, Illuminate O true bridegroom in your true prepared place
ϭⲓ ⲛⲁⲕ ⲛⲟⲩⲣⲁϣⲓ ⲛⲉⲙ ϯⲇⲱⲣⲉⲁ ⲛⲧⲉ ⲫϯ ⲉⲧⲁϥⲧⲏⲓⲧⲟⲩ ⲛⲁⲕ ⲛϫⲉ ⲡⲭⲥ ⲡⲉⲛⲛⲟⲩϯ	اقبل الفرح و موهبة الله التي أعطاها لك المسيح الهنا	Take unto you joy and the gift of God which Christ our God has given you

ⲙⲁϣⲉⲛⲁⲕ ϧⲉⲛ ⲟⲩⲣⲁϣⲓ ⲉⲡⲉⲕⲙⲁⲛϣⲉⲗⲏⲧ ⲉⲧⲥⲉⲗⲥⲱⲗ ⲉⲃⲟⲗ ϧⲉⲛ ⲟⲩⲑⲟ ⲛ̄ⲣⲏϯ	أمض بفرح الى خدرك المزين بكل نوع	Go with joy to your bridal chamber that is decorated in various ways
ⲁⲛⲟⲛ ϩⲱⲛ ⲧⲉⲛⲧⲱⲃϩ ⲉⲑⲣⲉⲛϣⲁϣⲛⲓ ⲉⲩⲛⲁⲓ ϩⲓⲧⲉⲛ ⲛⲉⲡⲣⲉⲥⲃⲓⲁ ⲛ̄ⲧⲟⲧϥ ⲙ̄ⲡⲓⲙⲁⲓⲣⲱⲙⲓ	و نحن نطلب أن نفوز بالرحمة بشفاعتك عند محب البشر	And we too hope to win mercy through your intercessions with the Lover of Mankind

The last verse is addressed to the Virgin Mary. It probably appears because the doxology is structured like the doxology for the Virgin from the Morning Doxology but otherwise it is out of place in this context. Then the priest says, "Place O Lord upon your servants [ⲉⲕⲉⲭⲱ Ⲡⲟⲥ ⲉϫⲉⲛ ⲛⲉⲕⲉⲃⲓⲁⲓⲕ]." Then the people say Our Father and the priest says the benediction which includes two prayers followed by the Absolution of the Son. Then the priest begins the commandments. The first commandment is to the groom. When the priest reaches "unto the end of ages Amen", the people chant "My peace I [ϫⲉ ⲧⲁϩⲓⲣⲏⲛⲏ ⲁⲛⲟⲕ]." The priest continues the commandment to the groom. When he says, "in this blessed hour" they say, "This is the time of blessing [ⲫⲛⲁⲩ ⲙ̄ⲡⲓⲥⲙⲟⲩ]." This is the first verse of a multi-verse hymn, and it is not specified if they say all of it or not. The priest says the last part of the groom's commandment. When he says, "in this world and the last" they say, "Listen O daughter [ⲥⲱⲧⲉⲙ ⲧⲁϣⲉⲣⲓ ⲉⲛⲁⲩ]." Then the priest says the commandment to the bride. The people say Lord Have Mercy, but it does not specify how many times. Finally, the people say the concluding canon "Rejoice O shining bride [Ⲭⲉⲣⲉ ⲧϣⲉⲗⲉⲧ ⲉⲧⲉⲣⲟⲩⲱⲓⲛⲓ]."

Then they prepare for liturgy. When the groom enters the sanctuary for the liturgy they say, "Blessed is the Father [ϫⲉ ϥⲥⲙⲁⲣⲱⲟⲩⲧ]." The readings of the liturgy are as follows: the Pauline Epistle is from Ephesians 4 beginning with "I ask you as a prisoner of the Lord [ϯϯϩⲟ ⲉⲣⲱⲧⲉⲛ ⲁⲛⲟⲕ] [اسألكم أنا الأسير بالرب]", the Catholic Epistle begins with "Likewise in ancient times [ⲛⲁⲓⲣⲏϯ ⲅⲁⲣ ⲛⲟⲩⲥⲏⲟⲩ] [هكذا كن قديما]" (1 Peter 3), the Acts begins with "As for the multitude who believed [فاما الجمع الذين آمنوا]" until "unto his need [كالذي يحتاج اليه]" (Acts 4:32-35), the Psalm reference is not mentioned, and the Gospel is John 2:1-11 which is the reading of the Wedding at Cana of Galilee. The communion of the Eucharist, which should conclude all sacramental rites, indicates that the marital union is not just between the bride and groom, but also between them and the Church.

CHAPTER 2

The 15th Century – Pope Gabriel V

Biography

Pope Gabriel V was the 88th patriarch of the Coptic Church. He was born in Giza and worked in the government until he was fired for being a Christian. He became a monk at the Monastery of St Samuel. He was later ordained the hegumen of The Hanging Church (al-Mu'allaqah). He was consecrated patriarch on April 21, 1409.[15] His reign was marked by intense hardship and persecution for the Copts. He himself was largely ignored by the leading figures of the day. The Sultan did not esteem him and demanded double the poll tax (jizya) from the Copts. The kings of Ethiopia stopped their financial support of the Coptic Church. The Copts were forced to dress in certain clothing to distinguish them from the Muslim citizens. All Christians were prohibited from employment in public service. On top of all that, the head of St. Mark was stolen by Venetian merchants. Pope Gabriel V can be described as a good administrator. He was not an outspoken miracle working firebrand like his predecessor Matthew I. He correctly saw that the challenges facing the Copts would lead many to leave the faith or try to change the faith to be more acceptable to Islam. He focused his efforts on liturgical reform and clerical instruction. He maintained emphasis on preserving the traditions in the face of persecution. He reigned from 1409 to 1427.

---

[15] Aziz Atiya, *Claremont Coptic Encyclopedia,* s.v. "Gabriel V," https://ccdl.claremont.edu/digital/collection/cce/id/876

Description of His Work

Pope Gabriel V's main contribution is the creation of the *Ritual Ordo* *(Arabic* كتاب ترتيب *Kitāb tartīb)*. He supervised a collaborative effort involving several contemporary clerics and scholars to compile a manual for priests and bishops to perform all liturgical functions. It includes information about movements, time of day when services should take place, silent prayers, variations for when the patriarch attends, etc. They studied many older similar works, comparing them and creating a single collection containing all the known rites of the day. They thereby reorganized the liturgy of the church, giving it the definitive form that it currently retains. On Sunday, May 3, 1411, at the Church of Abu Sifayn in Old Cairo, Pope Gabriel assembled the priests, notables, and deacons of the entire Coptic community and submitted the new Ordo to them. The assembly gave its unanimous approval to this Ordo and the patriarch consequently decreed its exclusive use in all Coptic churches.[16] This makes it different from the work of Ibn Kabar in that it was written intentionally to be used by clergy. Whereas Ibn Kabar wrote to observe, Pope Gabriel's Ordo was written to educate and train. Its manuscript is BnF Arabe 98. I used that manuscript along with the version published by 'Abdallah[17] to create an English translation in Appendix B.

Description of The Rite

The first thing he says is that it is customary to hold the wedding after midnight praise. Although this is the custom, it is not mandatory. Ibn Kabar never specified time of day; however, he did say a liturgy is part of the ceremony so it can be inferred that it took place in the morning. The groom arrives at the church with his party and attends Matins. Pope Gabriel says that the deacons and priests process the groom "from the

---

[16] Ibid.
[17] Alfonso 'Abdallah, *L'ordinamento liturgico di Gabriele V: 88° Patriarca Copto (1409-1427)* (Cairo: SOC Aegyptiaca,1962), 131 (Arabic).

door of the church to the place of contracting the properties ['aqd al-amlāk]."[18] The "place of 'aqd al-amlāk" could refer to the groom's house. It could also mean that there was another place, either adjacent to or close by the church, where this part was done. But the most likely explanation is that they were really processing the groom into the nave. Although it was previously stated that he and his party were already in the nave attending Matins, this was the formal beginning of the first part of the wedding. The "place of 'aqd al-amlāk" most likely refers to the chancel. They process him with this hymn: "Blessed is he who comes according to the order of angels. Alleluia, Alleluia, & Alleluia [Ⲉⲩⲗⲟⲅⲏⲙⲉⲛⲟⲥ Ⲟ ⲉⲣⲭⲱⲙⲉⲛⲟⲥ ⲕⲁⲧⲁⲧⲓⲥ ⲧⲁⲍⲓⲥ ⲁⲅⲅⲉⲗⲟⲛ. ⲁⲗ ⲁⲗ ⲕⲉ ⲁⲗ]." If time remains, then they sing "Christ the Logos of the Father [Ⲡⲭⲥ ⲡⲓⲗⲟⲅⲟⲥ ⲛⲧⲉ ⲫⲓⲱⲧ]" in the Palm Sunday tune. If they do not know it, they sing "Galilee of the nations [Ϯⲅⲁⲗⲓⲗⲉⲁ ⲛⲧⲉ ⲛⲧⲉ ⲛⲓⲉⲑⲛⲟⲥ]." This is the first mention we have of processional hymns. The deacons carry candles during the procession. Then they leave and meet the bride at the door of the church also with candles and cymbals singing "Rejoice O Mary [ⲭⲉⲣⲉ ⲛⲉ ⲙⲁⲣⲓⲁ]", the seventh part of the Sunday Theotokia until she enters the "house of women [بيت النساء]."[19] It is unknown what this "house of women" means. It could be a separate building that was attached to the church or a room within the main church building. It seems to have had the purpose of being used for specific needs of women such as preparation of the baptism of women, bridal preparation, preparation for funerals of women, etc. Regardless, the bride was not inside the nave of the church with the groom. She waited outside in the bridal chamber until the end of the first part.

Then the priests and deacons enter the chancel. The priest uncovers his head and wears his liturgical vestments. Likewise, the deacons dress in their liturgical vestments. Ibn Kabar did not mention specific vestments, but he did say a liturgy would be done. It was common for rich people or high-ranking people, especially in the capital, to invite the patriarch. If

---

[18] Appendix B, Section 1.
[19] Ibid.

the Patriarch is in attendance, then he is the one who officiates the ceremony, but he enters the church with his own procession. They process him from his room with candles until they reach the chancel. The patriarch uncovers his head as usual. It appears to have been a tradition to gift the patriarch with a new phelonion in return for his attendance. Pope Gabriel says that "if the groom made for him a phelonion, then he [the patriarch] vests with that. He removes the phelonion with which he left his room and wears the groom's phelonion."[20]

A tray is placed on the lectern containing the groom's vestment, the girdle, the white cloth, the cross, the ring, and incense. This list is similar to that mentioned by Ibn Kabar but extends it to include all the vestments that will be worn by the groom by the end of the ceremony. Pope Gabriel does not specify that these items are prepared by the godparents. The priest or patriarch starts with the Thanksgiving Prayer. The people chant the Verses of the Cymbals beginning with Lord Have Mercy in the festal tune, then "We worship the Father [Ⲧⲉⲛⲟⲩⲱϣⲧ ⲙⲫⲓⲱⲧ]", "Rejoice O Church [ⲭⲉⲣⲉ ϯⲉⲕⲕⲗⲏⲥⲓⲁ]", "Through the intercessions [ϩⲓⲧⲉⲛ ⲛⲓⲡⲣⲉⲥⲃⲓⲁ]", "Through the prayers [ϩⲓⲧⲉⲛ ⲛⲓⲉⲩⲭⲏ]" for the Patriarch, and they finish with "That we may praise [ⲉⲑⲣⲉⲛϩⲟⲥ]". Then they say "Lord Have Mercy [Ⲕⲩⲣⲓⲉ Ⲉⲗⲉⲏⲥⲟⲛ], Alleluia, Glory be to You [Ⲇⲟⲝⲁⲥⲓ]", Our Father, Psalm 50, and "We worship You [Ⲧⲉⲛⲟⲩⲱϣⲧ ⲙⲙⲟⲕ]." The priest raises incense and says the prayer associated with the Pauline Epistle but there is no mention of saying the Hymn of the Censer.[21] The Pauline Epistle is read. Pope Gabriel mentions that it is read in Coptic first then Arabic. Nowadays it is only read in one language. The Trisagion is said. The Patriarch says the litany of the gospel. Nowadays a priest would say this litany and the patriarch or bishop would read the Gospel. The Psalm is said in the short annual tune. The text of the Psalm is, "Mercy and truth

---

[20] Ibid.
[21] The Hymn of the Censer is often said in Coptic liturgical services before the reading of the Pauline Epistle. It is concluded by the verse, "We worship You.". It is explained in detail later in the section on Hegumen Philotheos Ibrahim's version of the rite.

are met together; righteousness and peace have kissed each other. Truth shall spring out of the earth, and righteousness shall look down from heaven.

[Ⲟⲩⲛⲁⲓ ⲛⲉⲙ ⲟⲩⲙⲉⲑⲙⲏⲓ ⲁⲩⲓ ⲉⲃⲟⲗ ⲉϩⲣⲉⲛ ⲛⲟⲩⲉⲣⲏⲟⲩ ⲟⲩⲇⲓⲕⲉⲟⲥⲩⲛⲏ ⲛⲉⲙ ⲟⲩϩⲓⲣⲏⲛⲏ ⲁⲩϣⲉⲃⲧⲱ ⲧⲟⲩ ⲛⲛⲟⲩⲉⲣⲏⲟⲩ ϯⲙⲉⲑⲙⲏⲓ ⲁⲥϣⲁⲓ ⲉⲃⲟⲗ ϧⲉⲛ ⲡⲕⲁϩⲓ ϯⲇⲓⲕⲉⲟⲩⲥⲓⲛⲓ ⲁⲥϫⲟⲩϣⲧ ⲉⲃⲟⲗ ϧⲉⲛ ⲧⲫⲉ ⲁⲗ]" (Ps 85:10,11). If the patriarch or a bishop is present, then "Let them exalt him [Ⲙⲁⲣⲟⲩϭⲁⲥϥ]" is added to the end of the psalm.[22] If present, the patriarch reads the Gospel. If not, the priest reads the Gospel in Coptic, and a deacon interprets it in Arabic. The following response is said in the Palm Sunday tune: "Rejoice O bridal chamber adorned in various ways which is for the true bridegroom who united humanity [ⲭⲉⲣⲉ ⲡⲓⲙⲁⲛϣⲉⲗⲉⲧ ⲉⲧⲥⲉⲗⲥⲱⲗ ϧⲉⲛ ⲟⲩⲑⲟ ⲛⲣⲏϯ ⲛⲧⲉ ⲡⲓⲛⲉⲙⲫⲓⲟⲥ ⲙⲙⲏⲓ ⲉⲧⲁϥϩⲱⲧⲡ ⲉϯⲙⲉⲧⲣⲱⲙⲓ]." If the Patriarch is in attendance, they add, "Likewise we magnify you [ⲱⲥⲁⲩⲧⲟⲥ]" but if not, they proceed with "Intercede on our behalf [ⲁⲣⲓⲡⲣⲉⲥⲃⲉⲩⲓⲛ ⲉϩⲣⲏⲓ ⲉϫⲟⲛ]" for the Virgin and after that "Blessed is the Father [Ϫⲉ ϥⲥⲙⲁⲣⲱⲟⲩⲧ]."

The priest recites the three great litanies. The people say the Creed followed by Lord Have Mercy three times. Then the four prayers are said along with their responses in the muḥayyar tune. Pope Gabriel does not mention the first words of the prayers themselves but includes the full Coptic text of the responses with no Arabic translations. Each of these prayers is preceded by the call to peace [ⲏⲣⲓⲛⲓ ⲡⲁⲥⲓⲛ]. It is interesting that it does not start with the usual call to pray followed by the deacon's command to stand up for prayer. Also, there is no congregational response. Perhaps this was because people were already standing. It was probably added to quiet down the crowd as people are usually causing a ruckus in the middle of the ceremony. The response of the first prayer is "Christ the Logos of the Father, the Only-Begotten God, grant us Your peace which

---

[22] "Let them exalt him" refers to a selection of psalms (Ps 107:32,41,42 & Ps 110:4) said after the main psalm in the presence of the bishop or patriarch.

is full of joy. For Blessed [Ⲡⲭⲥ ⲡⲓⲗⲟⲅⲟⲥ ⲛⲧⲉ ⲫⲓⲱⲧ ⲡⲓⲙⲟⲛⲟⲅⲉⲛⲏⲥ ⲛⲛⲟⲩϯ ⲉⲕⲉϯ ⲛⲁⲛ ⲛⲧⲉⲕϩⲓⲣⲓⲛⲓⲏ ⲑⲁⲓ ⲉⲑⲙⲉϩ ⲛⲣⲁϣⲓ ⲛⲓⲃⲉⲛ. Ⲇⲉ ϥⲥⲙⲁⲣⲱⲟⲩⲧ]." The response of the second prayer is "As You have given your holy Apostles, likewise, say unto us, "My peace I give to you" [Ⲕⲁⲧⲁ ⲫⲣⲏϯ ⲉⲧⲁⲕⲧⲏⲓⲥ ⲉⲛⲉⲕⲁⲅⲓⲟⲥ ⲛⲁⲡⲟⲥⲧⲟⲗⲟⲥ ⲉⲕⲉϫⲟⲥ ⲛⲁⲛ ⲙⲡⲟⲩⲣⲏϯ ϫⲁ ⲧⲁϩⲓⲣⲓⲛⲓ ϯϯⲙⲙⲟⲥ ⲛⲱⲧⲉⲛ. Ⲇⲉ ϥⲥⲙⲁⲣⲱⲟⲩⲧ]." The response of the third prayer is "My peace which I have taken from my Father I leave with you now and forever [Ⲧⲁϩⲓⲣⲏⲛⲏ ⲁⲛⲟⲕ ⲑⲏⲉⲧⲁⲥϭⲓⲧⲥ ⲛⲧⲉⲛ ⲡⲁⲓⲱⲧ ⲁⲛⲟⲕ ϯⲭⲱ ⲙⲙⲟⲥ ⲛⲉⲙⲱⲧⲉⲛ ⲓⲥϫⲉⲛ ϯⲛⲟⲩ ⲛⲉⲙ ϣⲁ ⲉⲛⲉϩ. Ⲇⲉ ϥⲥⲙⲁⲣⲱⲟⲩⲧ]." Then they say Our Father and the priest recites the benediction with the cross over the groom's head. Then they say Lord Have Mercy 43 times.

The priest says the call to peace. The godparent brings the vestment to the priest. He recites the prayer of the vestment over it. He vests the groom with it and ties the girdle around the groom's waist. He covers the groom's head with the broad white cloth. He puts one of the rings on the ring finger of the groom's right hand. Pope Gabriel does not include the priestly cap among the groom's vestments. This practice probably stopped because the groom already had the white cloth over his head. If the patriarch attends, then during the vesting of the groom, they sing in the Palm Sunday tune:[23]

ϯⲥⲧⲟⲗⲏ ⲙⲡⲛⲉⲩⲙⲁⲧⲓⲕⲟⲛ ⲁⲩⲧⲏⲓⲥ ϩⲓⲱⲧⲥ ϩⲓⲱⲧϥ ⲙⲙⲓⲭⲁⲏⲗ ⲟⲩⲟϩ ⲡⲓϩⲱⲕ ⲙⲙⲁⲣⲅⲁⲣⲓⲧⲏⲥ ⲁⲩⲙⲟⲩⲣ ⲙⲙⲓⲭⲁⲏⲗ ⲙⲙⲟⲥ	The spiritual raiment was clothed around Michael and the precious cloak was draped around Michael
ⲧⲱⲃϩ ⲙⲡⲟⲥ ⲡⲉⲛⲓⲱⲧ	Pray to the Lord (for the patriarch)
ⲁⲕϭⲓ ⲧⲭⲁⲣⲓⲥ ⲙⲙⲟⲩⲥⲏⲥ	You received the grace of Moses (until its end)

---

[23] Appendix B, Section 2

It is unclear if this hymn existed during the time of Ibn Kabar or was just a local tradition. It speaks of putting a cloak around Archangel Michael, thus linking the Archangel Michael to the groom. This is reminiscent of how the Bible sometimes refers to the bishop or shepherd of a community as its angel. This calls back the symbolism of viewing the groom as the priest of his house. Here the imagery expands such that he not only is a priest, but also an angel like Archangel Michael.

The last verse could refer to the Doxology of the Patriarch[24] said during Vespers or Matins when the patriarch is in attendance, or the concluding canon for the patriarch,[25] both of which start with "You received the grace of Moses." I think it is more likely the concluding canon because the doxology for the patriarch always concludes with the verse, "Pray to the Lord on our behalf O our father the Patriarch, Pope Abba (...) that He may forgive us our sins." That is already the second verse of this hymn. It would not make sense to say the last verse and then start the doxology from its beginning. Also, since this is the conclusion of the first part, it makes sense that this hymn serves a double function of being a hymn for the wedding vestment and a concluding canon, which, as previously explained, is usually said just before the benediction and dismissal, which is exactly what happens next. The patriarch dons his cap and says the blessing. He blesses the groom then retires to rest while they begin singing "Come see this bride." If the patriarch is not attending, then "The Spiritual Raiment" is not said but rather they say, "Come see this bride" and nothing else. The text of "Come see this bride" is:

| ⲁⲙⲟⲩ ⲧⲉⲕⲛⲁⲩ ⲉⲧⲁⲓϣⲉⲗⲉⲧ ⲉⲧⲁⲩⲥⲉⲗⲥⲱⲗⲥ ⲙⲡⲓϩⲓⲏⲃ ⲁⲥⲉⲣⲫⲟⲣⲓⲛ ⲙⲡⲁⲓⲛⲟⲩϫ ⲛⲱⲟⲩ ⲡⲉϫⲁϥ ⲛϫⲉ ⲡϣⲏⲣⲓ ⲛϯϧⲁⲣⲁⲃⲁⲓ | Come see this bride who is adorned for the lamb. She is engulfed in great glory according to the saying of the son of thunder. |

---

[24] The Doxology of the Patriarch can be found at http://tasbeha.org/hymn_library/view/1327.
[25] The text may be found at http://tasbeha.org/hymn_library/view/1336.

Iwa ⲡϣⲏⲣⲓ ⲛⲍⲉⲃⲉⲇⲉⲟⲥ ⲉϥⲱϣ ⲉⲃⲟⲗ ⲉϥϫⲱ ⲙⲙⲟⲥ ϫⲉ ⲁⲥⲉⲣⲟⲩⲱⲓⲛⲓ ⲛϫⲉ ⲧⲁⲓϣⲉⲗⲉⲧ ⲡⲁⲣⲁ ⲡⲓⲥⲓⲟⲩ ⲛⲧⲉ ϩⲁⲛⲁⲧⲟⲩⲓ	John the son of Zebedee cries out and says, "This bride shines more brightly than the stars of the morning.
Ⲉⲧⲉ ⲑⲁⲓ ⲧⲉ ⲥⲓⲱⲛ ⲙⲃⲉⲣⲓ ⲧⲡⲟⲗⲓⲥ ⲙⲡⲉⲛⲛⲟⲩⲧⲉ ⲉⲣⲉ ⲡⲟⲩⲛⲟϥ ⲛⲧⲉ ⲛⲓⲉⲑⲟⲩⲁⲃ ⲧⲏⲣⲟⲩ ϣⲱⲡⲓ ⲛϧⲣⲏⲓ ⲛϧⲏⲧⲥ	This is the new Zion, the city of our God. The joy of all the saints dwells within her."
Ϫⲉ ϥⲥⲙⲁⲣⲱⲟⲩⲧ	Blessed

Note that aside from a few spelling variations it is the same exact text as found in Ibn Kabar.

After vesting the groom, they depart with candles and cymbals to the "house of crowning" [بيت الاكليل].[26] This could refer to a different house, the same house, or the church. Assuming everything was done in a church, the house of crowning would still be the same place where the groom was, namely the chancel. The bride would still be waiting in the "house of women." So, the procession would take the groom out of the nave to meet the bride somewhere in the entrance or courtyard of the church. When the procession ends, the priest takes the bride by herself to where the groom is seated. He commands the groom to put the second ring upon which he "contracted the crowning" on her right ring finger. If she extends her hand and accepts the "cross of the contract", then it is a sign that she is willing to take the groom to be her husband. Then the priest hands the bride to the groom and commands the godparent to present them to the masses. If the ceremony took place in a house, then this ritualistic exchange of rings would have been done privately with just the priest, the bride, the groom, and the godparent. But if it took place in a church, then it probably occurred at the door of the church or at the foot of the chancel. Regardless, this marks the beginning of the second part of the wedding called the crowning. The bride stands at the right of the groom and the priest covers

---

[26] Appendix B., Section 3.

both their heads with the single broad white cloth. Pope Gabriel explains that the single cloth is a testimony to those present of the bride and groom's union with each other. The white cloth is a manifestation of pure righteous union. If the patriarch chooses, he may delegate to one of the priests to officiate the crowning. If he so chooses, then he may put the phelonion on the priest who will perform the crowning. That is his prerogative, and it is an honor to the groom.

The priest starts with the Thanksgiving Prayer. The people sing The Hymn of the Censer [Ταιϣογρη] instead of the verses of cymbals while priest says the prayers of the Pauline Incense. If the ceremony was in a house, then he censes the entire house.[27] Then they conclude with "We worship [Τενογωϣτ]." Then the Pauline Epistle is read. The people chant the Trisagion. The priest recites the Litany of Gospel. The Psalm is chanted in the short annual tune. The text of the Psalm comes from Psalms 19 and 128:

Μϕρηϯ νογπατϣελετ εϥνηογ εβολ ϧεν πεϥμανϣελετ. Εϥεθελμλ μμοϥ μϕρηϯ νογαϕωϕ εϥϭοϫι ϩι πεϥμωιτ ερε τεκϲϩιμι ερμϕρηϯ νογβω ναλολι εϲϕορι εβολ. Ϲαπιϲϕιρ ντε πεκηι. Νεκϣηρι μϕρηϯ νϩανϭο μβερι ντε ϩαναϫωιτ εγκωϯ ετεκτραπεζα	Which is like a bridegroom coming out of his chamber, and rejoices like a strong man to run its race. Your wife shall be like a fruitful vine in the very heart of your house, your children like olive plants all around your table

The deacon says, "Stand up [ϲταθητε]". Pope Gabriel says the priest reads the gospel in Coptic and the deacon interprets it into Arabic. Neither the exact passage nor its reference are included so it can be assumed it was the same as that found in Ibn Kabar (Mt 19:1-6). However, Pope

---

[27] Appendix B, Section 4.

Gabriel does include the text of the Gospel Response, which Ibn Kabar omitted. This response is said in its unique tune:

Ναι ετα϶βοτπγ εγϲοπ ⲛϫⲉ ⲡⲓⲡⲛⲁ ⲉⲑ ⲙ̀ⲫⲣⲏϯ ⲛⲟⲩⲕⲛⲑⲁⲣⲁ ⲉⲩⲉⲥⲙⲟⲩ ⲉϥϯ ⲛϭⲟⲩ ⲛⲓⲃⲉⲛ	Those whom the Holy Spirit attuned like a stringed instrument praise God continuously
Ⲧⲉⲛⲟⲩⲱϣⲧ ⲙⲙⲟⲕ ⲱ ⲡⲭⲥ	We worship You O Christ

This response comes from the Morning Doxology.[28] It has a unique tune[29] which is not used for any other hymn or any other occasion. The full context from the Morning Doxology is:

Behold how beneficent and how pleasant it is for brethren to dwell together in unity, united in true evangelic love like the Apostles. It is like the fragrant oil on the head of Christ running down the beard, down to the feet, that anoints, every day, the elders, the children, young men, and the deacons, those whom the Holy Spirit has attuned together as a stringed instrument always blessing God by psalms and hymns and spiritual songs by day and by night with an incessant heart.

This passage refers to the unity and harmony of the Church. In the wedding, the verse is used to refer to the unity and harmony of the bride and groom, who, as a new branch of the Church, are likewise attuned/united[30] by the Holy Spirit and praise God incessantly. Then they say Lord Have Mercy three times. This response did not appear in Ibn Kabar. It is possible it was a new addition in Pope Gabriel's time. The

---

[28] See http://tasbeha.org/hymn_library/view/1553 for the full text of the Morning Doxology.
[29] See http://tasbeha.org/hymn_library/view/1460?mid=10244 for this tune.
[30] The Coptic word ϩⲟⲧⲡ can mean both to unite or to tune a stringed instrument.

most likely explanation is that it was a local custom that Pope Gabriel standardized to be used moving forward.

The priest recites the Supplications. Pope Gabriel recommends he say the first three in Coptic facing East, then continue in Arabic until he reaches the part where he says, "bless this marriage" after which he turns and faces West from then on.[31] Again, this was an attempt to balance the amount of Coptic and Arabic. Whenever he says the name of the bride and groom, he signs them with the sign of the cross. He continues until he reaches, "O the compassionate." He then says, "O the beneficent the great in mercy" facing East. The people say Lord Have Mercy three times. Then he says the three great litanies: peace, fathers, congregations. Then they say the Creed. They say Lord Have Mercy three times. The priest says the call to peace followed by the first prayer in Coptic facing East. If time permits, they say the following in the muḥayyar tune, "As David said in the psalm, 'The queen stood at the right hand of the king. For blessed [Ⲕⲁⲧⲁ ⲫⲣⲏϯ ⲉⲧⲁϥϫⲟⲥ ⲛϫⲉ ⲇⲁⲩⲓⲇ ϧⲉⲛ ⲡⲓⲯⲁⲗⲙⲟⲥ ϫⲉ ⲁⲥⲟϩⲓ ⲉⲣⲁⲧⲥ ⲛϫⲉ ϯⲟⲩⲣⲱ ⲥⲁⲟⲩⲓⲛⲁⲙ ⲙⲙⲟⲕ ⲡⲟⲩⲣⲟ. Ϫⲉ ϥⲥⲙⲁⲣⲱⲟⲩⲧ]." They say Lord Have Mercy three times. The second litany is said in Coptic facing East followed by this verse in the same tune, "Solomon has called you in the Song of Songs My sister and my spouse my true city Jerusalem [Ⲥⲟⲗⲟⲙⲱⲛ ⲙⲟⲩϯ ⲉⲣⲟ ϧⲉⲛ ⲡⲓϫⲱ ⲛⲧⲉ ⲛⲓϫϩ ϫⲁ ⲧⲁⲥⲱⲛⲓ ⲟⲩⲟϩ ⲧⲁϣⲫⲏⲣⲓ ⲧⲁⲡⲟⲗⲓⲥ ⲙⲙⲏⲓ ⲓⲏⲗⲙ]." They say Lord Have Mercy three times. The priest says the third prayer facing the West either in Coptic or Arabic. They respond with, "Do not forget the covenant which you made with our fathers Abraham, Isaac, and Jacob Israel Your saints. For blessed [Ⲙⲡⲉⲣⲉⲣⲡⲱϣ ⲛϯⲇⲓⲁⲑⲏⲕⲏ ⲑⲏⲉⲧⲁⲕⲥⲉⲙⲛⲏⲧⲥ ⲛⲉⲙ ⲛⲉⲛⲓⲟϯ ⲁⲃⲣⲁⲁⲙ ⲓⲥⲁⲁⲕ ⲓⲁⲕⲱⲃ ⲡⲓⲥⲗ ⲡⲓⲉⲑⲟⲩⲁⲃ ⲛⲧⲁⲕ. Ϫⲉ ϥⲥⲙⲁⲣⲱⲟⲩⲧ]." They say Lord Have Mercy three times. The deacon says, "Bow your heads to the Lord [ⲧⲁⲥ ⲕⲁⲫⲁⲗⲁⲥ ⲏⲙⲱⲛ]." They respond with, "And with your spirit [ⲕⲁⲑⲟ ⲡⲛⲁ ⲑⲓⲥⲟⲩ]." The priest says the prayer of submission facing East. They

---

[31] Appendix B, Section 5.

respond in the same tune as before with, "May God bless us and let us bless us and let us bless His holy name and may His praise continually be always upon our mouths. For blessed [ⲉϥⲥⲙⲟⲩ ⲉⲣⲟⲛ ⲛϫⲉ Ⲫϯ ⲧⲉⲛⲛⲁⲥⲙⲟⲩ ⲉⲡⲉϥⲣⲁⲛ ⲉⲑⲩ ⲛⲥⲏⲟⲩ ⲛⲓⲃⲉⲛ ⲉⲣⲉ ⲡⲉϥⲥⲙⲟⲩ ⲛⲁϣⲱⲡⲓ ⲉϥⲙⲏⲛ ⲉⲃⲟⲗ ϧⲉⲛ ⲣⲱⲟⲩ. Ϫⲉ ϥⲥⲙⲁⲣⲱⲟⲩⲧ]." They say Lord Have Mercy three times.

The deacon says the following, "ⲧⲱ ⲕⲩ ⲉⲗⲉⲑⲱⲙⲉⲛ." This is clearly some form of a Greek response that was probably copied incorrectly. The closest form of a correction is ⲧⲟⲩ ⲕⲩⲣⲓⲟⲩ ⲇⲉⲑⲱⲙⲉⲛ which means "Let us beseech the Lord." They respond with Lord Have Mercy. The priest prays over the oil container. At the end of the prayer, he anoints the groom and bride while the people sing the response. Pope Gabriel only includes the first four verses from Ibn Kabar followed by the conclusory verse:

ⲁⲕⲑⲱϩⲥ ⲛⲧⲁⲁⲡⲉ ⲛⲟⲩⲛⲉϩ ⲟⲩⲟϩ ⲡⲉⲕⲁⲫⲟⲧ ⲉⲧⲑⲁϧⲓ ⲙⲫⲣⲏϯ ⲛⲟⲩⲁⲙⲁϩⲓ	You have anointed my head with oil and your cup intoxicated me
ⲡⲉⲕⲛⲁⲓ ⲉϥⲉⲃⲟϫⲓ ⲛⲥⲱⲓ ⲛⲛⲓⲉϩⲟⲟⲩ ⲧⲏⲣⲟⲩ ⲛⲧⲉ ⲡⲁⲱⲛϧ	Your mercy will seek me all the days of my life
ⲛⲓⲉⲑⲛⲟⲥ ⲧⲏⲣⲟⲩ ⲛⲧⲉ ⲡⲕⲁϩⲓ ⲛⲁⲉⲣⲙⲁⲕⲁⲣⲓⲍⲓⲛ ⲙⲙⲟⲓ	All the nations of the earth will bless me
ⲡⲗⲁⲟⲥ ⲧⲏⲣϥ ⲛⲁϫⲟⲥ ϫⲉ ⲉⲥⲉϣⲱⲡⲓ ⲉⲥⲉϣⲱⲡⲓ	All the people will say may it be may it be
Ϫⲉ ϥⲥⲙⲁⲣⲱⲟⲩⲧ	For blessed

The tune used for these verses is said to be "as previously explained" indicating that it was the muḥayyar tune.[32] This makes sense as the muḥayyar tune fits the length of each line. The Palm Sunday tune requires a four stanza quatrain so the stanzas would have to be combined in some

---

[32] Appendix B, Section 6.

way to form a quatrain in order to use that tune. While they sing "You have anointed", the priest rushes through the rest of the prayer of the oil.

Then he prays over the crowns. When the prayer of the crowns finishes, the priest puts the crowns on their heads and says:

Δοξη κε τιμι κε cτεφανογcαc αγτογ	بالمجد و الوقار توجته	You have crowned him with glory and honor
ο πατηρ εγλογι	الآب يبارك	The Father blesses
ο γιοc cτεφανι	و الابن يكلل	The Son crowns
τω πνατι αγιον παραγιθενε κε τελη	و الروح القدس يكمل و يتمم	The Holy Spirit perfects and completes

These verses are slightly different than what appeared in Ibn Kabar. The Greek is more correct than Ibn Kabar's version and thus the Arabic translation is more accurate. In the first line, the word cτεφανογcαc is clearly the second person singular past tense of the verb cτεφανω which means to crown. The Arabic confirms this by translating it as "you have crowned him [توجته]" instead of "he who is to be crowned." Also, the word for glory [Δοξη] is in the correct case. These corrections reveal the first line to be a quotation from Psalm 8:5, "You crowned him with glory and honor" which in Greek is, "Δοξη κε τιμη εcτεφανωcαc αγτον." In the third line, παραγιθενε is spelled with an iota after the gamma. Ibn Kabar had an epsilon in that spot. The Arabic in this version replaces the word surrounds [يشمله] with perfects [يكمل]. These changes reveal that the copyists probably did not recognize παραγιθενε as a valid Greek word and chose to simply ignore it and replace it in Arabic with a synonym of the final word τελη.

The congregation responds with "Worthy, worthy, worthy is the bridegroom and his helpmate [αξιοc αξιοc αξιοc πιπατϣελετ νεμ ⲧⲉϥⲃⲟⲏⲑⲟⲥ]" in "the same tune previously explained." But he never explained the tune of this response. Nevertheless, it is known. It is the Axios tune mentioned at the beginning of the book. The subsequent verses use the same tune. The priest says these verses "according to the custom of the Hanging Church and the majority of the other churches:"[33]

ⲁⲕϭⲓ ⲧⲭⲁⲣⲓⲥ ⲕⲉ ⲉⲩⲗⲟⲅⲓⲑⲟⲥ ϩⲓⲧⲉⲛ ⲡⲉⲛⲟⲥ ⲓⲏⲥ ⲡⲭⲥ	You received grace and blessing through our Lord Jesus Christ.
ⲁⲕϭⲓ ⲥⲧⲁⲫⲁⲛⲓ ⲛⲧⲉⲗⲓⲟⲥ ⲉⲑⲙⲉϩ ⲛⲉⲗⲉⲩⲑⲉⲣⲟⲥ	You received perfect crowns full of freedom.
ⲁⲕϭⲓ ⲛϯⲉⲡⲁⲅⲅⲉⲗⲓⲁ ⲉⲑⲛⲉⲥⲟⲥ ⲱ ⲡⲓⲛⲩⲙⲫⲓⲟⲥ ⲛⲉⲙ ⲧⲉϥⲃⲱⲏⲑⲟⲥ	You received the beautiful promise O bridegroom and his helpmate.

The priest then says the verses of blessing mentioned by Ibn Kabar in the Axios tune. After each one they respond with "Worthy, Worthy, Worthy is the bridegroom and his helpmate [ⲁⲝⲓⲟⲥ ⲁⲝⲓⲟⲥ ⲁⲝⲓⲟⲥ ⲡⲓⲡⲁⲧϣⲉⲗⲉⲧ ⲛⲉⲙ ⲧⲉϥⲃⲟⲏⲑⲟⲥ]." Pope Gabriel provides the entire Coptic text and an Arabic translation for each verse. The first three verses are for the groom:

| ⲫⲏⲉⲧⲁϥ ⲥⲙⲟⲩ ⲙⲡⲉⲛⲓⲱⲧ ⲁⲇⲁⲙ ⲛⲉⲙ ⲛⲱϩ ⲛⲉⲙ ⲁⲃⲣⲁⲁⲙ ⲛⲉⲙ ⲙⲱⲩⲥⲏⲥ | يا الذى بارك ابينا ادم و حوى[34] ابراهيم و موسى فى ارض مدين | He who blessed our father Adam and Noah and Abraham and Moses in the land of Midian blesses you O the |

---

[33] Appendix B, Section 7.
[34] This word in Arabic is Eve but the Coptic says Noah. The Arabic for Noah is نوح, which, if written properly, looks different enough than حوى to indicate the copyist intended to write Eve. However, the entire verse along with subsequent verses are specific to the holy men of the Old Testament so it makes more sense for Noah to be correct rather than Eve. It is unclear if the copyist felt Eve was more appropriate or if this was just a mistake or the handwriting really did distort نوح to look like حوى.

ϦEN ΠΚΑϨΙ ΜΜΑΔΙΑΝ EϤCΜΟΥ EΡΟΚ ω ΠΙΠΑΤϢΕΛΕΤ ΝΕΜ ΤΕϤΒϢΗΘΟC	يباركك ايها العريس و معينتك باسمه العظيم	bridegroom and his helpmate.
ΦΗΕΤΑϤCΜΟΥ ΜΠΕΝΙωΤ ΙCCΑΚ ΠΙΜΕΝΡΙΤ ΝΕΜ ΕΒΕΛ ΠΙΘΜΗΙ ΝϨΟΥΙΤ ΝΕΜ CΟΛΟΜωΝ ΝΕΜ ΠΕϤΙωΤ ΔΑΥΙΔ EϤCΜΟΥ EΡΟΚ ω ΠΑΠΙϢΑΛΕΤ ΝΕΜ ΤΕϤΒϢΗΘΟC	يا الذى بارك أسحق الحبيب و بارك هابيل الصديق و سليمن و ابيه داود يبارك عليكم باسمه القدس	He who blessed our father Isaac the beloved and Abel the first righteous and Solomon and his father David blesses you O the bridegroom and his helpmate.
ΦΗΕΤΑϤCΜΟΥ ΜΠΕΝΙωΤ ΙΑΚωΒ ΝΕΜ ΙΕCΟΥ ΝΕΜ ΠΙΘΜΗΙ ΔΙΙωΒ EϤCΜΟΥ.	يا الذى بارك ابينا يعقوب و يساه و البار ايوب و باركه سبع مرات يباركهم	He who blessed our father Jacob and Esau and the righteous Job blesses you O the bridegroom and his helpmate.

Note that conclusion of each verse in Coptic is the same but in Arabic is different. The Arabic conclusion of the first verse is "with His Great Name." The conclusion of the second verse is "with His Holy Name." The conclusion of the third verse is "bless you both sevenfold." It appears the endings were changed to create more assonance in the Arabic text. In the first verse the words great ['aẓīm] and Abraham [Ibrāhīm] end with the same vowel sound. In the second verse, the same is true for holy [quddūs] and David [Dāwūd]. In the third verse, the same applied to Esau [Yasāh] and fold [marrāt]. This is the first time we see the full text of these verses and already there is variation between languages. The remaining verses are said for the bride:

ΦΗΕΤΑϤCΜΟΥ ΜΠΕΝΙωΤ ΑΒΡΑΑΜ ΝΕΜ CΑΡΡΑ ϨΑΤΕΝ ΠΙϢϢΗΝ ΝΤΕ	يا الذى بارك لابينا أبراهيم فى ساره على شجرة ممرا الآن يبارك هذا الاتصال باسمه العظيم	O You who blessed our father Abraham with Sarah by the tree of Mamre now bless this

ⲙⲁⲙⲣⲏ ϯⲛⲟⲩ ⲛⲥⲙⲟⲩ ⲉⲡⲁⲓϫⲓⲛⲧⲟⲙⲓ ⲡⲁⲓ ⲉϥⲥⲙⲟⲩ ⲉⲣⲟⲕ ⲡⲓⲡⲁⲧϣⲉⲗⲉⲧ ⲛⲉⲙ…			union. He blesses you O the bridegroom and his helpmate.
Ⲫⲏⲉⲧⲁϥⲥⲙⲟⲩ ⲛⲓⲥⲁⲁⲕ ⲛⲉⲙ ⲓⲉⲣⲉⲃⲉⲕⲭⲁ ϯⲛⲟⲩ ⲟⲛ ⲥⲙⲟⲩ ⲉⲡⲁⲓϫⲓⲛⲧⲟⲙⲓ ⲫⲁⲓ	يا الذى بارك اسحق و رفقا الآن يبارك هذه العرسان باسمه القدوس		O You who blessed Isaac with Rebecca now also bless this union.
Ⲫⲏⲉⲧⲁϥⲥⲙⲟⲩ ⲙⲡⲉⲛⲓⲱⲧ ⲓⲁⲕⲱⲃ ⲉϫⲉⲛ ⲉⲗⲓⲁ ⲛⲉⲙ ⲣⲁⲭⲏⲗ ⲛⲏⲉⲧⲁⲩⲛⲕⲱⲧ ⲉⲡⲏⲓ ⲙⲡⲓⲥⲗ ϯⲛⲟⲩ ⲟⲛ ⲥⲙⲟⲩ ⲉⲡⲁⲓϫⲓⲛⲧⲟⲙⲓ ⲡⲁⲓ. Ⲉϥⲥⲙⲟⲩ ⲉⲣⲟⲕ…	يا الذى بارك لأبينا يعقوب اسرائيل فى اليا و راحيل يباركك بيركة عمانويل الآن يبارك هذا الاتصال باسمه القدوس		O You who blessed our father Jacob with Leah and Rachel who built the house of Israel now also bless this union. May He bless you O the bridegroom and his helpmate.
Ⲫⲏⲉⲧⲁϥⲥⲙⲟⲩ ⲛⲓⲟⲩⲥⲏⲃ ⲛⲉⲙ ⲉⲥⲏⲛⲛⲁⲧ ⲛⲉⲙ ⲍⲁⲭⲁⲣⲓⲁⲥ ⲉϫⲉⲛ ⲁⲗⲓⲥⲁⲃⲉⲧ ⲛⲉⲙ ⲓⲱⲁⲕⲓⲙ ⲛⲉⲙ ⲁⲛⲛⲁ ⲉⲧⲥⲙⲁⲙⲁⲧ ϯⲛⲟⲩ ⲟⲛ ⲥⲙⲟⲩ ⲉⲡⲁⲓϫⲓⲛⲧⲟⲙⲓ ⲡⲁⲓ. Ⲉϥⲥⲙⲟⲩ ⲉⲣⲟⲕ…	يا الذى بارك يوسف و اسنات و زكريا و اليصابات و يواقيم و حنه يبارك على هذا العريس و معينته باسمه العظيم		O You who blessed Joseph with Asenath and Zacharias with Elizabeth and Joachim and Anna the blessed now also bless this union. May He bless you O the bridegroom and his helpmate.
Ⲫⲏⲉⲧⲁϥⲥⲙⲟⲩ ⲙⲙⲓⲭⲁⲏⲗ ⲛⲉⲙ ⲅⲁⲃⲣⲓⲏⲗ ⲛⲉⲙ ⲣⲁⲫⲁⲏⲗ ⲛⲉⲙ ⲥⲟⲩⲣⲓⲏⲗ ⲛⲉⲙ ⲡⲓⲇ ⲛⲍⲟⲟⲛ ⲛⲁⲥⲟⲙⲁⲧⲟⲥ ⲛⲉⲙ ⲡⲓⲕⲇ ⲙⲡⲣⲉⲥⲃⲓⲧⲉⲣⲟⲥ ⲛⲉⲙ ⲛⲓⲭⲉⲣⲟⲩⲃⲓⲙ ⲛⲉⲙ ⲛⲓⲥⲁⲣⲁⲫⲓⲙ ⲛⲉⲙ ⲛⲓⲧⲁⲅⲙⲁ ⲛⲉⲡⲟⲩⲣⲁⲛⲓⲟⲛ ⲁϥⲥⲙⲟⲩ ⲉⲣⲟⲕ…	يا الذى بارك ميخائيل و غبريال و رافائيل و سوريال و الاربع حيوانات الغير متجسدين و الاربع و عشرين قسيس و الشاروبيم و السيرافيم يباركنا باسمه القدوس		He who blessed Michael and Gabriel and Raphael and Suriel and the four incorporeal creatures and the twenty four presbyters and the Cherubim and the Seraphim and the heavenly orders blesses you O the bridegroom and his helpmate.

ⲪⲎⲈⲦⲀϤⲤⲘⲞⲨ ⲚⲚⲀⲞⲤ ⲚⲒⲰⲦ ⲚⲀⲠⲞⲤⲦⲞⲖⲞⲤ ⲈⲦⲈ ⲠⲈⲦⲢⲞⲤ ⲚⲈⲘ ⲠⲈⲚⲤⲀϨ ⲠⲀⲨⲖⲞⲤ ⲚⲈⲘ ⲠⲤⲈⲠⲒ ⲚⲦⲈ ⲚⲒⲘⲀⲐⲎⲦⲎⲤ ⲚⲈⲘ ⲠⲀⲞⲤ ⲠⲞⲨⲢⲞ ⲄⲈⲰⲢⲄⲒⲞⲤ ⲚⲈⲘ ⲐⲈⲞⲆⲞⲢⲞⲤ ⲠⲒⲤⲒⲦⲢⲀϮⲖⲀⲦⲎⲤ ⲚⲈⲘ ⲐⲈⲞⲆⲞⲢⲞⲤ ⲠⲒⲈⲚⲀⲦⲞⲨⲖⲎⲞⲤ ⲚⲈⲘ ⲪⲎⲖⲞⲠⲀⲦⲎⲢ ⲘⲀⲢⲔⲞⲢⲒⲞⲤ ⲚⲈⲘ ⲀⲠⲀ ⲘⲒⲚⲀ ⲚⲈⲘ ⲀⲠⲀ ⲂⲞⲔⲐⲞⲢ ⲚⲈⲘ ⲬⲖⲞⲆⲒⲞⲤ ⲚⲈⲘ ⲠⲬⲰⲢⲞⲤ ⲦⲎⲢϤ ⲚⲦⲈ ⲚⲒⲘⲀⲢⲦⲨⲢⲞⲤ. ⲀϤⲤⲘⲞⲨ ⲈⲢⲞⲔ…	N/A – no Arabic translation is given for this verse	He who blessed our lords and fathers the Apostles, Peter and our teacher Paul, and the rest of the disciples, and my lord the prince George, and Theodore the general, and Theodore Anatolius, and Philopater Mercurius, and Abba Mina, and Abba Victor, and Claudius, and all the choir of the martyrs blesses you O the bridegroom and his helpmate.
ⲞⲨⲬⲖⲞⲘ ⲚⲚⲞⲨⲂ ⲞⲨⲬⲖⲞⲘ ⲚϨⲎⲦ ⲞⲨⲬⲖⲞⲘ ⲚⲰⲚⲒ ⲘⲘⲀⲢⲄⲀⲢⲒⲦⲎⲤ ⲀⲖ ⲀⲖ ⲔⲈ ⲀⲖ ⲠⲀⲒⲞⲨ ⲠⲈⲚⲚⲞⲨϮ ⲠⲈ.	N/A – no Arabic translation is given for this verse	[With] A crown of gold, a crown of silver, a crown of precious stone. Alleluia, Alleluia, Alleluia glory be to our God.

These verses for the bride not specified by Ibn Kabar. The last two verses are not accompanied by an Arabic translation. Once again, the Arabic translations end with different words in order to make the whole verse more poetic. My English translations follow the Coptic.

The priest then says the prayer after the crowning to the Lord. This prayer was probably said silently. Then they say this doxology in the Morning Doxology tune: "Unfading crowns the Lord has placed upon the bridegroom of Jesus Christ. Illuminate, Illuminate O bridegroom and your true bride who is in the prepared place [ϨⲀⲚⲬⲖⲞⲘ ⲚⲀⲦⲖⲞⲘ ⲀϤⲦⲎⲒⲦⲞⲨ ⲚϪⲈ ⲡⲟⲥ ⲉϫⲉⲛ ⲡⲓⲡⲁⲧϣⲉⲗⲉⲧ ⲛⲧⲉ ⲓⲏⲥ ⲡⲭⲥ. ϭⲓⲟⲩⲱⲓⲛⲓ ϭⲓⲟⲩⲱⲓⲛⲓ ⲱ ⲡⲓⲡⲁⲧϣⲉⲗⲉⲧ ⲛⲉⲙ ⲧⲉⲕϣⲉⲗⲉⲧ ⲙⲙⲏⲓ ⲉⲧϧⲉⲛ ⲡⲓⲙⲁ ⲉⲧⲥⲉⲃⲧⲱⲧ]." Pope Gabriel only includes these two verses. They say Our Father and the priest says, "Yes O Lord" followed by "You O Lord" and the Absolution of the Son "with the cross over the heads of the groom and bride and his hands placed crosswise as our father Jacob Israel blessed the sons of Joseph."[35]

After the Absolution of the Son, he says the commandment facing East until he finishes with saying "unto the ages of ages, Amen." The people say with the cymbals in its "special tune",[36] "My peace I give you [Ϫⲉ ⲧⲁϩⲓⲣⲏⲛⲏ ⲁⲛⲟⲕ]" followed by "O King of Peace [Ⲡⲟⲩⲣⲟ ⲛⲧⲉ ϯϩⲓⲣⲏⲛⲏ]." The special tune here is not clear. It could mean any of the tunes we've seen so far but it most likely is the muḥayyar tune. The priest says, "The peace of our Lord Jesus Christ" towards the West. Then he delivers the bride to the groom. The deacons sing the following verses in the muḥayyar tune. Pope Gabriel only includes the complete text of the first two verses and the first few words of the remaining verses:

Ⲫⲛⲁⲩ ⲙⲡⲓⲥⲙⲟⲩ ⲡⲉ ⲫⲁⲓ ⲫⲛⲁⲩ ⲙⲡⲓⲥⲑⲟⲓⲛⲟⲩϥⲓ ⲉⲧⲥⲱⲧⲡ. Ⲫⲛⲁⲩ ⲛⲧⲉⲛϩⲟⲥ ⲉⲡⲉⲛⲥⲱⲣ ⲡⲓⲙⲁⲓⲣⲱⲙⲓ ⲛⲁⲅⲁⲑⲟⲥ	This is the time of blessing, this is the time of chosen incense, this is the time for us to praise our Savior the Lover of mankind.
Ⲟⲩⲥⲑⲟⲓⲛⲟⲩϥⲓ ⲡⲉ Ⲙⲁⲣⲓⲁ ⲟⲩⲥⲑⲟⲓⲛⲟⲩϥⲓ ⲉⲥⲙⲓⲥⲓ ⲙⲙⲟϥ. Ⲟⲩⲥⲑⲟⲓⲛⲟⲩϥⲓ ⲉⲧϧⲉⲛ ⲧⲉⲥⲛⲉϫⲓ ϣⲁϥⲭⲁ ⲛⲉⲛⲛⲟⲃⲓ ⲛⲁⲛ ⲉⲃⲟⲗ	The incense is Mary, the incense is the one to whom she gave birth, the incense is the one in her womb. He forgives us our sins.
Ⲟⲩⲥⲑⲟⲓⲛⲟⲩϥⲓ ⲡⲉ Ⲓⲏⲥ. ⲁⲙⲱⲓⲛⲓ	The incense is Jesus. Come
Ⲛⲓϣⲉⲣⲟⲩⲃⲓⲙ ⲥⲉⲟⲩⲱϣⲧ ⲙⲙⲟϥ	The Cherubim worship Him

---

[35] Appendix B, Section 7.
[36] Ibid.

Ⲭⲟⲩⲁⲃ Ⲡⲟⲥ ϧⲉⲛ ⲛⲓⲁⲛⲁⲛⲙⲩⲟⲩ	Holy are You O Lord among the thousands
Ⲉⲕⲧⲁⲓⲟⲩⲧ ϧⲉⲛ ⲛⲓⲁⲛⲁⲛⲟⲃⲁ	You are honored among the myriads
Ⲛⲑⲟⲕ ⲟⲩⲥⲑⲟⲓⲛⲟⲩϥⲓ ⲡⲁⲥⲱⲣ ϫⲉ ⲁⲕⲓ ⲁⲕⲥⲱϯ ⲙⲙⲱⲛ ⲛⲁⲓ ⲛⲁⲛ	You are incense O my savior for You came and saved us. Have mercy on us.

The priest says the second commandment to the groom, "It behooves you O beloved brother, and blessed son" until "may it be good to you in this world and the next." They respond saying,

Ⲥⲱⲧⲉⲙ ⲧⲁϣⲉⲣⲓ ⲁⲛⲁⲩ ⲣⲉⲕ ⲡⲉⲕⲙⲁϣϫ ⲁⲣⲓⲡⲱⲃϣ ⲙⲡⲉⲗⲁⲟⲥ ⲛⲉⲙ ⲡⲁⲓ ⲧⲏⲣϥ ⲛⲧⲉ ⲡⲁⲓⲱⲧ. Ϫⲉⲧ ⲁ ⲡⲓⲟⲩⲣⲟ ⲉⲣⲉⲡⲓⲑⲩⲙⲓⲛ ⲉⲡⲉⲥⲁⲓ. Ϫⲉ ⲟⲩⲏⲓ ⲛⲑⲟϥ ⲡⲉ ⲡⲟⲥ.	Listen or daughter and see and incline your ear. Forget your people and your father's house. For the king has desired your beauty, for he alone is your lord. (Ps. 45:10,11)
Ⲡⲱⲟⲩ ⲧⲏⲣϥ ⲛⲧϣⲱⲣⲓ ⲙⲡⲟⲩⲣⲟ ⲟⲩⲛⲉⲥⲉⲃⲱⲛ ⲉⲥⲛⲓⲉⲃ ⲛⲛⲟⲩⲃ. ⲁⲗ ⲁⲗ ⲁⲗ ⲡⲓⲱⲟⲩ ⲫⲁ ⲡⲉⲛⲛⲟⲩϯ ⲡⲉ	All the glory of the daughter is within, her clothing is wrought with gold. (Ps. 45: 13) Alleluia, Alleluia, Alleluia Glory be to our God.

The priest says, "And you blessed and glad daughter" until the end of the commandment. They respond with Amen. The priest lifts the cross and they say Lord Have Mercy 43 times. They sing the concluding canon "Rejoice O groom [ⲭⲉⲣⲉ ⲡⲓⲡⲉⲧϣⲉⲗⲉⲧ]"[37] during which the priest says the blessing over the heads of the couple as in the case of the Absolution of the Son with his hands crosswise.

---

[37] This is probably a typographical error. The correct text of this hymn should start with Rejoice O bride. But the text starts with Rejoice O groom. The words for bride and groom in Coptic are almost identical.

Then he blesses the bride and bids her to sit and rest. Then he gives the groom the cross in his hand[38] and stands him in the East. Then, holding candles, they sing before him, "Blessed is he who comes" and "Galilee of the nations" while processing into the church until they reach the chancel. This may be going from a house back to the church from a church building back into the church proper. If the crowning was already in the church, then it is also possible that just a procession around the nave was done. This is usually a stand-in for a procession from a location to the church anyway. "Then they begin the service of the Divine Liturgy whether the Patriarch is in attendance or not. If the groom is a deacon, and is prepared, he serves in the sanctuary and carries the chalice."[39] This line is interesting because full deacons are not supposed to get married after ordination. At first glance, the only way this would make sense is if the groom got married, and then got ordained a deacon during the post-wedding liturgy. But the problem with that is that in order to be ordained a deacon, he must have already been ordained a subdeacon, and subdeacons are also prohibited from marriage after ordination. The gospel response of the liturgy is the response of the Feast of the Wedding at Cana of Galilee, "Six jars of water You transformed into choice wine through Your great power at the wedding at Cana of Galilee [ⲋ ⲛⲋⲩⲁⲣⲓⲁ ⲁⲙⲱⲟⲩ ⲟⲩⲏⲣⲡ ⲉⲧⲥⲱⲧⲡ ⲁⲕⲟⲩⲱⲧⲉⲃ ⲙⲙⲱⲟⲩ ⲉⲃⲟⲗϩⲓⲧⲉⲛ ⲡⲉϥⲛⲓϣϯ ⲛⲱⲟⲩ ϧⲉⲛ ⲡϩⲟ ⲛⲧⲉ ⲛⲁ ⲛⲧⲉ ϯⲅⲁⲗⲓⲗⲉⲁ]." When the liturgy concludes, they process the bride first to the doors of the church with "Rejoice O Mary [ⲭⲉⲣⲉ ⲛⲉ ⲙⲁⲣⲓⲁ]." They have the groom stand at the chancel and sing before him the hymn "Blessed is he who comes" and after it "May God Bless Us" and if time permits, "Galilee of the Nations", until they process him out to the doors of the church. After that, they return to their homes in peace.

---

[38] Giving the cross to hold in his hand is also something done to a newly ordained priest on the day of welcoming him to his church after his period of training.

[39] Appendix B, Section 8.

CHAPTER 3

The 19th Century – Hegumen Philotheos Ibrahim

Biography

The next source is from Hegumen Philotheos Ibrahim Baghdady (1837-1904). He lived during the time of the Muhammad Ali dynasty. He was ordained priest in 1863 and elevated to hegumen in 1865. He was transferred to the patriarchal cathedral in Cairo in 1874.[40] He was an expert in Coptic language and theology. During his time, Protestant missionaries were very active in Egypt. Most Copts did not know or practice their faith. Hegumen Philotheos traveled throughout Egypt giving sermons in defense of the Orthodox faith. He also taught Coptic language in various schools and later at the newly established seminary. He supported modernization efforts as well as using more Arabic in worship services to make them accessible to people.

Description of His Work

As the hegumen of the patriarchal cathedral, he was essentially in the same position as Ibn Kabar, and had the same level of influence. He wrote many sermons and training manuals for clergy. *The Dignified Rank of Crowning (Rutbat al-Iklīl al-Jalīl)* is just one of his works. Like Pope

---

[40] Aziz Atiya, *Claremont Coptic Encyclopedia,* s.v. "Philuthawus Ibrahim al-Baghdadi," https://ccdl.claremont.edu/digital/collection/cce/id/1574.

Gabriel V, he wrote it to standardize practices. He includes the full Coptic and Arabic text of all readings and prayers. He also includes a homily in Arabic to be used during weddings if desired. He foresaw that using the vernacular would become important in the future. Indeed, as the Church entered the 20th century, it became less acceptable to just use Coptic for all services without paying attention to the level of understanding by the common layperson. As an expert, and a pastor, Hegumen Philotheos knew the importance the Copts placed on their weddings. He introduced many new responses in Arabic to allow the general populace to participate and understand the ceremony. All of these additions are still present in the rite as it is practiced today.

Description of the Rite

He calls the first part the sequence of the pledge [ϯⲁⲕⲟⲩⲗⲟⲅⲉⲓⲁ̀ ⲛⲧⲉ ⲡⲓⲁⲣⲏⲃ] in Coptic and 'aqd al-amlāk in Arabic.[41] This is the first time a label other than the Arabic 'aqd al-amlāk appears in the literature. He does not mention where it starts but says it should be in a church. He makes no mention of processional hymns and no mention of what the priest wears. The rings and crowns are no longer placed on a tray with the other items. Instead, the rings and crowns are threaded through the broad white cloth that will be placed on the couple's heads later, and the whole thing is wrapped around the cross. The priest holds that same cross in his right hand and begins the first part with a set of declarations. These are brand new and in Arabic only. They are interspersed between the common Coptic blessings:

---

[41] Heg Philotheos Ibrahim. *Rutbat al-Iklīl al-Jalīl [The Dignified Rank of Crowning]* (Cairo: Al-Watan, 1888), 7.

	باسم ربنا و مخلصنا يسوع المسيح نعقد أملاك الابن الارثذوكسي المبارك البكر (فلان) على مخطوبته الابنة الارثذوكسية المباركة البكر (فلانة)	In the name of our Lord, God, and Savior Jesus Christ, we declare the marriage of the blessed Orthodox son the virgin (…) to his fiance the blessed Orthodox daughter the virgin (…).
Ϧⲉⲛ ⲫⲣⲁⲛ ⲙ̀ⲫⲓⲱⲧ ⲛⲉⲙ ⲡ̀ϣⲏⲣⲓ ⲛⲉⲙ ⲡⲓⲡ̀ⲛⲉⲩⲙⲁ ⲉⲑⲟⲩⲁⲃ ⲟⲩⲛⲟⲩϯ ⲛ̀ⲟⲩⲱⲧ ϥ̀ⲥⲙⲁⲣⲱⲟⲩⲧ ⲛ̀ϫⲉ ⲫ̀ⲛⲟⲩϯ ⲫⲓⲱⲧ ⲡⲓⲡⲁⲛⲧⲟⲕⲣⲁⲧⲱⲣ ⲁⲙⲏⲛ	باسم الآب و الابن و الروح القدس اله واحد مبارك الله الآب الضابط الكل آمين	In the name of the Father and the Son and the Holy Spirit one God, blessed be God the Father the Pantocrator. Amen.
	باسم ربنا و مخلصنا يسوع المسيح نعقد أملاك الابنة الارثذوكسية المباركة البكر (فلانة) على الابن الارثذوكسي المبارك البكر (فلان)	In the name of our Lord, God, and Savior Jesus Christ, we declare the marriage of the blessed Orthodox daughter the virgin (…) to the blessed Orthodox son the virgin (…).
ϥ̀ⲥⲙⲁⲣⲱⲟⲩⲧ ⲛ̀ϫⲉ ⲡⲉϥⲙⲟⲛⲟⲅⲉⲛⲏⲥ ⲛ̀ϣⲏⲣⲓ Ⲓⲏⲥ Ⲡⲭⲥ ⲡⲉⲛϭⲟⲓⲥ ⲁⲙⲏⲛ	مبارك ابنه الوحيد يسوع المسيح ربنا آمين	Blessed be His Only-Begotten Son Jesus Christ our Lord. Amen.
	باسم ربنا و مخلصنا يسوع المسيح نعقد أملاك الابن الارثذوكسي المبارك البكر (فلان) على مخطوبته الابنة الارثذوكسية المباركة البكر (فلانة)	In the name of our Lord, God, and Savior Jesus Christ, we declare the marriage of the blessed Orthodox son the virgin (…) to his fiance the blessed Orthodox daughter the virgin (…).
ϥ̀ⲥⲙⲁⲣⲱⲟⲩⲧ ⲛ̀ϫⲉ ⲡⲓⲡ̀ⲛⲉⲩⲙⲁ ⲉⲑⲟⲩⲁⲃ ⲙ̀ⲡⲁⲣⲁⲕⲗⲏⲧⲟⲛ ⲁⲙⲏⲛ	مبارك الروح القدس المعزي آمين	Blessed be the Holy Spirit the Paraclete. Amen.

The people respond to each one with Amen three times followed by Our Father. The second declaration has the bride is mentioned first then the groom. The third declaration is exactly like the first. The priest finishes the declarations by saying "Glory and honor, honor and glory to the All-Holy Trinity the Father the Son and the Holy Spirit now and forever and unto the age of ages Amen."

It is unknown why Hegumen Philotheos added these declarations to the beginning of the ceremony. My best guess is that he copied them over from the engagement ceremony that he created. Although beyond the scope of this study, there was never any formal rite for an engagement in the Coptic Church. But Hegumen Philotheos created one as he saw a need for people to start going through a period of engagement and courtship first before going straight to marriage. His engagement rite consisted of just these declarations followed by a few short prayers. Perhaps he thought that by inserting the same declarations to the beginning of the wedding, he would ensure the couple were always officially engaged before getting married. The logic he used is that engagement and marriage are ranks like the clerical ranks of priesthood.[42] Just as with any clerical hierarchy, one should not skip over ranks but attain each one sequentially. So in this case, one should not skip over engagement straight to marriage. However, this view of marital status as a clerical rank is not present in either Ibn Kabar or Pope Gabriel's Ordo, who both viewed it as a covenantal relationship rather than a rank.

After the declarations, the priest says Have mercy on us followed by Our Father. The priest says the Thanksgiving Prayer. Then the people chant the Hymn of the Censer [ⲧⲁⲓϣⲟⲩⲣⲏ]. There are no Verses of the Cymbals and no Psalm 50. The Pauline Epistle is read from 1 Corinthians. The Trisagion is said. The priest recites the Litany of Gospel. The Psalm is from Psalm 48 just as it was in Pope Gabriel (Mercy and Truth). The Gospel is John 1. The Gospel response is "Rejoice O bridal chamber" in the Palm Sunday tune. If the patriarch is in attendance, they add

---

[42] Ibid, 3.

"Likewise we magnify you." If not, then they say, "Intercede on our behalf." The priest says the three great litanies of peace, fathers, congregations. They say the Creed.

He calls the next four prayers "Prayers for the Contract of Properties [صلاة لعقد الاملاك]."[43] The responses are the same as in Pope Gabriel but do not include the final three Lord Have Mercies. They are said in the muḥayyar tune. There is no mention of a call to peace. It was probably abandoned for being repetitive or ineffective. He does not mention which way the priest faces for each prayer. After the fourth prayer, the people say Our Father while the priest says the Absolution of the Son. It is not specified that the cross be placed over the head of the groom. The people say Lord Have Mercy three times.

The priest begins the prayer of the vestment. There is no mention of the godparent preparing the vestment. It was probably the case that by this time it had fallen out of practice for people to make their own vestments for this prayer. The modern practice of using any priestly phelonion probably started around this time. After the prayer the people chant "The Spiritual Raiment." The hymn is expanded with four new verses:

ϮⲤⲦⲞⲖⲎ ⲘⲠⲚⲈⲨⲘⲀⲦⲒⲔⲞⲚ ⲀⲨⲦⲈⲒⲰⲦϤ ⲘⲘⲒⲬⲀⲎⲖ ⲞⲨⲞϨ ⲠⲒϨⲰⲔ ⲘⲘⲀⲢⲄⲀⲢⲒⲦⲎⲤ ⲀⲨⲘⲎⲢ ⲘⲘⲒⲬⲀⲎⲖ ⲘⲘⲞϤ	الحلة الروحية التحف بها ميخائيل و المنطقة الجوهرية تمنطق بها ميخائيل	The spiritual raiment was clothed around Michael and the precious cloak was draped around Michael
ϮⲤⲦⲞⲖⲎ ⲚⲞⲨⲤⲰⲪⲢⲞⲤⲨⲚⲎ ⲀⲨⲦⲎⲒⲤ ⲈϪⲈⲚ ⲠⲀⲒϢⲈⲖⲈⲦ ⲞⲨⲞϨ ⲠⲒⲬⲖⲞⲘ ⲚⲦⲈ ⲠⲐⲈⲖⲎⲖ ⲀⲨⲦⲎⲒϤ ⲈϪⲈⲚ ⲦⲈϤⲀⲪⲈ	حلة العفاف أعطيت لهذا العريس و اكليل البهجة وضع على رأسه	The raiment of chastity has been given to this bridegroom, and the crown of joy has been placed upon his head

---

[43] Ibid., 15.

ⲕⲁⲧⲁ ⲫⲣⲏϯ ⲉⲧⲁϥϫⲟⲥ ⲛϫⲉ ⲇⲁⲩⲓⲇ ⲡⲓϩⲩⲙⲛⲟⲧⲟⲥ ϫⲉ ⲟⲩⲱⲟⲩ ⲛⲉⲙ ⲟⲩⲧⲁⲓⲟ ⲁⲕⲧⲏⲓⲧⲟⲩ ⲛⲟⲩⲭⲗⲟⲙ ⲉϫⲟϥ	كالذي قاله داود المرتل مجدا و كرامة جعلتهما تاجا عليه	As it is said by David the Psalmist, "You have made glory and honor, a crown for him"
ⲁⲕⲉⲣϣⲟⲣⲡ ⲉⲣⲟϥ ϧⲉⲛ ⲡⲓⲥⲙⲟⲩ ⲛⲧⲉ ⲧⲉⲕⲙⲉⲧⲭⲣⲥ ⲁⲕⲭⲱ ϩⲓϫⲱϥ ⲛⲟⲩⲭⲗⲟⲙ ⲉⲃⲟⲗ ϧⲉⲛ ⲟⲩⲱⲛⲓ ⲉϥⲧⲁⲓⲏⲟⲩⲧ	أدركته بركة صلاحك و وضعت على رأسه اكليل من حجر كريم	You have manifested to him the blessing of Your kindness, and placed upon his head a crown of precious stone
ⲁϥⲉⲣⲉⲧⲓⲛ ⲙⲙⲟⲕ ⲛⲟⲩⲱⲛϧ ⲡⲟⲥ ⲟⲩⲟϩ ⲁⲕⲧⲏⲓϥ ⲛⲁϥ ⲫⲟⲩⲉⲓ ⲛⲧⲉ ⲡⲓⲉⲛⲉϩ ⲁⲙⲏⲛ	سألك حياة يا رب فأعطيته طول الايام الى أبد الأبد آمين	He asked You for life O Lord and You granted it to him to the furthest age. Amen

There is no mention of its tune but there is no reason to suspect its tune changed from the Palm Sunday tune. There is no mention of extra verses for the patriarch or intercessory verses. The new verses come from Psalms 8 and 21. They could be Hegumen Philotheos' own addition to the hymn. It is also possible that they were a local custom in some of the churches during his time. Regardless, they change the nature of the hymn from being focused on the Archangel Michael and the Patriarch to being focused on the groom and the fact that he is being vested and crowned in the wedding. It would make sense that Hegumen Philotheos is the one who added these verses because it is consistent with his other additions that restate hymns or biblical verses to link them more explicitly with the bride and groom.

This hymn marks the end of the first part of the wedding. In Pope Gabriel's Ordo there was a whole sequence of events that involved the exchange of rings between the bride and the groom. This is omitted in Hegumen Philotheos' description. In fact, there is no mention of any movements or processions, just that the bride is brought in from where she was to where the groom is already standing. There is no mention of the hymn "Come see this bride." It is possible that the bride was already in the nave at this point and that she was simply brought up to the chancel without a procession. Pope Gabriel has the priest in full clerical dress at this point. But here the priest is dressed as if he is in vespers or matins, only wearing the epitrachelion. This change probably came about as the post-wedding liturgy was abandoned and weddings were moved to the end of the day.

The priest begins the second part by uncovering his head and saying Have mercy on us, Our Father, and the Thanksgiving Prayer. The people sing the second half of the Hymn of the Censer [ϯϣουρη]. It is said during the incense raised after the Thanksgiving Prayer so again there are no Verses of the Cymbals and no Psalm 50. It is likely that in the times of Pope Gabriel and Ibn Kabar, they said Ταιϣουρη and Τϣουρη together. Here Ταιϣουρη is said in part 1 and Τϣουρη is said in part 2 probably as a time saver. But really, they from one unit. The full text is "This censer of pure gold, bearing the aroma, which is in the hands of Aaron the priest, offering up incense on the altar, the golden censer, is the Virgin. Her aroma is our Savior. She gave birth to Him. He saved us and forgave us our sins." Clearly, together they make a complete sentence but separately, they are only sentence fragments. Next, the Pauline Epistle is read. There is no mention of which language should be used in the readings but given that the full Coptic text appears, it can be assumed they were read in Coptic first then Arabic. The Trisagion is said. The priest recites the Litany of Gospel. The Psalm and Gospel are read. The Gospel Response is the same as that found in Pope Gabriel (Those whom the Holy Spirit attuned together) but "We worship" and the proceeding three Lord Have Mercies are omitted.

Then the Supplications are said. There is no deacon's call to prayer and no priest's call to peace. Nor are there directions to say a few of them in Coptic. The Supplications now end with the people saying "Christ the Logos of the Father, the Only-Begotten God, grant us Your peace that is full of joy. For blessed. [Ⲡⲭⲥ ⲡⲓⲗⲟⲅⲟⲥ ⲛⲧⲉ ⲫⲓⲱⲧ ⲡⲓⲙⲟⲛⲟⲅⲉⲛⲏⲥ ⲛⲛⲟⲩϯ

ⲈⲔⲈϮ ⲚⲀⲚ ⲚⲦⲈⲔϨⲒⲢⲎⲚⲎ ⲐⲀⲒ ⲈⲐⲘⲈϨ ⲚⲢⲀϢⲒ ⲚⲒⲂⲈⲚ. Ϫⲉ ϥⲤⲘⲀⲢⲰⲞⲨⲦ]." This verse is the response of the first post-creed prayer in the first part. It did not appear as a response to the Supplications in either Pope Gabriel or Ibn Kabar. It is unknown why Hegumen Philotheos added it in this position. The most likely explanation is that he did it based on the other changes he made to the responses of the subsequent prayers. In any case, the priest recites the three great litanies. The people say the Creed with no mention of Lord Have Mercy at all after the Creed.

The priest begins the Matrimonial Prayers. The responses include one verse for Christ and one for the Virgin with no "Blessed is the Father" or Lord Have Mercy three times. The verses are different than what Pope Gabriel had. Pope Gabriel listed the following as the responses: "As David has said", "Solomon called you", and "Do not forget". Each one was followed by "Blessed is the Father" and Lord Have Mercy three times. Hegumen Philotheos lists the following as the responses: "As You have given", "The door of the East", "My peace which I have taken", "All the kings of the Earth", "Solomon called you", "Do not forget", "O the angel of this day", "You're brighter than the sun." He added one or two more verses for the Virgin to each response and removed the concluding "Blessed is the Father" and three Lord Have Mercies. Hegumen Philotheos says the first and third responses are said by deacons, but the second prayer's response is said by the priest, but this was probably a typographical error.[44] It is unlikely that the priest would say any of the responses. There is no mention of the tune used but in the first part of the wedding the analogous verses were said in the muḥayyar tune. Given that the verses are different and higher in number, it is likely that this is when the muḥayyar tune began to be abandoned in favor of the Palm Sunday tune. The deacon's call to bow the heads and congregation response are omitted. The priest says the prayer of submission. Its response is "May God Bless us" as in Pope Gabriel and this time it is followed by "Blessed is the Father." Instead of saying "Blessed is the Father" with every

---

[44] Ibid., 47.

response, Hegumen Philotheos puts it at the very end to conclude the Matrimonial Prayers.

The priest prays over the oil with "O Master Lord God the Pantocrator." When he anoints the groom, the people sing, "May this oil destroy demons; this oil is against the evil spirits; this oil is the oil of holy spirits; this oil is against the assaults of unclean spirits through Jesus Christ the King of Glory. Blessed is the Father and the Son and the Holy Spirit the perfect Trinity, we worship Him and glorify Him. [Παινεϩ ϕαι ντεϥκωρϥ ναεμων παινεϩ ϕαι ογβε μπνεγμα μπονηρον παινεϩ ϕαι ννιπνεγμα ναγιον παι νεϩ ϕαι ογβε ναντια ννιπνεγμα νακαθαρτον ϩιτεν Ιηϲ Πχϲ πογρο ντε πωογ. Δε ϥϲμαρωογτ ̀ ναε ϕιωτ νεμ πϣηρι νεμ πιπνεγμα εθογαβ ϯτριαϲ εταηκ εβολ τενογωϣτ μμοϲ τενϯωογ ναϲ]."[45] This is the first time this verse appears as a response to this prayer. Its tune is not specified. It comes from the rite of baptism, but it is unknown if it appears there as a single response or if it is something composed of many smaller responses. It was probably added because the oil used during the wedding is the oil of gladness [Γαλιλεον] [غاليلاون].[46] Hegumen Philotheos probably associated this verse with any use of this oil and hence probably felt it appropriate to include it here. This is also probably why it appears with "Blessed is the Father" after it. He needed a way to say this new verse is not part of the existing "You have anointed" verses. But the addition does not make sense because weddings have little to do with fighting off demons and unclean spirits. Furthermore, it is not tradition to associate certain verses or hymns with specific elements like oil. The oil of gladness is used in many different scenarios, not all of which are related. When he anoints the bride, they sing the "You have

---

[45] Ibahim, 55.
[46] The Coptic Church uses three kinds of oil: regular olive oil, consecrated myron oil, and the oil of gladness which is made from the remnants of the process of making myron.

anointed" verses. Although he does not mention the tune, Hegumen Philotheos includes the following verses:

ⲁⲕⲑⲱϩⲥ ⲛⲧⲁⲁϥⲉ ⲛⲟⲩⲛⲉϩ ⲟⲩⲟϩ ⲡⲉⲕⲁⲫⲟⲧ ⲉⲧⲑⲁϧⲓ ⲙ̄ⲫⲣⲏϯ ⲛⲟⲩⲁⲙⲁϩⲓ	دهنت بالزيت رأسي وكأسك اسكرني مثل الصرف	You have anointed my head with oil and your cup intoxicated me.
ⲡⲉⲕⲛⲁⲓ ⲉϥⲉⲃⲟϫⲓ ⲛ̄ⲥⲱⲓ ⲛ̄ⲛⲓⲉϩⲟⲟⲩ ⲧⲏⲣⲟⲩ ⲛ̄ⲧⲉ ⲡⲁⲱⲛϧ	و رحمتك تدركني كل ايام حياتي	Your mercy will seek me all the days of my life.
ϩⲁⲛⲉⲑⲛⲟⲥ ⲧⲏⲣⲟⲩ ⲥⲉⲛⲁⲉⲣⲙⲁⲕⲁⲣⲓⲍⲓⲛ ⲙ̄ⲙⲱⲟⲩ ⲉϫⲟⲥ ⲉⲃⲟⲗ ⲉⲥⲉϣⲱⲡⲓ ⲁⲙⲏⲛ	يغبطهما الامم جميعها قائلين سيكون آمين	All the nations bless them saying may it be Amen.
ⲁ ⲡⲟⲥ ⲟⲩⲱⲣⲡ ⲙ̄ⲡⲉϥⲁⲅⲅⲉⲗⲟⲥ ⲁϥⲟⲗⲧ ⲉⲃⲟⲗ ϧⲉⲛ ⲛⲓⲉⲥⲱⲟⲩ ⲛ̄ⲧⲉ ⲡⲁⲓⲱⲧ ⲟⲩⲟϩ ⲁϥⲑⲁϩⲥ ⲙ̄ⲙⲟⲓ ϧⲉⲛ ⲡⲛⲉϩ ⲛ̄ⲧⲉ ⲡⲉϥⲑⲱϩⲥ	الرب أرسل ملاكه و اخذني من غنم أبي و مسحني بدهن مسحته	The Lord sent His angel; he lifted me from my father's sheep and anointed me with the oil of his anointing.
ⲛⲁⲥⲛⲏⲟⲩ ⲛⲁⲛⲉⲩ ⲟⲩⲟϩϩⲁⲛⲁϣϯ ⲛⲉ ⲥⲉⲛⲁⲉⲣⲙⲁⲕⲁⲣⲓⲍⲓⲛ ⲙ̄ⲙⲟⲓ ⲛⲁϫⲟⲥ ⲉⲃⲟⲗ ⲉⲥⲉϣⲱⲡⲓ ⲉⲥⲉϣⲱⲡⲓ ⲁⲙⲏⲛ	اخوتي حسان و هم عظماء يغبطوني قائلين سيكون سيكون آمين	My brothers are handsome and great; they will bless me saying may it be. Amen.
ϫⲉ ϥⲥⲙⲁⲣⲱⲟⲩⲧ	لأنه مبارك	For blessed

There are considerable differences that appear in this version. First, the third verse changed from "bless me" to "bless them." In the Arabic the word them is in the dual hinting that it probably was reinterpreted from quoting a bible verse to referring to the bride and groom. The fourth, fifth, and sixth verses of Ibn Kabar are missing. The last verse is expanded to say that the handsome brothers also bless David. However, that line is not part of Psalm 151 so Hegumen Philotheos must have felt it awkward to just end with "My brothers are handsome and great" and added the rest to make it a complete thought.

The priest begins the prayer of the crowns with "O Lord God of powers." The priest holds the crowns and says "O God the Holy who crowned the saints." He puts the crowns on the couple and says "Put O Lord on your servants." He puts the broad white cloth on them[47] and says while signing them with the cross:

كللهما بالمجد و الكرامة أيها الآب آمين	Crown them with glory and honor O Father Amen.
باركهما أيها الابن الوحيد آمين	Bless them O Only-Begotten Son Amen.
قدسهما أيها الروح القدس آمين	Sanctify them O Holy Spirit Amen.

The Greek text found in Pope Gabriel and Ibn Kabar is completely omitted here. There is only the Arabic. Note that it is not an exact translation of the original Greek. The text turned into the imperative mood. The Greek had it in the indicative mood. It appears that by this point nobody was saying the original Greek anyway so Hegumen Philotheos dispensed with it entirely and made the best Arabic interpretation he could create. The references to the Holy Spirit surrounding and perfecting are also omitted in favor of saying the Holy Spirit sanctifies. In previous versions the white cloth was put on at the beginning of the ceremony. But now the crowns come first and are placed when the priest says, "Put O Lord on your servants." The white cloth is placed on top of the crowns when the priest says, "Crown them with glory." The people respond saying "Worthy, Worthy, Worthy is the groom and his helpmate [ⲁⲝⲓⲟⲥ

---

[47] Ibid., 62.

ⲁⲍⲓⲟⲥ ⲁⲍⲓⲟⲥ ⲡⲓⲡⲁⲧϣⲉⲗⲉⲧ ⲛⲉⲙ ⲧⲉϥⲃⲟⲏⲑⲟⲥ]." This is said in the Axios tune. Then they say this doxology in the Morning Doxology tune:

ϩⲁⲛⲭⲗⲟⲙ ⲛⲁⲧⲗⲟⲙ ⲁϥⲑⲏⲓⲧⲟⲩ ⲛϫⲉ ⲡⲟⲥ ⲉϫⲉⲛ ⲡⲓⲡⲁⲧϣⲉⲗⲉⲧ ⲛⲧⲉ ⲓⲏⲥ ⲡⲭⲥ	أكاليل لا تبلى منحها الرب لهذا العريس الذي ليسوع المسيح	Unfading crowns the Lord has placed upon the bridegroom of Jesus Christ
ϭⲓⲟⲩⲱⲓⲛⲓ ϭⲓⲟⲩⲱⲓⲛⲓ ⲱ ⲡⲓⲡⲁⲧϣⲉⲗⲉⲧ ⲛⲉⲙ ⲧⲉⲕϣⲉⲗⲉⲧ ⲙⲙⲏⲓ ⲉⲧϧⲉⲛ ⲡⲓⲙⲁ ⲉⲧⲥⲉⲃⲧⲱⲧ	استضئ استضئ أيها العريس مع عروستك الحقيقية التي في موضعك المستعد	Illuminate, Illuminate O bridegroom and your true bride who is in the prepared place
ϭⲓ ⲛⲁⲕ ⲛⲟⲩⲣⲁϣⲓ ⲛⲉⲙ ϯⲱⲣⲉⲁ ⲛⲧⲉ ⲫϯ ⲉⲧⲁϥⲧⲏⲓⲧⲟⲩ ⲛⲁⲕ ⲛϫⲉ ⲡⲭⲥ ⲡⲉⲛⲛⲟⲩϯ	اقبل الفرح و موهبة الله التي أعطاها لك المسيح الهنا	Take unto you joy and the gift of God which Christ our God has given you
ⲙⲁϣⲉⲛⲁⲕ ϧⲉⲛ ⲟⲩⲣⲁϣⲓ ⲉⲡⲉⲕⲙⲁⲛϣⲉⲗⲉⲧ ⲉⲧⲥⲉⲗⲥⲱⲗ ⲉⲃⲟⲗ ϧⲉⲛ ⲟⲩⲑⲟ ⲛⲣⲏϯ	أمض بفرح الى خدرك المزين بكل نوع	Go with joy to your bridal chamber that is decorated in various way

Then they say Our Father and the priest says the Absolution of the Son.

The priest then says the verses of blessing while crossing the groom's head before each verse. This is another change. In both Ibn Kabar and Pope Gabriel, the order was the proclamation of worthiness, the verses of blessing, the doxology, and finally the absolution. Here, the order is proclamation of worthiness, doxology, absolution, verses of blessing. It is not clear why this change was made. The verses for the groom are:

Ⲫⲏⲉⲧⲁϥⲥⲙⲟⲩ ⲙⲡⲉⲛⲓⲱⲧ ⲁⲇⲁⲙ ⲛⲉⲙ ⲛⲱⲉ ⲛⲉⲙ ⲁⲃⲣⲣⲁⲙ ⲛⲉⲙ ⲙⲱⲩⲥⲏⲥ ϧⲉⲛ ⲡⲕⲁϩⲓ ⲙⲙⲁⲇⲓⲁⲙ ⲉϥⲥⲙⲟⲩ ⲉⲣⲟⲕ ⲱ ⲡⲓⲡⲁⲧϣⲉⲗⲏⲧ ⲛⲉⲙ ⲧⲉϥⲃⲟⲏⲑⲟⲥ	الذي بارك أبانا آدم و نوح و ابراهيم و موسى في أرض مدين يباركك أيها العريس و معينته	He who blessed our father Adam, Noah, Abraham, and Moses in the land of Midian, blesses you O bridegroom and his helpmate.
Ⲫⲏⲉⲧⲁϥⲥⲙⲟⲩ ⲛⲓⲥⲁⲁⲕ ⲡⲓⲙⲉⲛⲣⲓⲧ ⲛⲉⲙ ⲁⲃⲉⲗ ⲡⲓⲑⲙⲏⲓ ⲛϣⲟⲣⲡ ⲛⲉⲙ ⲥⲟⲗⲟⲙⲱⲛ ⲛⲉⲙ ⲡⲉϥⲓⲱⲧ ⲇⲁⲩⲓⲇ ⲉϥⲥⲙⲟⲩ ⲉⲣⲟⲕ ⲱ ⲡⲓⲡⲁⲧϣⲉⲗⲏⲧ ⲛⲉⲙ ⲧⲉϥⲃⲟⲏⲑⲟⲥ	الذي بارك اسحق الحبيب و هابيل الصديق الاول و سليمان و أبيه داود يباركك أيها العريس و معينته	He who blessed Isaac the beloved, and Abel the first righteous, and Solomon, and his father David, blesses you O bridegroom and his helpmate.
Ⲫⲏⲉⲧⲁϥⲥⲙⲟⲩ ⲙⲡⲉⲛⲓⲱⲧ ⲓⲁⲕⲱⲃ ⲡⲓⲥⲣⲁⲏⲗ ⲛⲉⲙ ⲏⲥⲁⲩ ⲛⲉⲙ ⲡⲓⲑⲙⲏⲓ ⲓⲱⲃ ⲉϥⲥⲙⲟⲩ ⲉⲣⲟⲕ ⲛϣⲁϣϥ ⲛⲕⲱⲃ ⲱ ⲡⲓⲡⲁⲧϣⲉⲗⲏⲧ ⲛⲉⲙ ⲧⲉϥⲃⲟⲏⲑⲟⲥ	الذي بارك أبانا يعقوب ايرائيل و عيسو و الصديق أيوب يباركك أيها العريس و معينته	He who blessed our father Jacob Israel and Esau and the righteous Job blesses you sevenfold O bridegroom and his helpmate.

These verses are identical to how they appeared in Pope Gabriel. They are followed by these verses, which the priest says while blessing the bride:

Ⲫⲏⲉⲧⲁϥⲥⲙⲟⲩ ⲙⲡⲉⲛⲓⲱⲧ ⲁⲇⲁⲙ ⲛⲉⲙ ⲉⲩⲁ ⲛⲉⲙ ⲁⲃⲣⲁⲁⲙ ⲛⲉⲙ ⲥⲁⲣⲣⲁ ⲛⲉⲙ ⲓⲥⲁⲁⲕ ⲛⲉⲙ ⲓⲉⲣⲉⲃⲉⲕⲕⲁ ⲉϥⲥⲙⲟⲩ ⲉⲡⲁⲓϭⲓⲛⲧⲟⲙⲓ ⲫⲁⲓ	الذي بارك أبينا آدم و حوى و ابراهيم مع سارة و اسحق و رفقا يبارك هذا الزواج	He who blessed our father Adam with Eve, and Abraham with Sarah, and Isaac with Rebecca blesses this union.

Ⲫⲏⲉⲧⲁϥⲥⲙⲟⲩ ⲛⲓⲁⲕⲱⲃ ⲡⲓⲥⲣⲁⲏⲗ ⲉϫⲉⲛ ⲗⲓⲁ ⲛⲉⲙ ⲣⲁⲭⲏⲗ ⲛⲉⲙ ⲁⲛⲛⲁ ⲑⲙⲁⲩ ⲛⲥⲁⲙⲟⲩⲏⲗ ⲉϥⲥⲙⲟⲩ ⲉⲡⲁⲓϫⲓⲛⲧⲟⲙⲓ ⲫⲁⲓ	الذي بارك يعقوب اسرائيل على ليا و راحيل و حنة أم صموئيل يبارك هذا الزواج	He who blessed Jacob Israel with Leah and Rachel and Hannah the mother of Samuel blesses this union.
Ⲫⲏⲉⲧⲁϥⲥⲙⲟⲩ ⲛⲓⲱⲥⲏⲫ ⲛⲉⲙ ⲁⲥⲉⲛⲏⲑ ⲛⲉⲙ ⲍⲁⲭⲁⲣⲓⲁⲥ ⲛⲉⲙ ⲉⲗⲓⲥⲁⲃⲉⲧ ⲛⲉⲙ ⲙⲁⲣⲓⲁⲙ ⲑⲙⲁⲩ ⲛϣⲉⲗⲉⲧ ⲛⲉⲙ ⲛⲓϩⲓⲟⲙⲓ ⲧⲏⲣⲟⲩ ⲉⲧⲥⲙⲁⲙⲁⲧ ⲉϥⲥⲙⲟⲩ ⲉⲡⲁⲓϫⲓⲛⲧⲟⲙⲓ ⲫⲁⲓ	الذي بارك يوسف و اسنات و زكريا مع اليصابات و مريم أم الختن و كافة النساء المباركات يبارك هذا الزواج	He who blessed Joseph with Asenath, and Zacharias with Elizabeth, and Mary the mother the bride, and the rest of the blessed women, blesses this union.

These verses are slightly different than those found in Pope Gabriel. They are in the indicative instead of the imperative mood. The first verse omitted the reference to the Tree of Mamre and combined the ones for Abraham and Isaac and their wives. The second verse replaced "who built the house of Israel" with "and Hanna the mother of Samuel." The third verse replaced the reference to Joachim and Anna with a reference to the Virgin Mary and a general reference to all other blessed women. I believe these changes are an effort to give the Arabic better assonance. Hegumen Philotheos sought to improve on the poetic edits made by Pope Gabriel. In the first verse, Eve [Ḥawwá], Sarah [Sārah], and Rebecca [Rifqa] all have the same ending vowel sound. In the second verse, Israel [Isrā'īl], Rachel [Rāḥīl], and Samuel [Ṣamū'īl] all end with the same vowel sound. The same is true in the third verse for Asenath [Asnāt], Elizabeth [Alyṣābāt], and blessed [al-Mubārakāt]. After that, the verses for the Archangels, the Apostles, and the Martyrs are omitted. All the verses end in the same way unlike in Pope Gabriel in which some verses ended with "May He bless you O the bridegroom and his helpmate." There is no mention of the tune used for these verses. The lack of detail in mentioning the tune is probably what led to their disuse over time. It is possible that they were not sung with any tune at all because the priest goes right into the first commandment after the last verse.

Out of all the things Hegumen Philotheos changed in the rite, the biggest change was made to the commandments. The commandments no longer have responses. Rather, the priest says them as one big contiguous section and the deacons interrupt the priest with a few carefully placed verses. The verses do not include a concluding piece like "Blessed is the Father" or Lord Have Mercy. There is no mention of the tunes used for the interruptions. Given that the text of the interruptions differs from Pope Gabriel, it is possible that the tune also changed at this time. However, "The Cherubim" and "Holy are You O Lord" from "This is the time of blessing" are included so it is also possible the muḥayyar tune continued to be used. The priest starts the commandment to the groom with "Glory to God." Hegumen Philotheos presents its full text. The people respond with "The Cherubim" and "Holy are You O Lord." The priest continues with "May the peace of our Lord Jesus Christ." When he reaches "and gave Himself up for her" the people say "My peace which I have taken." This is where he makes an incompatible change. Up till now the order was "Glory to God", "My peace which I have taken", "May the peace of our Lord Jesus Christ", and "This is the time of blessing", which included "The Cherubim." This change reverses the order and makes it "Glory to God", "The Cherubim", "May the peace", and "My peace which I have taken." This turns "My peace which I have taken" into a response of "May the peace." Previously it introduced "May the peace." The change of the verses from introductions to responses is applied to the rest of the commandments. This was probably done to cut up the commandments into smaller chunks to increase comprehension. The priest continues with "And now since you both attended" until he reaches "submit yourselves to one another." Hegumen Philotheos mentions that if the wedding takes place in a church, the priest adds a line saying that they attended in front of the altar of the Lord but if not then to just say it was an Orthodox gathering.[48] The people interrupt with "O King of Peace." The priest continues with "It behooves you O blessed son" until he finishes the commandment to the groom with "in this world and the next."

The people say these verses to introduce the commandment to the bride:

Ⲥⲱⲧⲉⲙ ⲧⲁϣⲉⲣⲓ ⲁⲛⲁⲩ ⲣⲉⲕ ⲛⲉⲙⲁϣϫ ⲁⲣⲓⲡⲱⲃϣ ⲙⲡⲉⲗⲁⲟⲥ ⲛⲉⲙ ⲡⲏⲓ ⲛⲧⲉ ⲡⲉⲓⲱⲧ ϫⲉ ⲁⲡⲓ ⲟⲩⲣⲟ ⲉⲣⲉⲡⲓⲑⲩⲙⲓⲛ ⲉⲡⲉⲥⲁⲓ ϫⲉ ⲟⲩⲏⲓ ⲛⲑⲟϥ ⲡⲉ ⲡⲉⲟⲥ	اسمعي يا ابنتي و انظري و ميلي بسمعك و انسي شعبك و بيت أبيك فان الملك قد اشتهى حسنك لانه هو ربك	Listen my daughter and see and incline your ear. Forget your people and your father's house. For the king has desired your beauty, for he alone is your lord
Ⲥⲱⲧⲉⲙ ⲱ ϯϣⲉⲗⲉⲧ ⲟⲩⲟϩ ⲕⲁϯ ⲛⲉⲙ ⲣⲉⲕ ⲡⲉⲙⲁϣϫ ϫⲉ ⲁⲡⲓϣⲉⲗⲉⲧ ⲉⲣⲉⲡⲓⲑⲩⲙⲓⲛ ⲛⲧⲉⲙⲉⲧⲁⲅⲁⲑⲟⲥ ϫⲉ ⲟⲩⲏⲓ ⲛⲑⲟϥ ⲡⲉϩⲁⲓ ⲟⲩⲟϩ ϥⲉⲙⲡϣⲁ ⲛⲥⲱⲧⲉⲙ ⲛⲥⲱϥ	اسمعي يا عروسة و افهمي و ميلي بسمعك لان الختن قد اشتهى صلاحك لانه رجلك فيجب أن تطيعه	Listen O bride and incline you ear. Forget your people and your father's house, for your goodness has appealed to the bridegroom, for He is your husband and to him you will submit

The second verse is a rewriting of the first one but addressed to the bride instead of the Virgin. This is yet another example of where Hegumen Philotheos inserted new things into the rite to explicitly link the existing bible verses with what is happening to the bride and groom during the ceremony. The priest says, "And you O blessed daughter and glad bride" until he reaches "by whom God will delight your eyes." The people say "O King of Peace" again. The priest continues with "Likewise may the Lord bless you" until he reaches "and grant you a long age and happy life with blessed children." The people say just the first verse of "This is the time of blessing." The priest says the last piece of the

---

[48] Ibid., 68.

commandments, "And unto Him we ask" until he finishes with "let us all say Lord Have Mercy." Then they say Our Father and the benediction. Note this is the second time Our Father is said. The deacons chant this concluding canon:

Ⲭⲉⲣⲉ ⲧϣⲉⲗⲉⲧ ⲉⲧⲉⲣⲟⲩⲱⲓⲛⲓ ⲑⲙⲁⲩ ⲙⲡⲓⲣⲉϥⲉⲣⲟⲩⲱⲟⲓⲛⲓ ⲭⲉⲣⲉ ⲑⲏⲉⲧϣⲱⲡ ⲉⲣⲟⲥ ⲙⲡⲓⲥⲁϫⲓ ⲫⲏ ⲉⲧϣⲟⲡ ϧⲉⲛ ⲧⲉⲥⲛⲉϫⲓ	السلام للعروس المضيئة أم الذي ينير السلام للتي قبلت اليها الكلمة الكائن في أحشاها	Rejoice O shining bride, the mother of One who enlightens; Rejoice she who accepted the Word who dwelt in her womb
Ⲭⲉⲣⲉ ⲑⲏⲉⲧⲧⲁⲓⲏⲟⲩⲧ ⲉϩⲟⲧⲉ ⲛⲓⲭⲉⲣⲟⲩⲃⲓⲙ ⲭⲉⲣⲉ ⲑⲏ ⲉⲧⲁⲥⲙⲓⲥⲓ ⲙⲡⲥⲱⲧⲏⲣ ⲛⲧⲉ ⲛⲉⲛⲯⲩⲭⲏ	السلام للتي هي أكرم من الشاروبيم السلام للتي ولدت لنا مخلص أنفسنا	Rejoice she who is honored more than the Cherubim; Rejoice she who gave birth to the Savior of our souls
Ⲇⲟⲝⲁ ⲡⲁⲧⲣⲓ ⲕⲁⲓ ⲩⲓⲱ ⲕⲁⲓ ⲁⲅⲓⲱ ⲡⲛⲉⲩⲙⲁⲧⲓ ⲛⲩⲛ	المجد للآب و الابن و الروح القدس الآن	Glory be to the Father and the Son and the Holy Spirit now and forever

Hegumen Philotheos includes the readings and gospel response for the liturgy. It should be noted that he put these at the tail end of his book indicating that they probably were less important since by his time it was likely that liturgies were not done after the wedding. He lists the same passages as Pope Gabriel and Ibn Kabar, namely the readings and hymns of the Feast of the Wedding at Cana of Galilee. He also has a poetic Arabic sermon that he personally wrote to be used either during the wedding or the liturgy. I include this sermon in Appendix E.

CHAPTER 4

The 20th Century

Social Changes

The 20th century saw many changes in the standard wedding format. The emergence of mass media made the white wedding the de facto standard. Copts entered the middle class and started emigrating to Western countries. Social mobility increased, even in Egypt. People started copying European traditions like having the father give away the bride and having receptions, which were not common in Egypt prior to the mid-twentieth century. Those who emigrated found themselves in foreign lands with no Coptic community from which to find a mate and no Coptic churches in which to get married. This led to the practice of renting any church building just to hold the ceremony. Back in Egypt, people started having their weddings toward the end of the day so that the reception could start immediately following the ceremony. These two things quickly led to the disappearance of the post-wedding liturgy. As the wedding reception industry grew, people relied less and less on their own homes for holding receptions. This led to the cessation of having the wedding in one's own house. Over time, it became cost-prohibitive to have a blanket open invitation to the entire community to attend the festivities, so people started to pick and choose exactly whom to invite to the reception. This was the beginning of the trend toward personal customization of everything related to the wedding. Finally, more and more people began to go on honeymoons as they became financially fit to do so. Time management became more important as the wedding had to be on the same day as the reception, and the departure for the honeymoon had to be soon afterwards.

Mid-century Description of the Rite

A snapshot of the rite during this time comes to us from Fr. Markos Hanna. He was the priest of St. Mark Coptic Orthodox Church of Los Angeles, California from 1988 to 2002. He was involved in translating many of the service books used by the clergy from Arabic to English. The first edition of his translation of the wedding service was published in June 1984. It is unknown on what Arabic source he based his translation. It is doubtful that he based it on Hegumen Philotheos. By this time, the two parts of the wedding ceremony had combined into a single service and Fr. Markos' work reflects that reality. The changes introduced by Hegumen Philotheos made their way into the popular Arabic service books of the day. It is most likely one of these books on which Fr. Markos based his translation. He did not create it to promote or create a new standard but to respond to an immediate need for clergy in North America to have an English translation.

He does not include anything about processions, but the ceremony starts with both the bride and groom standing together in the chancel. The priest starts with the declarations that were added by Hegumen Philotheos. But there is an additional description of the Lord Jesus Christ as "the founder of the statute of perfection and the author of the law of virtues [مشرع شريعة الكمال و واضع ناموس الأفضال]."[49] This additional text was in widespread use by this time and Fr. Markos' edition is not the first to include it. But it is unknown exactly when it was inserted into the rite after the time of Hegumen Philotheos. Then he says the Thanksgiving Prayer. The people chant the Verses of Cymbals with "Rejoice O bridal chamber" as the verse for the wedding. The priest then recites a single

---

[49] Fr. Markos Hanna. *The Coptic Offices for the Coptic Orthodox Church: Part 2 Holy Matrimony & Second Matrimony 4th edition* (Lost Angeles: self-published, 2004), 14.

prayer that replaces the entire first part. This prayer begins with "O God who created man with His own Hands." The people respond with "Christ the Logos" followed by "Blessed is the Father" in the Palm Sunday tune. The priest then says the prayer of the vestment beginning with "O Master Lord Jesus Christ who adorned the sky." The people chant "The Spiritual Raiment"[50] followed by Lord Have Mercy three times. The priest puts the girdle & rings on bride & groom, then he puts the vestment on groom.

The people say the Hymn of the Censer followed by "We worship." The Pauline Epistle is read from Ephesians 5:22-6:3. Then the people say the Hymn of the Holy Spirit [Ⲡⲓⲡⲛⲉⲩⲙⲁ]. This is the first mention of this hymn being said during weddings. It is unknown when this hymn entered the rite. Technically, it could have been said during the post-wedding liturgy. But since there was no more liturgy, and only one set of readings, this was the logical place to put it. Then they chant the Trisagion. The priest recites the Litany of Gospel. The Psalm is chanted from Psalms 19:5 & 128:3,4. It is not specified what tune to use for the psalm. The Gospel is read from Matthew 19:1-6. The Gospel Response is that of the crowning "Those whom the Holy Spirit attuned." The priest says the Supplications. The people respond with "Christ the Logos" and "Blessed is the Father" as found in Hegumen Philotheos. Although there are no guides for tunes mentioned, the convention is to use the same tune that was used previously, which is the Palm Sunday tune. The priest says the three great litanies. The people say the Creed.

The priest says the first matrimonial prayer beginning with "O God who is eternal and everlasting." The people respond with "As you have given" and "The gate of the east." The priest says the second prayer beginning with "O Father our God who formed all nature." The people respond with "My peace which I have taken" and "Blessed is the Father." The priest says the third prayer beginning with "O Lord our great and eternal God." The people respond with "Do not forget the covenant", "O Angel of this day", and Lord Have Mercy three times. The priest says the

---

[50] Fr. Markos only includes the first verse.

prayer of submission beginning with "Listen O God to us." The people respond with "May God bless us" and "Blessed be the Father." This section is exactly as it appeared in Hegumen Philotheos.

The priest says the Prayer of the Oil. The people respond with "May this oil"., "Blessed be the Father," only the first verse of "You have anointed", and finish with another "Blessed be the Father." It is likely that the remaining verses of "You have anointed" were skipped in order to save time hence Fr. Markos did not bother including them. The priest completes the prayer of the oil with "O God Lord of Hosts."

The priest says the prayer of the crowns, while holding the crowns, beginning with "O Holy God who crowned the saints." The deacon responds with "Place the crowns O priest of Emmanuel; Place the crowns O Shepherd of Israel; Place the crowns in joy and jubilation for (…) the bridegroom and (...) the bride [ضع الاكاليل يا كاهن عمانوئيل ضع الاكاليل يا راعي اسرائيل ضع الاكاليل بفرح و تهليل لفلان العريس و فلانة العروس].".[51] This is followed by Lord Have Mercy three times. This is a new deacon response that was absent in earlier versions. Its text is not presented in Coptic nor is its tune mentioned. The priest says, "Place O Lord upon your servants crowns of unvanquished grace." There is nothing about the white cloth. The people sing in the Axios tune "In the name of the Father and the Son and the Holy Spirit the coessential Trinity, Worthy, Worthy, Worthy is the bridegroom and his helpmate [ϧⲉⲛ ⲫⲣⲁⲛ ⲙⲫⲓⲱⲧ ⲛⲉⲙ ⲡϣⲏⲣⲓ ⲛⲉⲙ ⲡⲓⲡⲛⲉⲩⲙⲁ ⲉⲑⲟⲩⲁⲃ ϯⲧⲣⲓⲁⲥ ⲛⲟⲙⲟⲟⲩⲥⲓⲟⲥ ⲁⲍⲓⲟⲥ ⲁⲍⲓⲟⲥ ⲁⲍⲓⲟⲥ ⲡⲓⲡⲁⲧϣⲉⲗⲉⲧ ⲛⲉⲙ ⲧⲉϥⲃⲟⲏⲑⲟⲥ]." Then they sing the doxology of the crowns, "Unfading crowns", in the Morning Doxology tune. Fr. Markos lists all four verses mentioned by Hegumen Philotheos.

The priest says the verses of blessing for the groom followed by those for the bride. He does not include the Coptic text of these verses but uses the ones from Hegumen Philotheos. The people respond to the priest with "The Cherubim" and "Holy are You O Lord." Neither the verses of blessing nor the last two responsorial verses have a tune specified.

---

[51] Hanna, 100.

Hegumen Philotheos had an initial commandment after the verses of blessing and before "The Cherubim." This commandment begins with "Glory to God" and it is omitted in Fr. Markos' version. That is why "The Cherubim" immediately follows the verses of blessing and is itself followed by the commandment beginning with "May the peace of our Lord."

The Coptic commandment verses encountered so far have all been removed in favor of new Arabic responses. These responses are addressed to the bride and groom and follow in the trend of replacing bible verses with things specific to the couple. They are clearly originally composed in Arabic as they rhyme in that language. The first new response is, "You have been crowned O groom in this ceremony and on your right sat a virgin; the Lord Almighty gave her to you in purity and perfection among Jesus' congregation [توجت يا عريس في هذه الحضرة و عن يمينك جلست عذراء بها و خصك رب القدرة بكمال و طهر من شعب أيسوس]."[52] This and all subsequent responses end with Lord Have Mercy three times. Although no tune is specified, the convention is to say them in the festal tune instead of the Palm Sunday tune. The priest says, "Now since you have been present" until "but the wife does." The deacon responds with "Take unto you O bridegroom your bride; Jesus Christ has given her to you and at the hand of the priest He has given her to you and blessed you both with His Holy Name [استلم يا عريس عروسا هي لك يسوع المسيح وهبها لك و بيد الكاهن سلمها لك و بركككما باسمه القدوس]."[53] The priest says "It behooves you O blessed son" until "in this life and the one thereafter." The deacon responds with "Listen O bride and lend your ear; forsake your people and your father's home for your chastity has appealed to the bridegroom, and he is your husband and to him you will submit [اسمعي يا ابنة و اصغي بسمعك و انسي شعبك و بيت ابيك لأن العريس راق له طهرك فهو زوجك و له تخضعين]."[54] This was the second verse that Hegumen Philotheos wrote to clarify the original verse which quoted Psalm 45. Here the original quotation is completely

---

[52] Ibid., 110.
[53] Hanna, 112.
[54] Ibid., 114.

removed, and the paraphrase is preserved. The priest says, "And you blessed daughter" until "fill your heart with joy." The deacon responds with "A pure marriage and a revered crown bless it our God Emmanuel as You blessed the wedding of Cana of Galilee for (...) the bridegroom and (...) the bride [في بركة ربنا عمانوئيل باركته يا كاهن جليل و اكليل طاهر زواج عرس قانا الجليل لفلان العريس و فلانة العروس].''[55] The English translation of this verse does not exactly match the Arabic. The Arabic asks the priest of Emmanuel to bless the marriage. But the English asks God to bless it and calls Him Emmanuel directly. The priest says "May god bless both of you" until the end. The people say Our father. The priest says the Absolution of the Son. The people say the concluding canon "Amen alleluia." This is not the specific concluding canon for weddings previously mentioned in the other sources. It is the general annual concluding canon used for any service. The deacons lead the couple out of the church in a procession while singing "Rejoice O Mary the queen [ⲭⲉⲣⲉ ⲙⲁⲣⲓⲁ ϯⲟⲩⲣⲟ]." There is no mention of a list of readings to be said during a potential liturgy.

The 1999 Holy Synod

The version of the rite found in Fr. Markos represents the most drastic change ever experienced by this rite. As previously mentioned, the two separate parts were combined into one. There was no more post-wedding liturgy. Many hymns and prayers were removed. Coptic was no longer used as the main language of prayer. In practice, it was very common to start late due to the bridal party arriving late, so many parts were said quickly or skipped entirely. In 1999, the Holy Synod of the Coptic Orthodox Church codified these changes into official canon.[56] They labeled the first part, the part referred to in the literature as 'aqd al-amlāk

---

[55] Ibid., 116.
[56] Secretariat of the Holy Synod, *The Decisions of the Holy Synod during the reign of His Holiness Pope Shenouda III 3rd Edition* (Cairo: Coptic Orthodox Cultural Center, 2011), 158.

as the "prayer of the 'arbūn (عربون)."⁵⁷ They claimed that this comes from the Greek word ⲁⲣⲣⲁⲃⲱⲛⲁ, whose cognate is ⲁⲣⲏⲃ in Coptic. The word ⲁⲣⲏⲃ appeared in Hegumen Philotheos' description of the rite and appears many times in the post-Creed prayers of the first part. However, this is incorrect. The Greek word ⲁⲣⲣⲁⲃⲱⲛⲁ is of Semitic origin and entered Greek through either Phoenician or Hebrew. This word means pledge, promise, or covenant. It refers to the pledge the bride and groom make to remain faithful to each other. The Holy Synod ordered that the wedding start with the declarations introduced by Hegumen Philotheos, followed by the Thanksgiving Prayer, followed by a single prayer to take the place of the entire first part. The prayer they chose was the one that started with "O God who created man." This is the first of originally four prayers said before vesting the groom. This prayer was to be followed by the prayer of the vestment and the hymn of the vestment. From then on, the rite should follow the rite of the crowning starting with the readings of the crowning.

The Holy Synod claimed it produced this order "after researching the ancient rite of weddings in the Coptic manuscripts and the ancient Greek rite." Furthermore, it claimed that canceling nearly all of the first part save for two prayers was perfectly fine since in the Greek Church the analogous rite does not include any readings but focuses on the blessing of the rings and exchange of vows. They did not cite any published study in making these claims. While it is true that the Greek Church, and all other Eastern Orthodox Churches, only have one set of readings used during the wedding, it is also the case that those churches do not have the groom dressed in special vestments. The lack of citation for any serious study, or even citing the name of an old manuscript that might have supported their conclusions, certainly raises more questions than it answers. It appears the Holy Synod was looking for a reason to retroactively justify the existing practice and to make the existing practice the new normal rather than restoring the traditional practice explained in

---

⁵⁷ Appendix C.

the sources. Perhaps they thought that the Coptic tradition added extra prayers that were not original and hence felt unconcerned with officially changing the rite so much. Perhaps they felt that they had lost control over the practice of the rite and felt there was nothing they could do to restore the original practice. In any case, this decree was just rubber stamping what had already been happening as evidenced by Fr. Markos' edition of the rite.

The Current Rite

The 20th century trend of each person customizing their wedding to their liking continued unabated into the 21st century. Weddings are now controlled by external factors such as planners, photographers, schedules, venues, etc. It is common, especially for those who live outside Egypt, to engage in local cultural practices such as bachelor or bachelorette parties, rehearsal dinners, etc. Weddings are no longer a local community affair. With the availability of mass transportation, it is very common to invite friends and family who live far away. It is no longer assumed that a wedding taking place in the local parish may be attended by any parish member nor even that the wedding is that of a parish member. Destination weddings, although uncommon, are allowed and practiced. The amount of people invited determines the church and reception venue. Since most Coptic churches are of modest construction, many Coptic weddings take place in non-Coptic churches that are big enough to carry all the invited guests. The photographers like to take pictures of the bride and groom getting ready so that usually takes place mid-morning. The wedding ceremony usually takes place in the afternoon with no subsequent liturgy. The reception is usually on the same day as the wedding, and it typically starts in the evening and lasts till midnight. The reception venue may be hours away from the church depending on what the bride and groom were able to book for the day. Usually, the couple departs for their honeymoon the day after the reception. While grooms still wear tuxedos, bridal dresses have undergone many changes. Due to the large variety in dress design, it is now common for the bride to wear a white chasuble like vestment during the ceremony in case her dress is too revealing or inappropriate for a liturgical setting. Most couples print their own booklets to be used during the service. This is done for several reasons. First, the ceremony includes prayers in which the priest must mention the bride and groom by name. In cases where the multiple priests are invited, and not all priests know the names of the couple, it is better to have a booklet with the names printed out so the priests and deacons can just read from the booklet. Another reason is that couples like to specify what hymns are said in what language. Finally, sometimes time is short due to scheduling conflicts, so some prayers need to be skipped. Printing their own booklet allows the couple to specify what they are or are not willing to skip. The couple takes liberty in customizing every aspect of the rite. There is less emphasis on preserving tradition and more emphasis on making it a special day for the couple.

The most complete text of the rite that was published after the changes of the 1999 Holy Synod comes from *The Essentials in the Deacon's Service* by Albair Gamal Mikhail.[58] He starts with the bride entering the church with her father. The father gives her away to the groom at the door of the nave. This seems to be Mikhail's compromise in allowing a modern practice and also preserving the original rite. The bride is allowed to let her father give her away, but the couple still enter the church together for the beginning of the crowning. They both enter the nave with the deacons chanting "O King of Peace" during annual days or "Christ is risen" during the Holy 50 Days. There is no mention of the original processional hymn "Blessed is he who comes." The priest begins with the declarations as they appeared in Fr. Markos. Then he says the Thanksgiving Prayer. The deacons chant the Verses of the Cymbals with "Rejoice O bridal chamber." If a bishop is present, they add "We ask You O Son of God to preserve the life of our father the patriarch Pope Abba

---

[58] Albair Gamal Mikhail, *al-Asās fī khidmat al-Shammās [The Essentials in the Deacon's Service] 3rd Edition* (Shubra, Egypt: Shikolani, 2013), 1095.

(…) confirm him upon his throne [ⲧⲉⲛ†ⲍⲟ ⲉⲣⲟⲕ ⲱ ⲩⲓⲟⲥ ⲑⲉⲟⲥ ⲉⲑⲣⲉⲕⲁⲣⲉϩ ⲡⲱⲛϧ ⲙⲡⲉⲛⲡⲁⲧⲣⲓⲁⲣⲭⲏⲥ ⲡⲁⲡⲁ ⲁⲃⲃⲁ („‚) ⲙⲁⲧⲁϫⲣⲟϥ ϩⲓϫⲉⲛ ⲡⲉϥⲑⲣⲟⲛⲟⲥ] and his partner in the liturgy our righteous father Abba (…) the bishop confirm him upon his throne [ⲛⲉⲙ ⲡⲉϥⲕⲉϣⲫⲏⲣ ⲛⲗⲩⲧⲟⲩⲣⲅⲟⲥ ⲡⲉⲛⲓⲱⲧ ⲉⲑⲟⲩⲁⲃ ⲛⲇⲓⲕⲉⲟⲥ ⲁⲃⲃⲁ („‚) ⲡⲓⲉⲡⲓⲥⲕⲟⲡⲟⲥ ⲙⲁⲧⲁϫⲣⲟϥ ϩⲓϫⲉⲛ ⲡⲉϥⲑⲣⲟⲛⲟⲥ]." There verses are different from the ones mentioned by Pope Gabriel. But they are the current standard verses used for bishops.

The priest says the prayer that replaced the entire first part. Mikhail calls this the Prayer for the Pledge [عربون] following the explanation of the Holy Synod. It begins with "O God who created man with His own Hands." The people respond with "Christ the Logos", "Blessed is the Father", and Lord Have Mercy three times. The priest says the prayer of the vestment beginning with "O Master Lord Jesus Christ who adorned the sky." The people sing "The Spiritual Raiment." Mikhail includes all five verses that appeared in Hegumen Philotheos along with a concluding "Blessed is the Father." The priest puts the rings on bride & groom, then the vestment on groom but no white cloth and no girdle. It is specifically called out that the priest is the one who puts the rings on their fingers. They do not exchange the rings with each other.[59]

The people sing the Hymn of the Censer followed by "We worship." The Pauline Epistle is read from Ephesians 5:22-6:3. Then the Hymn of the Holy Spirit is chanted. Mikhail claims another hymn, "All the villages [ⲛⲓⲭⲱⲣⲁ]" was said here[60] when the full first part was done but none of the historical sources mention it. Furthermore, in the production of the hymns of the wedding in his app, he has a recording of a few verses said in the muḥayyar tune beginning with "God who is called by His saints [Ⲫϯ ⲫⲏⲉⲑⲙⲟⲧⲉⲛ ⲙⲙⲟϥ ϧⲉⲛ ⲛⲏⲉⲑⲟⲩⲁⲃ ⲛⲧⲁϥ]."[61] Mikhail includes these

---

[59] Ibid., 1100.
[60] Ibid.
[61] The Heritage of the Coptic Orthodox Church. "CopticHymns". Holy Crowning Track 19, 5.12.0 (2021). https://play.google.com/store/apps/details?id=com.subsplashconsulting.s_728J

in his app after the Hymn of the Holy Spirit, but they are neither in the sources nor his book. It is possible they were obtained from other lesser-known manuscripts. Then the people say the Trisagion. The priest recites the Litany of Gospel. The Psalm is read from Psalms 19:5 and 128:3,4. The Gospel is read from Matthew 19:1-6. The Gospel Response is "Those whom the Holy Spirit attuned." Mikhail concludes it with three Lord Have Mercies. The priest recites the Supplications. The people respond with "Christ the Logos" in the Palm Sunday tune, "Blessed is the Father", and Lord Have Mercy three times. The priest recites the three great litanies. The people say the Creed.

The priest says the first matrimonial prayer beginning with "O God who is eternal and everlasting." The people respond with "As you have given", "The door of the East", and Lord Have Mercy three times. The priest says the second matrimonial prayer beginning with "O Father our God who formed all nature." The people respond with "My peace which I have taken", "Blessed is the Father", and Lord Have Mercy three times. The priest says the third matrimonial prayer beginning with "O Lord our great and eternal God." The people respond with "Do not forget the covenant", "O Angel of this day", "Blessed is the Father", and Lord Have Mercy three times. The priest says the prayer of submission beginning with "Listen O God to us." Mikhail says the priest faces East while people bow their heads; however, there is no deacon's call to bow the heads. The people respond with "May God bless us", "Blessed is the Father", and Lord Have Mercy three times. All the aforementioned responses are said in the Palm Sunday tune.[62] Mikhail used the same verses as Hegumen Philotheos but also brought back the concluding "Blessed is the Father" and the three Lord Have Mercies from Pope Gabriel.

The priest recites the Prayer of the Oil. The people respond with "May this oil", "Blessed is the Father", and Lord Have Mercy three times. They continue with the first verse only of "You have anointed", followed by

---

TS&referrer=utm_source%3Dsubsplash%26utm_content%3DeyJoYW5kbGVy IjoiYXBwIiwiYXBwa2V5IjoiNzI4SlRTIn0=.
[62] Mikhail, 1103.

"Blessed is the Father", and Lord Have Mercy three times. During this the priest says "O God Lord of Hosts" silently. The priest holds the crowns and begins the prayer of the crowns with "O Holy God who crowned the saints." The deacon says this response: "Place the crowns O priest of Emmanuel; place the crowns O shepherd of Israel; place the crowns in glory and joy for (…) the groom and (…) the bride. Worthy, worthy, worthy bless the bride and groom with Your Holy Name [ضع الاكاليل يا كاهن عمانوئيل ضع الاكاليل يا راعي اسرائيل ضع الاكاليل بالمجد و تهليل لفلان العريس و فلانة العروس مستحق مستحق مستحق بارك العروسين باسمك القدوس].''[63] This is different than how it appeared in Fr. Markos' version. First, the word glory is substituted for jubilation. Second, the text includes a proclamation of worthiness. Furthermore, that proclamation is not the standard "worthy is the bridegroom and his helpmate" but rather an entirely new statement asking God to bless the couple with His Holy Name. More than likely this was a variant of the standard proclamation that Mikhail wanted to include in his rendition. Nevertheless, it is not part of the historical sources, and it has no Coptic equivalent. The fact that a proclamation of worthiness is included indicates that the response should be said in the Axios tune. In the app, there are two tunes for this response: one in the Axios tune and one in the Festal tune.[64]

The priest then says, "Place O Lord upon your servants crowns of unvanquished grace." The priest then puts the heads of the bride and groom together such that they remain touching and says "Crown them with glory and honor O Father" as it appeared in Fr. Markos. This touching of the heads is reminiscent of the ancient practice of kissing, which is still preserved in Western Christian traditions. It symbolizes their marital union. The joining of the heads was not mentioned in earlier sources, probably because they had already been covered by the white

---

[63] Ibid., 1105.
[64] The Heritage of the Coptic Orthodox Church. "CopticHymns". Holy Crowning Track 38, 5.12.0 (2021).
https://play.google.com/store/apps/details?id=com.subsplashconsulting.s_728J TS&referrer=utm_source%3Dsubsplash%26utm_content%3DeyJoYW5kbGVy IjoiYXBwIiwiYXBwa2V5IjoiNzI4SlRTIn0=.

cloth. Here, instead of the broad white cloth that covered their heads, their hands are joined together, and a small white veil is placed over their hands. The people sing "In the name" followed by the standard proclamation of worthiness in the Axios tune. Mikhail includes one extra verse that was present in Pope Gabriel beginning with "You received grace."[65] He does not say that this verse is only to be said if the patriarch is present. He then lists the verses of blessing for the groom only followed by the doxology for the crowns. The doxology includes all four verses found in Hegumen Philotheos. He then lists a set of alternative verses that may be said in addition to verses of blessing. These alternative verses are clearly originally composed in Arabic and probably come from a local tradition somewhere in Egypt. I include them along with an English translation in the full reconstruction at the end of the book.

Like Fr. Markos, Mikhail does not have any of the original Coptic commandment responses except "The Cherubim" and "Holy are You O Lord." But he goes one step further and removes the entire commandment beginning with "May the peace." Thus, Mikhail starts the commandments with "The Cherubim" and "Holy are You O Lord" in the muḥayyar tune.[66] The first commandment said by the priest is "And now since you both attended." The deacon responds with "Take unto you O bridegroom your bride." The priest says, "It behooves you O blessed son." The deacon responds with "Listen O bride." The priest says the commandment to the bride "And you blessed daughter." The deacon responds with "A pure marriage." The priest continues with "May God bless both of you" until "a long happy life with blessed children." The deacon responds with "You have been crowned O groom." The priest finishes with "And unto Him we ask" until the end. Then the people say Our Father and the priest says the Absolution of the Son. The people sing the concluding canon "Amen Alleluia" as explained in Fr. Markos. The bride and groom are both processed out of the church with the deacons chanting "Rejoice O Mary the queen." Although it is no longer the norm, Mikhail does include the

---

[65] Mikhail, 1105
[66] Ibid., 1108.

instructions for the post-wedding liturgy. He lists the Pauline Epistle from Ephesians 4:1-13, the Catholic Epistle from 1 Peter 3:1-12, the Acts from Acts 4:32-35, Psalm 21:1-2, and the Gospel from John 2:1-11. The Gospel Response is that of the Feast of Cana of Galilee. He also includes a melody to be sung during the communion distribution of the liturgy. I have included this melody in my reconstruction at the end of the book.

It is worth pointing out that there are differences between the rite as described by Fr. Markos Hanna and Albair Mikhail as well as discrepancies with how the rite is currently practiced. In practice, many of the responses to the matrimonial prayers and commandments are skipped. If they are said at all, then only the verse for Christ is said followed immediately by Lord Have Mercy three times. The verses for the Virgin and "Blessed be the Father" are almost never said. This could be because the schedule is running late, the available deacons do not know how to sing those responses, or the booklets being used do not have the full text. In a real time, crunch, only Lord Have Mercy would be said three times as the response to all the prayers. After the crowning and before the doxology for the crowns, there is another verse that may be said after the verses of blessing. The text of this verse is "O David, sing today, make melody, and psaltery play, shout for joy and celebrate, for (...) the groom and (...) the bride [رتل يا داود في وسطنا بالمزمار و العود بالفرح و السرور لفلان العريس و فلانة العروس].." This verse is not in the source material and is probably a local variation that got popular due to social media. The verses of blessing themselves are almost never said, neither is "The Cherubim" nor "Holy are You O Lord." The most likely reason is simply that most people have never observed these verses being said so they are not familiar. Some people instead say the Hymn of the Holy Spirit during that time following the crowning and before the commandments. This could be done to give the photographers more time to capture the bride and groom from different angles or because some people really like that hymn, and this is one of the things that couples like to customize about their wedding. In the commandment responses, it is common to insert the bride and groom's name instead of the general words bride and groom. This is inspired by the changes made by Hegumen Philotheos in which he rewrote some of the text to be direct commands instead of the original bible verses. Albair Mikhail removed two entire sections of the commandments, namely the piece beginning with "Glory to God" and the piece beginning with "May the peace." This meant that there was no place for the "You have been crowned" response. So, he divided the final commandment into two parts and put that response after the first part. At "May God Bless both of you", if the ceremony takes place in a Coptic Church, the curtain of the sanctuary is opened, and the couple is brought before it and kneel with their heads touching. They stay in this position until the concluding canon. Priests do not place their hands on the couple crosswise as directed by Pope Gabriel. It is likely that this practice fell out of use because the priest would have to have someone else hold the book for them or have the commandment memorized. Or it could simply be that priests stopped being trained to do it that way. Sometimes the full absolution is dispensed with in the interest of saving time. The concluding canon "Amen Alleluia" is said immediately after "And unto Him we ask." Sometimes the couple invites the bridal party up to the chancel to take photos before they exit. In this case the deacons either wait, start singing the exit hymn "Rejoice O Mary the queen", sing the Hymn of the Holy Spirit, or sing something else. It really depends on the deacons present and their discretion and how long the bridal party plans to delay their exit.

CHAPTER 5

Reconstructing the Rite

The biggest thing that stands out from the 1999 Holy Synod decree is that it was not theologically motivated. It was a practical response to a pastoral reality. However, it must be asked, what if they decided to go in the other direction? What if they reaffirmed the version of the rite that was in the *Ritual Ordo* of Pope Gabriel V and observed by Ibn Kabar? Would they have been ignored by the general populace? I do not think so. I think people would have been thankful that they chose to preserve the tradition. The Internet age has led to a renaissance movement to rediscover traditional rites and hymns and I think there is a great opportunity for the Coptic Church to restore the wedding rite to its original practice.

Restoring the rite is not just about preserving tradition. It is about the principle of how much customization should be allowed. A high degree of customization without official review would not be tolerated in any other rite. The Eucharistic liturgical service started as a completely open event in which each bishop or priest made up his own prayers on the spot. But over time, and with conciliar approval, it evolved into a set of agreed upon texts designed to standardize practice, reinforce correct theology, and prevent heresy. The same thing can be done with the wedding rite. Officially the sole authority to define the rites lies with the Holy Synod but in reality, it lies with the people and what they consider acceptable. People want their rites to mean something and rightfully so. The Church should oblige this need by making the wedding rite whole again. The entire first part prayed over the groom should be restored and a liturgy should be done after the crowning. A base edition of the text should be published along with guidelines explaining areas of flexibility that may be customized. I present such an edition in the next section.

But the question remains of how to convince people to go back to these practices. I believe the answer lies in the uniqueness of the Coptic wedding rite. The Orthodox Church teaches that the fundamental unit of the Church is the family and therefore, marriage is a creation of a new Church unit. As the head of the new household, the groom needs to be "ordained" like the priest who leads the flock of Christ. The original first part of Coptic wedding rite was analogous to a priest's ordination. The capstone of that part was the vesting of the groom to essentially look like a priest. The wedding vestment is a priest's phelonion. The groom also wears a girdle like the priest's girdle. Ibn Kabar said that the groom wears a priest's cap. Pope Gabriel said the groom wears the white cloth instead of the cap. Wearing the white cloth would make the groom reminiscent of what the priest would look like when serving a liturgy in clerical vestments. The bride meets the groom in this fashion as if she meets Christ. The second part of the rite, the crowning, binds the two in a spiritual union. Hegumen Philotheos called it the rank of crowning as if it were just like the other clerical ranks. The two become one flesh. That single new flesh then unites with the broader Church through the partaking of the Eucharist in the post-wedding liturgy. By restoring the post-wedding liturgy, this link with the creation of a new branch of the Church is made obvious.

In this section, I present my own proposal for restoring the rite to its original form. This proposal is based on the aforementioned sources and includes practical considerations for modern day needs. It is not purely based on my preferences nor is it an authoritative declaration. Ultimately the authority to officially change the rite lies with the Holy Synod and I humbly offer this proposal for their review. If accepted, the Holy Synod should establish a center of excellence for family affairs that should be in charge of educating the faithful on this rite and publishing a base text to be used in all future weddings.

The first consideration to make when attempting to reconstruct the rite is to first fill in the existing gaps. Terminology should be updated and clarified. Every prayer and hymn need to be identified with a unique name. The minute details like when the ceremony can occur need to be clearly specified. Extra care should be taken against just combining everything into one. Not all the changes that were made to the rite are still necessary. Although saving time is not a valid reason for removing anything, practicality and experience should be considered. It would not make sense to restore something that will end up being a burden.

The most important thing to restore is the practice of having the wedding in the morning followed by a liturgy. Regarding when the rite should take place, it can be done any day of the week but preferably should be done on weekends. For time of day, it should be done after Matins and before the afternoon. It should not be done during fasts. It should be done in a consecrated Coptic Church because it will be followed by a Coptic liturgy. Destination weddings, in which the bride and groom get married in a foreign country or a location in their home country far away from where they live, should be avoided, unless it can be done in a Coptic Church in that destination.

The first part should be called the Vesting of the Groom and not the prayer of the pledge. It ends with the vesting of the groom. Yes the prayers feature the word pledge/covenant a lot. But just as the second part is called the Crowning because the crowns are the physical artifacts used, the first part should be called the Vesting because the vestment is the physical artifact that caps that part. Furthermore, it does not make sense to make a pledge or vow with the other person absent and the first part only involves the groom.

The priest and deacons should wear the full liturgical vestments after Matins. The groom should arrive to the church first with his party, preferably during or right at the end of Matins. The deacons should process him in with the hymn "Blessed is he who comes according to the order of angels." The vestment, girdle, broad white cloth, rings, and crowns should be prepared in a tray by the priest instead of the godparents.

These items are now usually owned by the Church. The groom stands in the chancel behind the priest. The priest should not thread the rings and crowns through the white cloth or through the girdle. The priest should begin with Have Mercy on us and the Thanksgiving Prayer. I would remove the declarations of Hegumen Philotheos. They are not necessary. People know it is a wedding. There is no practical or theological reason to declare it three times. This is not done for any other rite. After the Thanksgiving Prayer, the deacons should chant the Hymn of the Censer. I would not reintroduce Psalm 50 nor would I keep the Verses of the Cymbals. It is no longer the standard to say Psalm 50 after the Thanksgiving Prayer and the Verses of the Cymbals are not part of the original rite. The Hymn of the Censer may be said in full (ⲧⲁⲓϣⲟⲩⲣⲏ & ϯϣⲟⲩⲣⲏ) or just half (ⲧⲁⲓϣⲟⲩⲣⲏ).

Then the Pauline Epistle should be read. It may be sung in its Coptic tune first if desired and time permits. Then the Trisagion is chanted followed by the Litany of the Gospel, the reading of the Psalm in the annual tune, and the Gospel. The Gospel Response should be "Rejoice O bridal chamber" in the Palm Sunday tune. If a bishop is present, then additional verses may be added. The priest should pray the three great litanies, but he may pray these silently during the reading of the Gospel as is commonly done nowadays. The Creed should then be said followed by a call to prayer by the priest.

The priest should then say the four prayers. I give them a new label: The Prayers of the Covenant. Their responses should be chanted in the muḥayyar tune but I would not have each one concluded with "Blessed is the Father" and Lord Have Mercy three times as that is unnecessarily repetitive. After the last prayer, they say Our Father and the priest says the Absolution of the Son with the cross on the groom's head. The deacons respond with Lord Have Mercy three times. Although Pope Gabriel's Ordo called for it to be said forty-three times, I do not think that is necessary. The deacons then chant "The Spiritual Raiment" in the Palm Sunday tune. I would keep all its verses. The priest puts the vestment, girdle, and ring on the groom. The vestment should be a white phelonion.

By now the bride should have arrived. If she arrived earlier, she waits outside the nave. If the first part finishes and the bride has not arrived, they may chant some extra hymns after "The Spiritual Raiment" such as "Christ the Logos" and "Galilee of the Nations." If it is the time of the Holy 50 Days, then they may chant the hymns of the Resurrection. When the bride arrives, the priest and deacons go out of the nave to meet her. The priest puts a white chasuble on her shoulders if necessary. She should not enter the nave wearing anything inappropriate. They bring her in with "Come see this bride" in the Palm Sunday tune. She may enter with her father if she wants but her father gives her to the priest at the base of the chancel. I choose "Come see this bride" instead of any of the hymns to the Virgin Mary as a practical matter. If the bride enters to one of the hymns of the Virgin Mary, then "Come see this bride" would have to be said with everyone standing in place doing nothing. I do not think that would be sustainable in the long term. It would be the first thing to go as soon as people start cutting things out to save time. The way to prevent future potential cuts is to associate the hymn with movement and action. Furthermore, the hymns to the Virgin Mary are said many times throughout the year but "Come see this bride" is only said during the wedding rite so it receives priority of preservation.

The groom goes down to meet her. The priest gives the other ring to the groom. The groom offers it to the bride. She extends her hand and allows the groom to put it on her. The priest then leads them up to the chancel and puts the broad white cloth over their heads. It should be long enough to cover both of their heads and drape down their sides, but it does not have to reach the floor. It should not be taut since the crowns will be place over it. If desired, a small white veil may be placed over the joined hands of the bride and groom as well. They stand in front of the sanctuary facing east. The priest begins the second part, which I still call the Crowning, with Have mercy on us and the Thanksgiving Prayer. The deacons chant the Hymn of the Censer while the priest recites the Pauline incense. Again, it may be said in full or half (ϯϣⲟⲩⲣⲏ).

The Pauline Epistle is read. The Trisagion is chanted. I do not add any hymns before the Trisagion because it is not necessary. These hymns do not add any meaning and they just take up time. There is an opportunity to say those hymns during the liturgy. There is even controversy regarding the Hymn of the Holy Spirit. This hymn was added with the intention of reminding everyone that the Holy Spirit is active in uniting the bride and groom during the wedding. However, by that logic, this hymn should be sung at all church services because the Holy Spirit is active at all services, especially sacramental services. The hymn itself is not about the Holy Spirit per se but rather about the events of Pentecost. It has nothing to do with weddings, marriage, union, or purity. The physical symbol of the divine work of the Holy Spirit is supposed to be the large white cloth draped over the heads of the couple. When the correct rite is restored, this need to have something, whether an artifact or a hymn, represent the Holy Spirit is resolved naturally. Furthermore, Albair Mikhail mentions in his book that this hymn should not be said during the Holy 50 Days because it should not be said until after the Feast of Pentecost.[67] However, in practice, this rule is rarely followed. It is customary to say the hymns of the Resurrection at this point, but this was never mentioned in any of the sources. Mikhail also mentions that another hymn, "All the villages [Nιχωρα]", was said at this time but again the sources do not mention it. This hymn is for the Feast of the Wedding at Cana of Galilee. While I think this hymn is more appropriate for the occasion then the Hymn of the Holy Spirit, I leave it as an option to be said during the liturgy instead of during the Crowning.

After the Trisagion, the priest says the Litany of the Gospel. The Psalm is read in the annual tune. If it is the season of the Holy 50 Days, then it is said in the festal tune. The Gospel is read. The Gospel Response is "Those whom the Holy Spirit attuned." I find it unnecessary to conclude it with "Blessed is the Father" or Lord Have Mercy. The priest issues the call to prayer and begins the Supplications. Then the priest says

---

[67] Mikhail, 791, 1100.

the three great litanies. The people say the Creed. It is common for there to be commotion and ululation, so I reintroduce the calls to peace at this point. I would also include the diaconal directives due to it being common for non-Coptic guests to attend.

The matrimonial prayer responses are said in the muḥayyar tune. I would restore them to Pope Gabriel's versions, since they are the originals, but have only the last one be concluded with "Blessed is the Father" and Lord Have Mercy three times. The prayer of the oil is said. The people respond with the "You have anointed" verses in the muḥayyar tune. I would remove "May this oil." As previously explained, it is not part of the original rite and has nothing to do with weddings. The priest says the prayer of the crowns. He puts the crowns on the heads of the couple and over the broad white cloth while saying "You crowned him with glory and honor. The Father blesses..." I would keep that passage in the indicative mood rather than the imperative because it reveals that it is God who performs the sacrament at the priest's hand and not the priest himself with some internal power to command God to do something. The crowns being over the white cloth forces the couple to walk in sync and that is intentional. It is another physical sign of their unity. The deacons sing the proclamation of worthiness followed by the extra verses beginning with "You received grace."

The priest crosses the groom while saying the verses of blessing for the groom. He should say them in the Axios tune but if he does not know it, he may say them with no tune or he may delegate saying them to the deacons. He then does the same for the bride. I would restore the second verse to Pope Gabriel's version since it does not make sense to mention Hanna and Samuel because they are not a married couple. I would also restore the reference to Joachim and Anna since they were an officially married couple unlike the Virgin Mary and Joseph the Carpenter. I would leave the verses for the heavenly orders, the Apostles, and the martyrs as optional. The deacons should conclude the verses of blessing with "A crown of gold." I would allow the alternative versions of these blessing verses to be said either instead of or in addition to the originals. The priest finishes the crowning prayer. The deacons sing the doxology "Unfading crowns" in its entirety.

The priest then begins the commandments. The Arabicization that Hegumen Philotheos did is not necessary anymore because people can read and are educated. So I do not think it is useful to restate the originals as commands to the couple. The problem with direct commands is that people think they can change them at will. Also, they are affected by the surrounding culture. There are many who do not like the "Listen O daughter" command which says that she should submit to her husband. If it were still the original bible verse, then this controversy would not exist. Removing the link to the bible makes it sound like an arbitrary command that someone made up. It is easy to change or dismiss it as being contemporaneously irrelevant in an era in which equality is considered ethically desirable. But by keeping it tied to the Bible it effectively presents what the Virgin Mary did and invites the bride to draw her own conclusion. This strategy is superior and time-proof.

The priest begins with the first commandment "Glory to God." The deacons sing "My peace I give" and "O King of peace" in the muḥayyar tune. The priest says "May the peace of our Lord Jesus Christ" to the groom. The deacons sing all the verses of "This is the time of blessing." The priest says the final commandment to the groom. The deacons sing the original "Listen O daughter" verse that quotes Psalm 45. The priest says the commandment to the bride. I see no reason to break up the commandment into smaller sections as Hegumen Philotheos did. The deacons respond with Lord Have Mercy three times. The priest says the final commandment "May God bless both of you" until the end. The people say Our Father. The priest says the Absolution of the Son with his hands placed crosswise over the heads of the bride and groom and touching their heads together. The deacons say Lord Have Mercy three times followed by the concluding canon for the wedding "Rejoice O shining bride."

The priest then removes the crowns, white cloth, and vestment. He bids the bride to take a seat in the nave while they begin the liturgy. If the groom belongs to the minor orders of the deaconate, he may vest and serve in the sanctuary as is allowed in the Coptic Orthodox Church. Otherwise, he may stand on the men's side with his party. The liturgy begins with the prayers of the third and sixth hours from the horologion followed by the Prothesis. The Pauline Epistle is from Ephesians 4:1-13, the Catholic Epistle from 1 Peter 3:1-9, the Acts from Acts 4:32-35. The hymn "All the villages [Nιχωρα]" may be said after the Acts. The Psalm is Psalm 21:1-2, and the Gospel from John 2:1-11. The Gospel response is that of the Feast of Cana of Galilee. The canons of the Church already prescribe that a wedding should not take place on the same day as another occasion. However, that scenario must be considered. The convention in the Coptic Church is that if an occasion occurs more than once throughout the year, it may be superseded by a different occasion that only occurs once. For example, if the Feast of Annunciation falls during Pascha Week, it is not celebrated then since Pascha Week is only celebrated once a year whereas the Coptic Church commemorates the Feast of Annunciation on the 29th of every Coptic month. I would apply the same principle in the case of the wedding. If it falls on an occasion that is repeated[68], then the wedding rite supersedes the rite of that day. If it falls on an occasion that not repeated, such as a Lordly feast, then that occasion supersedes the wedding, and its readings and hymns are prayed. The only exception to this is the Holy 50 Days, which always supersede any other occasion. When the liturgy concludes, they process the bride and groom together with the bridal party to the doors of the church singing "Rejoice O Mary the queen."

As a practical matter, I include an estimate of how long all this may take. The Vesting of the Groom may take thirty minutes. The Crowning may take one and a half hours. The liturgy usually takes three hours but can vary depending on the speed of the officiant. So, in total the whole

---

[68] The Coptic Church has feasts for the Virgin Mary and Archangel Michael that repeat monthly. Many saints have multiple feasts throughout the year such as the date of their death and the date of the consecration of their church. The Feast of the Cross is celebrated twice a year.

thing takes about four to five hours. If done in the morning as prescribed, then most of the day is still available for the bride and groom to take photographs and interact with their guests. A reception may still be held on the same day.

CHAPTER 6

The Fully Restored Rite

In this section, I present the full text of the rite as I reconstructed it from the sources. I include the text of every prayer, response, and hymn in English, Coptic, and Arabic. I include in italics direction for clergy regarding processions, movements, anointings, etc. After the rite of the wedding, I include readings and hymns to be used during the subsequent liturgy. The Coptic text was collected from all the sources and the spelling and vocabulary was corrected according to current standards. The Arabic text was also collected from all the sources. The English was taken mostly from *The Coptic Offices for the Coptic Orthodox Church Part II* by Fr. Markos Hanna. The prayers in the first part that I label the Prayers of the Covenant are taken from *The Rites of the Coptic Church* by B.T.A. Evetts and *Coptic Offices* by Reginald Wooley. I updated the wording to reflect contemporary English. In any case in which a source did not include a translation in a particular language, I made my own translation such that all the text is available in all three languages. The only exception to this are things that were originally composed in Arabic like the commandments and alternative verses of blessing. I intend for this section to be available for immediate use by clergy or couples wishing to copy it as a starter for their own wedding booklets. In those prayers in which the names of the bride and groom are mentioned, I have inserted the markers {GROOM} and {BRIDE} to allow for easy search and replace.

The Vesting of the Groom

The groom and his party arrive to the church in the morning. They may attend Matins, but it is not necessary. The priests and deacons vest in their liturgical vestments. They process the groom into the church with Blessed is He, Christ the Logos, and Galilee of the Gentiles, unless it is during the Holy 50 Days, in which they only say Christ is Risen. They finish when everyone is in their place.

Blessed is He who comes

(In the tune of Eflogimenos)

Blessed is He • who comes • according to the order of angels	Ⲉⲩⲗⲟⲅⲓⲙⲉⲛⲟⲥ ⲟ̀ ⲉⲣⲭⲱⲙⲉⲛⲟⲥ ⲕⲁⲧⲁ ⲧⲏⲛ ⲧⲁⲝⲏⲛ ⲁⲅⲅⲉⲗⲱⲛ	مبارك الآتي كطقس الملائكة
Let us chant saying, "Alleluia Alleluia Alleluia."	Ⲧⲉⲛⲉⲣⲯⲁⲗⲓⲛ ⲉⲛϫⲱ ⲙⲙⲟⲥ ⲁⲗ ⲁⲗ ⲁⲗ ⲡⲓⲱⲟⲩ ⲫⲁ ⲡⲉⲛⲛⲟⲩϯ ⲡⲉ	فلنرتل قائلين هلليلويا هلليلويا هلليلويا المجد لالهنا

Christ the Logos

(In the melismatic Palm Sunday tune)

| Christ the Logos of the Father, the Only-Begotten God, grant us Your peace, which is full of all joy. | Ⲡⲭⲥ Ⲡⲓⲗⲟⲅⲟⲥ ⲛⲧⲉ ⲫⲓⲱⲧ ⲡⲓⲙⲟⲛⲟⲅⲉⲛⲏⲥ ⲛⲛⲟⲩϯ ⲉⲕⲉϯ ⲛⲁⲛ ⲛⲧⲉⲕϩⲓⲣⲏⲛⲏ ⲑⲁⲓ ⲉⲑⲙⲉϩ ⲛⲣⲁϣⲓ ⲛⲓⲃⲉⲛ | أيها المسيح كلمة الآب الاله الواحيد الجنس أعطنا سلامك هذا المملوء كل فرح |

Galilee of the Nations

| Galilee of the nations • who sit in darkness • and in the shadow of death • had the great Light shine to them. | Ⲧⲅⲁⲗⲓⲗⲉⲁ ⲛⲧⲉ ⲛⲓⲉⲑⲛⲟⲥ ⲛⲏⲉⲧϩⲉⲙⲥⲓ ϧⲉⲛ ⲡⲕⲁⲕⲓ ⲛⲉⲙ ⲧϧⲏⲓⲃⲓ ⲙⲫⲙⲟⲩ | جليل الأمم الجالسون في الظلمة وظلال الموت أشرق عليهم النور العظيم |

	ⲟⲩⲛⲓϣϯ ⲛⲟⲩⲱⲓⲛⲓ ⲁϥϣⲁⲓ ⲛⲱⲟⲩ	
God who rests • among His saints • became incarnate of the Virgin • for our salvation.	Ⲫⲛⲟⲩϯ ⲫⲏⲉⲑⲙⲟⲧⲉⲛ ⲙⲙⲟϥ ϧⲉⲛ ⲛⲏⲉⲑⲟⲩⲁⲃ ⲛⲧⲁϥ ⲁϥϭⲓⲥⲁⲣⲝ ϧⲉⲛ ϯⲡⲁⲣⲑⲉⲛⲟⲥ ⲉⲑⲃⲉ ⲫⲏⲉⲧⲉ ⲫⲱⲛ ⲛⲟⲩϫⲁⲓ	الله المستريح في قديسيه تجسد من العذراء لأجل خلاصنا
Come behold and be amazed. • Joyfully sing on account • of this mystery • which was revealed unto us.	Ⲁⲙⲱⲓⲛⲓ ⲁⲛⲁⲩ ⲁⲣⲓϣⲫⲏⲣⲓ ϩⲱⲥ ⲑⲉⲗⲏⲗ ϧⲉⲛ ⲟⲩϣⲗⲏⲗⲟⲩⲓ ⲉϫⲉⲛ ⲡⲁⲓⲙⲩⲥⲧⲏⲣⲓⲟⲛ ⲉⲧⲁϥⲟⲩⲱⲛϩ ⲛⲁⲛ ⲉⲃⲟⲗ	تعالوا أنظروا وتعجبوا وسبحوا وهللوا بإبتهاج لهذا السر الذي ظهر لنا
For the Incorporeal was incarnate, • and the Word became flesh. • The One without beginning began. • The Eternal came under time.	Ϫⲉ ⲡⲓⲁⲧⲥⲁⲣⲝ ⲁϥϭⲓⲥⲁⲣⲝ ⲟⲩⲟϩ ⲡⲓⲗⲟⲅⲟⲥ ⲁϥϣⲁⲓ ⲡⲓⲁⲧⲁⲣⲭⲏ ⲁϥⲉⲣϩⲏⲧⲥ ⲡⲓⲁⲧⲥⲛⲟⲩ ⲁϥϣⲱⲡⲓ ϧⲁ ⲟⲩⲭⲣⲟⲛⲟⲥ	لأن غير المتجسد تجسد والكلمة تجسمت غير المبتدئ إبتدأ وغير الزمني صار زمنياً
The Incomprehensible has been touched, • and the Unseen has been seen. • The Son of the living God • truly became the Son of Man.	Ⲡⲓⲁⲧϣⲧⲁϩⲟϥ ⲁⲩϫⲉⲙϫⲱⲙϥ ⲡⲓⲁⲑⲛⲁⲩ ⲉⲣⲟϥ ⲥⲉⲛⲁⲩ ⲉⲣⲟϥ ⲡϣⲏⲣⲓ ⲙⲪⲛⲟⲩϯ ⲉⲧⲟⲛϧ ⲁϥϣⲱⲡⲓ ⲛϣⲏⲣⲓ ⲛⲣⲱⲙⲓ ϧⲉⲛ ⲟⲩⲙⲉⲑⲙⲏⲓ	غير المدرك لمسوه وغير المرئي رأوه إبن الله الحي صار بشرياً بالحقيقة
Jesus Christ is the same yesterday, • today and forever • in one hypostasis. • We worship and glorify Him.	Ⲓⲏⲥⲟⲩⲥ Ⲡⲓⲭⲣⲓⲥⲧⲟⲥ ⲛⲥⲁϥ ⲛⲉⲙ ⲫⲟⲟⲩ ⲛⲑⲟϥ ⲛⲑⲟϥ ⲡⲉ ⲛⲉⲙ ϣⲁ ⲉⲛⲉϩ ϧⲉⲛ ⲟⲩϩⲩⲡⲟⲥⲧⲁⲥⲓⲥ ⲛⲟⲩⲱⲧ ⲧⲉⲛⲟⲩⲱϣⲧ ⲙⲙⲟϥ ⲧⲉⲛϯⲱⲟⲩ ⲛⲁϥ	يسوع المسيح هو هو أمس واليوم وإلى الأبد بأقنوم واحد نسجد له ونمجده
The Father looked from heaven • and found no one like you. • He sent His Only-Begotten • who came and took flesh from you.	Ⲁ Ⲫⲓⲱⲧ ϫⲟⲩϣⲧ ⲉⲃⲟⲗϧⲉⲛ ⲧⲫⲉ ⲙⲡⲉϥϫⲉⲙ ⲫⲏⲉⲧⲟⲛⲓ ⲙⲙⲟ ⲁϥⲟⲩⲱⲣⲡ ⲙⲡⲉϥⲙⲟⲛⲟⲅⲉⲛⲏⲥ ⲓ ⲁϥϭⲓⲥⲁⲣⲝ ⲉⲃⲟⲗⲛϧⲏϯ	تطلع الآب من السماء فلم يجد من يشبهك أرسل وحيده أتى وتجسد منك

A Textual History of the Coptic Wedding Rite

Christ is Risen

(To be said during the Holy 50 Days)

Christ is risen from the dead, trampling down death by death, and upon those in the tombs bestowing life.	Ⲭⲣⲓⲥⲧⲟⲥ ⲁⲛⲉⲥⲧⲏ ⲉⲕ ⲛⲉⲕⲣⲱⲛ ⲑⲁⲛⲁⲧⲱ ⲑⲁⲛⲁⲧⲟⲛ ⲡⲁⲧⲏⲥⲁⲥ ⲕⲉ ⲧⲏⲥ ⲉⲛ ⲧⲏⲥ ⲙⲛⲓⲙⲁⲥⲓ ⲍⲱⲏⲛ ⲭⲁⲣⲓⲥⲁⲙⲉⲛⲟⲥ	المسيح قام من بين الأموات بالموت داس الموت والذين في القبور أنعم عليهم بالحياة الأبدية
Glory to the Father and the Son and the Holy Spirit, now and forever and unto the age of all ages. Amen.	Ⲇⲟⲝⲁ Ⲡⲁⲧⲣⲓ ⲕⲉ Ⲩⲓⲱ ⲕⲉ ⲁⲅⲓⲱ Ⲡⲛⲉⲩⲙⲁⲧⲓ ⲕⲉ ⲛⲩⲛ ⲕⲉ ⲁⲓ ⲕⲉ ⲓⲥ ⲧⲟⲩⲥ ⲉⲱⲛⲁⲥ ⲧⲱⲛ ⲉⲱⲛⲱⲛ. ⲁⲙⲏⲛ.	المجد للآب والإبن والروح القدس الآن وكل أوان وإلى دهر الدهور آمين

The groom stands in front of the sanctuary in the chancel behind the priest.

Priest:

Have mercy on us, O God, the Father, the Pantocrator. All-Holy Trinity, have mercy on us. O Lord, God of the powers, be with us, for we have no helper in our tribulations and afflictions but You.	Ⲉⲗⲉⲏⲥⲟⲛ ⲏⲙⲁⲥ ⲟ Ⲑⲉⲟⲥ ⲟ Ⲡⲁⲧⲏⲣ ⲟ Ⲡⲁⲛⲧⲟⲕⲣⲁⲧⲱⲣ Ⲡⲁⲛⲁⲅⲓⲁ Ⲧⲣⲓⲁⲥ ⲉⲗⲉⲏⲥⲟⲛ ⲏⲙⲁⲥ. Ⲡ̄ϭⲟⲓⲥ Ⲫⲛⲟⲩϯ ⲛⲧⲉ ⲛⲓϫⲟⲙ ϣⲱⲡⲓ ⲛⲉⲙⲁⲛ ϫⲉ ⲙⲙⲟⲛ ⲛⲧⲁⲛ ⲛⲟⲩⲃⲟⲏⲑⲟⲥ ϧⲉⲛ ⲛⲉⲛⲑⲗⲓⲯⲓⲥ ⲛⲉⲙ ⲛⲉⲛϩⲟϫϩⲉϫ ⲉⲃⲏⲗ ⲉⲣⲟⲕ	إرحمنا يا الله الآب ضابط الكل أيها الثالوث القدوس إرحمنا أيها الرب اله القوات كن معنا لأنه ليس لنا معين في شدائدنا وضيقاتنا سواك
Make us worthy to pray thankfully:	ⲁⲣⲓⲧⲉⲛ ⲛⲉⲙⲡϣⲁ ⲛϫⲟⲥ ϧⲉⲛ ⲟⲩϣⲉⲡϩⲙⲟⲧ	اجعلنا مستحقين أن نقول بشكر

Congregation:

Our Father who art in heaven, hallowed be Thy name. Thy kingdom come. Thy will be done, on earth as it is in heaven. Give us this day our daily bread; and forgive us our trespasses, as we forgive those who trespass against us; and lead us not into temptation, but deliver us from the evil one. In Christ Jesus our Lord, for Thine is the kingdom and the power and the glory forever. Amen.	Ϫⲉ ⲡⲉⲛⲓⲱⲧ ⲉⲧϧⲉⲛ ⲛⲓⲫⲏⲟⲩⲓ ⲙⲁⲣⲉϥⲧⲟⲩⲃⲟ ⲛϫⲉ ⲡⲉⲕⲣⲁⲛ ⲙⲁⲣⲉⲥⲓ ⲛϫⲉ ⲧⲉⲕⲙⲉⲧⲟⲩⲣⲟ ⲡⲉⲧⲉϩⲛⲁⲕ ⲙⲁⲣⲉϥϣⲱⲡⲓ ⲙ̀ⲫⲣⲏϯ ϧⲉⲛ ⲧⲫⲉ ⲛⲉⲙ ϩⲓϫⲉⲛ ⲡⲓⲕⲁϩⲓ. Ⲡⲉⲛⲱⲓⲕ ⲛⲧⲉ ⲣⲁⲥϯ ⲙⲏⲓϥ ⲛⲁⲛ ⲙ̀ⲫⲟⲟⲩ. Ⲟⲩⲟϩ ⲭⲁ ⲛⲏⲉⲧⲉⲣⲟⲛ ⲛⲁⲛ ⲉⲃⲟⲗ ⲙ̀ⲫⲣⲏϯ ϩⲱⲛ ⲛⲧⲉⲛⲭⲱ ⲉⲃⲟⲗ ⲛ̀ⲛⲏⲉⲧⲉ ⲟⲩⲟⲛ̀ⲛⲧⲁⲛ ⲉⲣⲱⲟⲩ. Ⲟⲩⲟϩ ⲙ̀ⲡⲉⲣⲉⲛⲧⲉⲛ ⲉϧⲟⲩⲛ ⲉⲡⲓⲣⲁⲥⲙⲟⲥ ⲁⲗⲗⲁ ⲛⲁϩⲙⲉⲛ ⲉⲃⲟⲗϩⲁ ⲡⲓⲡⲉⲧϩⲱⲟⲩ ϧⲉⲛ Ⲡⲭⲥ Ⲓⲏⲥ Ⲡⲉⲛϭⲟⲓⲥ ⲑⲱⲕ ⲧⲉ ϯⲙⲉⲧⲟⲩⲣⲟ ⲛⲉⲙ ϯϫⲟⲙ ⲛⲉⲙ ⲡⲓⲱⲟⲩ ϣⲁ ⲉⲛⲉϩ. Ⲁⲙⲏⲛ.	أبانا الذي في السموات ليتقدس إسمك ليأت ملكوتك لتكن مشيئتك كما في السماء كذلك على الأرض خبزنا كفافنا أعطنا اليوم وأغفر لنا ذنوبنا كما نغفر نحن أيضاً للمذنبين إلينا ولا تدخلنا في تجربة لكن نجنا من الشرير بالمسيح يسوع ربنا لأن لك الملك والقوة والمجد إلى الأبد آمين

Congregation:

In Christ Jesus our Lord	ϧⲉⲛ Ⲡⲓⲭⲣⲓⲥⲧⲟⲥ Ⲓⲏⲥⲟⲩⲥ Ⲡⲉⲛϭⲟⲓⲥ	بالمسيح يسوع ربنا

Priest:

Let us pray	Ϣⲗⲏⲗ	صلوا

Deacon:

| Stand up for prayer | Ⲉⲡⲓ ⲡⲣⲟⲥⲉⲩⲭⲏ ⲥⲧⲁⲑⲏⲧⲉ | للصلاة قفوا |

Priest:

| Peace be with all. | Ⲓⲣⲏⲛⲏ ⲡⲁⲥⲓ | السلام لجميعكم |

Congregation:

| And with your spirit. | Ⲕⲉ ⲧⲱ ⲡⲛⲉⲩⲙⲁⲧⲓ ⲥⲟⲩ | ولروحك أيضاً |

The Thanksgiving Prayer

Priest:

| Let us give thanks to the beneficent and merciful God, the Father of our Lord, God and Savior Jesus Christ, for He has covered us, helped us, guarded us, accepted us to Himself, spared us, supported us, and brought us to this hour. Let us also ask Him, the Lord our God the Pantocrator, to guard us in all peace this holy day and all the days of our life. | Ⲙⲁⲣⲉⲛϣⲉⲡϩⲙⲟⲧ ⲛⲧⲟⲧϥ ⲙⲡⲓⲣⲉϥⲉⲣⲡⲉⲑⲛⲁⲛⲉϥ ⲟⲩⲟϩ ⲛⲛⲁⲏⲧ Ⲫⲛⲟⲩϯ Ⲫⲓⲱⲧ ⲙⲠⲉⲛϭⲟⲓⲥ ⲟⲩⲟϩ Ⲡⲉⲛⲥⲱⲧⲏⲣ ⲟⲩⲟϩ Ⲡⲉⲛⲟⲩⲣⲟ ⲧⲏⲣⲉⲛ Ⲓⲏⲥⲟⲩⲥ Ⲡⲓⲭⲣⲓⲥⲧⲟⲥ ϫⲉ ⲁϥⲉⲣⲥⲕⲉⲡⲁⲍⲓⲛ ⲉϫⲱⲛ ⲁϥⲉⲣⲃⲟⲏⲑⲓⲛ ⲉⲣⲟⲛ ⲁϥⲁⲣⲉϩ ⲉⲣⲟⲛ ⲁϥϣⲟⲡⲧⲉⲛ ⲉⲣⲟϥ ⲁϥϯⲁⲥⲟ ⲉⲣⲟⲛ ⲁϥϯⲧⲟⲧⲉⲛ ⲁϥⲉⲛⲧⲉⲛ ϣⲁ ⲉϩⲣⲏⲓ ⲉⲧⲁⲓⲟⲩⲛⲟⲩ ⲑⲁⲓ. Ⲛⲑⲟϥ ⲟⲛ ⲙⲁⲣⲉⲛϯϩⲟ ⲉⲣⲟϥ ϩⲟⲡⲱⲥ ⲛⲧⲉϥⲁⲣⲉϩ ⲉⲣⲟⲛ ϧⲉⲛ ⲡⲁⲓⲉϩⲟⲟⲩ ⲉⲑⲟⲩⲁⲃ ⲫⲁⲓ ⲛⲉⲙ ⲛⲓⲉϩⲟⲟⲩ ⲧⲏⲣⲟⲩ ⲛⲧⲉ ⲡⲉⲛⲱⲛϧ ϧⲉⲛ | فلنشكر صانع الخيرات الرحوم الله أبا ربنا وإلهنا ومخلصنا يسوع المسيح لأنه سترنا وأعاننا وحفظنا وقبلنا إليه وشفق علينا وعضدنا وأتى بنا إلى هذه الساعة هو أيضاً فلنسأله أن يحفظنا في هذا اليوم المقدس وكل أيام حياتنا بكل سلام ضابط الكل الرب إلهنا |

| | ϩιρнин ниβєн ηδє Παητοκρατωρ Πσοιс Πєnnoyϯ. | |

Deacon:

| Let us pray. | Προсєγzαсθє | صلوا |

Congregation:

| Lord have mercy. | Κγριє Ἐλєнсοn | يا رب إرحم |

Priest:

| O Master, Lord God, the Pantocrator, the Father of our Lord, God, and Savior Jesus Christ, we thank you, for everything, concerning everything and in everything, | Ⲫⲛⲏⲃ Ⲡϭⲟⲓⲥ Ⲫⲛⲟⲩϯ Ⲡⲓⲡⲁⲛⲧⲟⲕⲣⲁⲧⲱⲣ Ⲫⲓⲱⲧ ⲙⲠⲉⲛϭⲟⲓⲥ ⲟⲩⲟϩ Ⲡⲉⲛⲛⲟⲩϯ ⲟⲩⲟϩ Ⲡⲉⲛⲥⲱⲧⲏⲣ Ⲓⲏⲥⲟⲩⲥ Ⲡⲓⲭⲣⲓⲥⲧⲟⲥ ⲧⲉⲛϣⲉⲡϩⲙⲟⲧ ⲛⲧⲟⲧⲕ ⲕⲁⲧⲁ ϩⲱⲃ ⲛⲓⲃⲉⲛ ⲛⲉⲙ ⲉⲑⲃⲉ ϩⲱⲃ ⲛⲓⲃⲉⲛ ⲛⲉⲙ ϧⲉⲛ ϩⲱⲃ ⲛⲓⲃⲉⲛ | أيها السيد الرب الإله ضابط الكل أبو ربنا وإلهنا ومخلصنا يسوع المسيح نشكرك على كل حال ومن أجل كل حال وفي كل حال. |
| for You have covered us, helped us, guarded us, accepted us to Yourself, spared us, supported us, and have brought us to this hour. | ϫⲉ ⲁⲕⲉⲣⲥⲕⲉⲡⲁⲍⲓⲛ ⲉϫⲱⲛ ⲁⲕⲉⲣⲃⲟⲏⲑⲓⲛ ⲉⲣⲟⲛ ⲁⲕⲁⲣⲉϩ ⲉⲣⲟⲛ ⲁⲕϣⲟⲡⲧⲉⲛ ⲉⲣⲟⲕ ⲁⲕϯⲁⲥⲟ ⲉⲣⲟⲛ ⲁⲕϯⲧⲟⲧⲉⲛ ⲁⲕⲉⲛⲧⲉⲛ ϣⲁ ⲉϩⲣⲏⲓ ⲉⲧⲁⲓⲟⲩⲛⲟⲩ ⲑⲁⲓ | لأنك سترتنا وأعنتنا وحفظتنا وقبلتنا إليك وشفقت علينا وعضدتنا وأتيت بنا إلى هذه الساعة |

A Textual History of the Coptic Wedding Rite

Deacon:

| Pray that God have mercy and compassion on us, hear us, help us, and accept the supplications and prayers of His saints for that which is good on our behalf at all times, | Ⲧⲱⲃⲏ ϩⲓⲛⲁ ⲛⲧⲉ Ⲫⲛⲟⲩϯ ⲛⲁⲓ ⲛⲁⲛ ⲛⲧⲉϥϣⲉⲛϩⲏⲧ ϧⲁⲣⲟⲛ ⲛⲧⲉϥⲥⲱⲧⲉⲙ ⲉⲣⲟⲛ ⲛⲧⲉϥⲉⲣⲃⲟⲏⲑⲓⲛ ⲉⲣⲟⲛ ⲛⲧⲉϥϭⲓ ⲛⲛⲓϯϩⲟ ⲛⲉⲙ ⲛⲓⲧⲱⲃϩ ⲛⲧⲉ ⲛⲏⲉⲑⲟⲩⲁⲃ ⲛⲧⲁϥ ⲛⲧⲟⲧⲟⲩ ⲉϩⲣⲏⲓ ⲉϫⲱⲛ ⲉⲡⲓⲁⲅⲁⲑⲟⲛ ⲛⲥⲏⲟⲩ ⲛⲓⲃⲉⲛ | أطلبوا لكي يرحمنا الله ويتراءف علينا ويسمعنا ويعيننا ويقبل سؤالات وطلبات قديسيه منهم بالصلاح عنا في كل حين |

(In the presence of a bishop)

| and to keep the life and standing of our honored father the high priest Pope Abba (...), and his partner in the liturgy our father the bishop Abba (...), | ⲛⲧⲉϥⲁⲣⲉϩ ⲉⲡⲱⲛϧ ⲛⲉⲙ ⲡⲧⲁϩⲟ ⲉⲣⲁⲧϥ ⲙⲡⲉⲛⲓⲱⲧ ⲉⲧⲧⲁⲓⲏⲟⲩⲧ ⲛⲁⲣⲭⲏⲉⲣⲉⲩⲥ ⲡⲁⲡⲁ ⲁⲃⲃⲁ (...) ⲛⲉⲙ ⲡⲉϥⲕⲉϣⲫⲏⲣ ⲛⲗⲓⲧⲟⲩⲣⲅⲟⲥ ⲡⲉⲛⲓⲱⲧ ⲛⲉⲡⲓⲥⲕⲟⲡⲟⲥ/ⲙⲙⲏⲧⲣⲟⲡⲟⲗⲓⲧⲏⲥ ⲁⲃⲃⲁ (...) | وأن يحفظ حياة وقيام أبينا المكرم البابا الأنبا (...) وشريكه في الخدمة الرسولية أبينا الأسقف (المطران) أنبا |
| and forgive us our sins. | ⲛⲧⲉϥⲭⲁ ⲛⲉⲛⲛⲟⲃⲓ ⲛⲁⲛ ⲉⲃⲟⲗ | ويغفر لنا خطايانا |

Congregation:

| Lord have mercy. | Ⲕⲩⲣⲓⲉ Ⲉⲗⲉⲏⲥⲟⲛ | يا رب إرحم |

Priest:

| Therefore, we ask and entreat Your goodness, O Lover of mankind, grant us to complete this holy day and all the days of | Ⲉⲑⲃⲉ ⲫⲁⲓ ⲧⲉⲛϯϩⲟ ⲟⲩⲟϩ ⲧⲉⲛⲧⲱⲃϩ ⲛⲧⲉⲕⲙⲉⲧⲁⲅⲁⲑⲟⲥ Ⲡⲓⲙⲁⲓⲣⲱⲙⲓ ⲙⲏⲓⲥ ⲛⲁⲛ | من أجل هذا نسأل ونطلب من صلاحك يا محب البشر إمنحنا أن نكمل هذا اليوم المقدس وكل أيام |

| our life in all peace with Your fear. All envy, all temptation, all the work of Satan, the counsel of wicked men, and the rising up of enemies, hidden and manifest, take them away from us, and from all Your people, and from this holy place that is Yours. But those things which are good and profitable, do provide for us, for it is You who have given us the authority to tread on serpents and scorpions and upon all the power of the enemy. | ⲉⲑⲣⲉⲛϫⲱⲕ ⲉⲃⲟⲗ ⲙⲡⲁⲓⲕⲉⲉϩⲟⲟⲩ ⲉⲑⲟⲩⲁⲃ ⲫⲁⲓ ⲛⲉⲙ ⲛⲓⲉϩⲟⲟⲩ ⲧⲏⲣⲟⲩ ⲛⲧⲉ ⲡⲉⲛⲱⲛϧ ϧⲉⲛ ϩⲓⲣⲏⲛⲏ ⲛⲓⲃⲉⲛ ⲛⲉⲙ ⲧⲉⲕϩⲟϯ. Ⲫⲑⲟⲛⲟⲥ ⲛⲓⲃⲉⲛ ⲡⲓⲣⲁⲥⲙⲟⲥ ⲛⲓⲃⲉⲛ ⲉⲛⲉⲣⲅⲓⲁ ⲛⲓⲃⲉⲛ ⲛⲧⲉ ⲡⲥⲁⲧⲁⲛⲁⲥ ⲡⲥⲟϭⲛⲓ ⲛⲧⲉ ϩⲁⲛⲣⲱⲙⲓ ⲉⲩϩⲱⲟⲩ ⲛⲉⲙ ⲡⲧⲱⲛϥ ⲉⲡϣⲱⲓ ⲛⲧⲉ ϩⲁⲛϫⲁϫⲓ ⲛⲏⲉⲧϩⲏⲡ ⲛⲉⲙ ⲛⲏⲉⲑⲟⲩⲱⲛϩ ⲁⲗⲓⲧⲟⲩ ⲉⲃⲟⲗϩⲁⲣⲟⲛ ⲛⲉⲙ ⲉⲃⲟⲗ ϩⲁ ⲡⲉⲕⲗⲁⲟⲥ ⲧⲏⲣϥ ⲛⲉⲙ ⲉⲃⲟⲗ ϩⲁ ⲧⲁⲓⲉⲕⲕⲗⲏⲥⲓⲁ ⲑⲁⲓ ⲛⲉⲙ ⲉⲃⲟⲗϩⲁ ⲡⲁⲓⲙⲁ ⲉⲑⲟⲩⲁⲃ ⲛⲧⲁⲕ ⲫⲁⲓ. Ⲛⲏ ⲇⲉ ⲉⲑⲛⲁⲛⲉⲩ ⲛⲉⲙ ⲛⲏⲉⲧⲉⲣⲛⲟⲩⲣⲓ ⲥⲁϩⲛⲓ ⲙⲙⲱⲟⲩ ⲛⲁⲛ ϫⲉ ⲛⲑⲟⲕ ⲡⲉ ⲉⲧⲁⲕϯ ⲙⲡⲓⲉⲣϣⲓϣⲓ ⲛⲁⲛ ⲉϩⲱⲙⲓ ⲉϫⲉⲛ ⲛⲓϩⲟϥ ⲛⲉⲙ ⲛⲓϭⲗⲏ ⲛⲉⲙ ⲉϫⲉⲛ ϯϫⲟⲙ ⲧⲏⲣⲥ ⲛⲧⲉ ⲡⲓϫⲁϫⲓ. | حياتنا بكل سلام مع مخافتك كل حسد وكل تجربة وكل فعل الشيطان ومؤامرة الناس الأشرار وقيام الأعداء الخفيين والظاهرين إنزعها عنا وعن سائر شعبك وعن هذه الكنيسة وعن موضعك المقدس هذا أما الصالحات والنافعات فارزقنا إياها لأنك أنت الذي أعطيتنا السلطان أن ندوس على الحيات والعقارب وكل قوة العدو |

The Hymn of the Censer

| This censer of pure gold, bearing the aroma which is in the hands of Aaron the priest, offering up incense on the altar — | Ⲧⲁⲓϣⲟⲩⲏ ⲛⲛⲟⲩⲃ ⲛⲕⲁⲑⲁⲣⲟⲥ ⲉⲧϥⲁⲓ ϩⲁ ⲡⲓⲁⲣⲱⲙⲁⲧⲁ ⲉⲧϧⲉⲛ ⲛⲉⲛϫⲓϫ ⲛⲁⲁⲣⲱⲛ ⲡⲓⲟⲩⲏⲃ ⲉϥⲧⲁⲗⲉ ⲟⲩⲥⲑⲟⲓⲛⲟⲩϥⲓ ⲉⲡϣⲱⲓ ⲉϫⲉⲛ ⲡⲓⲙⲁⲛⲉⲣϣⲱⲟⲩϣⲓ | هذه المجمرة الذهب النقي الحاملة العنبر التي في يدي هرون الكاهن يرفع بخوراً فوق المذبح |

the golden censer is the Virgin. • Her aroma is our Savior. • She gave birth to Him. He saved us • and forgave us our sins.	Ϯϣⲟⲩⲣⲏ ⲛⲛⲟⲩⲃ ⲧⲉ Ϯⲡⲁⲣⲑⲉⲛⲟⲥ ⲡⲉⲥⲁⲣⲱⲙⲁⲧⲁ ⲡⲉ Ⲡⲉⲛⲥⲱⲧⲏⲣ. ⲁⲥⲙⲓⲥⲓ ⲙⲙⲟϥ ⲁϥⲥⲱϯ ⲙⲙⲟⲛ ⲟⲩⲟϩ ⲁϥⲭⲁ ⲛⲉⲛⲛⲟⲃⲓ ⲛⲁⲛ ⲉⲃⲟⲗ.	المجمرة الذهب هي العذراء وعنبرها هو مخلصنا قد ولدته وخلصنا وغفر لنا خطايانا
We worship You O Christ, • with Your good Father, • and the Holy Spirit, • for You have come and saved us.	Ⲧⲉⲛⲟⲩⲱϣⲧ ⲙⲙⲟⲕ ⲱ Ⲡⲭⲥ ⲛⲉⲙ ⲡⲉⲕⲓⲱⲧ ⲛⲁⲅⲁⲑⲟⲥ ⲛⲉⲙ Ⲡⲓⲡⲛⲉⲩⲙⲁ Ⲉⲑⲟⲩⲁⲃ ϫⲉ ⲁⲕⲓ ⲁⲕⲥⲱϯ ⲙⲙⲟⲛ ⲛⲁⲓ ⲛⲁⲛ	نسجد لك ايها المسيح مع أبيك الصالح والروح القدس لأنك اتيت وخلصتنا إرحمنا.

Pauline Epistle

(1 Corinthians 1:1 – 10)

Reader:

Paul, the servant of our Lord Jesus Christ, called to be an apostle, appointed to the Gospel of God. A reading from the first Epistle of our teacher St. Paul to the Corinthians, may his holy blessings be with us all, Amen.	Ⲡⲁⲩⲗⲟⲥ ϥⲃⲱⲕ ⲙⲡⲉⲛϭⲟⲓⲥ Ⲓⲏⲥ Ⲡⲭⲥ ⲫⲏⲉⲧⲁϩⲉⲙ ⲉⲡⲓϩⲓϣⲉⲛⲛⲟⲩϥⲓ ⲛⲧⲉ Ⲫϯ	البولس فصل من رسالة معلمنا بولس الى أهل كورنثوس الأولى بركاته تكون معنا أمين
Paul, called to be an apostle of Jesus Christ through the will of God, and Sosthenes our brother, to the church of God which is at Corinth, to those who are sanctified in Christ Jesus, called to be saints,	Ⲡⲁⲩⲗⲟⲥ ⲡⲓⲁⲡⲟⲥⲧⲟⲗⲟⲥ ⲉⲧⲑⲁϩⲉⲙ ⲛⲧⲉ Ⲓⲏⲥ Ⲡⲭⲥ ⲉⲃⲟⲗϩⲓⲧⲉⲛ ϥⲟⲩⲱϣ ⲙⲫϯ ⲛⲉⲙ Ⲥⲱⲥⲑⲉⲛⲏⲥ ⲡⲓⲥⲟⲛ ⲛϯⲉⲕⲕⲗⲏⲥⲓⲁ ⲛⲧⲉ Ⲫϯ ⲑⲏⲉⲧϣⲟⲡ ϧⲉⲛ Ⲕⲟⲣⲓⲛⲑⲟⲥ	بولس المدعو رسولا ليسوع المسيح بمشيئة الله وسوستانيس الاخ الى كنيسة الله التي في كورنثوس المقدسين في المسيح يسوع المدعوين قديسين مع جميع الذين يدعون باسم ربنا يسوع المسيح في كل مكان لهم ولنا

with all who in every place call on the name of Jesus Christ our Lord, both theirs and ours: Grace to you and peace from God our Father and the Lord Jesus Christ. I thank my God always concerning you for the grace of God which was given to you by Christ Jesus, that you were enriched in everything by Him in all utterance and all knowledge, even as the testimony of Christ was confirmed in you, so that you come short in no gift, eagerly waiting for the revelation of our Lord Jesus Christ, who will also confirm you to the end, that you may be blameless in the day of our Lord Jesus Christ. God is faithful, by whom you were called into the fellowship of His Son, Jesus Christ our Lord. Now I plead with you, brethren, by the name of our Lord Jesus Christ, that you all speak the same thing, and that there be no divisions among you, but that you be perfectly joined together in the same mind and in the same judgment.	ⲛⲏⲉⲧⲁⲩⲧⲟⲩⲃⲱⲟⲩ ϧⲉⲛ Ⲡ̄ⲭ̄ⲥ̄ Ⲓⲏ̄ⲥ̄ ⲛⲏⲉⲧⲁⲩⲑⲁϩⲉⲙ ⲉⲑⲟⲩⲁⲃ ⲛⲉⲙ ⲟⲩⲟⲛ ⲛⲓⲃⲉⲛ ⲉⲑⲙⲟⲩϯ ⲉⲫⲣⲁⲛ ⲙ̄ⲡⲉⲛϭⲟⲓⲥ Ⲓⲏ̄ⲥ̄ Ⲡ̄ⲭ̄ⲥ̄ ϧⲉⲛ ⲙⲁⲓ ⲛⲓⲃⲉⲛ ⲛ̄ⲧⲱⲟⲩ ⲛⲉⲙ ⲛ̄ⲧⲁⲛ. Ⲡϩⲙⲟⲧ ⲛⲱⲧⲉⲛ ⲛⲉⲙ ⲓⲣⲏⲛⲏ ⲉⲃⲟⲗϩⲓⲧⲉⲛ Ⲫϯ ⲡⲉⲛⲓⲱⲧ ⲛⲉⲙ ⲡⲉⲛϭⲟⲓⲥ Ⲓⲏ̄ⲥ̄ Ⲡ̄ⲭ̄ⲥ̄. Ϯϣⲉⲡϩⲙⲟⲧ ⲛ̄ⲧⲉⲛ ⲡⲁⲛⲟⲩϯ ⲛ̄ⲥⲏⲟⲩ ⲛⲓⲃⲉⲛ ⲉϩⲣⲏⲓ ⲉϫⲉⲛ ⲑⲏⲛⲟⲩ ⲉϫⲉⲛ ⲡⲓϩⲙⲟⲧ ⲛ̄ⲧⲉ Ⲫϯ ⲉⲧⲁⲩⲧⲏⲓϥ ⲛⲱⲧⲉⲛ ϧⲉⲛ Ⲡ̄ⲭ̄ⲥ̄ Ⲓⲏ̄ⲥ̄. ϫⲉ ϧⲉⲛ ϩⲱⲃ ⲛⲓⲃⲉⲛ ⲁ ⲧⲉⲧⲉⲛⲉⲣⲣⲁⲙⲁⲟ ⲛ̄ϧⲣⲏⲓ ⲛ̄ϧⲏⲧϥ ϧⲉⲛ ⲥⲁϫⲓ ⲛⲓⲃⲉⲛ ⲛⲉⲙ ⲉⲙⲓ ⲛⲓⲃⲉⲛ ⲕⲁⲧⲁ ⲉⲫⲣⲏϯ ⲉⲧⲁ ϯⲙⲉⲧⲙⲉⲑⲣⲉ ⲛ̄ⲧⲉ Ⲡ̄ⲭ̄ⲥ̄ ⲧⲁϫⲣⲟ ϧⲉⲛ ⲑⲏⲛⲟⲩ. ϩⲱⲧⲉ ⲛ̄ⲧⲉⲧⲉⲛϣⲱⲡⲓ ⲛ̄ⲧⲉⲧⲉⲛϣⲁⲧ ⲁⲛ ϧⲉⲛ ϩⲗⲓ ⲛ̄ϩⲙⲟⲧ ⲉⲣⲉⲧⲉⲛϫⲟⲩϣⲧ ⲉⲃⲟⲗ ϧⲁ ⲧϩⲏ ⲙ̄ⲡⲓϭⲱⲣⲡ ⲉⲃⲟⲗ ⲛ̄ⲧⲉ ⲡⲉⲛϭⲟⲓⲥ Ⲓⲏ̄ⲥ̄ Ⲡ̄ⲭ̄ⲥ̄. Ⲫⲁⲓ ⲉⲧⲉ ⲉϥⲉⲧⲁϫⲣⲉ ⲑⲏⲛⲟⲩ ϣⲁ ⲉⲃⲟⲗ ⲛ̄ⲁⲧⲁⲣⲓⲕⲓ ϧⲉⲛ ⲡⲉϩⲟⲟⲩ ⲙ̄ⲡⲉⲛϭⲟⲓⲥ Ⲓⲏ̄ⲥ̄ Ⲡ̄ⲭ̄ⲥ̄. Ϥⲉⲛϩⲟⲧ ⲛ̄ϫⲉ Ⲫϯ ⲫⲏⲉⲧⲁϥⲑⲁϩⲉⲙ ⲑⲏⲛⲟⲩ ⲉϧⲟⲩⲛ ⲉϯⲙⲉⲧϣⲫⲏⲣ ⲛ̄ⲧⲉ ⲡⲉϥϣⲏⲣⲓ Ⲓⲏ̄ⲥ̄ Ⲡ̄ⲭ̄ⲥ̄ Ⲡⲉⲛⲟ̄ⲥ̄. Ϯϯϩⲟ ⲇⲉ ⲉⲣⲱⲧⲉⲛ ⲛⲁⲥⲛⲏⲟⲩ ⲉⲃⲟⲗϩⲓⲧⲉⲛ	نعمة لكم وسلام من الله ابينا والرب يسوع المسيح اشكر الهي في كل حين من جهتكم على نعمة الله المعطاة لكم في يسوع المسيح انكم في كل شيء استغنيتم فيه في كل كلمة وكل علم كما ثبتت فيكم شهادة المسيح حتى انكم لستم ناقصين في موهبة ما وانتم متوقعون استعلان ربنا يسوع المسيح الذي سيثبتكم ايضا الى النهاية بلا لوم في يوم ربنا يسوع المسيح. امين هو الله الذي به دعيتم الى شركة ابنه يسوع المسيح ربنا ولكني اطلب اليكم ايها الاخوة باسم ربنا يسوع المسيح ان تقولوا جميعكم قولا واحدا ولا يكون بينكم انشقاقات بل كونوا كاملين في فكر واحد ورأي واحد

	ⲫⲣⲁⲛ ⲙⲡⲉⲛϭⲟⲓⲥ Ⲓⲏⲥ Ⲡⲭⲥ ϩⲓⲛⲁ ⲟⲩⲥⲁϫⲓ ⲛⲟⲩⲱⲧ ⲉⲣⲉⲧⲉⲛϫⲱ ⲙⲙⲟϥ ⲧⲏⲣⲟⲩ ⲟⲩⲟϩ ⲛⲧⲉϣⲧⲉⲙ ϩⲁⲛⲫⲱⲣϫ ϣⲱⲡⲓ ϧⲉⲛ ⲑⲏⲛⲟⲩ ⲛⲧⲉⲧⲉⲛϣⲱⲡⲓ ⲇⲉ ⲉⲣⲉⲧⲉⲛⲥⲉⲃⲧⲱⲧ ϧⲉⲛ ⲟⲩϩⲏⲧ ⲛⲟⲩⲱⲧ ⲛⲉⲙ ⲟⲩⲅⲛⲱⲙⲏ ⲛⲟⲩⲱⲧ.	
The grace of God the Father be with you all. Amen.	Ⲡⲓϩⲙⲟⲧ ⲅⲁⲣ ⲛⲉⲙⲱⲧⲉⲛ ⲧⲏⲣⲟⲩ. ⲇⲉ ⲁⲙⲏⲛ ⲉⲥⲉϣⲱⲡⲓ.	نعمة الله الآب تكون مع جميعكم آمين

The Trisagion

Holy God, Holy Mighty, Holy Immortal. was born of the Virgin, have mercy upon us.	ⲁⲅⲓⲟⲥ ⲟ Ⲑⲉⲟⲥ ⲁⲅⲓⲟⲥ ⲓⲥ ⲭⲩⲣⲟⲥ ⲁⲅⲓⲟⲥ ⲁⲑⲁⲛⲁⲧⲟⲥ ⲟ ⲉⲕ Ⲡⲁⲣⲑⲉⲛⲟⲩ ⲅⲉⲛⲛⲉⲑⲏⲥ ⲉⲗⲉⲏⲥⲟⲛ ⲏⲙⲁⲥ	قدوس الله قدوس القوي قدوس الحي الذي لا يموت الذي ولد من العذراء إرحمنا
Holy God, Holy Mighty, Holy Immortal. who was crucified for us, have mercy upon us.	ⲁⲅⲓⲟⲥ ⲟ Ⲑⲉⲟⲥ ⲁⲅⲓⲟⲥ ⲓⲥ ⲭⲩⲣⲟⲥ ⲁⲅⲓⲟⲥ ⲁⲑⲁⲛⲁⲧⲟⲥ ⲟ ⲥⲧⲁⲩⲣⲱⲑⲉⲓⲥ ⲇⲓ ⲏⲙⲁⲥ ⲉⲗⲉⲏⲥⲟⲛ ⲏⲙⲁⲥ	قدوس الله قدوس القوي قدوس الحي الذي لا يموت الذي صلب عنا إرحمنا
Holy God, Holy Mighty, Holy Immortal. Who rose from the dead and ascended into the heavens, have mercy upon us.	ⲁⲅⲓⲟⲥ ⲟ Ⲑⲉⲟⲥ ⲁⲅⲓⲟⲥ ⲓⲥ ⲭⲩⲣⲟⲥ ⲁⲅⲓⲟⲥ ⲁⲑⲁⲛⲁⲧⲟⲥ ⲟ ⲁⲛⲁⲥⲧⲁⲥ ⲉⲕ ⲧⲱⲛ ⲛⲉⲕⲣⲱⲛ ⲕⲉ ⲁⲛⲉⲗⲑⲱⲛ ⲓⲥ ⲧⲟⲩⲥ ⲟⲩⲣⲁⲛⲟⲩⲥ ⲉⲗⲉⲏⲥⲟⲛ ⲏⲙⲁⲥ	قدوس الله قدوس القوي قدوس الحي الذي لا يموت الذي قام من الأموات وصعد إلى السموات إرحمنا

Glory be to the Father, and to the Son and to the Holy Spirit. Both now and ever, and unto the age of the ages, Amen	Δοξα πατρι κε γιω κε αγιω πνεγματι κε νγν κε αι κε ιc τογc εωναc των εωνων. αμην.	المجد للآب والإبن والروح القدس الآن وكل أوان وإلى دهر الدهور آمين
O Holy Trinity, Have mercy upon us.	αγια Τριαc ελεηcον ημαc	أيها الثالوث القدوس إرحمنا

Litany of the Gospel

Priest:

Let us pray	Ϣλнλ	صلوا

Deacon:

Stand up for prayer	Επι προcεγχη cταθητε	للصلاة قفوا

Priest:

Peace be with all.	Ιρηνη παcι	السلام لجميعكم

Congregation:

And with your spirit.	Κε τω πνεγματι cογ	ولروحك أيضاً

Priest:

O Master, Lord Jesus Christ our God, who said to His saintly disciples and honored Apostles, "Many prophets and	ⲫⲛⲏⲃ Ⲡⲟⲥ Ιⲏⲥ Ⲡⲭⲥ Ⲡⲉⲛⲛⲟⲩϯ ⲫⲏⲉⲧⲁϥϫⲟⲥ ⲛⲛⲉϥⲁⲅⲓⲟⲥ ⲉⲧⲧⲁⲓⲏⲟⲩⲧ ⲙⲙⲁⲑⲏⲧⲏⲥ ⲟⲩⲟϩ	أيها السيد الرب يسوع المسيح إلهنا الذي خاطب لتلاميذه القديسين ورسله الأطهار المكرمين قائلا إن

righteous men have desired to see the things which you see, and have not seen them, and to hear the things which you hear, and have not heard them.	ⲛⲁⲡⲟⲥⲧⲟⲗⲟⲥ ⲉⲑⲟⲩⲁⲃ ⲇⲉ ϩⲁⲛⲙⲏϣ ⲙⲡⲣⲟⲫⲏⲧⲏⲥ ⲛⲉⲙ ϩⲁⲛⲑⲙⲏⲓ ⲁⲩⲉⲣⲉⲡⲓⲑⲩⲙⲓⲛ ⲉⲛⲁⲩ ⲉⲛⲏⲉⲧⲉⲧⲉⲛⲛⲁⲩ ⲉⲣⲱⲟⲩ ⲟⲩⲟϩ ⲙⲡⲟⲩⲛⲁⲩ ⲟⲩⲟϩ ⲉⲥⲱⲧⲉⲙ ⲉⲛⲏⲉⲧⲉⲧⲉⲛⲥⲱⲧⲉⲙ ⲉⲣⲱⲟⲩ ⲟϩⲟϩ ⲙⲡⲟⲩⲥⲱⲧⲉⲙ.	أنبياء وأبراراً كثيرين إشتهوا أن يروا ما أنتم ترون ولم يروا وأن يسمعوما أنتم تسمعون ولم يسمعوا
But as for you, blessed are your eyes for they see, and your ears for they hear." May we be worthy to hear and to act according to Your Holy Gospel through the prayers of Your saints.	ⲛⲑⲱⲧⲉⲛ ⲇⲉ ⲱⲟⲩⲛⲓⲁⲧⲟⲩ ⲛⲛⲉⲧⲉⲛⲃⲁⲗ ϫⲉ ⲥⲉⲛⲁⲩ ⲛⲉⲙ ⲛⲉⲧⲉⲛⲙⲁϣϫ ϫⲉ ⲥⲉⲥⲱⲧⲉⲙ. ⲙⲁⲣⲉⲛⲉⲣⲡⲉⲙⲡϣⲁ ⲛⲥⲱⲧⲉⲙ ⲟⲩⲟϩ ⲉⲓⲣⲓ ⲛⲛⲉⲕⲉⲩⲁⲅⲅⲉⲗⲓⲟⲛ ⲉⲑⲟⲩⲁⲃ ϧⲉⲛ ⲛⲓⲧⲱⲃϩ ⲛⲧⲉ ⲛⲏⲉⲑⲟⲩⲁⲃ ⲛⲧⲁⲕ.	أما أنتم فطوبى لأعينكم لأنها تبصرولآذانكم لأنها تسمع فلنستحق أن نسمع ونعمل بأناجيلك المقدسة بطلبات قديسيك

Deacon:

Pray for the Holy Gospel.	Ⲡⲣⲟⲥⲉⲩⲝⲁⲥⲑⲉ ⲩⲡⲉⲣ ⲧⲟⲩ ⲁⲅⲓⲟⲩ ⲉⲩⲁⲅⲅⲉⲗⲓⲟⲩ	صلوا من أجل الإنجيل المقدس

Congregation:

Lord have mercy.	Ⲕⲩⲣⲓⲉ ⲉⲗⲉⲏⲥⲟⲛ	يا رب إرحم

Priest:

Remember also, O our Master, all those who have bidden us to	Ⲁⲣⲓⲫⲙⲉⲩⲓ ⲇⲉ ⲟⲛ Ⲡⲉⲛⲛⲏⲃ ⲛⲟⲩⲟⲛ ⲛⲓⲃⲉⲛ ⲉⲧⲁⲩϩⲟⲛϩⲉⲛ ⲛⲁⲛ	أذكر أيضاً يا سيدنا كل الذين أوصونا أن نذكرهم في تضرعاتنا

remember them in our supplications and prayers which we offer up unto You, O Lord our God. Those who have already fallen asleep repose them, those who are sick, heal them. For You are the life of us all, the salvation of us all, the hope of us all, the healing of us all, and the resurrection of us all.	ⲉⲉⲣⲡⲟⲩⲙⲉⲩⲓ ϧⲉⲛ ⲛⲉⲛϯϩⲟ ⲛⲉⲙ ⲛⲉⲛⲧⲱⲃϩ ⲉⲧⲉⲛⲓⲣⲓ ⲙⲙⲱⲟⲩ ⲉⲡϣⲱⲓ ϩⲁⲣⲟⲕ Ⲡⲟⲥ Ⲡⲉⲛⲛⲟⲩϯ. Ⲛⲏⲉⲧⲁⲩⲉⲣϣⲟⲣⲡ ⲛⲉⲛⲕⲟⲧ ⲙⲁⲙⲧⲟⲛ ⲙⲙⲱⲟⲩ. Ⲛⲏⲉⲧϣⲱⲛⲓ ⲙⲁⲧⲁⲗϭⲱⲟⲩ ϫⲉ ⲛⲑⲟⲕ ⲅⲁⲣ ⲡⲉ ⲡⲉⲛⲱⲛϧ ⲧⲏⲣⲟⲩ ⲛⲉⲙ ⲡⲉⲛⲟⲩϫⲁⲓ ⲧⲏⲣⲟⲩ ⲛⲉⲙ ⲧⲉⲛϩⲉⲗⲡⲓⲥ ⲧⲏⲣⲟⲩ ⲛⲉⲙ ⲡⲉⲛⲧⲁⲗϭⲟ ⲧⲏⲣⲟⲩ ⲛⲉⲙ ⲧⲉⲛⲁⲛⲁⲥⲧⲁⲥⲓⲥ ⲧⲏⲣⲉⲛ.	وطلباتنا التي نصعدها إليك أيها الرب إلهنا الذين سبقوا فرقدوا نيحهم المرضى إشفهم لأنك أنت حياتنا كلنا وخلاصنا كلنا ورجاؤنا كلنا وشفاؤنا كلنا وقيامتنا كلنا

Psalm and Gospel

Reader:

A Psalm of David. Alleluia.	Ⲯⲁⲗⲙⲟⲥ ⲧⲱ Ⲇⲁⲩⲓⲇ. ⲁⲗⲗⲏⲗⲟⲩⲓⲁ.	من مزامير داود النبي بركاته تكون معنا آمين
(Psalm 84) "Mercy and truth have met together; • Righteousness and peace have kissed. • Truth shall spring out of the earth, • and righteousness shall look down from heaven." Alleluia.	Ⲟⲩⲛⲁⲓ ⲛⲉⲙ ⲟⲩⲙⲉⲑⲙⲏⲓ ⲁⲩⲓ ⲉⲃⲟⲗ ⲉϩⲣⲉⲛ ⲛⲟⲩⲉⲣⲏⲟⲩ. Ⲟⲩⲇⲓⲕⲉⲟⲥⲩⲛⲏ ⲛⲉⲙ ⲟⲩϩⲓⲣⲏⲛⲏ ⲁⲩϣⲉⲡ ⲧⲟⲧⲟⲩ ⲛⲛⲟⲩⲉⲣⲏⲟⲩ. Ϯⲙⲉⲑⲙⲏⲓ ⲁⲥϣⲁⲓ ⲉⲃⲟⲗϧⲉⲛ ⲡⲕⲁϩⲓ. Ϯⲇⲓⲕⲉⲟⲥⲩⲛⲏ ⲁⲥϫⲟⲩϣⲧ ⲉⲃⲟⲗϧⲉⲛ ⲧⲫⲉ.	الرحمة والحق التقيا والعدل والسلام تلاقيا الحق من الأرض أشرق والعدل من السماء تطلع هلليلويا

A Textual History of the Coptic Wedding Rite

(In the presence of a bishop)

"Let them exalt Him in the church of His people, • and praise Him in the seat of the elders, • for He has made the family like a flock of sheep, the upright shall see and rejoice. • The Lord has sworn and will have no regret, • You are a priest forever, after the order of Melchizedek." • The Lord is at your right hand, our saintly father, the patriarch, Pope Abba (...) • and our father the bishop, Abba (...) • May the Lord keep your lives.	Ⲙⲁⲣⲟⲩⲃⲁⲥϥ ϧⲉⲛ ⲧⲉⲕⲕⲗⲏⲥⲓⲁ ⲛⲧⲉ ⲡⲉϥⲗⲁⲟⲥ ⲟⲩⲟϩ ⲙⲁⲣⲟⲩⲥⲙⲟⲩ ⲉⲣⲟϥ ϩⲓ ⲧⲕⲁⲑⲉⲇⲣⲁ ⲛⲧⲉ ⲛⲓⲡⲣⲉⲥⲃⲩⲧⲉⲣⲟⲥ ϫⲉ ⲁϥⲭⲱ ⲛⲟⲩⲙⲉⲧⲓⲱⲧ ⲙⲫⲣⲏϯ ⲛϩⲁⲛⲉⲥⲱⲟⲩ ⲉⲩⲉⲛⲁⲩ ⲛϫⲉ ⲛⲏⲉⲧⲥⲟⲩⲧⲱⲛ ⲟⲩⲟϩ ⲉⲩⲉⲟⲩⲛⲟϥ. Ⲁϥⲱⲣⲕ ⲛϫⲉ Ⲡⲟⲥ ⲟⲩⲟϩ ⲛⲛⲉϥⲟⲩⲱⲙ ⲛϩⲑⲏϥ ϫⲉ ⲛⲑⲟⲕ ⲡⲉ ⲫⲟⲩⲏⲃ ϣⲁ ⲉⲛⲉϩ ⲕⲁⲧⲁ ⲧⲧⲁⲝⲓⲥ ⲙⲙⲉⲗⲭⲓⲥⲉⲇⲉⲕ. Ⲡⲟⲥ ⲥⲁⲟⲩⲓⲛⲁⲙ ⲙⲙⲟⲕ ⲡⲉⲛⲓⲱⲧ ⲉⲑⲟⲩⲁⲃ ⲙⲡⲁⲧⲣⲓⲁⲣⲭⲏⲥ ⲡⲁⲡⲁ ⲁⲃⲃⲁ (...) ⲡⲓⲙⲁϩⲥⲛⲁⲩ ⲛⲉⲙ ⲡⲉⲛⲓⲱⲧ ⲛⲉⲡⲓⲥⲕⲟⲡⲟⲩϣ ⲁⲃⲃⲁ (...). Ⲡⲟⲥ ⲉϥⲉⲁⲣⲉϩ ⲉⲡⲉⲧⲉⲛⲱⲛϧ.	فليرفعوه في كنيسة شعبه وليباركوه على منابر الشيوخ لأنه جعل أبوة مثل الخراف يصير المستقيمون ويفرحون أقسم الرب ولن يندم أنك أنت هو الكاهن إلى الأبد على طقس ملكي صادق الرب عن يمينك يا أبانا القديس البطريرك البابا المعظم الأنبا (تواضروس الثاني) (وأبانا الأسقف) (...) الرب يحفظ حياتك (...) أنبا (حياتكما)

Congregation:

Alleluia	ⲁⲗⲗⲏⲗⲟⲩⲓⲁ	هلليلوي

Deacon:

Stand in the fear of God and let us listen to the Holy Gospel.	Ⲥⲧⲁⲑⲏⲧⲉ ⲙⲉⲧⲁ ⲫⲟⲃⲟⲩ Ⲑⲉⲟ ⲁⲕⲟⲩⲥⲱⲙⲉⲛ ⲧⲟⲩ ⲁⲅⲓⲟⲩ ⲉⲩⲁⲅⲅⲉⲗⲓⲟⲩ	قفوا بخوف الله لسماع الإنجيل المقدس

Reader:

| Blessed is He who comes in the name of the Lord of Hosts. Bless O Lord the reading of the Holy Gospel according to St. John, may his holy blessings | Ϥⲥⲙⲁⲣⲱⲟⲩⲧ ⲛϫⲉ ⲫⲏⲉⲑⲛⲏⲟⲩ ϧⲉⲛ ⲫⲣⲁⲛ ⲙⲠϭⲟⲓⲥ ⲛⲧⲉ ⲛⲓϫⲟⲙ. Ⲕⲩⲣⲓⲉ ⲉⲩⲗⲟⲅⲏⲥⲟⲛ ⲉⲕ ⲧⲟⲩ ⲕⲁⲧⲁ Ⲓⲱⲁⲛⲛⲏⲛ ⲁⲅⲓⲟⲩ ⲉⲩⲁⲅⲅⲉⲗⲓⲟⲛ ⲧⲟ ⲁⲛⲁⲅⲛⲱⲥⲙⲁ | مبارك الآتي بإسم رب القوات يا رب بارك الفصل من الإنجيل المقدس من يوحنا القديس |

Congregation:

| be with us all Amen. | Ⲇⲟⲝⲁ ⲥⲓ Ⲕⲩⲣⲓⲉ | المجد لك يا رب |

Reader:

| Our Lord, God, Savior, and King of us all, Jesus Christ, the Son of the Living God, to whom is due all glory | Ⲡⲉⲛϭⲟⲓⲥ ⲟⲩⲟϩ ⲡⲉⲛⲛⲟⲩϯ ⲟⲩⲟϩ ⲡⲉⲛⲥⲱⲧⲏⲣ ⲟⲩⲟϩ ⲡⲉⲛⲟⲩⲣⲟ ⲧⲏⲣⲉⲛ Ⲓⲏⲥ Ⲡⲭⲥ Ⲡϣⲏⲣⲓ ⲙⲪϯ ⲉⲧⲟⲛϧ ⲡⲓⲱⲟⲩ ⲛⲁϥ ϣⲁ ⲉⲛⲉϩ | ربنا وإلهنا ومخلصنا وملكنا كلنا يسوع المسيح إبن الله الحي الذي له المجد دائما |

Congregation:

| forever amen | | إلى الأبد آمين |

Reader: *(John 1:1-17)*

| In the beginning was the Word, and the Word was with God, and the Word was God. He was in the beginning with God. All things were made through Him, and | ϧⲉⲛ ⲧⲁⲣⲭⲏ ⲛⲉ ⲡⲥⲁϫⲓ ⲡⲉ ⲟⲩⲟϩ ⲡⲓⲥⲁϫⲓ ⲛⲁϥⲭⲏ ϩⲁⲧⲉⲛ Ⲫϯ ⲟⲩⲟϩ ⲛⲉ ⲟⲩⲛⲟⲩϯ ⲡⲉ ⲡⲓⲥⲁϫⲓ. Ⲫⲁⲓ ⲉⲛⲁϥⲭⲏ ⲓⲥϫⲉⲛ ϩⲏ ϩⲁⲧⲉⲛ Ⲫϯ. Ϩⲱⲃ ⲛⲓⲃⲉⲛ ⲁⲩϣⲱⲡⲓ | في البدء كان الكلمة والكلمة كان عند الله وكان الكلمة الله هذا كان في البدء عند الله |

without Him nothing was made that was made. In Him was life, and the life was the light of men. And the light shines in the darkness, and the darkness did not comprehend it. There was a man sent from God, whose name was John. This man came for a witness, to bear witness of the Light, that all through him might believe. He was not that Light, but was sent to bear witness of that Light. That was the true Light which gives light to every man coming into the world. He was in the world, and the world was made through Him, and the world did not know Him. He came to His own, and His own did not receive Him. But as many as received Him, to them He gave the right to become children of God, to those who believe in His name: who were born, not of blood, nor of the will of the flesh, nor of the will of man, but of God. And the Word became flesh and dwelt among us, and we beheld His glory, the glory as of the only begotten of the Father, full of grace and truth.	ⲉⲃⲟⲗϩⲓⲧⲟⲧϥ ⲟⲩⲟϩ ⲁⲧϭⲛⲟⲩϥ ⲙⲡⲉ ϩⲗⲓ ϣⲱⲡⲓ ⲉⲃⲟⲗϧⲉⲛ ⲫⲏⲉⲧⲁϥϣⲱⲡⲓ ⲛⲉ ⲡⲱⲛϩ ⲡⲉ ⲉⲧⲉⲛϧⲏⲧϥ ⲟⲩⲟϩ ⲡⲱⲛϩ ⲛⲉ ϥⲟⲩⲱⲓⲛⲓ ⲛⲛⲓⲣⲱⲙⲓ ⲡⲉ ⲟⲩⲟϩ ⲡⲓⲟⲩⲱⲓⲛⲓ ⲁϥⲉⲣⲟⲩⲱⲓⲛⲓ ϧⲉⲛ ⲡⲓⲭⲁⲕⲓ ⲟⲩⲟϩ ⲙⲡⲉ ⲡⲓⲭⲁⲕⲓ ϣⲧⲁϩⲟϥ. ⲁϥϣⲱⲡⲓ ⲛϫⲉ ⲟⲩⲣⲱⲙⲓ ⲉⲁⲩⲟⲩⲟⲣⲡϥ ⲉⲃⲟⲗϩⲓⲧⲉⲛ ⲫϯ ⲉⲡⲉϥⲣⲁⲛ ⲡⲉ ⲓⲱⲁⲛⲛⲏⲥ. ⲫⲁⲓ ⲁϥⲓ ⲉⲩⲙⲉⲧⲙⲉⲑⲣⲉ ϩⲓⲛⲁ ⲛⲧⲉϥⲉⲣⲙⲉⲑⲣⲉ ϧⲁ ⲡⲓⲟⲩⲱⲓⲛⲓ ϩⲓⲛⲁ ⲛⲧⲉ ⲟⲩⲟⲛ ⲛⲓⲃⲉⲛ ⲛⲁϩϯ ⲉⲃⲟⲗϩⲓⲧⲟⲧϥ. ⲛⲉ ⲛⲑⲟϥ ⲁⲛ ⲡⲉ ⲡⲓⲟⲩⲱⲓⲛⲓ ⲁⲗⲗⲁ ϩⲓⲛⲁ ⲛⲧⲉϥⲉⲣⲙⲉⲑⲣⲉ ϧⲁ ⲡⲓⲟⲩⲱⲓⲛⲓ. ⲛⲁϥϣⲟⲡ ⲅⲁⲣ ⲛϫⲉ ⲡⲓⲟⲩⲱⲓⲛⲓ ⲉⲣⲱⲙⲓ ⲛⲓⲃⲉⲛ ⲉⲑⲛⲏⲟⲩ ⲉⲡⲓⲕⲟⲥⲙⲟⲥ ⲛⲁϥⲭⲏ ϧⲉⲛ ⲡⲓⲕⲟⲥⲙⲟⲥ ⲡⲉ ⲟⲩⲟϩ ⲡⲓⲕⲟⲥⲙⲟⲥ ⲁϥϣⲱⲡⲓ ⲉⲃⲟⲗϩⲓⲧⲟⲧϥ ⲟⲩⲟϩ ⲙⲡⲉ ⲡⲓⲕⲟⲥⲙⲟⲥ ⲥⲟⲩⲱⲛϥ. ⲁϥⲓ ϩⲁ ⲛⲏⲉⲧⲉ ⲛⲟⲩϥ ⲟⲩⲟϩ ⲛⲏⲉⲧⲉ ⲛⲟⲩϥ ⲙⲡⲟⲩϣⲟⲡϥ ⲉⲣⲱⲟⲩ. ⲁϥϯⲉⲣϣⲓϣⲓ ⲙⲙⲱⲟⲩ ⲉⲉⲣϣⲏⲣⲓ ⲛⲛⲟⲩϯ ⲛⲏⲉⲑⲛⲁϩϯ ⲉⲡⲉϥⲣⲁⲛ ⲛⲏⲉⲧⲉ ⲉⲃⲟⲗϧⲉⲛ ⲥⲛⲟϥ ⲁⲛ ⲛⲉ ⲟⲩⲇⲉ ⲉⲃⲟⲗϧⲉⲛ ϥⲟⲩⲱϣ ⲛⲥⲁⲣⲝ ⲁⲛ ⲛⲉ	كل شيء به كان وبغيره لم يكن شيء مما كان فيه كانت الحياة والحياة كانت نور الناس والنور يضيء في الظلمة والظلمة لم تدركه كان انسان مرسل من الله اسمه يوحنا هذا جاء للشهادة ليشهد للنور لكي يؤمن الكل بواسطته لم يكن هو النور بل ليشهد للنور كان النور الحقيقي الذي ينير كل انسان آتيا الى العالم كان في العالم وكوّن العالم به ولم يعرفه العالم الى خاصته جاء وخاصته لم تقبله واما كل الذين قبلوه فاعطاهم سلطانا ان يصيروا اولاد الله اي المؤمنون باسمه الذين ولدوا ليس من دم ولا من مشيئة جسد ولا من مشيئة رجل بل من الله والكلمة صار جسدا وحل بيننا ورأينا مجده مجدا كما لوحيد من الآب مملوءا نعمة وحقا يوحنا شهد له ونادى قائلا هذا هو الذي قلت عنه ان الذي يأتي بعدي صار قدامي لانه كان قبلي ومن ملئه نحن جميعا اخذنا ونعمة فوق نعمة لان الناموس بموسى اعطي اما النعمة والحق فبيسوع المسيح صارا

John bore witness of Him and cried out, saying, "This was He of whom I said, 'He who comes after me is preferred before me, for He was before me.'" And of His fullness we have all received, and grace for grace. For the law was given through Moses, but grace and truth came through Jesus Christ.	ⲟⲩⲇⲉ ⲉⲃⲟⲗϧⲉⲛ ⲫⲟⲩⲱϣ ⲛⲣⲱⲙⲓ ⲁⲛ ⲛⲉ ⲁⲗⲗⲁ ⲉⲧⲁⲩⲙⲁⲥⲟⲩ ⲉⲃⲟⲗϧⲉⲛ Ⲫϯ. Ⲟⲩⲟϩ ⲡⲓⲥⲁϫⲓ ⲁϥⲉⲣ ⲟⲩⲥⲁⲣⲝ ⲟⲩⲟϩ ⲁϥϣⲱⲡⲓ ⲛϧⲣⲏⲓ ⲛϧⲏⲧⲉⲛ ⲟⲩⲟϩ ⲁⲛⲛⲁⲩ ⲉⲡⲉϥⲱⲟⲩ ⲙⲫⲣⲏϯ ⲛⲟⲩϣⲏⲣⲓ ⲙⲙⲁⲩⲁⲧϥ ⲛⲧⲟⲧϥ ⲙⲡⲉϥⲓⲱⲧ ⲉϥⲙⲉϩ ⲛϩⲙⲟⲧ ⲛⲉⲙ ⲙⲉⲑⲙⲏⲓ. Ⲓⲱⲁⲛⲛⲏⲥ ⲁϥⲉⲣⲙⲉⲑⲣⲉ ⲉⲑⲃⲏⲧϥ ⲟⲩⲟϩ ⲁϥⲱϣ ⲉⲃⲟⲗ ⲉϥϫⲱ ⲙⲙⲟⲥ ϫⲉ ⲫⲁⲓ ⲡⲉ ⲫⲏⲉⲧⲁⲓϫⲟⲥ ⲁⲛⲟⲕ ⲉⲑⲃⲏⲧϥ ϫⲉ ⲫⲏⲉⲑⲛⲏⲟⲩ ⲙⲉⲛⲉⲛⲥⲱϥ ⲁϥⲉⲣϣⲟⲣⲡ ⲉⲟⲓ ϫⲉ ⲛⲉ ⲟⲩϣⲟⲣⲡ ⲉⲣⲟⲓ ⲣⲱ ⲡⲉ. ϫⲉ ⲁⲛⲟⲛ ⲧⲏⲣⲉⲛ ⲁⲛϭⲓ ⲉⲃⲟⲗ ϧⲉⲛ ⲡⲉϥⲙⲟϩ ⲛⲉⲙ ⲟⲩϩⲙⲟⲧ ⲛⲧϣⲉⲃⲓⲱⲛⲟⲩϩⲙⲟⲧ ϫⲉ ⲡⲓⲛⲟⲙⲟⲥ ⲁⲩⲧⲏⲓϥ ⲉⲃⲟⲗϩⲓⲧⲉⲛ ⲙⲱⲩⲥⲏⲥ ⲡⲓϩⲙⲟⲧ ⲇⲉ ⲛⲉⲙ ϯⲙⲉⲑⲙⲏⲓ ⲁⲩϣⲱⲡⲓ ⲉⲃⲟⲗϩⲓⲧⲉⲛⲒⲏⲥ Ⲡⲭⲥ. Ⲡⲓⲱⲟⲩ ⲫⲁ ⲡⲉⲛⲛⲟⲩϯ ⲡⲉ ϣⲁ ⲉⲛⲉϩ ⲛⲧⲉ ⲛⲓⲉⲛⲉϩ ⲧⲏⲣⲟⲩ. ⲁⲙⲏⲛ.	

Congregation:

Glory be to God forever.	Ⲇⲟⲝⲁ ⲥⲓ Ⲕⲩⲣⲓⲉ	واجملد لله دائماً

Gospel Response
(In the Palm Sunday tune)

| Rejoice O bridal chamber • that is adorned with all types • for the true Bridegroom • who became united with humanity. | Ⲭⲉⲣⲉ ⲡⲓⲙⲁⲛϣⲉⲗⲉⲧ ⲉⲧⲥⲉⲗⲥⲱⲗ ϧⲉⲛ ⲟⲩⲑⲟ ⲛⲣⲏϯ ⲛⲧⲉ ⲡⲓⲛⲩⲙⲫⲓⲟⲥ ⲙⲙⲏⲓ ⲉⲧⲁϥϩⲱⲧⲡ ⲉϥⲙⲉⲧⲣⲱⲙⲓ | السلام للخدر المزين بكل نوع الذي للعريس الحقيقي الذي إتحد بالبشرية |

(If a bishop is present)

| Likewise we exalt you • with David the psalmist saying, • "You are the priest forever • according to the order of Melchizedek." | Ⲱⲥⲁⲩⲧⲟⲥ ⲧⲉⲛϭⲓⲥⲓ ⲙⲙⲟⲕ ⲛⲉⲙ ⲡⲓϩⲩⲙⲛⲟⲇⲟⲥ Ⲇⲁⲩⲓⲇ ϫⲉ ⲛⲑⲟⲕ ⲡⲉ ⲡⲓⲟⲩⲏⲃ ϣⲁ ⲉⲛⲉϩ ⲕⲁⲧⲁ ⲧⲧⲁⲝⲓⲥ ⲙⲘⲉⲗⲭⲓⲥⲉⲇⲉⲕ | كذلك نعظمك مع المرتل داود قائلين أنت هو الكاهن إلى الأبد على طقس ملكي صادق |

(Otherwise, continue with)

| Intercede on our behalf, • O the Lady of us all the Theotokos, • Mary the mother of Jesus Christ, • that He may forgive us our sins. | Ⲁⲣⲓⲡⲣⲉⲥⲃⲉⲩⲓⲛ ⲉϩⲣⲏ ⲉϫⲱⲛ ⲱ ⲧⲉⲛϬⲟⲓⲥ ⲛⲛⲏⲃ ⲧⲏⲣⲉⲛ ϯⲑⲉⲟⲧⲟⲕⲟⲥ Ⲙⲁⲣⲓⲁ ⲑⲙⲁⲩ ⲛⲒⲏⲥ Ⲡⲭⲥ ⲛⲧⲉϥⲭⲁ ⲛⲉⲛⲛⲟⲃⲓ ⲛⲁⲛ ⲉⲃⲟⲗ | إشفعي فينا يا سيدتنا كلنا السيدة والدة الإله مريم أم مخلصنا ليغفر لنا خطايانا |

(If a bishop is present)

| Pray to the Lord on our behalf, • our holy father the patriarch, • Pope Abba (…), that He may forgive us our sins. | Ⲧⲱⲃϩ ⲙⲠⲟⲥ ⲉϩⲣⲏⲓ ⲉϫⲱⲛ ⲡⲉⲛⲓⲱⲧ ⲉⲑⲟⲩⲁⲃ ⲙⲡⲁⲧⲣⲓⲁⲣⲭⲏⲥ ⲡⲁⲡⲁ ⲁⲃⲃⲁ (…) ⲛⲧⲉϥⲭⲁ ⲛⲉⲛⲛⲟⲃⲓ ⲉⲃⲟⲗ | اطلب من الرب عنا يا أبانا القديس البطريرك أنبا (…) رئيس الكهنة ليغفر لنا خطايانا |

| Pray to the Lord on our behalf, • our holy righteous father, • Abba (…) the bishop, • that He may forgive us our sins. | Ⲧⲱⲃϩ ⲙⲠⲟⲥ ⲉϩⲣⲏⲓ ⲉϫⲱⲛ ⲡⲉⲛⲓⲱⲧ ⲉⲑⲟⲩⲁⲃ ⲛⲁⲓⲕⲉⲟⲩϣ ⲁⲃⲃⲁ (…) ⲡⲓⲉⲡⲓⲥⲕⲟⲡⲟⲥ ⲛⲧⲉϥⲭⲁ ⲛⲉⲛⲛⲟⲃⲓ ⲉⲃⲟⲗ | اطلب من الرب عنا يا أبينا القديس البار أنبا (…) الأسقف (المطران) ليغفر لنا خطايانا |

(Conclude with)

| Blessed is the Father and the Son • and the Holy Spirit • the perfect Trinity. • We worship him and glorify him. | Ϫⲉ ϥⲥⲙⲁⲣⲱⲟⲩⲧ ⲛϫⲉ Ⲫⲓⲱⲧ ⲛⲉⲙ Ⲡϣⲏⲣⲓ ⲛⲉⲙ Ⲡⲓⲡⲛⲉⲩⲙⲁ ⲉⲑⲟⲩⲁⲃ ϯⲧⲣⲓⲁⲥ ⲉⲧϫⲏⲕ ⲉⲃⲟⲗ ⲧⲉⲛⲟⲩⲱϣⲧ ⲙⲙⲟⲥ ⲧⲉⲛϯⲱⲟⲩ ⲛⲁⲥ. | مبارك الآب و الابن و الروح القدس الثالوث الكامل نسبحه و نمجده |

The Three Great Litanies

Priest:

| Let us pray | Ϣⲗⲏⲗ | صلوا |

Deacon:

| Stand up for prayer | Ⲉⲡⲓ ⲡⲣⲟⲥⲉⲩⲭⲏ ⲥⲧⲁⲑⲏⲧⲉ | للصلاة قفوا |

Priest:

| Peace be with all. | Ⲓⲣⲏⲛⲏ ⲡⲁⲥⲓ | السلام لجميعكم |

Congregation:

| And with your spirit. | Ⲕⲉ ⲧⲱ ⲡⲛⲉⲩⲙⲁⲧⲓ ⲥⲟⲩ | ولروحك أيضاً |

A Textual History of the Coptic Wedding Rite

Priest:

Again, let us ask God the Pantocrator, the Father of our Lord, God, and Savior Jesus Christ. We ask and entreat Your goodness, O Lover of Mankind, remember, O Lord, the peace of your one, only, holy, catholic, and apostolic Orthodox Church.	Ⲡⲁⲗⲓⲛ ⲟⲛ ⲙⲁⲣⲉⲛϯϩⲟ ⲉⲫϯ ⲡⲓⲡⲁⲛⲧⲟⲕⲣⲁⲧⲱⲣ Ⲫⲓⲱⲧ ⲙⲠⲉⲛⲟⲥ ⲟⲩⲟϩ Ⲡⲉⲛⲛⲟⲩϯ ⲟⲩⲟϩ Ⲡⲉⲛⲥⲱⲧⲏⲣ Ⲓⲏⲥ Ⲡⲭⲥ. Ⲧⲉⲛϯϩⲟ ⲟⲩⲟϩ ⲧⲉⲛⲧⲱⲃϩ ⲛⲧⲉⲕⲙⲉⲧⲁⲅⲁⲑⲟⲥ ⲡⲓⲙⲁⲓⲣⲱⲙⲓ ⲁⲣⲓⲫⲙⲉⲩⲓ Ⲡⲟⲥ ⲛϯϩⲓⲣⲏⲛⲏ ⲛⲧⲉ ⲧⲉⲕⲟⲩⲓ ⲙⲙⲁⲩⲁⲧⲥ ⲉⲑⲟⲩⲁⲃ ⲛⲕⲁⲑⲟⲗⲓⲕⲏ ⲛⲁⲡⲟⲥⲧⲟⲗⲓⲕⲏ ⲛⲉⲕⲕⲗⲏⲥⲓⲁ	وأيضاً فلنسأل الله الضابط الكل أبا ربنا وإلهنا ومخلصنا يسوع المسيح نسأل ونطلب من صلاحك يا محب البشر اذكر يا رب سلام كنيستك الواحدة الوحيدة المقدسة الجامعة الرسولية

Deacon:

Pray for the peace of the one, holy, catholic, and apostolic Orthodox Church of God.	Ⲡⲣⲟⲥⲉⲩⲝⲁⲥⲑⲉ ⲩⲡⲉⲣ ⲧⲏⲥ ⲓⲣⲏⲛⲏⲥ ⲧⲏⲥ ⲁⲅⲓⲁⲥ ⲙⲟⲛⲏⲥ ⲕⲁⲑⲟⲗⲓⲕⲏⲥ ⲕⲉ ⲁⲡⲟⲥⲧⲟⲗⲓⲕⲏⲥ ⲟⲣⲑⲟⲇⲟⲝⲟⲩ ⲧⲟⲩ Ⲑⲉⲟⲩ ⲉⲕⲕⲗⲏⲥⲓⲁⲥ	صلوا من اجل سلام الواحدة المقدسة الجامعة الرسولية كنيسة الله الارثوذكسية

Congregation:

Lord have mercy.	Ⲕⲩⲣⲓⲉ Ⲉⲗⲉⲏⲥⲟⲛ	يا رب إرحم

Priest:

that which exists from one end of the world to the other. All peoples and all flocks, bless. The heavenly peace, send	Ⲑⲁⲓ ⲉⲧϣⲟⲡ ⲓⲥϫⲉⲛ ⲁⲩⲣⲏϫⲥ ⲛⲧⲟⲓⲕⲟⲩⲙⲉⲛⲏ ϣⲁ ⲁⲩⲣⲏϫⲥ. Ⲛⲓⲗⲁⲟⲥ ⲧⲏⲣⲟⲩ ⲛⲉⲙ ⲛⲓⲟϩⲓ ⲧⲏⲣⲟⲩ	هذه الكائنة من أقاصي المسكونة إلى أقاصيها كل الشعوب وكل القطعان باركهم السلامة التي من السموات

down into all our hearts; even the peace of this life, graciously grant to us. The king [leader], the armies, the chiefs, the counselors, the multitudes, our neighbors, our coming in and our going out, adorn them with all peace. O King of Peace, grant us Your peace; for You have given us all things. Acquire us to Yourself, O God our Savior, for we know none other but You. Your Holy name we utter. May our souls live by Your Holy Spirit. And let not the death of sin have dominion over us, we Your servants, nor over all Your people.	ⲥⲙⲟⲩ ⲉⲣⲱⲟⲩ. Ϯⲉⲓⲣⲏⲛⲏ ϯⲉⲃⲟⲗ ϧⲉⲛ ⲛⲓⲫⲏⲟⲩⲓ ⲙⲏⲓⲥ ⲉϩⲣⲏⲓ ⲉⲛⲉⲛϩⲏⲧ ⲧⲏⲣⲟⲩ ⲁⲗⲗⲁ ⲛⲉⲙ ϯⲕⲉϩⲓⲣⲏⲛⲏ ⲛⲧⲉ ⲡⲁⲓⲃⲓⲟⲥ ⲫⲁⲓ ⲁⲣⲓⲭⲁⲣⲓⲍⲉⲥⲑⲉ ⲙⲙⲟⲥ ⲛⲁⲛ ⲛϩⲙⲟⲧ. Ⲡⲓⲟⲩⲣⲟ (Ⲡⲓⲁⲣⲭⲏ) ⲛⲓⲙⲉⲧⲙⲁⲧⲟⲓ ⲛⲓⲁⲣⲭⲱⲛ ⲛⲓⲥⲟϭⲛⲓ ⲛⲙⲏϣ ⲛⲉⲛⲑⲉϣⲉⲩ ⲛⲉⲛⲇⲓⲛⲙⲟϣⲓ ⲉϧⲟⲩⲛ ⲛⲉⲙ ⲛⲉⲛⲇⲓⲛⲙⲟϣⲓ ⲉⲃⲟⲗ ⲥⲉⲗⲥⲱⲗⲟⲩ ϧⲉⲛ ϩⲓⲣⲏⲛⲏ ⲛⲓⲃⲉⲛ. Ⲡⲟⲩⲣⲟ ⲛⲧⲉ ϯϩⲓⲣⲏⲛⲏ ⲙⲟⲓ ⲛⲁⲛ ⲛⲧⲉⲕϩⲓⲣⲏⲛⲏ ϩⲱⲃ ⲅⲁⲣ ⲛⲓⲃⲉⲛ ⲁⲕⲧⲏⲓⲧⲟⲩ ⲛⲁⲛ. Ⲇⲫⲟⲛ ⲛⲁⲕ Ⲫϯ ⲡⲉⲛⲥⲱⲧⲏⲣ ⲇⲉ ⲧⲉⲛⲱⲟⲩⲛ ⲛⲕⲉⲟⲩⲁⲓ ⲁⲛ ⲉⲃⲏⲗ ⲉⲣⲟⲕ. Ⲡⲉⲕⲣⲁⲛ ⲉⲑⲟⲩ ⲡⲉⲧⲉⲛϫⲱ ⲙⲙⲟϥ. Ⲙⲁⲣⲟⲩⲟⲩⲛϩ ⲛϫⲉ ⲛⲏⲉⲧⲉ ⲛⲟⲩⲛ ⲙⲯⲩⲭⲏ ϩⲓⲧⲉⲛ ⲡⲉⲕⲡⲛⲉⲩⲙⲁ ⲉⲑⲟⲩⲁⲃ. Ⲟⲩⲟϩ ⲙⲡⲉⲛⲑⲣⲉϥϫⲉⲙϫⲟⲙ ⲉⲣⲟⲛ ⲁⲛⲟⲛ ϧⲁ ⲛⲉⲕⲉⲃⲓⲁⲓⲕ ⲛϫⲉ ⲫⲙⲟⲩ ⲛⲧⲉ ϩⲁⲛⲛⲟⲃⲓ ⲟⲩⲇⲉ ⲁϩ ⲡⲉⲕⲗⲁⲟⲥ ⲧⲏⲣϥ.	إنزلها على قلوبنا جميعا بل وسلامة هذا العمر أنعم بها علينا إنعاما الملك (الرئيس) والجند والأراخنة والمشيرين والجموع وجيراننا ومداخلنا ومخارجنا زينهم بكل سلام يا ملك السلام أعطنا سلامك لان كل شئ قد أعطيتنا اقتننا لك يا الله مخلصنا لاننا لا نعرف آخر سواك إسمك القدوس هو الذى نقوله فلتحيا نفوسنا بروحك القدوس ولا تدع موت الخطية يقوى علينا نحن عبيدك ولا على كل شعبك

Congregation:

Lord have mercy.	Ⲕⲩⲣⲓⲉ ⲉⲗⲉⲏⲥⲟⲛ	يا رب إرحم

Priest:

Again, let us ask God the Pantocrator, the Father of our Lord, God, and Savior Jesus Christ. We ask and entreat Your goodness, O Lover of Mankind. Remember, O Lord, our blessed and honored father, the archbishop our patriarch, Abba (…) and his partner in the liturgy, our father the bishop Abba (…).	Ⲡⲁⲗⲓⲛ ⲟⲛ ⲙⲁⲣⲉⲛϯⲟ ⲉⲫϯ ⲡⲓⲡⲁⲛⲧⲟⲕⲣⲁⲧⲱⲣ Ⲫⲓⲱⲧ ⲙⲡⲉⲛⲟⲥ ⲟⲩⲟϩ ⲡⲉⲛⲛⲟⲩϯ ⲟⲩⲟϩ ⲡⲉⲛⲥⲱⲧⲏⲣ Ⲓⲏⲥ Ⲡⲭⲥ ⲧⲉⲛϯⲟ ⲟⲩⲟϩ ⲧⲉⲛⲧⲱⲃϩ ⲛⲧⲉⲕⲙⲉⲧⲁⲅⲁⲑⲟⲥ ⲡⲓⲙⲁⲓⲣⲱⲙⲓ ⲁⲣⲓⲫⲙⲉⲩⲓ Ⲡⲟⲥ ⲙⲡⲉⲛⲡⲁⲧⲣⲓⲁⲣⲭⲏⲥ ⲛⲓⲱⲧ ⲉⲧⲧⲁⲓⲏⲟⲩⲧ ⲛⲁⲣⲭⲓⲉⲣⲉⲩⲥ ⲡⲁⲡⲁ ⲁⲃⲃⲁ (…) ⲛⲉⲙ ⲡⲉϥⲕⲉϣⲫⲏⲣ ⲛⲗⲓⲧⲟⲩⲣⲅⲟⲥ ⲡⲉⲛⲓⲱⲧ ⲛⲉⲡⲓⲥⲕⲟⲡⲟⲥ ⲁⲃⲃⲁ (…)	وأيضا فلنسأل الله ضابط الكل أبا ربنا وإلهنا ومخلصنا يسوع المسيح نسأل ونطلب من صلاحك يا محب البشر اذكر يا رب بطريركنا الأب المكرم رئيس الكهنة البابا المعظم أنبا (…) وشريكة في الخدمة الرسولية أبينا الأسقف المكرم الأنبا (…)

Deacon:

Pray for our high priest, Pope Abba (…), pope and patriarch and archbishop of the great of Alexandria, and his partner in the liturgy, our father the bishop Abba (…), and for our orthodox bishops.	Ⲡⲣⲟⲥⲉⲩⲝⲁⲥⲑⲉ ⲩⲡⲉⲣ ⲧⲟⲩ ⲁⲣⲭⲏⲉⲣⲉⲱⲥ ⲏⲙⲱⲛ ⲡⲁⲡⲁ ⲁⲃⲃⲁ (…) ⲡⲁⲡⲁ ⲕⲉ ⲡⲁⲧⲣⲓⲁⲣⲭⲟⲩ ⲕⲉ ⲁⲣⲭⲏ ⲉⲡⲓⲥⲕⲟⲡⲟⲩ ⲧⲏⲥ ⲙⲉⲅⲁⲗⲟ ⲡⲟⲗⲉⲱⲥ ⲁⲗⲉⲝⲁⲛⲇⲣⲓⲁⲥ ⲛⲉⲙ ⲡⲉϥⲕⲉϣⲫⲏⲣ ⲛⲗⲓⲧⲟⲩⲣⲅⲟⲥ ⲡⲉⲛⲓⲱⲧ ⲛⲉⲡⲓⲥⲕⲟⲡⲟⲥ ⲁⲃⲃⲁ (…) ⲕⲉ ⲧⲟⲛ ⲟⲣⲑⲟⲇⲟⲝⲱⲛ ⲏⲙⲱⲛ ⲉⲡⲓⲥⲕⲟⲡⲱⲛ	صلوا من أجل رئيس كهنتنا البابا أنبا (…) بابا وبطريرك ورئيس أساقفة المدينة العظمى الاسكندرية وشريكة في الخدمة الرسولية أبينا الأسقف المكرم الأنبا (…) وسائر أساقفتنا الارثوذكسيين

Congregation:

Lord have mercy.	Ⲕⲩⲣⲓⲉ Ⲉⲗⲉⲏⲥⲟⲛ	يا رب إرحم

Priest:

In keeping keep them for us for many years and peaceful times. fulfilling that holy high priesthood with which You have entrusted him from Yourself, according to Your holy and blessed will, rightly dividing the word of truth, shepherding Your people in purity and righteousness, and all the orthodox bishops, hegumens, priests, and deacons, and all the fullness of Your one, only, holy, catholic, and apostolic Church. Grant them and us peace and safety in every place. Their prayers which they offer on our behalf, and on behalf of all Your people, as well as ours on their behalf, receive upon Your holy, rational Altar of heaven, as a sweet savor of incense. All their enemies, visible and invisible, trample and humiliate under their feet speedily.	ϧⲉⲛ ⲟⲩⲁⲣⲉϩ ⲁⲣⲉϩ ⲉⲣⲱⲟⲩ ⲛⲁⲛ ⲛϩⲁⲛⲙⲏϣ ⲛⲣⲟⲙⲡⲓ ⲛⲉⲙ ϩⲁⲛⲥⲏⲟⲩ ⲛϩⲓⲣⲏⲛⲓⲕⲟⲛ ⲉϥϫⲱⲕ ⲉⲃⲟⲗ ⲛⲑⲉⲑⲟⲩⲁⲃ ⲉⲧⲁⲕⲧⲉⲛϩⲟⲩⲧⲱⲟⲩ ⲉⲣⲟⲥ ⲉⲃⲟⲗϩⲓⲧⲟⲧⲕ ⲙⲙⲉⲧⲁⲣⲭⲏⲉⲣⲉⲩⲥ ⲕⲁⲧⲁ ⲡⲉⲕⲟⲩⲱϣ ⲉⲑⲟⲩⲁⲃ ⲟⲩⲟϩ ⲙⲙⲁⲕⲁⲣⲓⲟⲛ. ⲉⲩϣⲱⲧ ⲉⲃⲟⲗ ⲙⲡⲥⲁϫⲓ ⲛⲧⲉ ϯⲙⲉⲑⲙⲏⲓ ϧⲉⲛ ⲟⲩⲥⲱⲟⲩⲧⲉⲛ ⲉⲩⲁⲙⲟⲛⲓ ⲙⲡⲉⲕⲗⲁⲟⲥ ϧⲉⲛ ⲟⲩⲧⲟⲩⲃⲟ ⲛⲉⲙ ⲟⲩⲙⲉⲑⲙⲏⲓ ⲛⲉⲙ ⲛⲓⲉⲡⲓⲥⲕⲟⲡⲟⲥ ⲧⲏⲣⲟⲩ ⲛⲟⲣⲑⲟⲇⲟⲝⲟⲥ ⲛⲉⲙ ⲛⲓϩⲏⲅⲟⲩⲙⲉⲛⲟⲥ ⲛⲉⲙ ⲛⲓⲡⲣⲉⲥⲃⲩⲧⲉⲣⲟⲥ ⲛⲉⲙ ⲛⲓⲇⲓⲁⲕⲱⲛ ⲛⲉⲙ ⲫⲙⲟϩ ⲧⲏⲣϥ ⲛⲧⲉ ⲧⲉⲕⲟⲩⲓ ⲙⲙⲁⲩⲁⲧⲥ ⲉⲑⲟⲩⲁⲃ ⲛⲕⲁⲑⲟⲩⲗⲓⲕⲏ ⲛⲁⲡⲟⲥⲧⲟⲗⲓⲕⲏ ⲛⲉⲕⲕⲗⲏⲥⲓⲁ. ⲉⲕⲉⲉⲣⲭⲁⲣⲓⲍⲉⲥⲑⲉ ⲛⲱⲟⲩ ⲛⲉⲙⲁⲛ ⲛⲟⲩϩⲓⲣⲏⲛⲏ ⲛⲉⲙ ⲟⲩⲟⲩϫⲁⲓ ⲉⲃⲟⲗϧⲉⲛ ⲙⲁⲓ ⲛⲓⲃⲉⲛ. ⲛⲟⲩⲡⲣⲟⲥⲉⲩⲭⲏ ⲇⲉ ⲉⲧⲟⲩⲓⲣⲓ ⲙⲙⲱⲟⲩ ⲉϩⲣⲏⲓ ⲉϫⲱⲛ ⲛⲉⲙ ⲉϫⲉⲛ ⲡⲉⲕⲗⲁⲟⲥ ⲧⲏⲣϥ ⲛⲉⲙ ⲛⲟⲩⲛ ϩⲱⲛ ⲉϩⲣⲏⲓ ⲉϫⲱⲟⲩ ϣⲟⲡⲟⲩ ⲉⲣⲟⲕ ⲉϫⲉⲛ ⲡⲉⲕⲑⲩⲥⲓⲁⲥⲧⲏⲣⲓⲟⲛ	حفظاً إحفظهم لنا سنين كثيرة وأزمنة سلامية مكملين رئاسة الكهنوت المقدسة التي ائتمنتهم عليها من قِبلك كإرادتك المقدسة الطوباوية مفصلاً كلمة الحق باستقامة راعيا شعبك بطهارة وبر وجميع الاساقفة الارثوذكسيين والقمامصة والقسوس والشمامسة وكل امتلاء كنيستك الواحدة الوحيدة المقدسة الجامعة الرسولية أنعم عليهم وعلينا بالسلام والعافية في كل موضع وصلواتهم التي يقدمونها عنا وعن كل شعبك وصلواتنا نحن أيضا عنهم إقبلها إليك على مذبحك المقدس الناطق السمائي رائحة بخور فسائر أعدائهم الذين يرون والذين لا يرون اسحقهم وأذلهم تحت أرجلهم سريعا وأما هم فاحفظهم في سلام وعدل في كنيستك المقدسة

| | ⲉⲑⲟⲩⲁⲃ ⲛⲉⲗⲗⲟⲅⲓⲙⲟⲛ ⲛⲧⲉ ⲧⲫⲉ ⲉⲟⲩⲥⲑⲟⲓ ⲛⲥⲑⲟⲓⲛⲟⲩϥⲓ. ⲛⲟⲩϫⲁϫⲓ ⲙⲉⲛ ⲧⲏⲣⲟⲩ ⲛⲏⲉⲧⲟⲩⲛⲁⲩ ⲉⲣⲱⲟⲩ ⲛⲉⲙ ⲛⲏⲉⲧⲉ ⲛⲥⲉⲛⲁⲩ ⲉⲣⲱⲟⲩ ⲁⲛ ϫⲉⲙϣⲱⲙⲟⲩ ⲟⲩⲟϩ ⲙⲁⲑⲉⲃⲓⲱⲟⲩ ⲥⲁⲡⲉⲥⲏⲧ ⲛⲛⲟⲩϭⲁⲗⲁⲩϫ ⲛⲭⲱⲗⲉⲙ. ⲛⲑⲱⲟⲩ ⲇⲉ ⲁⲣⲉϩ ⲉⲣⲱⲟⲩ ϧⲉⲛ ⲟⲩϩⲓⲣⲏⲛⲏ ⲛⲉⲙ ⲟⲩⲇⲓⲕⲉⲟⲥⲩⲛⲏ ϧⲉⲛ ⲧⲉⲕⲉⲕⲕⲗⲏⲥⲓⲁ ⲉⲑⲟⲩⲁⲃ. | |

Congregation:

| Lord have mercy. | Ⲕⲩⲣⲓⲉ ⲉⲗⲉⲏⲥⲟⲛ | يا رب إرحم |

Priest:

| Again, let us ask God the Pantocrator, the Father of our Lord, God and Savior Jesus Christ. We ask and entreat Your goodness, O Lover of Mankind, remember O Lord, our assemblies. Bless them. | Ⲡⲁⲗⲓⲛ ⲟⲛ ⲙⲁⲣⲉⲛϯϩⲟ ⲉⲫϯ ⲡⲓⲡⲁⲛⲧⲟⲕⲣⲁⲧⲱⲣ ⲫⲓⲱⲧ ⲙⲡⲉⲛⲟⲥ ⲟⲩⲟϩ ⲡⲉⲛⲛⲟⲩϯ ⲟⲩⲟϩ ⲡⲉⲛⲥⲱⲧⲏⲣ Ⲓⲏⲥ Ⲡⲭⲥ ⲧⲉⲛϯϩⲟ ⲟⲩⲟϩ ⲧⲉⲛⲧⲱⲃϩ ⲛⲧⲉⲕⲙⲉⲧⲁⲅⲁⲑⲟⲥ ⲡⲓⲙⲁⲓⲣⲱⲙⲓ ⲁⲣⲓⲫⲙⲉⲩⲓ Ⲡⲟⲥ ⲛⲛⲉⲛϫⲓⲛⲑⲱⲟⲩϯ. Ⲥⲙⲟⲩ ⲉⲣⲱⲟⲩ. | وأيضاً فلنسأل الله ضابط الكل أبا ربنا وإلهنا ومخلصنا يسوع المسيح نسأل ونطلب من صلاحك يا محب البشر اذكر يا رب اجتماعاتنا باركها |

Deacon:

Pray for this holy church and for our assemblies.	Ⲡⲣⲟⲥⲉⲩⲝⲁⲥⲑⲉ ⲩⲡⲉⲣ ⲧⲏⲥ ⲁⲅⲓⲁⲥ ⲉⲕⲕⲗⲏⲥⲓⲁⲥ ⲧⲁⲩⲧⲏⲥ ⲕⲉ ⲧⲱⲛ ⲥⲩⲛⲉⲗⲉⲩⲥⲉⲱⲛ ⲏⲙⲱⲛ	صلوا من أجل هذه الكنيسة المقدسة واجتماعاتنا

Congregation:

Lord have mercy.	Ⲕⲩⲣⲓⲉ Ⲉⲗⲉⲏⲥⲟⲛ	يا رب إرحم

Priest:

Grant that they may be to us without obstacle or hindrance, that we may hold them according to Your Holy and blessed will: houses of prayer, houses of purity, houses of blessing. Grant them to us, O Lord, and Your servants who shall come after us, forever. The worship of idols, utterly uproot from the world. Satan and all his evil powers, trample and humiliate under our feet speedily. All offenses and their instigators, abolish. May all dissensions of corrupt heresies cease. The enemies of Your Holy Church, O Lord, as at all times, now also humiliate. Strip their	Ⲙⲏⲓⲥ ⲉⲑⲣⲟⲩϣⲱⲡⲓ ⲛⲁⲛ ⲛⲁⲧⲉⲣⲕⲱⲗⲓⲛ ⲛⲁⲧⲧⲁϩⲛⲟ ⲉⲑⲣⲉⲛⲁⲓⲧⲟⲩ ⲕⲁⲧⲁ ⲡⲉⲕⲟⲩⲱϣ ⲉⲑⲟⲩⲁⲃ ⲟⲩϩ ⲙⲙⲁⲕⲁⲣⲓⲟⲛ. Ϩⲁⲛⲏⲓ ⲛⲉⲩⲭⲏ ϩⲁⲛⲏⲓ ⲛⲧⲟⲩⲃⲟ ϩⲁⲛⲏⲓ ⲛⲥⲙⲟⲩ ⲁⲣⲓⲭⲁⲣⲓⲍⲉⲥⲑⲉ ⲙⲙⲱⲟⲩ Ⲡϭⲟⲓⲥ ⲛⲉⲙ ⲛⲉⲕⲉⲃⲓⲁⲓⲕ ⲉⲑⲛⲏⲟⲩ ⲙⲉⲛⲉⲛⲥⲱⲛ ϣⲁ ⲉⲛⲉϩ. Ⲧⲙⲉⲧϣⲁⲙϣⲉ ⲓⲇⲱⲗⲟⲛ ϧⲉⲛ ⲟⲩϫⲱⲕ ϥⲟϫⲥ ⲉⲃⲟⲗϧⲉⲛ ⲡⲓⲕⲟⲥⲙⲟⲥ. Ⲡⲥⲁⲧⲁⲛⲁⲥ ⲛⲉⲙ ϫⲟⲙ ⲛⲓⲃⲉⲛ ⲉⲧϩⲱⲟⲩ ⲛⲧⲁϥ ϩⲉⲙϩⲱⲙⲟⲩ ⲟⲩⲟϩ ⲙⲁⲑⲉⲃⲓⲱⲟⲩ ⲥⲁⲡⲉⲥⲏⲧ ⲛⲛⲉⲛϭⲁⲗⲁⲩϫ ⲛⲭⲱⲗⲉⲙ. Ⲛⲓⲥⲕⲁⲛⲇⲁⲗⲟⲛ ⲛⲉⲙ ⲛⲏⲉⲧⲓⲣⲓ ⲙⲙⲱⲟⲩ ⲕⲟⲣϥⲟⲩ ⲙⲁⲣⲟⲩⲕⲏⲛ ⲛϫⲉ ⲛⲓⲫⲱⲣϫ ⲙⲡⲧⲁⲕⲟ ⲛⲧⲉ ⲛⲓϩⲉⲣⲉⲥⲓⲥ. Ⲛⲓϫⲁϫⲓ ⲛⲧⲉ	اعط أن تكون لنا بغير مانع ولا عائق لنصنعها كمشيئتك المقدسة الطوباوية بيوت صلاة بيوت طهارة بيوت بركة. انعم بها لنا يارب ولعبيدك الآتين بعدنا إلي الأبد عبادة الأوثان بتمامها اقلعها من العالم الشيطان وكل قواته الشريرة اسحقهم وأذلهم تحت أقدامنا سريعا الشكوك وفاعلوها ابطلهم ولينقض افتراق فساد البدع. أعداء كنيستك المقدسة يارب مثل كل زمان الآن أيضاً أذلهم حل تعاظمهم عرفهم ضعفهم سريعا ابطل حسدهم وسعايتهم وجنونهم وشرهم ونميمتهم التي يصنعونها فينا يا رب اجعلهم كلهم كلا شئ وبدد

vanity, show them their weakness speedily. Bring to naught their envy, their intrigues, their madness, their wickedness, and their slander, which they commit against us. O Lord, bring them all to no avail. Disperse their counsel, O God, who dispersed the counsel of Ahithophel.	Ⲧⲉⲕⲉⲕⲕⲗⲏⲥⲓⲁ ⲉⲑⲟⲩⲁⲃ Ⲡϭⲟⲓⲥ ⲙ̀ⲫⲣⲏϯ ⲛ̀ⲥⲏⲟⲩ ⲛⲓⲃⲉⲛ ⲛⲉⲙ ϯⲛⲟⲩ ⲙⲁⲑⲉⲃⲓⲱⲟⲩ. Ⲃⲱⲗ ⲛ̀ⲧⲟⲩⲙⲉⲧϭⲁⲥⲓϩⲏⲧ ⲉⲃⲟⲗ ⲙⲁⲧⲁⲙⲱⲟⲩ ⲉⲧⲟⲩⲙⲉⲧϫⲱⲃ ⲛ̀ⲭⲱⲗⲉⲙ. Ⲕⲱⲣϥ ⲛ̀ⲛⲟⲩⲫⲑⲟⲛⲟⲥ ⲛⲟⲩⲉⲡⲓⲃⲟⲗⲏ ⲛⲟⲩⲙⲁⲛⲕⲁⲛⲓⲁ ⲛⲟⲩⲕⲁⲕⲟⲩⲣⲅⲓⲁ ⲛⲟⲩⲕⲁⲧⲁⲗⲁⲗⲓⲁ ⲉⲧⲟⲩⲓⲣⲓ ⲙ̀ⲙⲱⲟⲩ ϧⲁⲣⲟⲛ. Ⲡϭⲟⲓⲥⲉ ⲁⲣⲓⲧⲟⲩ ⲧⲏⲣⲟⲩ ⲛ̀ⲁⲡⲣⲁⲕⲧⲟⲛ ⲟⲩⲟϩ ϫⲱⲣ ⲉⲃⲟⲗ ⲙ̀ⲡⲟⲩⲥⲟϭⲛⲓ Ⲫϯ ⲫⲏⲉⲧⲁϥϫⲱⲣ ⲉⲃⲟⲗ ⲙ̀ⲡⲥⲟϭⲛⲓ ⲛ̀ⲁⲭⲓⲧⲟⲫⲉⲗ.	مشورتهم يا الله بدد مشورة أخيتوفل

Congregation:

Lord have mercy.	Ⲕⲩⲣⲓⲉ Ⲉⲗⲉⲏⲥⲟⲛ	يا رب إرحم

Priest:

Arise, O Lord God, let all Your enemies be scattered, and let all who hate Your holy name flee before Your face. But let Your people be in blessing, thousands of thousands and ten thousand times ten thousand doing Your Will.	Ⲧⲱⲛⲕ Ⲡⲟⲥ Ⲫϯ ⲙⲁⲣⲟⲩϫⲱⲣ ⲉⲃⲟⲗ ⲛ̀ϫⲉ ⲛⲉⲕϫⲁϫⲓ ⲧⲏⲣⲟⲩ ⲙⲁⲣⲟⲩⲫⲱⲧ ⲉⲃⲟⲗ ϧⲁ ⲧϩⲏ ⲙ̀ⲡⲉⲕϩⲟ ⲛ̀ϫⲉ ⲟⲩⲟⲛ ⲛⲓⲃⲉⲛ ⲉⲑⲙⲟⲥϯ ⲙ̀ⲡⲉⲕⲣⲁⲛ ⲉⲑⲟⲩⲁⲃ. Ⲡⲉⲕⲗⲁⲟⲥ ⲇⲉ ⲙⲁⲣⲉϥϣⲱⲡⲓ ϧⲉⲛ ⲡⲓⲥⲙⲟⲩ ⲉϩⲁⲛⲁⲛϣⲟ	قم أيها الرب الاله وليتفرق جميع أعدائك وليهرب من قدام وجهك كل مبغضي إسمك القدوس وأما شعبك فليكن بالبركة ألوف ألوف وربوات ربوات يصنعون إرادتك

| | ⲛϣⲟ ⲛⲉⲙ ϩⲁⲛⲑⲃⲁ ⲛⲉⲃⲁ ⲉⲩⲓⲣⲓ ⲙⲡⲉⲕⲟⲩⲱϣ. | |

Deacon:

| In the wisdom of God, let us attend. Lord have mercy. Lord have mercy. Truly | Ⲉⲛ ⲥⲟⲫⲓⲁ Ⲑⲉⲟⲩ ⲡⲣⲟⲥⲭⲱⲙⲉⲛ. Ⲕⲩⲣⲓⲉ ⲉⲗⲉⲏⲥⲟⲛ Ⲕⲩⲣⲓⲉ ⲉⲗⲉⲏⲥⲟⲛ. ϧⲉⲛ ⲟⲩⲙⲉⲑⲙⲏⲓ | إنصتوا بحكمة الله يا رب إرحم يا رب إرحم بالحقيقة |

The Creed

Congregation:

| We believe in one God, God the Father the Pantocrator, who created heaven and earth, and all things seen and unseen. We believe in one Lord Jesus Christ, the Only-Begotten Son of God, begotten of the Father before all ages; Light of Light, true God of true God, begotten not created, of one essence with the Father, by whom all things were made. Who for us men and for our salvation came down from heaven, and was incarnate of the Holy Spirit, and the Virgin Mary, and became Man. And He was crucified for us under Pontius Pilate, suffered, and was buried. And on the third | Ⲧⲉⲛⲛⲁϩϯ ⲉⲟⲩⲛⲟⲩϯ ⲛⲟⲩⲱⲧ Ⲫⲛⲟⲩϯ Ⲫⲓⲱⲧ Ⲡⲓⲡⲁⲛⲧⲟⲕⲣⲁⲧⲱⲣ ⲫⲏⲉⲧⲁϥⲑⲁⲙⲓⲟ ⲛⲧⲫⲉ ⲛⲉⲙ ⲡⲕⲁϩⲓ ⲛⲏⲉⲧⲟⲩⲛⲁⲩ ⲉⲣⲱⲟⲩ ⲛⲉⲙ ⲛⲏⲉⲧⲉ ⲛⲥⲉⲛⲁⲩ ⲉⲣⲱⲟⲩ ⲁⲛ. Ⲧⲉⲛⲛⲁϩϯ ⲉⲟⲩϭⲟⲓⲥ ⲛⲟⲩⲱⲧ Ⲓⲏⲥⲟⲩⲁ Ⲡⲓⲭⲣⲓⲥⲧⲟⲥ Ⲡϣⲏⲣⲓ ⲙⲪⲛⲟⲩϯ ⲡⲓⲙⲟⲛⲟⲅⲉⲛⲏⲥ ⲡⲓⲙⲓⲥⲓ ⲉⲃⲟⲗϧⲉⲛ Ⲫⲓⲱⲧ ϧⲁϫⲱⲟⲩ ⲛⲛⲓⲉⲱⲛ ⲧⲏⲣⲟⲩ ⲟⲩⲟⲩⲱⲓⲛⲓ ⲉⲃⲟⲗϧⲉⲛ ⲟⲩⲟⲩⲱⲓⲛⲓ ⲟⲩⲛⲟⲩϯ ⲛⲧⲁⲫⲙⲏⲓ ⲉⲃⲟⲗϧⲉⲛ ⲟⲩⲛⲟⲩϯ ⲛⲧⲁⲫⲙⲏⲓ ⲟⲩⲙⲓⲥⲓ ⲡⲉ ⲟⲩⲑⲁⲙⲓⲟ ⲁⲛ ⲡⲉ ⲟⲩⲟⲙⲟⲟⲩⲥⲓⲟⲥ ⲡⲉ ⲛⲉⲙ Ⲫⲓⲱⲧ ⲫⲏⲉⲧ ⲁ ϩⲱⲃ ⲛⲓⲃⲉⲛ ϣⲱⲡⲓ ⲉⲃⲟⲗϩⲓⲧⲟⲧϥ. Ⲫⲁⲓ ⲉⲧⲉ | نؤمن بإله واحد الله الآب ضابط الكل خالق السماء والأرض ما يرى وما لا يرى نؤمن برب واحد يسوع المسيح إبن الله الوحيد المولود من الآب قبل كل الدهور نور من نور إله حق من إله حق مولود غير مخلوق مساوي للآب في الجوهر الذي به كان كل شيء هذا الذي من أجلنا نحن البشر ومن أجل خلاصنا نزل من السماء وتجسد من الروح القدس ومن مريم العذراء وتأنس وصلب عنا على عهد بيلاطس البنطي وتألم وقبر وقام من بين الأموات في اليوم الثالث كما في الكتب |

day He rose from the dead, according to the Scriptures, ascended into the heavens. He sits at the right hand of His Father, and He is coming again in His glory to judge the living and the dead, whose kingdom shall have no end. Yes, we believe in the Holy Spirit, the Lord, the Life-Giver, who proceeds from the Father, who with the Father and the Son is worshiped and glorified, who spoke by the prophets. And in one holy, catholic and apostolic church, we confess one baptism for the remission of sins. We look for the resurrection of the dead, and the life of the coming age. Amen.	ⲉⲑⲃⲏⲧⲉⲛ ⲁⲛⲟⲛ ϧⲁ ⲛⲓⲣⲱⲙⲓ ⲛⲉⲙ ⲉⲑⲃⲉ ⲡⲉⲛⲟⲩϫⲁⲓ ⲁϥⲉⲡⲉⲥⲏⲧ ⲉⲃⲟⲗϧⲉⲛ ⲧⲫⲉ ⲁϥϭⲓⲥⲁⲣϩ ⲉⲃⲟⲗϧⲉⲛ Ⲡⲓⲡⲛⲉⲩⲙⲁ Ⲉⲑⲟⲩⲁⲃ ⲛⲉⲙ ⲉⲃⲟⲗϧⲉⲛ Ⲙⲁⲣⲓⲁ ϯⲡⲁⲣⲑⲉⲛⲟⲥ ⲟⲩⲟϩ ⲁϥⲉⲣⲣⲱⲙⲓ. Ⲟⲩⲟϩ ⲁⲩⲉⲣⲥⲧⲁⲩⲣⲱⲛⲓⲛ ⲙⲙⲟϥ ⲉϩⲣⲏⲓ ⲉϫⲱⲛ ⲛⲁϩⲣⲉⲛ Ⲡⲟⲛⲧⲓⲟⲥ Ⲡⲓⲗⲁⲧⲟⲥ ⲁϥϣⲉⲡⲙⲕⲁϩ ⲟⲩⲟϩ ⲁⲩⲕⲟⲥϥ. Ⲟⲩⲟϩ ⲁϥⲧⲱⲛϥ ⲉⲃⲟⲗϧⲉⲛ ⲛⲏⲉⲑⲙⲱⲟⲩⲧϧⲉⲛ ⲡⲓⲉϩⲟⲟⲩ ⲙⲙⲁϩϣⲟⲙⲧ ⲕⲁⲧⲁ ⲛⲓⲅⲣⲁⲫⲏ. Ⲁϥϣⲉⲛⲁϥ ⲉⲡϣⲱⲓ ⲉⲛⲓⲫⲏⲟⲩⲓ ⲁϥϩⲉⲙⲥⲓ ⲥⲁⲟⲩⲓⲛⲁⲙ ⲙⲡⲉϥⲓⲱⲧ ⲕⲉ ⲡⲁⲗⲓⲛ ϥⲛⲏⲟⲩ ϧⲉⲛ ⲡⲉϥⲱⲟⲩ ⲉϯϩⲁⲡ ⲉⲛⲏⲉⲧⲟⲛϧ ⲛⲉⲙ ⲛⲏⲉⲑⲙⲱⲟⲩⲧ ⲫⲏⲉⲧⲉ ⲧⲉϥⲙⲉⲧⲟⲩⲣⲟ ⲟⲩⲁⲑⲙⲟⲩⲛⲕ ⲧⲉ. Ⲥⲉ ⲧⲉⲛⲛⲁϩϯ ⲉⲠⲓⲡⲉⲛⲩⲙⲁ Ⲉⲑⲟⲩⲁⲃ Ⲡϭⲟⲓⲥ ⲛⲣⲉϥϯ ⲙⲡⲱⲛϧ ⲫⲏⲉⲑⲛⲏⲟⲩ ⲉⲃⲟⲗϧⲉⲛ Ⲫⲓⲱⲧ ⲥⲉⲟⲩⲱϣⲧ ⲙⲙⲟϥ ⲥⲉϯⲱⲟⲩ ⲛⲁϥ ⲛⲉⲙ Ⲫⲓⲱⲧ ⲛⲉⲙ Ⲡϣⲏⲣⲓ ⲫⲏⲉⲧⲁϥⲥⲁϫⲓ ϧⲉⲛ ⲛⲓⲡⲣⲟⲫⲏⲧⲏⲥ. Ⲉⲟⲩⲓ ⲛⲁⲅⲓⲁ ⲛⲕⲁⲑⲟⲗⲓⲕⲏ ⲛⲁⲡⲟⲥⲧⲟⲗⲓⲕⲏ ⲛⲉⲕⲕⲗⲏⲥⲓⲁ	وصعد إلى السموات وجلس عن يمين أبيه وأيضاً يأتي في مجده ليدين الأحياء والأموات الذي ليس لملكه إنقضاء نعم نؤمن بالروح القدس الرب المحيي المنبثق من الآب نسجد له ونمجده مع الآب والإبن الناطق في الأنبياء وبكنيسة واحدة مقدسة جامعة رسولية ونعترف بمعمودية واحدة لمغفرة الخطايا وننتظر قيامة الأموات وحياة الدهر الآتي آمين

	ⲧⲉⲛⲉⲣⲟⲙⲟⲗⲟⲅⲓⲛ ⲛⲟⲩⲱⲙⲥ ⲛⲟⲩⲱⲧ ⲉⲡⲭⲱ ⲉⲃⲟⲗ ⲛⲧⲉ ⲛⲓⲛⲟⲃⲓ. Ⲧⲉⲛϫⲟⲩϣⲧ ⲉⲃⲟⲗ ϧⲁ ⲧⲋⲏ ⲛϯⲁⲛⲁⲥⲧⲁⲥⲓⲥ ⲛⲧⲉ ⲛⲓⲣⲉϥⲙⲱⲟⲩⲧ ⲛⲉⲙ ⲡⲓⲱⲛϧ ⲛⲧⲉ ⲡⲓⲉⲱⲛ ⲉⲑⲛⲏⲟⲩ. ⲁⲙⲏⲛ.	

The Prayers of the Covenant

Priest:

Let us pray	Ϣⲗⲏⲗ	صلوا

Deacon:

Stand up for prayer	Ⲉⲡⲓ ⲡⲣⲟⲥⲉⲩⲭⲏ ⲥⲧⲁⲑⲏⲧⲉ	للصلاة قفوا

Priest:

Peace be with all.	Ⲓⲣⲏⲛⲏ ⲡⲁⲥⲓ	السلام لجميعكم

Congregation:

And with your spirit.	Ⲕⲉ ⲧⲱ ⲡⲛⲉⲩⲙⲁⲧⲓ ⲥⲟⲩ	ولروحك أيضاً

Priest *(facing the groom)*:

O God who formed man by His own hands, and gave him the woman for his help and strength, now also our Master, be	Ⲫϯ ⲫⲏⲉⲧⲁϥⲉⲣⲡⲗⲁⲍⲓⲛ ⲙⲡⲣⲱⲙⲓ ϧⲉⲛ ⲛⲉϥϫⲓϫ ⲙⲙⲓⲛ ⲙⲙⲟϥ ⲁϥϯⲛⲁϥ ⲛⲧⲉϥⲥϩⲓⲙⲓ ⲛⲟⲩⲃⲟⲏⲑⲟⲥ ⲟⲩⲟϩ ⲛⲧⲁϫⲣⲟ ⲛⲁϥ ⲛⲑⲟⲕ	يا الله الذي جبل الانسان بيديه وحده و أعطاه المرأة عونا و قوة له أنت أيضا الآن يا سيدنا كن وسيطا لهذين الفتيين العروس و معينته

A Textual History of the Coptic Wedding Rite

a mediator for the groom and his helpmate. Adjoin {GROOM} and {BRIDE} through the pledge of fellowship, and grant them the sign of their union so that they may be unified in harmony through the bond of love. And say unto them, "My peace I give you both, My peace I leave with you both." For You are the peace of us all, and unto You do we offer the glory and honor, with Your only begotten Son and the Holy Spirit, the Giver of Life, now and at all times and unto the age of all ages. Amen	ⲟⲛ ϯⲛⲟⲩ ⲡⲉⲛⲛⲏⲃ ϣⲱⲡⲓ ⲙⲙⲉⲥⲓⲧⲏⲥ ⲛⲛⲁⲓ ⲁⲗⲱⲟⲩⲓ ⲛⲁⲓ ⲡⲓⲛⲩⲙⲫⲓⲟⲥ ⲛⲉⲙ ⲧⲉϥⲃⲟⲏⲑⲟⲥ. ϩⲟⲧⲡⲟⲩ ⲉⲟⲩⲁⲣⲏⲃ ⲛⲧⲉ ⲟⲩⲙⲉⲧϣⲫⲏⲣ ⲉⲁⲕϭⲙⲏⲓⲛⲓ ⲛⲱⲟⲩ ⲙⲡⲓⲥⲩⲙⲃⲟⲩⲗⲟⲛ ⲛⲧⲉ ⲡⲟⲩϫⲓⲛϩⲱⲧⲡ ⲛⲧⲟⲩϣⲱⲡⲓ ϧⲉⲛ ⲟⲩⲙⲉⲧⲟⲩⲁⲓ ϧⲉⲛ ⲡⲓⲙⲟⲩⲣ ⲛⲧⲉ ϯⲁⲅⲁⲡⲏ. ⲉⲕϫⲱ ⲙⲙⲟⲥ ⲛⲱⲟⲩ ϫⲉ ⲧⲁϩⲓⲣⲏⲛⲏ ϯϯ ⲙⲙⲟⲥ ⲛⲱⲧⲉⲛ ⲧⲁϩⲓⲣⲏⲛⲏ ⲁⲛⲟⲕ ϯⲭⲱ ⲙⲙⲟⲥ ⲛⲉⲙⲱⲧⲉⲛ. ⲛⲑⲟⲕ ⲡⲉ ⲧⲉⲛϩⲓⲣⲏⲛⲏ ⲧⲏⲣⲉⲛ ⲧⲉⲛⲟⲩⲱⲣⲡ ⲛⲁⲕ ⲉⲡϣⲱⲓ ⲙⲡⲓⲱⲟⲩ ⲛⲉⲙ ⲡⲓⲧⲁⲓⲟ ⲛⲉⲙ ⲡⲉⲕⲙⲟⲛⲟⲅⲉⲛⲏⲥ ⲛϣⲏⲣⲓ ⲛⲉⲙ ⲡⲓⲡⲛⲉⲩⲙⲁ ⲉⲑⲟⲩⲁⲃ ⲛⲣⲉϥⲧⲁⲛϧⲟ ϯⲛⲟⲩ ⲛⲉⲙ ⲛⲥⲏⲟⲩ ⲛⲓⲃⲉⲛ ⲛⲉⲙ ϣⲁ ⲉⲛⲉϩ ⲛⲧⲉ ⲛⲓⲉⲛⲉϩ ⲧⲏⲣⲟⲩ. ⲁⲙⲏⲛ.	صلهما بعربون الشركة و أعطهما علامة اشارة اتصالهما اذ تقول لهما واحدة برباط المحبة لكيكونا بآلفية سلامي أعطيه لكما سلامي أنا أتركه معكما فأنت سلامة جميعنا و نرسل المجد و الكرامة مع ابنك الوحيد الجنس و الروح القدس المحيي الان وكل أوان وإلى دهر الدهور آمين

Congregation *(in the muḥayyar tune)*:

Christ the Logos of the Father, • the Only-Begotten God, • grant us Your peace • which is full of all joy.	Ⲡⲭⲥ Ⲡⲓⲗⲟⲅⲟⲥ ⲛⲧⲉ ⲫⲓⲱⲧ ⲡⲓⲙⲟⲛⲟⲅⲉⲛⲏⲥ ⲛⲛⲟⲩϯ ⲉⲕⲉϯ ⲛⲁⲛ ⲛⲧⲉⲕϩⲓⲣⲏⲛⲏ ⲑⲁⲓ ⲉⲑⲙⲉϩ ⲛⲣⲁϣⲓ ⲛⲓⲃⲉⲛ	أيها المسيح كلمة الآب الاله الواحد الجنس أعطنا سلامك هذا المملوء كل فرح

Priest *(facing the groom)*:

O Master the Lover of Mankind, who fulfilled the prophetic voice saying, "Through the Lord man is united with woman." Now O Lord, bless the covenant of your servants which is present before us. Perfect and unite your servants without blame as it pleases Your life-giving will. For You are our God who created man from the ground, and created woman from him, that she may be a wife, a companion, and a helpmate, that she may bear sons and daughters, that the human race may grow. Now also O Lord, bless the covenant of Your servants the groom and his helpmate. Let them grow and multiply through Your many compassions. Give them the fruit of blessing, the life of godliness, the unity of faith, wisdom, purity, and works of righteousness, that through their body and soul they may become one. Let the fear of You dwell within them that they may become worthy of Your blessings through Christ Jesus our Lord to whom the glory,	Ⲫⲛⲏⲃ ⲡⲓⲙⲁⲓⲣⲱⲙⲓ ⲫⲏⲉⲧⲁϥϫⲱⲕ ⲛ̀ϯⲥⲙⲏ ⲙ̀ⲡⲣⲟⲫⲏⲧⲓⲕⲏ ⲇⲉ ⲉⲃⲟⲗϩⲓⲧⲉⲛ Ⲡⲟⲥ ⲉϥⲉϩⲱⲧⲡ ⲛ̀ϫⲉ ⲡⲓⲣⲱⲙⲓ ⲉϥϭⲥⲓⲙⲓ ⲛ̀ⲑⲟⲕ Ⲡⲟⲥ ⲡⲁⲓⲁⲣⲏⲃ ⲛ̀ⲧⲉ ⲛⲉⲕⲉⲃⲓⲁⲓⲕ ⲫⲁⲓ ⲉⲧⲁϥⲣ̀ⲁⲟⲩⲱ ϩⲁⲣⲟⲛ ⲛⲉⲙⲡϣⲁ ⲙ̀ⲡⲓⲥⲙⲟⲩ ⲡⲓⲉⲃⲟⲗϩⲓⲧⲟⲧⲕ. Ⲟⲩⲟϩ ϫⲱⲕ ⲉⲃⲟⲗ ⲟⲩⲟϩ ⲥⲱⲧⲡ ⲛ̀ⲛⲉⲕⲉⲃⲓⲁⲓⲕ ϧⲉⲛ ⲟⲩⲙⲉⲧⲁⲧⲁⲣⲓⲕⲓ ⲉⲩⲣⲁⲛⲁϥ ⲙ̀ⲡⲉⲕⲟⲩⲱϣ ⲛ̀ⲣⲉϥϯⲙ̀ⲡⲱⲛϧ. Ⲛⲑⲟⲕ ⲅⲁⲣ ⲡⲉⲛⲛⲟⲩϯ ⲫⲏⲉⲧⲁϥⲉⲣⲡⲗⲁⲍⲓⲛ ⲙ̀ⲡⲓⲣⲱⲙⲓ ⲉⲃⲟⲗϩⲉⲛ ⲡⲕⲁϩⲓ ⲁⲕϯⲛⲁϥ ⲁⲕⲑⲁⲙⲓⲟⲥ ⲉⲃⲟⲗⲛ̀ϧⲏⲧϥ ⲉⲑⲣⲉⲥϣⲱⲡⲓ ⲛⲟⲩⲥϩⲓⲙⲓ ⲛⲁϥ ⲛⲉⲙ ⲟⲩⲣⲉϥⲉⲣϣⲫⲉⲣⲓ ⲛⲉⲙ ⲟⲩϫⲓⲛϯⲧⲟⲧϥ ⲉⲑⲣⲉⲥⲙⲓⲥⲓ ⲛ̀ϩⲁⲛϣⲏⲣⲓ ⲛⲉⲙ ϩⲁⲛϣⲉⲣⲓ ⲛⲉⲙ ⲟⲩϫⲓⲛⲁⲓⲁⲓ ⲙ̀ⲡⲅⲉⲛⲟⲥ ⲛ̀ⲛⲓⲣⲱⲙⲓ. Ϯⲛⲟⲩ ⲟⲛ Ⲡⲟⲥ ⲉⲕⲉⲥⲙⲟⲩ ⲉⲡⲓⲁⲣⲏⲃ ⲛ̀ⲧⲉ ⲛⲉⲕⲉⲃⲓⲁⲓⲕ ⲡⲓⲡⲁⲧϣⲉⲗⲉⲧ ⲛⲉⲙ ⲧⲉϥⲃⲟⲏⲑⲟⲥ. Ⲙⲁⲣⲟⲩⲁⲓⲁⲓ ⲟⲩⲟϩ ⲙⲁⲣⲟⲩⲁϣⲁⲓ ϧⲉⲛ ⲛⲉⲕⲙⲉⲧϣⲉⲛϩⲏⲧ ⲉⲧⲟϣ. Ⲙⲟⲓ ⲛⲱⲟⲩ ⲛⲟⲩⲕⲁⲣⲡⲟⲥ ⲛ̀ⲧⲉ ⲟⲩⲥⲙⲟⲩ ⲛⲉⲙ ⲟⲩⲧⲣⲟⲡⲟⲥ ⲛ̀ⲧⲉ ϯⲙⲉⲧⲉⲩⲥⲉⲃⲏⲥ ⲛⲉⲙ	أيها السيد محب البشر الذي أكمل الصوت النبوي أن من قبل الرب يتصل الرجل بالمرأة أنت أيضا يا رب عربون عبيدك هذا الحاضر لدينا اجعله أهلا للبركة التي من قبلك و كمل و اقرن عبيدك بغير لوم مرضيين لارادتك المحيية لانك أنت الهنا الذي جبل الانسان من الارض و أعطيته معينة نظيرة صنعتها منه لتكون له زوجة و شريكة و مساعدة لتلد بنين و بنات و لينمو جنس البشر الآن أيضا يا رب بارك عربون عبيدك العريس ومعينته لينميا و يكثرا من قبل رأفاتك الكثيرة اعطهما ثمرة البركة و مثال التقوى و اتصال الايمان و حكمة و طهارة و اعمال البر لكي بجسدهما ونفسهما يكونا بوحدانية كائنا خوفك فيهما ليستحقا البركات التي من قبلك بالمسيح يسوع ربنا هذا الذي من قبله المجد والإكرام والعزة والسجود تليق بك معه مع الروح القدس المحيي المساوي لك الآن وكل أوان وإلى دهر الدهور آمين

honor, majesty, and worship are due together with you and the Holy Spirit, the coessential and life-giver, now and forever and unto the age of all ages. Amen.	ⲟⲩϫⲓⲛϩⲱⲧⲡ ⲛⲧⲉ ⲡⲓⲛⲁϩϯ ⲛⲉⲙ ⲟⲩⲙⲉⲧⲥⲁⲃⲉ ⲛⲉⲙ ⲟⲩⲧⲟⲩⲃⲟ ⲛⲉⲙ ϩⲁⲛϩⲃⲏⲟⲩⲓ ⲛⲧⲉ ϯⲇⲓⲕⲉⲟⲥⲩⲛⲏ ϩⲓⲛⲁ ϧⲉⲛ ⲧⲟⲩⲥⲁⲣⲝ ⲛⲉⲙ ⲧⲟⲩⲯⲩⲭⲏ ⲛⲧⲟⲩϣⲱⲡⲓ ϧⲉⲛ ⲟⲩⲙⲉⲧⲟⲩⲁⲓ ⲉⲣⲉⲧⲉⲕϩⲟϯ ϣⲱⲡⲓ ⲛϧⲏⲧⲟⲩ ⲛⲧⲟⲩⲉⲣⲡⲉⲙⲡϣⲁ ⲛϩⲁⲛⲥⲙⲟⲩ ⲛⲓ ⲉⲃⲟⲗϩⲓⲧⲟⲧⲕ ϧⲉⲛ Ⲡⲭⲥ Ⲓⲏⲥ Ⲡⲉⲛⲟⲥ ⲫⲁⲓ ⲉⲧⲉ ⲉⲃⲟⲗϩⲓⲧⲟⲧϥ ⲉⲣⲉ ⲡⲓⲱⲟⲩ ⲛⲉⲙ ⲡⲓⲧⲁⲓⲟ ⲛⲉⲙ ⲡⲓⲁⲙⲁϩⲓ ⲛⲉⲙ ϯⲡⲣⲟⲥⲕⲩⲛⲏⲥⲓⲥ ⲉⲣⲡⲣⲉⲡⲓ ⲛⲁⲕ ⲛⲉⲙⲁϥ ⲛⲉⲙ ⲡⲓⲡⲛⲉⲩⲙⲁ ⲉⲑⲟⲩⲁⲃ ⲛⲣⲉϥⲧⲁⲛϧⲟ ⲟⲩⲟϩ ⲛⲟⲙⲟⲟⲩⲥⲓⲟⲥ ⲛⲉⲙⲁⲕ ϯⲛⲟⲩ ⲛⲉⲙ ⲛⲥⲏⲟⲩ ⲛⲓⲃⲉⲛ ⲛⲉⲙ ϣⲁ ⲉⲛⲉϩ ⲛⲧⲉ ⲛⲓⲉⲛⲉϩ ⲧⲏⲣⲟⲩ. ⲁⲙⲏⲛ.	

Congregation *(in the muḥayyar tune)*:

As You have given • your holy apostles, • likewise say unto us, • "My peace I give to you"	Ⲕⲁⲧⲁ ⲫⲣⲏϯ ⲉⲧⲁⲕⲧⲏⲓⲥ ⲛⲛⲉⲕⲁⲅⲓⲟⲥ ⲛⲁⲡⲟⲥⲧⲟⲗⲟⲥ ⲉⲕⲉϫⲟⲥ ⲛⲁⲛ ⲙⲡⲟⲩⲣⲏϯ ϫⲉ ⲧⲁϩⲓⲣⲏⲛⲏ ϯϯ ⲙⲙⲟⲥ ⲛⲱⲧⲉⲛ	كما عطيته لرسلك القديسين هكذا أيضا قل لنا مثلهم اني أعطيكم سلامي

Priest *(facing the groom):*

O Master Lord our God who accompanied the servant of Abraham the patriarch in Mesopotamia, who sent him to take a wife for his son Isaac, who by means of the drawing of water saw his marriage to Rebecca. Now also O our Master the Lover of Mankind, be a partner and take pleasure in this covenant of your servants, the groom and his bride, and bless them. Keep the agreements that took place between them. Strengthen them through Your perfection. May their covenant be unshakable. Nourish their youth. For You from the beginning created male and female and through You the wife received a promise from her husband as an aid and succession for the human race. As for our fathers and brethren those gathered together joining us in prayer, purify and preserve these Your servants through the intercessions of our Lady the Theotokos St. Mary and all the choir of Your saints. Amen.	Ⲫⲛⲏⲃ Ⲡⲟⲥ ⲡⲉⲛⲛⲟⲩϯ ⲫⲏⲉⲧⲁϥⲉⲣϣⲫⲏⲣ ⲙⲙⲟϣⲓ ⲛⲉⲙ ⲡⲓⲁⲗⲟⲩ ⲛⲧⲉ ⲁⲃⲣⲁⲁⲙ ⲡⲓⲡⲁⲧⲣⲓⲁⲣⲭⲏⲥ ϧⲉⲛ ϯⲙⲉⲥⲟⲡⲟⲧⲁⲙⲓⲁ ⲉⲟⲩⲱⲣⲡ ⲙⲙⲟϥ ⲉϭⲓ ⲛⲟⲩⲥϩⲓⲙⲓ ⲙⲡⲉϥⲁⲗⲟⲩ Ⲓⲥⲁⲁⲕ ⲟⲩⲟϩ ⲉⲃⲟⲗϩⲓⲧⲉⲛ ϯⲙⲉⲥⲓⲧⲓⲁ ⲛⲧⲉ ϯϫⲓⲛⲙⲁϩ ⲙⲱⲟⲩ ⲛⲧⲉϥⲛⲁⲩ ⲉⲡⲉϥϩⲁⲣⲏⲃ ϩⲓϫⲉⲛ ⲉⲣⲉⲃⲉⲕⲕⲁ. Ⲛⲑⲟⲕ ⲟⲛ ϯⲛⲟⲩ ⲡⲉⲛⲛⲏⲃ ⲡⲓⲙⲁⲓⲣⲱⲙⲓ Ⲡⲟⲥ ⲁⲣⲓϣⲫⲏⲣ ⲛϯⲙⲁϯ ϩⲓϫⲉⲛ ⲡⲓⲁⲣⲏⲃ ⲛⲧⲉ ⲛⲉⲕⲉⲃⲓⲁⲓⲕ ⲡⲓⲛⲩⲙⲫⲓⲟⲥ ⲛⲉⲙ ⲧⲉϥ ⲛⲩⲙⲫⲏ ⲟⲩⲟϩ ⲥⲙⲟⲩ ⲉⲣⲱⲟⲩ ⲁⲣⲉϩ ⲉⲡⲓⲥⲁϫⲓ ⲉⲧⲁϥϣⲱⲡⲓ ⲟⲩⲧⲱⲟⲩ ⲛⲉⲙ ⲛⲟⲩⲉⲣⲏⲟⲩ. Ⲙⲁϫⲟⲙ ⲛⲱⲟⲩ ϧⲉⲛ ⲑⲏⲉⲧⲉ ⲑⲱⲕ ⲙⲙⲉⲧⲧⲉⲗⲓⲟⲥ ⲟⲩⲟϩ ⲛⲟⲩⲥⲩⲛⲑⲏⲕⲏ ⲉⲩⲟⲓ ⲛⲁⲧⲕⲓⲙ ⲟⲩⲟϩ ⲙⲁⲧⲟⲧⲥ ⲛⲑⲏⲉⲧⲉ ⲑⲱⲟⲩ ⲙⲙⲉⲧⲁⲗⲟⲩ. Ⲛⲑⲟⲕ ⲅⲁⲣ ⲓⲥϫⲉⲛ ϯⲁⲣⲭⲏ ⲁⲕⲑⲁⲙⲓⲟ ⲛⲟⲩϩⲱⲟⲩⲧ ⲛⲉⲙ ⲟⲩⲥϩⲓⲙⲓ ⲟⲩⲟϩ ⲉⲃⲟⲗ ϩⲓⲧⲟⲧⲕ ⲁⲥϭⲓⲁⲣⲏⲃ ⲛϫⲉ ϯⲥϩⲓⲙⲓ ⲉⲟⲩϩⲁⲓ ⲙⲃⲟⲏⲑⲓⲁ ⲛⲉⲙ ⲟⲩⲇⲓⲁⲇⲟⲭⲏ ⲙⲡⲅⲉⲛⲟⲥ ⲛⲛⲓⲣⲱⲙⲓ. Ⲛⲏⲉⲧⲁⲩⲑⲱⲟⲩϯ ⲇⲉ ⲟⲩⲟϩ ⲁⲩⲉⲣϣⲫⲏⲣ ⲛⲧⲱⲃϩ	أيها السيد الرب الهنا الذي رافق غلام ابراهيم رئيس الأباء في بين النهرين لما أرسله ليأخذ امرأة فتياه اسحق و بواسطة ملء الماء نظر املاكه على رفقة أنت أيضا الآن يا سيدنا محب البشر يا رب رافق و سر على عربون عبيدك العريس و عروسته و باركهما و احفظ القول الذي صار بينهما بعضهما لبعض قوهما بكمالك و ليكن عهدهما وطيدا و عضد شبوبيتهما لانك أنت من البدء خلقت ذكرا و انثى و من قبلك املكت المرأة لبعل عونا و خلافة لجنس البشر و الذين اجتمعوا و اشتركوا معنا في الطلبة أباؤنا و اخوتنا طهر عبيدك هؤلاء و احفظهم بشفاعة سيدتنا كلنا والدة الاله مريم و كل مصاف قديسيك أمين

111

| | ⲚⲈⲘⲀⲚ ⲚⲈⲚⲒⲞϮ ⲚⲈⲘ ⲚⲈⲚⲤⲚⲎⲞⲨ ⲘⲀⲦⲞⲨⲂⲞ ⲚⲚⲈⲔⲈⲂⲒⲀⲒⲔ ⲚⲀⲒ ⲞⲨⲞϨ ⲀⲢⲈϨ ⲈⲢⲰⲞⲨ ϨⲒⲦⲈⲚ ⲚⲒⲠⲢⲈⲤⲂⲒⲀ ⲚⲦⲈ ⲦⲈⲚⲞⲤ ⲦⲎⲢⲈⲚ ϮⲐⲈⲞⲦⲞⲔⲞⲤ ⲘⲀⲢⲒⲀ ⲚⲈⲘ ⲠⲬⲞⲢⲞⲤ ⲦⲎⲢϤ ⲚⲦⲈ ⲚⲎⲈⲐⲞⲨⲀⲂ ⲚⲦⲀⲔ. ⲀⲘⲎⲚ. | |

Congregation *(in the muḥayyar tune):*

| My peace, • which I have taken from My Father, • I leave unto you • both now and forever. | ⲦⲀϨⲒⲢⲎⲚⲎ ⲀⲚⲞⲔ ⲐⲎⲈⲦⲀⲒϬⲒⲦⲤ ϨⲒⲦⲈⲚ ⲠⲀⲒⲰⲦ ⲀⲚⲞⲔ ϮⲬⲰ ⲘⲘⲞⲤ ⲚⲈⲘⲰⲦⲈⲚ ⲒⲤϪⲈⲚ ϮⲚⲞⲨ ⲚⲈⲘ ϢⲀ ⲈⲚⲈϨ. | سلامي أنا الذي أخذته من أبي أنا أتركه معكم من الآن و الى الأبد |

Priest *(facing East):*

| We thank You O Lord God the Pantocrator, who exists before all ages, the Master of all, who adorned the ˡeavens with His word, and established the earth and everyone in it, who gathered those scattered abroad to one congregation, and form the two into one. Now also we ask You O our Master, let Your servants be worthy of the character of the sign of Your word through the bonds of covenant. May | ⲦⲈⲚϢⲈⲠϨⲘⲞⲦ ⲚⲦⲞⲦⲔ Ⲡⲟⲥ Ⲫϯ ⲠⲒⲠⲀⲚⲦⲞⲔⲢⲀⲦⲰⲢ ⲪⲎⲈⲦϢⲞⲠ ϨⲀϪⲰⲞⲨ ⲚⲚⲒⲈⲰⲚ ⲪⲚⲎⲂ ⲚⲦⲈ ⲠⲒⲈⲠⲦⲎⲢϤ ⲪⲎⲈⲦⲀϤⲤⲞⲖⲤⲈⲖ ⲚⲚⲒⲪⲎⲞⲨⲒ ϦⲈⲚ ⲠⲈϤⲤⲀϪⲒ ⲞⲨⲞϨ ⲀϤϨⲒⲤⲈⲚϮ ⲘⲠⲒⲔⲀϨⲒ ⲚⲈⲘ ⲞⲨⲞⲚ ⲚⲒⲂⲈⲚ ⲈⲦϢⲞⲠ ⲚϦⲎⲦϤ ⲪⲎⲈⲦⲀϤⲐⲞⲨⲰⲦ ⲈϦⲞⲨⲚ ⲚⲚⲎⲈⲦⲀⲨϢⲰⲢ ⲈⲂⲞⲖ ⲈⲞⲨⲘⲀⲚⲐⲰⲞⲨϮ ⲚⲞⲨⲰⲦ ⲞⲨⲞϨ ⲀⲔⲤⲰⲚⲦ ⲘⲠⲒⲤⲚⲀⲨ ⲚⲞⲨⲀⲒ. ϮⲚⲞⲨ ⲞⲚ ⲠⲈⲚⲚⲎⲂ ⲦⲈⲚϮϨⲞ | نشكرك أيها الرب الاله الضابط الكل الكائن قبل الدهور سيد الكل الذي زين السموات بكلمته و أسس الارض و كل من يسكن فيها الذي جمع المتفرقين الى مجمع واحد و خلقت الاثنين واحدا الآن أيضا يا سيدنا نسألك فليستحق عبيدك سمة علامة كلمتك برباط العربون اذ تكون لهما المحبة الغير المفترقة لبعضهما من قبل استحقاق ثبات اتحادها ابنهما على أساس كنيستك المقدسة لكي يسيرا بتقويم و رباط القول الذي قراره مع بعضهما لأنك |

they have undivided love through the assurance of the confirmation of their union. Build them on the foundation of the Holy Church that they may walk in conformity and adherence to the bonds of the promise they have made with each other, for You are the bond of love and ordainer of the law of their union. For You have made oneness come through the union of two through Your perfect word of the commandment of Your Only-Begotten Son Jesus Christ our Lord to whom the glory, honor, majesty, and worship are due together with you and the Holy Spirit, the coessential and life-giver, now and forever and unto the age of all ages. Amen.	ⲉⲣⲟⲕ ⲙⲁⲣⲉ ⲛⲉⲕⲉⲃⲓⲁⲓⲕ ⲉⲣⲡⲉⲙⲡϣⲁ ⲙⲡⲓⲭⲁⲣⲁⲕⲧⲏⲣ ⲙⲫⲙⲏⲓⲛⲓ ⲙⲡⲉⲕⲥⲁϫⲓ ϩⲓⲧⲉⲛ ⲫⲙⲟⲩⲣ ⲛⲧⲉ ⲡⲓⲁⲣⲏⲃ. Ⲉⲥϣⲟⲡ ⲛⲱⲟⲩ ⲛϫⲉ ϯⲁⲅⲁⲡⲏ ⲛⲁⲧⲫⲱⲣϫ ⲉϧⲟⲩⲛ ⲉⲛⲟⲩⲉⲣⲏⲟⲩ ϩⲓⲧⲉⲛ ⲧⲁⲥⲫⲁⲗⲓⲁ ⲙⲡⲧⲁϫⲣⲟ ⲛⲧⲉ ⲡⲟⲩϫⲓⲛϩⲱⲧⲡ. Ⲕⲟⲧⲟⲩ ϩⲓϫⲉⲛ ϯⲥⲉⲛϯ ⲛⲧⲉ ⲧⲉⲕⲉⲕⲕⲗⲏⲥⲓⲁ ⲉⲑⲟⲩⲁⲃ ϩⲓⲛⲁ ⲉⲑⲣⲟⲩⲙⲟϣⲓ ϧⲉⲛ ⲟⲩⲇⲓⲁⲑⲏⲥⲓⲥ ⲛⲉⲙ ⲟⲩⲥⲩⲛⲧⲓⲥⲙⲟⲥ ⲙⲫⲙⲟⲩⲣ ⲙⲡⲓⲥⲁϫⲓ ⲉⲧⲁⲩⲥⲉⲙⲛⲏⲧϥ ⲛⲉⲙ ⲛⲟⲩⲉⲣⲏⲟⲩ. Ⲛⲑⲟⲕ ⲅⲁⲣ ⲡⲉ ⲫⲙⲟⲩⲣ ⲛⲧⲉ ϯⲁⲅⲁⲡⲏ ⲛⲉⲙ ⲡⲓⲣⲉϥⲟⲩⲁϩⲥⲁϩⲛⲓ ⲛⲧⲉ ⲡⲓⲛⲟⲙⲟⲥ ⲛⲧⲉ ⲡⲟⲩϫⲓⲛϩⲱⲧⲡ ⲉⲁⲕⲉⲣ ϯⲙⲉⲧⲟⲩⲁⲓ ϣⲱⲡⲓ ϧⲉⲛ ⲡϫⲓⲛϩⲱⲧⲡ ⲙⲡⲓⲥⲛⲁⲩ ⲉⲃⲟⲗϩⲓⲧⲉⲛ ⲡⲉⲕⲥⲁϫⲓ ⲟⲩⲛϫⲱⲕ ⲉⲃⲟⲗ Ⲡⲟⲥ ⲙⲡⲓⲟⲩⲁϩⲥⲁϩⲛⲓ ⲛⲧⲉ ⲡⲉⲕⲙⲟⲛⲟⲅⲉⲛⲏⲥ ⲛϣⲏⲣⲓ Ⲓⲏⲥ Ⲡⲭⲥ ⲡⲉⲛϭⲟⲓⲥ ⲫⲁⲓ ⲉⲧⲉ ⲉⲃⲟⲗϩⲓⲧⲟⲧϥ ⲉⲣⲉ ⲡⲓⲱⲟⲩ ⲛⲉⲙ ⲡⲓⲧⲁⲓⲟ ⲛⲉⲙ ⲡⲓⲁⲙⲁϩⲓ ⲛⲉⲙ ϯⲡⲣⲟⲥⲕⲩⲛⲏⲥⲓⲥ ⲉⲣⲡⲣⲉⲡⲓ ⲛⲁⲕ ⲛⲉⲙⲁϥ ⲛⲉⲙ ⲡⲓⲡⲛⲉⲩⲙⲁ ⲉⲑⲟⲩⲁⲃ ⲛⲣⲉϥⲧⲁⲛϧⲟ ⲟⲩⲟϩ ⲛⲟⲙⲟⲟⲩⲥⲓⲟⲥ ⲛⲉⲙⲁⲕ	أنت هو رباط المحبة و الآمر بشريعة اتصالهما إذ جعلت الألفة باتصال اثنيهما بكلمتك إذ نكمل لها يا رب بأمر ابنك الوحيد الجنس يسوع المسيح ربنا هذا الذي من قبله المجد والإكرام والعزة والسجود تليق بك معه مع الروح القدس المحيي المساوي لك الآن وكل أوان وإلى دهر الدهور آمين

	ϯⲛⲟⲩ ⲛⲉⲙ ⲛⲭⲟⲩ ⲛⲓⲃⲉⲛ ⲛⲉⲙ ϣⲁ ⲉⲛⲉϩ ⲛⲧⲉ ⲛⲓⲉⲛⲉϩ ⲧⲏⲣⲟⲩ. ⲁⲙⲏⲛ.	

Congregation *(in the muḥayyar tune)*:

May God bless us • and let us bless His Holy Name • and may His praise continuously be • always upon our mouths.	Ⲉϥⲉⲥⲙⲟⲩ ⲉⲣⲟⲛ ⲛϫⲉ Ⲫϯ ⲧⲉⲛⲛⲁⲥⲙⲟⲩ ⲉⲡⲉϥⲣⲁⲛ ⲉⲑⲟⲩⲁⲃ ⲛⲭⲟⲩ ⲛⲓⲃⲉⲛ ⲉⲣⲉ ⲡⲉϥⲥⲙⲟⲩ ⲛⲁϣⲱⲡⲓ ⲉϥⲙⲏⲛ ⲉⲃⲟⲗ ϧⲉⲛ ⲣⲱⲛ.	يباركنا الله و لينبارك اسمه القدوس في كل حين تسبحته دائمة في أفواهنا

Congregation *(in the Palm Sunday tune):*

Blessed is the Father and the Son • and the Holy Spirit • the perfect Trinity. • We worship him and glorify him.	Ϫⲉ ϥⲥⲙⲁⲣⲱⲟⲩⲧ ⲛϫⲉ Ⲫⲓⲱⲧ ⲛⲉⲙ ⲡϣⲏⲣⲓ ⲛⲉⲙ ⲡⲓⲡⲛⲉⲩⲙⲁ ⲉⲑⲟⲩⲁⲃ ϯⲧⲣⲓⲁⲥ ⲉⲧϫⲏⲕ ⲉⲃⲟⲗ ⲧⲉⲛⲟⲩⲱϣⲧ ⲙⲙⲟⲥ ⲧⲉⲛϯⲱⲟⲩ ⲛⲁⲥ.	مبارك الآب و الابن و الروح القدس الثالوث الكامل نسبحه و نمجده
Lord Have Mercy Lord Have Mercy Lord Have Mercy	Ⲕⲩⲣⲓⲉ ⲉⲗⲉⲏⲥⲟⲛ Ⲕⲩⲣⲓⲉ ⲉⲗⲉⲏⲥⲟⲛ Ⲕⲩⲣⲓⲉ ⲉⲗⲉⲏⲥⲟⲛ	يا رب ارحم يا رب ارحم يا رب ارحم

Congregation:

Our Father who art in heaven, hallowed be Thy name. Thy kingdom come. Thy will be done, on earth as it is in heaven. Give us this day our daily bread; and forgive us our trespasses,	Ϫⲉ ⲡⲉⲛⲓⲱⲧ ⲉⲧϧⲉⲛ ⲛⲓⲫⲏⲟⲩⲓ ⲙⲁⲣⲉϥⲧⲟⲩⲃⲟ ⲛϫⲉ ⲡⲉⲕⲣⲁⲛ ⲙⲁⲣⲥⲓ ⲛϫⲉ ⲧⲉⲕⲙⲉⲧⲟⲩⲣⲟ ⲡⲉⲧⲉϩⲛⲁⲕ ⲙⲁⲣⲉϥϣⲱⲡⲓ ⲙⲫⲣⲏϯ ϧⲉⲛ ⲧⲫⲉ ⲛⲉⲙ ϩⲓϫⲉⲛ ⲡⲓⲕⲁϩⲓ ⲡⲉⲛⲱⲓⲕ ⲛⲧⲉ ⲣⲁⲥϯ	أبانا الذي في السموات ليتقدس إسمك ليأت ملكوتك لتكن مشيئتك كما في السماء كذلك على الأرض خبزنا كفافنا أعطنا اليوم وأغفر لنا ذنوبنا كما نغفر نحن أيضاً للمذنبين

as we forgive those who trespass against us; and lead us not into temptation, but deliver us from the evil one. In Christ Jesus our Lord, for Thine is the kingdom and the power and the glory forever. Amen.	ⲙⲏⲓϥ ⲛⲁⲛ ⲙ̀ⲫⲟⲟⲩ ⲟⲩⲟϩ ⲭⲁ ⲛⲏⲉⲧⲉⲣⲟⲛ ⲛⲁⲛ ⲉⲃⲟⲗ ⲙ̀ⲫⲣⲏϯ ϩⲱⲛ ⲛ̀ⲧⲉⲛⲭⲱ ⲉⲃⲟⲗ ⲛ̀ⲛⲏⲉⲧⲉ ⲟⲩⲟⲛ ⲛ̀ⲧⲁⲛ ⲉⲣⲱⲟⲩ ⲟⲩⲟϩ ⲙ̀ⲡⲉⲣⲉⲛⲧⲉⲛ ⲉϧⲟⲩⲛ ⲉ̀ⲡⲓⲣⲁⲥⲙⲟⲥ ⲁⲗⲗⲁ ⲛⲁϩⲙⲉⲛ ⲉⲃⲟⲗϩⲁ ⲡⲓⲡⲉⲧϩⲱⲟⲩ ϧⲉⲛ Ⲡⲭⲥ Ⲓⲏⲥ ⲡⲉⲛϬⲟⲓⲥ ϫⲉ ⲑⲱⲕ ⲧⲉ ϯⲙⲉⲧⲟⲩⲣⲟ ⲛⲉⲙ ϯϫⲟⲙ ⲛⲉⲙ ⲡⲓⲱⲟⲩ ϣⲁ ⲉⲛⲉϩ ⲁⲙⲏⲛ	إلينا ولا تدخلنا في تجربة لكن نجنا من الشرير بالمسيح يسوع ربنا لأن لك الملك والقوة والمجد إلى الأبد آمين

The Absolutions

Priest *(inaudibly)*:

Yes, O Lord, the Lord who have given us authority to tread on serpents and scorpions and upon all the power of the enemy, crush his heads beneath our feet speedily and scatter before us his every design of wickedness against us. For You are King of us all, O Christ our God, and unto You we send up the glory, the honor, and the worship with Your good Father and the Holy Spirit, the Giver of Life, who is of one essence with You, now and at all times and unto	Ⲥⲉ Ⲡϭⲟⲓⲥ Ⲡϭⲟⲓⲥ ⲫⲏⲉⲧⲁϥϯ ⲙ̀ⲡⲓⲉⲣϣⲓϣⲓ ⲛⲁⲛ ⲉϩⲱⲙⲓ ⲉϫⲉⲛ ⲛⲓϩⲟϥ ⲛⲉⲙ ⲛⲓϭⲗⲏ ⲛⲉⲙ ⲉϫⲉⲛ ϯϫⲟⲙ ⲧⲏⲣⲥ ⲛ̀ⲧⲉ ⲡⲓϫⲁϫⲓ ϧⲟⲙϧⲉⲙ ⲛ̀ⲛⲉϥⲁ̀ⲫⲏⲟⲩⲓ ⲥⲁⲡⲉⲥⲏⲧ ⲛ̀ⲛⲉⲛϭⲁⲗⲁⲩϫ ⲛ̀ⲭⲱⲗⲉⲙ ⲟⲩⲟϩ ϫⲱⲣ ⲉⲃⲟⲗϩⲁⲣⲟⲛ ⲛ̀ⲧⲉϥⲉ̀ⲡⲓⲛⲟⲓⲁ ⲧⲏⲣⲥ ⲙ̀ⲙⲉⲧⲣⲉϥⲉⲣⲡⲉⲧϩⲱⲟⲩ ⲉⲧⲧⲟⲩⲃⲏⲛ ϫⲉ ⲛ̀ⲑⲟⲕ ⲅⲁⲣ ⲡⲉ ⲡⲉⲛⲟⲩⲣⲟ ⲧⲏⲣⲉⲛ Ⲡⲭⲥ ⲡⲉⲛⲛⲟⲩϯ ⲟⲩⲟϩ ⲛ̀ⲑⲟⲕ ⲡⲉⲧⲉⲛⲟⲩⲱⲣⲡ ⲛⲁⲕ ⲉ̀ⲡϣⲱⲓ ⲙ̀ⲡⲓⲱⲟⲩ ⲛⲉⲙ ⲡⲓⲧⲁⲓⲟ ⲛⲉⲙ ϯⲡⲣⲟⲥⲕⲩⲛⲏⲥⲓⲥ ⲛⲉⲙ ⲡⲉⲕⲓⲱⲧ ⲛ̀ⲁⲅⲁⲑⲟⲥ ⲛⲉⲙ	نعم يا رب يا رب الذي أعطانا السلطان أن ندوس الحيات والعقارب وكل قوة العدو إسحق رؤوسه تحت أقدامنا سريعاً وبدد عنا كل معقولاته الشريرة المقاومة لنا لأنك أنت هو ملكنا كلنا أيها المسيح إلهنا وأنت الذي نرسل لك إلى فوق المجد والإكرام والسجود مع أبيك الصالح والروح القدس المحيي المساوي لك الآن وكل أوان وإلى دهر الدهور كلها آمين

| the age of all ages. Amen. | Ⲡⲓⲡⲛⲉⲩⲙⲁ ⲉⲑⲟⲩⲁⲃ ⲛⲣⲉϥⲧⲁⲛϧⲟ ⲟⲩⲟϩ ⲛⲟⲙⲟⲟⲩⲥⲓⲟⲥ ⲛⲉⲙⲁⲕ ϯⲛⲟⲩ ⲛⲉⲙ ⲛⲥⲏⲟⲩ ⲛⲓⲃⲉⲛ ⲛⲉⲙ ϣⲁ ⲉⲛⲉϩ ⲛⲧⲉ ⲛⲓⲉⲛⲉϩ ⲧⲏⲣⲟⲩ ⲁⲙⲏⲛ | |

Deacon:

| Bow your heads to the Lord. | Ⲧⲁⲥ ⲕⲉⲫⲁⲗⲁⲥ ⲩⲙⲱⲛ ⲧⲱ ⲕⲩⲣⲓⲱ ⲕⲗⲓⲛⲁⲧⲉ | إحنوا رؤوسكم للرب |

Congregation:

| Before You, O Lord. | Ⲉⲛⲱⲡⲓⲟⲛ ⲥⲟⲩ Ⲕⲩⲣⲓⲉ | أمامك يا رب. |

Priest *(inaudibly)*:

| You, O Lord, who bowed the heavens, You descended and became man for the salvation of the mankind. You are He who sits upon the Cherubim and the Seraphim, and beholds those who are lowly. You also now, O our Master, are He to whom we lift up the eyes of our heart; the Lord who forgives our iniquities and saves our souls from corruption. We worship Your ineffable compassion, and we ask You to give us Your | Ⲛⲑⲟⲕ Ⲡϭⲟⲓⲥ ⲫⲏⲉⲧⲁⲕⲣⲉⲕ ⲛⲓⲫⲏⲟⲩⲓ ⲁⲕⲓ ⲉⲡⲉⲥⲏⲧ ⲟⲩⲟϩ ⲁⲕⲉⲣⲣⲱⲙⲓ ⲉⲑⲃⲉ ⲡⲟⲩϫⲁⲓ ⲙⲡⲅⲉⲛⲟⲥ ⲛⲛⲓⲣⲱⲙⲓ. Ⲛⲑⲟⲕ ⲡⲉ ⲫⲏⲉⲧϩⲉⲙⲥⲓ ϩⲓϫⲉⲛ ⲛⲓⲭⲉⲣⲟⲩⲃⲓⲙ ⲛⲉⲙ ⲛⲓⲥⲉⲣⲁⲫⲓⲙ ⲟⲩⲟϩ ⲉⲧϫⲟⲩϣⲧ ⲉϫⲉⲛ ⲛⲏⲉⲑⲑⲉⲃⲓⲏⲟⲩⲧ. Ⲛⲑⲟⲕ ⲟⲛ ϯⲛⲟⲩ ⲡⲉⲛⲛⲏⲃ ⲛⲧⲉⲛϥⲁⲓ ⲛⲛⲓⲃⲁⲗ ⲛⲧⲉ ⲡⲉⲛϩⲏⲧ ⲉⲡϣⲱⲓ ϩⲁⲣⲟⲕ Ⲡϭⲟⲓⲥ ⲫⲏⲉⲧⲭⲱ ⲉⲃⲟⲗ ⲛⲛⲉⲛⲁⲛⲟⲙⲓⲁ ⲟⲩⲟϩ ⲉⲧⲥⲱϯ ⲛⲛⲉⲛⲯⲩⲭⲏ ⲉⲃⲟⲗϧⲉⲛ ⲡⲧⲁⲕⲟ. | أنت يا رب الذي طأطأت السموات ونزلت وتأنست من أجل خلاص جنس البشر أنت هو الجالس على الشاروبيم والسيرافيم والناظر إلى المتواضعين أنت أيضاً الآن يا سيدنا الذي نرفع أعين قلوبنا إليك أيها الرب الغافر آثامنا ومخلص نفوسنا من الفساد نسجد لتعطفك الذي لا ينطق به ونسألك أن تعطينا سلامك لأنك أعطيتنا كل شئ اقتننا لك يا الله مخلصنا لأننا لا نعرف أحداً سواك إسمك القدوس هو الذي نقوله ردنا يا الله إلى |

peace, for You have given us all things. Acquire us to Yourself, O God our Savior, for we know none other but You. Your holy name we utter. Turn us, O God, unto the fear of You and the desire of You. Be pleased that we may abide in the enjoyment of Your good things. And those who have bowed their heads beneath Your hand, exalt them in [their] ways of life and adorn them with virtues. And may we all be worthy of Your kingdom in the heavens, through the good will of God, Your good Father, with whom You are blessed with the Holy Spirit, the Giver of Life, who is of one essence with You, now and at all times and unto the age of all ages. Amen.	Ⲧⲉⲛⲟⲩⲱϣⲧ ⲛⲧⲉⲕⲙⲉⲧϣⲁⲛⲟⲙⲁϣⲧ ⲛⲁⲧϣⲥⲁϫⲓ ⲙⲙⲟⲥ ⲟⲩⲟϩ ⲧⲉⲛϯϩⲟ ⲉⲣⲟⲕ ⲉⲑⲣⲉⲕϯ ⲛⲁⲛ ⲛⲧⲉⲕϩⲓⲣⲏⲛⲏ ϩⲱⲃ ⲅⲁⲣ ⲛⲓⲃⲉⲛ ⲁⲕⲧⲁⲛⲓⲧⲟⲩ ⲛⲁⲛ ϫⲫⲟⲛ ⲛⲁⲕ Ⲫϯ ⲡⲉⲛⲥⲱⲧⲏⲣ ϫⲉ ⲧⲉⲛⲥⲱⲟⲩⲛ ⲛⲕⲉⲟⲩⲁⲓ ⲁⲛ ⲉⲃⲏⲗ ⲉⲣⲟⲕ ⲡⲉⲕⲣⲁⲛ ⲉⲑⲟⲩⲁⲃ ⲡⲉⲧⲉⲛϫⲱ ⲙⲙⲟϥ. Ⲙⲁⲧⲁⲥⲑⲟⲛ Ⲫϯ ⲉϧⲟⲩⲛ ⲉⲧⲉⲕϩⲟϯ ⲛⲉⲙ ⲡⲉⲕϭⲓϣϣⲱⲟⲩ ⲙⲁⲙⲁϯ ⲉⲑⲣⲉⲛϣⲱⲡⲓ ϧⲉⲛ ⲧⲁⲡⲟⲗⲁⲩⲥⲓⲥ ⲛⲧⲉ ⲛⲉⲕⲁⲅⲁⲑⲟⲛ ⲟⲩⲟϩ ⲛⲏⲉⲧⲁⲩⲣⲓⲕⲓ ⲛⲛⲟⲩⲁⲫⲏⲟⲩⲓ ϧⲁ ⲧⲉⲕϫⲓϫ ϭⲁⲥⲟⲩ ϧⲉⲛ ⲛⲓⲡⲟⲗⲏⲧⲓⲁ ⲥⲉⲗⲥⲱⲗⲟⲩ ϧⲉⲛ ⲛⲓⲁⲣⲉⲧⲏ ⲟⲩⲟϩ ⲙⲁⲣⲉⲛⲉⲣⲡⲉⲙⲡϣⲁ ⲧⲏⲣⲉⲛ ⲛⲧⲉⲕⲙⲉⲧⲟⲩⲣⲟ ⲉⲧϧⲉⲛ ⲛⲓⲫⲏⲟⲩⲓ ϧⲉⲛ ⲡϯⲙⲁϯ ⲙⲪϯ ⲡⲉⲕⲓⲱⲧ ⲛⲁⲅⲁⲑⲟⲥ ⲫⲁⲓ ⲉⲧⲉⲕⲥⲙⲁⲣⲱⲟⲩⲧ ⲛⲉⲙⲁϥ ⲛⲉⲙ Ⲡⲓⲡⲛⲉⲩⲙⲁ ⲉⲑⲟⲩⲁⲃ ⲛⲣⲉϥⲧⲁⲛϧⲟ ⲟⲩⲟϩ ⲛⲟⲙⲟⲟⲩⲥⲓⲟⲥ ⲛⲉⲙⲁⲕ ϯⲛⲟⲩ ⲛⲉⲙ ⲛⲥⲏⲟⲩ ⲛⲓⲃⲉⲛ ⲛⲉⲙ ϣⲁ ⲉⲛⲉϩ ⲛⲧⲉ ⲛⲓⲉⲛⲉϩ ⲧⲏⲣⲟⲩ ⲁⲙⲏⲛ	خوفك وشوقك سر أن نكون في تمتع خيراتك والذين أحنوا رؤوسهم تحت يدك إرفعهم في السيرة ذينهم بالفضائل ولنستحق كلنا ملكوتك الذي في السموات بمسرة أبيك الصالح هذا الذي أنت مبارك معه مع الروح القدس المحيي المساوي لك الآن وكل أوان وإلى دهر الدهور كلها آمين

Deacon:

Let us attend in the fear of God. Amen.	Προσχωμεν Θεου μετα φοβου αμην	أنصتوا بخوف الله آمين

Priest:

Peace be with all.	Ιρηνη πασι	السلام لجميعكم

Congregation:

And with your spirit.	Κε τω πνευματι σου	ولروحك أيضاً.

Priest *(with the cross on the groom's head)*:

O Master, Lord Jesus Christ, the only-begotten Son and Logos of God the Father, who has broken every bond of our sins through His saving, life-giving sufferings. Who breathed into the face of His holy Disciples and saintly Apostles, and said to them, "Receive the Holy Spirit. If you forgive the sins of any, they are forgiven. If you retain the sins of any, they are retained." You also now, O our Master, have given grace through Your holy Apostles to those who for a time labor in the priesthood in Your holy	ⲫⲛⲏⲃ Ⲡϭⲟⲓⲥ Ⲓⲏⲥⲟⲩⲥ Ⲡⲓⲭⲣⲓⲥⲧⲟⲥ ⲡⲓⲙⲟⲛⲟⲅⲉⲛⲏⲥ ⲛϣⲏⲣⲓ ⲟⲩⲟϩ ⲛⲗⲟⲅⲟⲥ ⲛⲧⲉ Ⲫϯ Ⲫⲓⲱⲧ ⲫⲏⲉⲧⲁϥⲥⲱⲗⲡ ⲛⲥⲛⲁⲩϩ ⲛⲓⲃⲉⲛ ⲛⲧⲉ ⲛⲉⲛⲛⲟⲃⲓ ϩⲓⲧⲉⲛ ⲛⲉϥⲙⲕⲁⲩϩ ⲛⲟⲩϫⲁⲓ ⲛⲣⲉϥⲧⲁⲛϧⲟ ⲫⲏⲉⲧⲁϥⲛⲓϥⲓ ⲉϧⲟⲩⲛ ϧⲉⲛ ⲡϩⲟ ⲛⲛⲉϥⲁⲅⲓⲟⲥ ⲙⲙⲁⲑⲏⲧⲏⲥ ⲟⲩⲟϩ ⲛⲁⲡⲟⲥⲧⲟⲗⲟⲥ ⲉⲑⲟⲩⲁⲃ ⲉⲁϥϫⲟⲥ ⲛⲱⲟⲩ ϫⲉ ϭⲓ ⲛⲱⲧⲉⲛ ⲛⲟⲩⲡⲛⲉⲩⲙⲁ ⲉϥⲟⲩⲁⲃ ⲛⲏⲉⲧⲉⲧⲉⲛⲛⲁⲭⲁ ⲛⲟⲩⲛⲟⲃⲓ ⲛⲱⲟⲩ ⲉⲃⲟⲗ ⲥⲉⲭⲏ ⲛⲱⲟⲩ ⲉⲃⲟⲗ ⲟⲩⲟϩ ⲛⲏⲉⲧⲉⲧⲉⲛⲛⲁⲁⲙⲟⲛⲓ ⲙⲙⲱⲟⲩ ⲥⲉⲛⲁⲁⲙⲟⲛⲓ	أيها السيد الرب يسوع المسيح الإبن الوحيد الجنس وكلمة الله الآب الذي قطع كل رباطات خطايانا من قبل آلامه المخلصة المحيية الذي نفخ في وجه تلاميذه القديسين ورسله الأطهار وقال لهم إقبلوا الروح القدس من غفرتم لهم خطاياهم غفرت لهم ومن أمسكتموها عليهم أمسكت أنت الآن أيضاً يا سيدنا من قبل رسلك الأطهار أنعمت للذين يعملون في الكهنوت كل زمان في كنيستك المقدسة أن يغفروا الخطايا على الأرض ويربطوا ويحلوا كل رباطات الظلم

Church to forgive sin upon the earth and to bind and to loose every bond of iniquity. Now also we ask and entreat Your goodness, O Lover of Mankind, for Your servants, my fathers and my brothers, and my weakness those who bow their heads before Your holy glory. Dispense to us Your mercy and loose every bond of our sins, and if we have committed any sin against You knowingly or unknowingly, or through anguish of heart, or in deed or word, or from faintheartedness, O Master who know the weakness of men, as a Good One and Lover of Mankind, O God, grant us the forgiveness of our sins. Bless us, purify us, absolve us, and all Your people. Fill us with Your fear and straighten us for Your holy good will, for You are our God, and the glory, the honor, the dominion, and the worship are due unto You, with Your good Father and the Holy Spirit, the Giver of Life, who is of one essence with You, now and at all	ⲙ̅ⲙⲱⲟⲩ. Ⲛ̅ⲑⲟⲕ ⲟⲛ ϯⲛⲟⲩ ⲡⲉⲛⲛⲏⲃ ϩⲓⲧⲉⲛ ⲛⲉⲕⲁⲡⲟⲥⲧⲟⲗⲟⲥ ⲉⲑⲟⲩⲁⲃ ⲁⲕⲉⲣϩⲙⲟⲧ ⲛ̅ⲛⲏⲉⲧⲉⲣϩⲱⲃ ϧⲉⲛ ⲟⲩⲙⲉⲧⲟⲩⲏⲃ ⲕⲁⲧⲁ ⲥⲏⲟⲩ ϧⲉⲛ ⲧⲉⲕⲉⲕⲕⲗⲏⲥⲓⲁ ⲉⲑⲟⲩⲁⲃ ⲉⲭⲁ ⲛⲟⲃⲓ ⲉⲃⲟⲗ ϩⲓϫⲉⲛ ⲡⲓⲕⲁϩⲓ ⲟⲩⲟϩ ⲉⲥⲱⲛϩ ⲟⲩⲟϩ ⲉⲃⲱⲗ ⲉⲃⲟⲗ ⲛ̅ⲥⲛⲁⲩϩ ⲛⲓⲃⲉⲛ ⲛ̅ⲧⲉ ϯⲁⲇⲓⲕⲓⲁ ϯⲛⲟⲩ ⲟⲛ ⲧⲉⲛϯϩⲟ ⲟⲩⲟϩ ⲧⲉⲛⲧⲱⲃϩ ⲛ̅ⲧⲉⲕⲙⲉⲧⲁⲅⲁⲑⲟⲥ ⲡⲓⲙⲁⲓⲣⲱⲙⲓ ⲉϩⲣⲏⲓ ⲉϫⲉⲛ ⲛⲉⲕⲉⲃⲓⲁⲓⲕ ⲛⲁⲓⲟϯ ⲛⲉⲙ ⲛⲁⲥⲛⲏⲟⲩ ⲛⲉⲙ ⲧⲁⲙⲉⲧϫⲱⲃ ⲛⲁⲓ ⲉⲧⲕⲱⲗϫ ⲛ̅ⲛⲟⲩⲁⲫⲏⲟⲩⲓ ⲙ̅ⲡⲉⲙⲑⲟ ⲙ̅ⲡⲉⲕⲱⲟⲩ ⲉⲑⲟⲩⲁⲃ ⲥⲁϩⲛⲓ ⲛⲁⲛ ⲙ̅ⲡⲉⲕⲛⲁⲓ ⲟⲩⲟϩ ⲥⲱⲗⲡ ⲛ̅ⲥⲛⲁⲩϩ ⲛⲓⲃⲉⲛ ⲛ̅ⲧⲉ ⲛⲉⲛⲛⲟⲃⲓ ⲓⲥϫⲉ ⲇⲉ ⲁⲛⲉⲣϩⲗⲓ ⲛ̅ⲛⲟⲃⲓ ⲉⲣⲟⲕ ϧⲉⲛ ⲟⲩⲉⲙⲓ ⲓⲉ ϧⲉⲛ ⲟⲩⲙⲉⲧⲁⲧⲉⲙⲓ ⲓⲉ ϧⲉⲛ ⲟⲩⲙⲉⲧϣⲗⲁϩ ⲛ̅ϩⲏⲧ ⲓⲧⲉ ϧⲉⲛ ⲡϩⲱⲃ ⲓⲧⲉ ϧⲉⲛ ⲡⲥⲁϫⲓ ⲓⲧⲉ ⲉⲃⲟⲗϧⲉⲛ ⲟⲩⲙⲉⲧⲕⲟⲩϫⲓ ⲛ̅ϩⲏⲧ ⲛ̅ⲑⲟⲕ ⲫⲛⲏⲃ ⲫⲏⲉⲧⲥⲱⲟⲩⲛ ⲛ̅ⲑⲙⲉⲧⲁⲥⲑⲉⲛⲏⲥ ⲛ̅ⲧⲉ ⲛⲓⲣⲱⲙⲓ ϩⲱⲥ ⲁⲅⲁⲑⲟⲥ ⲟⲩⲟϩ ⲙ̅ⲙⲁⲓⲣⲱⲙⲓ Ⲫϯ ⲁⲣⲓⲭⲁⲣⲓⲍⲉⲥⲑⲉ ⲛⲁⲛ ⲙ̅ⲡⲭⲱ ⲉⲃⲟⲗ ⲛ̅ⲧⲉ ⲛⲉⲛⲛⲟⲃⲓ ⲥⲙⲟⲩ ⲉⲣⲟⲛ ⲙⲁⲧⲟⲩⲃⲟⲛ ⲁⲣⲓⲧⲉⲛ	الآن أيضاً نسأل ونطلب من صلاحك يا محب البشر عن عبيدك أبائي وأخوتي وضعفي هؤلاء المنحنين برؤوسهم أمام مجدك المقدس إرزقنا رحمتك وأقطع كل رباطات خطايانا وإن كنا أخطأنا إليك في شيء بعلم أو بغير علم أو بجزع القلب أو بالفعل أو بالقول أو بصغر القلب فأنت أيها السيد العارف بضعف البشر كصالح ومحب البشر اللهُمَّ أنعم لنا بغفران خطايانا باركنا طهرنا حاللنا وحال سائر شعبك إملأنا من خوفك وقومنا إلى إرادتك المقدسة الصالحة لأنك أنت إلهنا والمجد والكرامة والعز والسجود تليق بك مع أبيك الصالح والروح القدس المحيي المساوي لك الآن وكل أوان وإلى دهر الدهور آمين

times and unto the age of all ages. Amen.	ⲚⲢⲈⲘϨⲈ ⲚⲈⲘ ⲠⲈⲔⲖⲀⲞⲤ ⲦⲎⲢϤ ⲚⲢⲈⲘϨⲈ ⲘⲀϨⲦⲈⲚ ⲈⲂⲞⲖϨⲈⲚ ⲦⲈⲔϨⲞϮ ⲞⲨⲞϨ ⲤⲞⲨⲦⲰⲚⲈⲚ ⲈϨⲞⲨⲚ ⲈⲠⲈⲔⲞⲨⲰϢ ⲈⲐⲞⲨⲀⲂ ⲚⲀⲄⲀⲐⲞⲚ. ⲆⲈ ⲚⲐⲞⲔ ⲄⲀⲢ ⲠⲈ ⲠⲈⲚⲚⲞⲨϮ ⲈⲢⲈ ⲠⲰⲞⲨ ⲚⲈⲘ ⲠⲒⲦⲀⲒⲞ ⲚⲈⲘ ⲠⲒⲀⲘⲀϨⲒ ⲚⲈⲘ ϮⲠⲢⲞⲤⲔⲨⲚⲎⲤⲒⲤ ⲈⲢⲠⲢⲈⲠⲒ ⲚⲀⲔ ⲚⲈⲘ ⲠⲈⲔⲒⲰⲦ ⲚⲀⲄⲀⲐⲞⲤ ⲚⲈⲘ ⲠⲒⲠⲚⲈⲨⲘⲀ ⲈⲐⲞⲨⲀⲂ ⲚⲢⲈϤⲦⲀⲚϨⲞ ⲞⲨⲞϨ ⲚⲞⲘⲞⲞⲨⲤⲒⲞⲤ ⲚⲈⲘⲀⲔ ϮⲚⲞⲨ ⲚⲈⲘ ⲚⲤⲎⲞⲨ ⲚⲒⲂⲈⲚ ⲚⲈⲘ ϢⲀ ⲈⲚⲈϨ ⲚⲦⲈ ⲚⲒⲈⲚⲈϨ ⲦⲎⲢⲞⲨ ⲀⲘⲎⲚ	

Congregation:

Lord Have Mercy	Ⲕⲩⲣⲓⲉ ⲉⲗⲉⲏⲥⲟⲛ	يا رب ارحم
Lord Have Mercy	Ⲕⲩⲣⲓⲉ ⲉⲗⲉⲏⲥⲟⲛ	يا رب ارحم
Lord Have Mercy	Ⲕⲩⲣⲓⲉ ⲉⲗⲉⲏⲥⲟⲛ	يا رب ارحم

The Prayer of the Vestment

Priest *(said over the vestment)*:

O Master, Lord Jesus Christ, our God, who ornamented the sky with the stars and adorned the earth with the splendor of the many different kinds of fruitful plants, who granted humanity the heavenly things and	ⲪⲚⲎⲂ Ⲡⲟⲥ Ⲓⲏⲥ Ⲡⲭⲥ ⲠⲈⲚⲚⲞⲨϮ ⲪⲎⲈⲦⲀϤⲤⲞⲖⲤⲈⲖ ⲚⲦⲪⲈ ϨⲈⲚ ϨⲀⲚⲤⲒⲞⲨ ⲀϤϬⲰⲢⲠ ⲘⲠⲒⲔⲀϨⲒ ϨⲒⲦⲈⲚ ⲐⲘⲈⲦⲤⲀⲒⲈ ⲚⲦⲈ ϨⲀⲚϢⲎⲢⲒ ⲚⲢⲈϤϮ ⲔⲀⲢⲠⲞⲤ ⲈⲦⲞⲒ ⲚⲞⲨⲐⲞ ⲚⲢⲎϮ	أيها السيد الرب يسوع المسيح الهنا الذي زين السماء بالنجوم و أظهر الأرض ببهاء الأزهر المثمرة ذات الأنواع الكثيرة الذي أنعم على البشرية بالسمائيات و أعطاهم راحة الأرض أنت الآن أيضا أيها الصالح

bestowed upon it rest on the earth. Now also, we ask You, O Good One, the Lover of Mankind, to bless these vestments, so that they may become for Your two servants who will wear them, through the pleasure of Your goodness, Vestments of glory and salvation, Amen. Vestments of joy and delight, Amen. Preserve them both, pure in soul, body, and spirit, Amen. That their life be healthy, peaceful, and chaste through the act of righteousness. Grant them both heavenly and earthly comfort, that they become rich through the acts of righteousness. Fill their houses and storage places with all blessings, and may they become worthy of doing Your pleasure at all times, for You are merciful, plenteous in mercy, and righteous. And to You is due glory with Your good Father, and the Holy Spirit, the Giver of Life, who is of one essence with you, now and forever and unto the age of all ages. Amen.	ⲫⲏⲉⲧⲁϥⲉⲣϩⲙⲟⲧ ⲛ̀ϯⲙⲉⲧⲣⲱⲙⲓ ⲛ̀ⲛⲁ ⲛⲓⲫⲏⲟⲩⲓ ⲁⲕϯ ⲛⲱⲟⲩ ⲛ̀ⲛⲓⲁⲡⲟⲗⲁⲩⲥⲓⲥ ⲛ̀ⲧⲉ ⲡ̀ⲕⲁϩⲓ ⲛⲑⲟⲕ ⲟⲛ ϯⲛⲟⲩ ⲡⲓⲁⲅⲁⲑⲟⲥ ⲟⲩⲟϩ ⲙ̀ⲙⲁⲓⲣⲱⲙⲓ ⲧⲉⲛϯϩⲟ ⲉⲣⲟⲕ ⲥⲙⲟⲩ ⲉⲛⲁⲓⲥⲧⲟⲗⲏ ⲛⲁⲓ ⲉⲧⲭⲏ ⲉϩⲣⲏⲓ ϩⲓⲛⲁ ⲛ̀ⲧⲟⲩϣⲱⲡⲓ ⲛ̀ⲛⲉⲕⲉⲃⲓⲁⲓⲕ ⲉⲑⲛⲁⲉⲣⲫⲟⲣⲓⲛ ⲙ̀ⲙⲱⲟⲩ ϩⲓⲧⲉⲛ ⲡ̀ϯⲙⲁϯ ⲛ̀ⲧⲉ ⲧⲉⲕⲙⲉⲧⲁⲅⲁⲑⲟⲥ ⲛ̀ϩⲁⲛⲥⲧⲟⲗⲏ ⲛ̀ⲧⲉ ⲟⲩⲱⲟⲩ ⲛⲉⲙ ⲟⲩ ⲟⲩϫⲁⲓ ϩⲁⲛⲥⲧⲟⲗⲏ ⲛ̀ⲧⲉ ⲫⲣⲁϣⲓ ⲛⲉⲙ ⲡ̀ⲑⲉⲗⲏⲗ ⲟⲩⲟϩ ⲁⲣⲉϩ ⲉⲣⲱⲟⲩ ⲉⲩⲧⲟⲩⲃⲏⲟⲩⲧ ϧⲉⲛ ⲧⲟⲩⲯⲩⲭⲏ ⲛⲉⲙ ⲡⲟⲩⲥⲱⲙⲁ ⲛⲉⲙ ⲡⲟⲩⲡⲛⲉⲩⲙⲁ. Ⲙⲁⲣⲉ ⲡⲟⲩϫⲓⲛⲱⲛϧ ϣⲱⲡⲓ ϧⲉⲛ ⲟⲩϩⲓⲣⲏⲛⲏ ⲛⲉⲙ ⲟⲩⲉⲩⲫⲣⲟⲥⲩⲛⲏ ϩⲓⲧⲉⲛ ⲧⲉⲣⲅⲁⲥⲓⲁ ⲛ̀ⲧⲉ ϯⲙⲉⲑⲙⲏⲓ. Ⲁⲣⲓϩⲙⲟⲧ ⲛⲱⲟⲩ ⲛ̀ⲧⲁⲡⲟⲗⲁⲩⲥⲓⲥ ⲛ̀ⲧⲉ ⲛⲁⲧⲫⲉ ⲛⲉⲙ ⲛⲁ ⲡ̀ⲕⲁϩⲓ. Ⲙⲁⲣⲟⲩⲉⲣⲣⲁⲙⲁⲟ ϧⲉⲛ ⲛⲓϩⲃⲏⲟⲩⲓ ⲛ̀ⲧⲉ ϯⲙⲉⲑⲙⲏⲓ ⲛⲟⲩϩⲟⲩ ⲛⲟⲩⲧⲁⲙⲓⲟⲛ ⲙⲁϩⲟⲩ ⲉⲃⲟⲗ ϧⲉⲛ ⲁⲅⲁⲑⲟⲛ ⲛⲓⲃⲉⲛ ⲙⲁⲣⲟⲩⲉⲣⲡⲉⲙⲡϣⲁ ⲉⲗⲣⲟⲩⲅⲓⲣⲓ ⲙ̀ⲡⲉⲧⲉϩⲛⲁⲕ ⲛ̀ⲥⲏⲟⲩ ⲛⲓⲃⲉⲛ ϫⲉ ⲛⲑⲟⲕ ⲟⲩⲛⲁⲏⲧ ⲛⲁϣⲉ ⲡⲉⲕⲛⲁⲓ ⲟⲩⲟϩ ⲛ̀ⲑⲙⲏⲓ ⲉⲣⲉ ⲡ̀ⲱⲟⲩ	محب البشر نسألك أن تبارك هذه الحلل الموضوعة لكي تصير لعبديك اللذين يلبسانها بمسرة صلاحك حلل المجد و الخلاص حلل الفرح و التهليل و احفظهما نقيين في النفس و الجسد و الروح لتكون حياتهما في صحة و سلام و عفاف بواسطة فعل البر هب لهما الراحة السمائية و الأرضية ليستغنيا بأفعال البر و أملأ منازلهما و مخازنهما من كل الخيرات و ليستحقا أن يعملا رضاك كل حين لأنك رحيم كثير الرحمة و بار و يليق بك المجد مع أبيك الصالح و الروح القدس المحيي المساوي لك الآن و كل أوان و الى دهر الدهور آمين

A Textual History of the Coptic Wedding Rite

| | ⲉⲣⲡⲣⲉⲡⲓ ⲛⲁⲕ ⲛⲉⲙ ⲡⲉⲕⲓⲱⲧ ⲛⲁⲅⲁⲑⲟⲥ ⲛⲉⲙ ⲡⲓⲡⲛⲉⲩⲙⲁ ⲉⲑⲟⲩⲁⲃ ⲛⲣⲉϥⲧⲁⲛϧⲟ ⲟⲩⲟϩ ⲛⲟⲙⲟⲟⲩⲥⲓⲟⲥ ⲛⲉⲙⲁⲕ ϯⲛⲟⲩ ⲛⲉⲙ ⲛⲥⲏⲟⲩ ⲛⲉⲃⲉⲛ ⲛⲉⲙ ϣⲁ ⲉⲛⲉϩ ⲁⲙⲏⲛ. | |

(The priest puts the vestment on the groom along with the girdle. He puts one ring on the groom's hand. During this the congregation sings the following hymn.)

Congregation *(in the Palm Sunday tune)*:

The spiritual garment • with which Michael is arrayed, • and the girdle of pearls • with which Michael is adorned,	ϯⲥⲧⲟⲗⲏ ⲙⲡⲛⲉⲩⲙⲁⲧⲓⲕⲟⲛ ⲁⲩϯⲥⲓⲱⲧϥ ⲙⲙⲓⲭⲁⲏⲗ ⲟⲩⲟϩ ⲡⲓϩⲱⲕ ⲙⲙⲁⲣⲅⲁⲣⲓⲧⲏⲥ ⲁⲩⲙⲏⲣ ⲙⲙⲓⲭⲁⲏⲗ ⲙⲙⲟϥ	الحلة الروحية التحف بها ميخائيل والمنطقة الجوهرية تمنطق بها ميخائيل
the raiment of chastity • has been given to this bridegroom, • and the crown of joy • has been placed upon his head.	ϯⲥⲧⲟⲗⲏ ⲛⲟⲩⲥⲱⲫⲣⲟⲥⲩⲛⲏ ⲁⲩⲧⲏⲓⲥ ⲉϫⲉⲛ ⲡⲁⲓⲡⲁⲧϣⲉⲗⲉⲧ ⲟⲩⲟϩ ⲡⲓⲭⲗⲟⲙ ⲛⲧⲉ ⲡⲑⲉⲗⲏⲗ ⲁⲩⲧⲏⲓϥ ⲉϫⲉⲛ ⲧⲉϥⲁⲫⲉ	حلة العفاف أعطيت لهذا العريس وإكليل البهجة وضع على رأسه
As it is said • by David the Psalmist, • "You have made glory and honor, • a crown for him."	ⲕⲁⲧⲁ ⲫⲣⲏϯ ⲉⲧⲁϥϫⲟⲥ ⲛϫⲉ ⲇⲁⲩⲓⲇ ⲡⲓϩⲩⲙⲛⲟⲇⲟⲥ ϫⲉ ⲟⲩⲱⲟⲩ ⲛⲉⲙ ⲟⲩⲧⲁⲓⲟ ⲁⲕⲧⲏⲓⲧⲟⲩ ⲛⲟⲩⲭⲗⲟⲙ ⲉϫⲟϥ	مثل الذي قاله داود المرتل مجداً وكرامة جعلتها تاجاً عليه
You have manifested to him • the blessing of Your kindness, • and placed upon his head • a crown of precious stone.	ⲁⲕⲉⲣϣⲟⲣⲡ ⲉⲣⲟϥ ϧⲉⲛ ⲡⲓⲥⲙⲟⲩ ⲛⲧⲉ ⲧⲉⲕⲙⲉⲧⲭⲣⲏⲥⲧⲟⲥ ⲁⲕⲭⲱ ϩⲓϫⲱϥ ⲛⲟⲩⲭⲗⲟⲙ	أدركته بركة صلاحك ووضعت على رأسه إكليلاً من حجر كريم

	ⲈⲂⲞⲖϨⲈⲚ ⲞⲨⲰⲚⲒ ⲈϤⲦⲀⲒⲎⲞⲨⲦ	
He asked You • for life O Lord • and You granted it to him • to the furthest age. Amen.	ⲀϤⲈⲢⲈⲦⲒⲚ ⲘⲘⲞⲔ ⲚⲞⲨⲰⲚϨ Ⲡⲟⲥ ⲞⲨⲞϨ ⲀⲔⲦⲎⲒϤ ⲚⲀϤ ⲪⲞⲨⲈⲒ ⲚⲦⲈ ⲠⲒⲈⲚⲈϨ ⲀⲘⲎⲚ	سألك حياة يا رب فأعطيته طول الأيام إلى أبد الآبد أمين
Blessed be the Father and the Son • and the Holy Spirit, • the perfect Trinity. • We worship Him and glorify Him.	Ⲭⲉ ϤⲤⲘⲀⲢⲰⲞⲨⲦ ⲚⲆⲈ ⲪⲒⲰⲦ ⲚⲈⲘ ⲠⲒϢⲎⲢⲒ ⲚⲈⲘ ⲠⲒⲠⲚⲈⲨⲘⲀ ⲈⲐⲞⲨⲀⲂ ϮⲦⲢⲒⲀⲤ ⲈⲦϪⲎⲔ ⲈⲂⲞⲖ ⲦⲈⲚⲞⲨⲰϢⲦ ⲘⲘⲞⲤ ⲦⲈⲚϮⲰⲞⲨ ⲚⲀⲤ	مبارك الآب و الابن و الروح القدس الثالوث الكامل نسبحه و نمجده

(If the bride has not yet arrived, they may continue The Spiritual Raiment saying all the verses in the long tune. After that, they may sing the other processional hymns until the bride arrives. If she has already arrived, the priest and deacons leave the groom in the chancel and go out to bring in the bride. The priest puts on her the white chasuble if necessary. They form a procession and bring her in while singing Come See This Bride.)

The Crowning

Come See This Bride

(in the Palm Sunday tune)

| "Come see this bride • who is adorned for the lamb. • She is engulfed in great glory", • said the son of thunder. | ⲀⲘⲞⲨ ⲚⲦⲈⲔⲚⲀⲨ ⲈⲦⲀⲒϢⲈⲖⲈⲦ ⲈⲦⲀⲨⲤⲈⲖⲤⲰⲖⲤ ⲘⲠⲒϨⲎⲂ ⲀⲤⲈⲢⲪⲞⲢⲒⲚ ⲘⲠⲀⲒⲚⲞⲨϪ ⲚⲰⲞⲨ ⲠⲈϪⲀϤ ⲚϪⲈ ⲠϢⲎⲢⲒ ⲚⲦⲈ ϨⲀⲢⲀⲂⲀⲒ | تعال أنظر هذه العروس التي زينت للحمل اشتملت بمجد عظيم كقول ابن الرعد |

John, the son of Zebedee, • cries out and says, • "This bride shines more brightly • than the stars of the morning.	Ⲓⲱⲁⲛⲛⲏⲥ ⲡϣⲏⲣⲓ ⲛⲌⲉⲃⲉⲇⲉⲟⲥ ⲉϥⲱϣ ⲉⲃⲟⲗ ⲉϥϫⲱ ⲙⲙⲟⲥ ϫⲉ ⲁⲥⲉⲣⲟⲩⲱⲓⲛⲓ ⲛϫⲉ ⲧⲁⲓϣⲉⲗⲉⲧ ⲡⲁⲣⲁ ⲡⲓⲥⲓⲟⲩ ⲛⲧⲉ ϩⲁⲛⲁⲧⲟⲩⲓ	يوحنا بن زبدي يصرخ و يقول هذه العروسة مضيئة اكثر من كوكب الصباح
This is the new Zion, • the city of our God. • The joy of all the saints • dwells within her."	Ⲉⲧⲉ ⲑⲁⲓ ⲧⲉ Ⲥⲓⲱⲛ ⲙⲃⲉⲣⲓ ⲧⲡⲟⲗⲓⲥ ⲙⲡⲉⲛⲛⲟⲩϯ ⲉⲣⲉ ⲡⲟⲩⲛⲟϥ ⲛⲧⲉ ⲛⲓⲉⲑⲟⲩⲁⲃ ⲧⲏⲣⲟⲩ ϣⲱⲡⲓ ⲛϧⲣⲏⲓ ⲛϧⲏⲧⲥ	هذه صهيون الجديدة مدينة الهنا و فرح جميع القديسين حال فيها
Blessed be the Father and the Son • and the Holy Spirit, • the perfect Trinity. • We worship Him and glorify Him.	Ϫⲉ ϥⲥⲙⲁⲣⲱⲟⲩⲧ ⲛϫⲉ Ⲫⲓⲱⲧ ⲛⲉⲙ ⲡϣⲏⲣⲓ ⲛⲉⲙ ⲡⲓⲡⲛⲉⲩⲙⲁ ⲉⲑⲟⲩⲁⲃ ϯⲧⲣⲓⲁⲥ ⲉⲧϫⲏⲕ ⲉⲃⲟⲗ ⲧⲉⲛⲟⲩⲱϣⲧ ⲙⲙⲟⲥ ⲧⲉⲛϯⲱⲟⲩ ⲛⲁⲥ	مبارك الآب و الابن و الروح القدس الثالوث الكامل نسبحه و نمجده

(When the bride reaches the foot of the chancel, the groom comes down to meet her. The priest gives the other ring to the groom. The groom offers it to the bride. She extends her hand and allows the groom to put it on her. The priest then leads them up to the chancel and puts the broad white cloth over their heads. He may also join their hands together and cover them with a small white veil. They should stand facing the sanctuary toward the East. The priest begins with Have mercy on us, the people say Our Father, the priest says the Thanksgiving Prayer. The priest recites the litany for the Pauline incense while the congregation says the Hymn of the Censer followed by We Worship. Then the Pauline Epistle is read.)

Pauline Epistle

(Ephesians 5:22 – 6:3)

Paul, the servant of our Lord Jesus Christ, called to be an apostle, appointed to the Gospel of God. A reading from the Epistle of our teacher St. Paul to the Ephesians, may his holy blessings be with us all, Amen.	Ⲡⲁⲩⲗⲟⲥ ⲫⲃⲱⲕ ⲙⲡⲉⲛϬⲟⲓⲥ Ⲓⲏⲥ Ⲡⲭⲥ ⲫⲏⲉⲧⲑⲁϩⲉⲙ ⲉⲡⲓϩⲓϣⲉⲛⲛⲟⲩϥⲓ ⲛⲧⲉ Ⲫϯ	أبولس فصل من رسالة معلمنا بولس الى أهل أفسس بركاته تكون معنا أمين
Wives, submit to your own husbands, as to the Lord. For the husband is head of the wife, as also Christ is head of the church; and He is the Savior of the body. Therefore, just as the church is subject to Christ, so let the wives be to their own husbands in everything. Husbands, love your wives, just as Christ also loved the church and gave Himself for her, that He might sanctify and cleanse her with the washing of water by the word, that He might present her to Himself a glorious church, not having spot or wrinkle or any such thing, but that she should be holy and without blemish. So husbands ought to love their own wives as their own	Ⲛⲓϩⲓⲟⲙⲓ ⲙⲁⲣⲟⲩϬⲛⲉϫⲱⲟⲩ ⲛⲛⲟⲩϩⲁⲓ ⲙⲫⲣⲏϯ ⲙⲡⲟⲥ ϫⲉ ⲡⲓⲱⲣⲱⲙⲓ ⲧⲁⲫⲉ ⲛϯⲥϩⲓⲙⲓ ⲡⲉ ⲙⲫⲣⲏϯ ⲙⲡⲭⲥ ⲉⲧⲉⲧⲁⲫⲉ ⲛϯⲉⲕⲕⲗⲏⲥⲓⲁ ⲡⲉ ⲛⲑⲟϥ ⲡⲉ ⲡⲥⲱⲧⲏⲣ ⲙⲡⲓⲥⲱⲙⲁ ⲁⲗⲗⲁ ⲙⲫⲣⲏϯ ⲉⲧⲉ ϯⲉⲕⲕⲗⲏⲥⲓⲁ ϬⲛⲟⲛⲛϪⲱⲥ ⲙⲡⲭⲥ ⲡⲁⲓⲣⲏϯ ϩⲱⲟⲩ ⲛⲓϩⲓⲟⲙⲓ ⲙⲁⲣⲟⲩϬⲛⲉϫⲱⲟⲩ ⲛⲛⲟⲩϩⲁⲓ ϧⲉⲛ ϩⲱⲃ ⲛⲓⲃⲉⲛ. Ⲛⲓⲣⲱⲙⲓ ⲁⲣⲓⲁⲅⲁⲡⲁⲛ ⲛⲛⲉⲧⲉⲛϩⲓⲟⲙⲓ ⲕⲁⲧⲁ ⲫⲣⲏϯ ⲉⲧⲁ Ⲡⲭⲥ ⲉⲣⲁⲅⲁⲡⲁⲛ ⲛϯⲉⲕⲕⲗⲏⲥⲓⲁ ⲟⲩⲟϩ ⲁϥⲧⲏⲓϥ ⲉϩⲣⲏⲓ ⲉϫⲱⲥ ϩⲓⲛⲁ ⲛⲧⲉϥⲧⲟⲩⲃⲟⲥ ⲉⲁϥⲧⲟⲩⲃⲟⲥ ϧⲉⲛ ⲡⲓⲱⲙⲥ ⲛⲧⲉ ⲡⲓⲙⲱⲟⲩ ⲛϩⲣⲏⲓ ϧⲉⲛ ⲡⲥⲁϫⲓ ϩⲓⲛⲁ ⲛⲧⲉϥⲧⲁϩⲉ ϯⲉⲕⲕⲗⲏⲥⲓⲁ ⲛⲁϥ ⲉⲣⲁⲧⲥ ⲉⲥϧⲉⲛ ⲟⲩⲱⲟⲩ ⲙⲙⲟⲛ	أيها النساء اخضعن لرجالكن كما للرب لأن الرجل هو رأس المرأة كما أن المسيح أيضا رأس الكنيسة وهو مخلص الجسد ولكن كما تخضع الكنيسة للمسيح كذلك النساء لرجالهن في كل شيئ أيها الرجال حبوا نساءكم كما أحب المسيح أيضا الكنيسة وأسلم نفسه لأجلها لكي يقدسها مطهرا إياها بغسل الماء بالكلمة لكي يحضرها لنفسه كنيسة مجيدة لا عيب فيها و لا دنس و لا شئ مثل ذلك بل تكون مقدسة وبلا عيب كذلك يجب على الرجال أن يحبوا نساءهم كأجسادهم من يحب امرأته يحب نفسه فإنه لم يبغض أحد جسده قط بل يقوته ويربيه كما الرب أيضا للكنيسة

bodies; he who loves his wife loves himself. For no one ever hated his own flesh, but nourishes and cherishes it, just as the Lord does the church. For we are members of His body, of His flesh and of His bones. "For this reason, a man shall leave his father and mother and be joined to his wife, and the two shall become one flesh." This is a great mystery, but I speak concerning Christ and the church. Nevertheless, let each one of you in particular so love his own wife as himself, and let the wife see that she respects her husband. Children, obey your parents in the Lord, for this is right. Honor your father and mother," which is the first commandment with promise: that it may be well with you and you may live long on the earth."	ⲁϭⲛⲓ ⲛϩⲏⲧⲥ ⲓⲉ ⲑⲱⲗⲉⲃ ⲓⲉ ⲕⲉ ⲉⲛⲭⲁⲓ ⲙ̀ⲫⲣⲏϯ ⲛ̀ⲛⲁⲓ ⲁⲗⲗⲁ ϩⲓⲛⲁ ⲛ̀ⲧⲉⲥϣⲱⲡⲓ ⲉⲥⲟⲩⲁⲃ ⲟⲩⲟϩ ⲉⲥⲟⲓ ⲛⲁⲑⲱⲗⲉⲃ. Ⲡⲁⲓⲣⲏϯ ϩⲱⲟⲩ ⲛⲓⲣⲱⲙⲓ ⲥⲉⲙⲡϣⲁ ⲛ̀ⲧⲟⲩⲉⲣⲁⲅⲁⲡⲁⲛ ⲛ̀ⲛⲟⲩϩⲓⲟⲙⲓ ⲙ̀ⲫⲣⲏϯ ⲛ̀ⲛⲟⲩⲥⲱⲙⲁ. Ⲫⲏ ⲅⲁⲣ ⲉⲧⲉⲣⲉⲁⲅⲁⲛ ⲛ̀ⲧⲉϥⲥϩⲓⲙⲓ ⲁϥⲉⲣⲁⲅⲁⲡⲁⲛ ⲙ̀ⲙⲟϥ ⲙ̀ⲙⲁⲩⲁⲧϥ. Ⲙ̀ⲡⲉ ϩⲗⲓ ⲅⲁⲣ ⲙⲉⲥⲧⲉ ⲧⲉϥⲥⲁⲣⲝ ⲉⲛⲉϩ ⲁⲗⲗⲁ ϣⲁϥϣⲁⲛⲟⲩϣⲥ ⲟⲩⲟϩ ϣⲁϥⲉⲣⲑⲁⲗⲡⲓⲛ ⲙ̀ⲙⲟⲥ ⲕⲁⲧⲁ ⲫⲣⲏϯ ϩⲱϥ ⲙ̀Ⲡⲭⲥ ⲉⲧⲁϥⲓⲣⲓ ⲛ̀ϯⲉⲕⲕⲗⲏⲥⲓⲁ ⲇⲉ ⲁⲛⲟⲛ ϩⲁⲛⲙⲉⲗⲟⲥ ⲛⲧⲉ ⲡⲉϥⲥⲱⲙⲁ. Ⲉⲑⲃⲉ ⲫⲁⲓ ⲉⲣⲉ ⲡⲓⲣⲱⲙⲓ ⲭⲁ ⲡⲉϥⲓⲱⲧ ⲛⲉⲙ ⲧⲉϥⲙⲁⲩ ⲛⲥⲱϥ ⲟⲩⲟϩ ⲉϥⲉⲧⲟⲙϥ ⲉⲧⲉϥⲥϩⲓⲙⲓ ⲉⲩⲉϣⲱⲡⲓ ⲙ̀ⲡⲓⲥⲛⲁⲩ ⲉⲩⲥⲁⲣⲝ ⲛ̀ⲟⲩⲱⲧ. Ⲡⲁⲓ ⲙⲩⲥⲧⲏⲣⲓⲟⲛ ⲟⲩⲛⲓϣϯ ⲡⲉ ⲁⲛⲟⲕ ⲇⲉ ϯϫⲱ ⲙ̀ⲙⲟⲥ ⲉⲠⲭⲥ ⲛⲉⲙ ϯⲉⲕⲕⲗⲏⲥⲓⲁ. Ⲡⲗⲏⲛ ⲛ̀ⲑⲱⲧⲉⲛ ϩⲱⲧⲉⲛ ⲕⲁⲧⲁ ⲫⲟⲩⲁⲓ ⲫⲟⲩⲁⲓ ⲙ̀ⲙⲱⲧⲉⲛ ⲙⲁⲣⲉϥⲉⲣⲁⲅⲁⲡⲁⲛ ⲛ̀ⲧⲉϥⲥϩⲓⲙⲓ ⲙ̀ⲡⲉϥⲣⲏϯ. Ⲧⲥϩⲓⲙⲓ ⲇⲉ ϩⲱⲥ ϩⲓⲛⲁ ⲛ̀ⲧⲉⲥⲉⲣϩⲟϯ ϧⲁⲧϩⲏ ⲙ̀ⲡⲉⲥϩⲁⲓ. Ⲛⲓϣⲏⲣⲓ ⲥⲱⲧⲉⲙ ⲛ̀ⲥⲁⲛⲉⲧⲉⲛⲓⲟϯ	لأننا أعضاء جسمه من لحمه ومن عظامه من أجل هذا يترك الرجل أباه وأمه ويلتصق بامرأته ويكون الإثنان جسدا واحدا

هذا السر عظيم ولكنني أنا أقول من نحو المسيح والكنيسة وأما الأفراد فليحب كل واحد امرأته هكذا كنفسه وأما المرأة فلتهب رجلها

أيها الأولاد أطيعوا والديكم في الرب لأن هذا حق أكرم أباك وأمك التي هي أول وصية بوعد لكي يكون لكم خير وتكونوا طوال الأعمار على الأرض |

	ϪΕΝ Ποc ϥⲁⲓ ⲅⲁⲣ ⲟⲩϩⲱⲃ ⲙⲙⲏⲓ ⲡⲉ. Ⲙⲁⲧⲁⲓⲉ ⲡⲉⲕⲓⲱⲧ ⲛⲉⲙ ⲧⲉⲕⲙⲁⲩ ⲉⲧⲉ ⲑⲁⲓ ⲧⲉ ϯⲉⲛⲧⲟⲗⲏ ⲛϩⲟⲩⲓϯ ⲉⲧϪⲉⲛ ⲡⲓⲱϣ ϩⲓⲛⲁ ⲛⲧⲉ ⲡⲓⲡⲉⲑⲛⲁⲛⲉϥ ϣⲱⲡⲓ ⲙⲙⲟⲕ ⲟⲩⲟϩ ⲛⲧⲉⲕⲉⲣ ⲟⲩⲛⲓϣϯ ⲛⲭⲣⲟⲛⲟⲥ ϩⲓϪⲉⲛ ⲡⲓⲕⲁϩⲓ.	
The grace of God the Father be with you all. Amen.	Ⲡⲓϩⲙⲟⲧ ⲅⲁⲣ ⲛⲉⲙⲱⲧⲉⲛ ⲧⲏⲣⲟⲩ. Ϫⲉ ⲁⲙⲏⲛ ⲉⲥⲉϣⲱⲡⲓ.	نعمة الله الآب تكون مع جميعكم آمين

(The congregation says The Trisagion. The priest recites the Litany of the Gospel.)

Psalm and Gospel

Reader:

A Psalm of David. Alleluia. (Psalm 19:5 & 128:3)	Ⲯⲁⲗⲙⲟⲥ ⲧⲱ Ⲇⲁⲩⲓⲇ. ⲁⲗⲗⲏⲗⲟⲩⲓⲁ.	من مزامير داود النبي بركاته تكون معنا أمين
"Which is like a bridegroom coming out of his chamber, • and rejoices like a strong man to run his race. • Your wife shall be like a fruitful vine in the very heart of your house, • your children like olive plants all around your table." Alleluia.	Ⲙ̀ⲫⲣⲏϯ ⲛⲟⲩⲡⲁⲧϣⲉⲗⲉⲧ ⲉϥⲛⲏⲟⲩ ⲉⲃⲟⲗ Ϫⲉⲛ ⲡⲉϥⲙⲁⲛϣⲉⲗⲉⲧ ⲉϥⲉⲑⲉⲗⲏⲗ ⲙⲙⲟϥ ⲙⲫⲣⲏϯ ⲛⲟⲩⲁⲫⲱϥ ⲉϥϭⲟϪⲓ ϩⲓ ⲡⲉϥⲙⲱⲓⲧ. Ⲉⲣⲉ ⲧⲉⲕⲥϩⲓⲙⲓ ⲙⲫⲣⲏϯ ⲛⲟⲩⲃⲱ ⲛⲁⲗⲟⲗⲓ ⲉⲥⲫⲟⲣⲓ ⲉⲃⲟⲗ ⲥⲁⲡⲥⲫⲓⲣ ⲛⲧⲉ ⲡⲉⲕⲏⲓ. Ⲛⲉⲕϣⲏⲣⲓ ⲙⲫⲣⲏϯ ⲛϩⲁⲛϭⲟ ⲙⲃⲉⲣⲓ ⲛⲧⲉ ϩⲁⲛϪⲱⲓⲧ ⲉⲩⲕⲱϯ	مثل العريس الخارج من خدره يتهلل مثل الجبار المسرع في طريقه إمرأتك تكون كالكرمة التي تزهر في جوانب بيتك وبنوك مثل غروس الزيتون محيطين بمائدتك هلليلونا

| | ⲉⲧⲉⲕⲧⲣⲁⲡⲉⲍⲁ. ⲁⲗⲗⲏⲗⲟⲩⲓⲁ. | |

(In the presence of a bishop)

| "Let them exalt Him in the church of His people, • and praise Him in the seat of the elders, • for He has made the family like a flock of sheep, the upright shall see and rejoice. • The Lord has sworn and will have no regret, • You are a priest forever, after the order of Melchizedek." • The Lord is at your right hand, our saintly father, the patriarch, Pope Abba (...) • and our father the bishop, Abba (...) • May the Lord keep your lives. | Ⲙⲁⲣⲟⲩⲃⲁⲥϥ ϧⲉⲛ ⲧⲉⲕⲕⲗⲏⲥⲓⲁ ⲛⲧⲉ ⲡⲉϥⲗⲁⲟⲥ ⲟⲩⲟϩ ⲙⲁⲣⲟⲩⲥⲙⲟⲩ ⲉⲣⲟϥ ϩⲓ ⲧⲕⲁⲑⲉⲇⲣⲁ ⲛⲧⲉ ⲛⲓⲡⲣⲉⲥⲃⲩⲧⲉⲣⲟⲥ ϫⲉ ⲁϥⲭⲱ ⲛⲟⲩⲙⲉⲧⲓⲱⲧ ⲙ̅ⲫⲣⲏϯ ⲛ̅ϩⲁⲛⲉⲥⲱⲟⲩ ⲉⲩⲉⲛⲁⲩ ⲛ̅ϫⲉ ⲛⲏⲉⲧⲥⲟⲩⲧⲱⲛ ⲟⲩⲟϩ ⲉⲩⲉⲟⲩⲛⲟϥ. ⲁϥⲱⲣⲕ ⲛ̅ϫⲉ Ⲡⲟⲥ ⲟⲩⲟϩ ⲛ̅ⲛⲉϥⲟⲩⲱⲙ ⲛ̅ϩⲑⲏϥ ϫⲉ ⲛ̅ⲑⲟⲕ ⲡⲉ ⲫⲟⲩⲏⲃ ϣⲁ ⲉⲛⲉϩ ⲕⲁⲧⲁ ⲧⲧⲁⲝⲓⲥ ⲙ̅Ⲙⲉⲗⲭⲓⲥⲉⲇⲉⲕ. Ⲡⲟⲥ ⲥⲁⲟⲩⲓⲛⲁⲙ ⲙ̅ⲙⲟⲕ ⲡⲉⲛⲓⲱⲧ ⲉⲑⲟⲩⲁⲃ ⲙ̅ⲡⲁⲧⲣⲓⲁⲣⲭⲏⲥ ⲡⲁⲡⲁ ⲁⲃⲃⲁ (...) ⲡⲓⲙⲁϩⲥⲛⲁⲩ ⲛⲉⲙ ⲡⲉⲛⲓⲱⲧ ⲛ̅ⲉⲡⲓⲥⲕⲟⲡⲟⲩ ⲁⲃⲃⲁ (...). Ⲡⲟⲥ ⲉϥⲉⲁⲣⲉϩ ⲉⲡⲉⲧⲉⲛⲱⲛϧ. | فليرفعوه في كنيسة شعبه وليباركوه على منابر الشيوخ لأنه جعل أبوة مثل الخراف يبصر المستقيمون ويفرحون أقسم الرب ولن يندم أنك أنت هو الكاهن إلى الأبد على طقس ملكي صادق الرب عن يمينك يا أبانا القديس البطريرك البابا المعظم الأنبا (...) الرب (...) (وأبانا الأسقف أنبا (...)) يحفظ حياتك (حياتكما) |

Congregation:

| Alleluia | ⲁⲗⲗⲏⲗⲟⲩⲓⲁ | هلليلوي |

Deacon:

| Stand in the fear of God and let us listen to the Holy Gospel. | Ⲥⲧⲁⲑⲏⲧⲉ ⲙⲉⲧⲁ ⲫⲟⲃⲟⲩ Ⲑⲉⲟ ⲁⲕⲟⲩⲥⲱⲙⲉⲛ ⲧⲟⲩ ⲁⲅⲓⲟⲩ ⲉⲩⲁⲅⲅⲉⲗⲓⲟⲩ | قفوا بخوف الله لسماع الإنجيل المقدس |

Reader:

| Blessed is He who comes in the name of the Lord of Hosts. Bless O Lord the reading of the Holy Gospel according to St. Matthew, may his holy blessings. | Ϥⲥⲙⲁⲣⲱⲟⲩⲧ ⲛ̀ϫⲉ ⲫⲏⲉⲑⲛⲏⲟⲩ ϧⲉⲛ ⲫ̀ⲣⲁⲛ ⲙ̀Ⲡ̀ϭⲟⲓⲥ ⲛ̀ⲧⲉ ⲛⲓϫⲟⲙ. Ⲕⲩⲣⲓⲉ ⲉⲩⲗⲟⲅⲏⲥⲟⲛ ⲉⲕ ⲧⲟⲩ ⲕⲁⲧⲁ Ⲙⲁⲧⲑⲉⲟⲛ ⲁⲅⲓⲟⲩ ⲉⲩⲁⲅⲅⲉⲗⲓⲟⲛ ⲧⲟ ⲁⲛⲁⲅⲛⲱⲥⲙⲁ | مبارك الآتي بإسم رب القوات يا رب بارك الفصل من الإنجيل المقدس من متى القديس |

Congregation:

| be with us all Amen. | Ⲇⲟⲝⲁ ⲥⲓ Ⲕⲩⲣⲓⲉ | المجد لك يا رب |

Reader:

| Our Lord, God, Savior, and King of us all, Jesus Christ, the Son of the Living God, to whom is due all glory | Ⲡⲉⲛϭⲟⲓⲥ ⲟⲩⲟϩ ⲡⲉⲛⲛⲟⲩϯ ⲟⲩⲟϩ ⲡⲉⲛⲥⲱⲧⲏⲣ ⲟⲩⲟϩ ⲡⲉⲛⲟⲩⲣⲟ ⲧⲏⲣⲉⲛ Ⲓⲏⲥ Ⲡⲭⲥ Ⲡ̀ϣⲏⲣⲓ ⲙ̀Ⲫϯ ⲉⲧⲟⲛϧ ⲡⲓⲱⲟⲩ ⲛⲁϥ ϣⲁ ⲉⲛⲉϩ | ربنا وإلهنا ومخلصنا وملكنا كلنا يسوع المسيح إبن الله الحي الذي له المجد دائما |

Congregation:

| forever amen | | إلى الأبد |

Reader: (*Matthew 19:1-6*)

Now it came to pass, when Jesus had finished these sayings, that He departed from Galilee and came to the region of Judea beyond the Jordan. And great multitudes followed Him, and He healed them there. The Pharisees also came to Him, testing Him, and saying to Him, "Is it lawful for a man to divorce his wife for just any reason?" And He answered and said to them, "Have you not read that He who made them at the beginning 'made them male and female,' and said, 'For this reason a man shall leave his father and mother and be joined to his wife, and the two shall become one flesh?' So then, they are no longer two but one flesh. Therefore what God has joined together, let not man separate."	Ⲟⲩⲟϩ ⲉⲧⲁ Ⲓⲏⲥ ϫⲉⲕ ⲛⲁⲓ ⲥⲁϫⲓ ⲧⲏⲣⲟⲩ ⲉⲃⲟⲗ ⲁϥⲟⲩⲱⲧⲉⲃ ⲉⲃⲟⲗ ϧⲉⲛ Ϯⲅⲁⲗⲓⲗⲉⲁ ⲁϥⲓ ⲉⲛⲓϭⲓⲏ ⲛⲧⲉ Ϯⲓⲟⲩⲇⲉⲁ ϩⲓ ⲙⲏⲣ ⲙⲡⲓⲓⲟⲣⲇⲁⲛⲏⲥ ⲁⲩⲟⲩⲁϩⲟⲩ ⲛⲥⲱϥ ⲛϫⲉ ϩⲁⲛⲛⲓϣϯ ⲙⲙⲏϣ ⲟⲩⲟϩ ⲁϥⲉⲣⲫⲁϧⲣⲓ ⲉⲣⲱⲟⲩ ⲙⲙⲁⲩ. Ⲟⲩⲟϩ ⲁⲩⲓ ϩⲁⲣⲟϥ ⲛϫⲉ ϩⲁⲛⲫⲁⲣⲓⲥⲉⲟⲥ ⲉⲩⲉⲣⲡⲓⲣⲁⲍⲓⲛ ⲙⲙⲟϥ ⲉⲩϫⲱ ⲙⲙⲟⲥ ⲛⲁϥ ϫⲉ ⲁⲛ ϣϣⲉ ⲛⲧⲉ ⲡⲓⲣⲱⲙⲓ ϩⲓ ⲧⲉϥⲥϩⲓⲙⲓ ⲉⲃⲟⲗ ϧⲉⲛ ⲛⲟⲃⲓ ⲛⲓⲃⲉⲛ. Ⲛⲑⲟϥ ⲇⲉ ⲁϥⲉⲣⲟⲩⲱ ⲡⲉϫⲁϥ ⲛⲱⲟⲩ ϫⲉ ⲙⲡⲉⲧⲉⲛⲱϣ ϫⲉ ⲓⲥϫⲉⲛ ϩⲏ ⲟⲩϩⲱⲟⲩⲧ ⲛⲉⲙ ⲟⲩⲥϩⲓⲙⲓ ⲡⲉ ⲉⲧⲁϥⲥⲟⲛⲧⲟⲩ. Ⲡⲉϫⲁϥ ⲇⲉ ϫⲉ ⲉⲑⲃⲉ ⲫⲁⲓ ⲉⲣⲉ ⲡⲓⲣⲱⲙⲓ ⲭⲁ ⲡⲉϥⲓⲱⲧ ⲛⲉⲙ ⲧⲉϥⲙⲁⲩ ⲛⲥⲱϥ ⲟⲩⲟϩ ⲉϥⲉⲧⲟⲙϥ ⲉⲧⲉϥⲥϩⲓⲙⲓ ⲟⲩⲟϩ ⲉⲩϣⲱⲡⲓ ⲙⲡⲥⲛⲁⲩ ⲉⲩⲥⲁⲣⲝ ⲛⲟⲩⲱⲧ ϩⲱⲥ ⲥⲛⲁⲩ ⲁⲛ ϫⲉ ⲁⲗⲗⲁ ⲟⲩⲥⲁⲣⲝ ⲛⲟⲩⲱⲧ ⲫⲏ ⲟⲩⲛ ⲉⲧⲁ Ⲫϯ ⲧⲟⲙϥ ⲙⲡⲉⲛⲑⲣⲉ ⲫⲣⲱⲙⲓ ⲫⲟⲣϫϥ.	ولما أكمل يسوع هذا الكلام جميعه انتقل من الجليل وجاء إلى تخوم اليهودية من عبر الأردن وتبعته جموع كثيرة فشفاهم هناك

وجاء إليه الفريسيون ليجربوه قائلين له هل يحل للرجل أن يطلق إمرأته من أجل كل سبب

فأجاب وقال لهم أما قرأتم أن من البدء خلقهما ذكرا وأنثى وقال من أجل ذلك يترك الرجل أباه وأمه ويلتصق بإمرأته ويكونا الإثنان جسدا واحدا إذا ليسا بعد اثنين بل جسد واحد فالذي جمعه الله لا يفرقه إنسان |

Congregation:

Glory be to God forever.	Ⲇⲟⲝⲁ ⲥⲓ Ⲕⲩⲣⲓⲉ	والمجد لله دائما

Gospel Response

Those attuned together • by the Holy Spirit • as a stringed instrument, • always blessing God	Ⲛⲁⲓ ⲉⲧⲁⲩⲥⲟⲧⲡⲟⲩ ⲉⲩⲥⲟⲡ ⲛϫⲉ Ⲡⲓⲡⲛⲉⲩⲙⲁ Ⲉⲑⲟⲩⲁⲃ ⲙ̅ⲫⲣⲏϯ ⲛⲟⲩⲕⲩⲑⲁⲣⲁ ⲉⲩⲥⲙⲟⲩ ⲉⲪⲛⲟⲩϯ ⲛ̅ⲥⲏⲟⲩ ⲛⲓⲃⲉⲛ	هؤلاء الذين ألفهم الروح القدس معا مثل قيثارة مسبحين الله كل حين
with psalms and hymns, • and spiritual songs, • by day and by night, • with an incessant heart.	ϧⲉⲛ ϩⲁⲛⲯⲁⲗⲙⲟⲥ ⲛⲉⲙ ϩⲁⲛϩⲱⲥ ⲛⲉⲙ ϩⲁⲛϩⲱⲇⲏ ⲙ̅ⲡⲛⲉⲩⲙⲁⲧⲓⲕⲟⲛ ⲙ̅ⲡⲓⲉϩⲟⲟⲩ ⲛⲉⲙ ⲡⲓⲉϫⲱⲣϩ ϧⲉⲛ ⲟⲩϩⲏⲧ ⲛⲁⲧⲭⲁⲣⲱϥ	بمزامير وتسابيح وترانيم روحية النهار والليل بقلب لا يفتر

The Supplications

Priest *(facing East)*:

O Lord God the Pantocrator, who is in heaven, the Lord of our forefathers, we ask You O Lord to hear us and have mercy on us.	Ⲡⲟⲥ Ⲫϯ ⲡⲓⲡⲁⲛⲧⲟⲕⲣⲁⲧⲱⲣ ⲫⲏⲉⲧ ϧⲉⲛ ⲧⲫⲉ Ⲫϯ ⲛ̅ⲧⲉ ⲛⲉⲛⲓⲟϯ ⲧⲉⲛⲧⲱⲃϩ ⲙ̅ⲙⲟⲕ Ⲡⲟⲥ ⲥⲱⲧⲉⲙ ⲉⲣⲟⲛ ⲟⲩⲟϩ ⲛⲁⲓ ⲛⲁⲛ.	أيها الرب الإله ضابط الكل الكائن في السماء إله آبائنا نطلب إليك أن تسمعنا وترحمنا
O You who created the heaven, the earth, and the sea, and everything therein, and ornamented them with Your wisdom, we ask You, O Lord, to hear us and have mercy on us.	Ⲫⲏⲉⲧⲁϥⲑⲁⲙⲓⲟ ⲛ̅ⲧⲫⲉ ⲛⲉⲙ ⲡⲕⲁϩⲓ ⲛⲉⲙ ⲫⲓⲟⲙ ⲛⲉⲙ ϩⲱⲃ ⲛⲓⲃⲉⲛ ⲉⲧⲉ ⲛ̅ϧⲏⲧⲟⲩ ⲟⲩⲟϩ ⲁⲕⲥⲉⲗⲥⲱⲗⲟⲩ ϧⲉⲛ ⲧⲉⲕⲥⲟⲫⲓⲁ ⲧⲉⲛⲧⲱⲃϩ ⲙ̅ⲙⲟⲕ Ⲡⲟⲥ ⲥⲱⲧⲉⲙ ⲉⲣⲟⲛ ⲟⲩⲟϩ ⲛⲁⲓ ⲛⲁⲛ.	يا الذي خلق السماء والأرض والبحر وكل ما فيها وزينتها بحكمتك نطلب إليك يا رب أن تسمعنا وترحمنا

O You who made man in His image, after His likeness, and put him in the paradise of joy, we ask You O Lord to hear us and have mercy on us.	Ⲫⲏ ⲉⲧⲁϥⲑⲁⲙⲓⲟ ⲙⲡⲓⲣⲱⲙⲓ ⲕⲁⲧⲁ ⲡⲉϥⲓⲛⲓ ⲛⲉⲙ ⲧⲉϥϩⲓⲕⲱⲛ ⲟⲩⲟϩ ⲁϥⲭⲁϥ ϧⲉⲛ ⲡⲓⲡⲁⲣⲁⲇⲓⲥⲟⲥ ⲛⲧⲉ ⲡⲟⲩⲛⲟϥ ⲧⲉⲛⲧⲱⲃϩ ⲙⲙⲟⲕ Ⲡⲟⲥ ⲥⲱⲧⲉⲙ ⲉⲣⲟⲛ ⲟⲩⲟϩ ⲛⲁⲓ ⲛⲁⲛ.	يا من صنع الإنسان على صورته ومثاله وجعله في فردوس النعيم نسألك يا رب أن تستجيب لنا وترحمنا
O You who created woman from Adam's side and gave her to him as a helper fit for him, we ask You to hear us and have mercy on us.	Ⲫⲏ ⲉⲧⲁϥⲥⲱⲛⲧ ⲛ̀ⲧϩⲓⲙⲓ ⲉⲃⲟⲗ ϧⲉⲛ ⲡⲓⲥⲫⲓⲣ ⲛⲁⲇⲁⲙ ⲟⲩⲟϩ ⲁϥⲧⲏⲓⲥ ⲛⲁϥ ⲙⲃⲟⲏⲑⲟⲥ ⲕⲁⲧⲁ ⲣⲟϥ ⲧⲉⲛⲧⲱⲃϩ ⲙⲙⲟⲕ Ⲡⲟⲥ ⲥⲱⲧⲉⲙ ⲉⲣⲟⲛ ⲟⲩⲟϩ ⲛⲁⲓ ⲛⲁⲛ.	يا من خلق المرأة من جنب آدم وأعطاها له معينة نظيره نطلب إليك يا رب أن تسمعنا وترحمنا
O You who blessed Abraham and Sarah, and made her a wife for him, and granted him the title of Head of all Patriarchs, we ask You to hear us and have mercy on us.	Ⲫⲏⲉⲧⲁϥⲥⲙⲟⲩ ⲉⲁⲃⲣⲁⲁⲙ ⲛⲉⲙ ⲥⲁⲣⲣⲁ ⲁϥⲧⲟⲙⲥ ⲉⲣⲟϥ ⲉⲟⲩⲥϩⲓⲙⲓ ⲟⲩⲟϩ ⲁϥⲧⲛⲁϥ ⲛ̀ϯⲧⲁϩⲓⲥ ⲛⲧⲉ ϯⲙⲉⲧⲡⲁⲧⲣⲓⲁⲣⲭⲏⲥ ⲧⲉⲛⲧⲱⲃϩ ⲙⲙⲟⲕ Ⲡⲟⲥ ⲥⲱⲧⲉⲙ ⲉⲣⲟⲛ ⲟⲩⲟϩ ⲛⲁⲓ ⲛⲁⲛ.	يا من بارك إبراهيم وسارة وجعلها له زوجة ومنحه رتبة رئاسة الآباء نطلب إليك يا رب أن تسمعنا وترحمنا
O You who preserved Isaac, and chose for him Rebecca, and delivered him from his enemies, we ask You O Lord to hear us and have mercy on us.	Ⲫⲏⲉⲧⲁϥⲁⲣⲉϩ ⲉⲓⲥⲁⲁⲕ ⲟⲩⲟϩ ⲁϥⲧⲟⲙⲓ ⲉⲣⲟϥ ⲛⲓⲉⲣⲉⲃⲉⲕⲕⲁ ⲟⲩⲟϩ ⲁϥⲥⲟⲧϥ ⲉⲃⲟⲗ ϧⲉⲛ ⲛⲉϥϫⲁϫⲓ ⲧⲉⲛⲧⲱⲃϩ ⲙⲙⲟⲕ Ⲡⲟⲥ ⲥⲱⲧⲉⲙ ⲉⲣⲟⲛ ⲟⲩⲟϩ ⲛⲁⲓ ⲛⲁⲛ.	يا من حفظ إسحق ووفق له رفقة وأنقذه من أعدائه نطلب إليك يا رب أن تسمعنا وترحمنا

O You who blessed Jacob, and gave him Rachel as a wife, and granted them to be heirs of the promise, we ask You O Lord to hear us and have mercy on us.	Ⲫⲏⲉⲧⲁϥⲥⲙⲟⲩ ⲉⲓⲁⲕⲱⲃ ⲟⲩⲟϩ ⲁϥⲧⲟⲙⲓ ⲉⲣⲟϥ ⲛⲣⲁⲭⲏⲗ ⲉⲟⲩⲥϩⲓⲙⲓ ⲛⲁϥ ⲟⲩⲟϩ ⲁϥⲁⲧⲟⲩ ⲛⲕⲗⲏⲣⲟⲛⲟⲙⲟⲥ ⲛⲧⲉ ϯⲉⲡⲁⲅⲅⲉⲗⲓⲁ ⲧⲉⲛⲧⲱⲃϩ ⲙⲙⲟⲕ Ⲡⲟⲥ ⲥⲱⲧⲉⲙ ⲉⲣⲟⲛ ⲟⲩⲟϩ ⲛⲁⲓ ⲛⲁⲛ.	يا من بارك يعقوب وأعطاه راحيل زوجة وجعله وارث الموعد نسألك يا رب أن تسمعنا وترحمنا
O You who raised Joseph up as a leader, and granted him Asenath as a wife, and through him You sustained all the land of Egypt, we ask You O Lord to hear us and have mercy on us.	Ⲫⲏⲉⲧⲁϥϭⲓⲥⲓ ⲛⲓⲱⲥⲏⲫ ⲟⲩⲟϩ ⲁϥⲧⲟⲙⲓ ⲉⲣⲟϥ ⲛⲁⲥⲉⲛⲏⲑ ⲟⲩⲟϩ ⲉⲃⲟⲗ ϩⲓⲧⲟⲧϥ ⲁⲕϣⲁⲛϣ ⲙⲡⲕⲁϩⲓ ⲧⲏⲣϥ ⲛⲭⲏⲙⲓ ⲧⲉⲛⲧⲱⲃϩ ⲙⲙⲟⲕ Ⲡⲟⲥ ⲥⲱⲧⲉⲙ ⲉⲣⲟⲛ ⲟⲩⲟϩ ⲛⲁⲓ ⲛⲁⲛ.	يا من رفع يوسف ووهب له أسينات زوجة وبواسطته علت كل أرض مصر نطلب إليك يا رب أن تسمعنا وترحمنا
O You who was pleased to be born of a virgin in the fullness of time to enlighten mankind, we ask You O Lord to hear us and have mercy on us.	Ⲫⲏⲉⲧⲁϥϯⲙⲁϯ ϧⲉⲛ ⲧϫⲁⲉ ⲛⲧⲉ ⲛⲓⲉϩⲟⲟⲩ ⲉⲑⲣⲟⲩⲙⲁⲥϥ ⲉⲃⲟⲗϧⲉⲛ ⲟⲩⲥϩⲓⲙⲓ ⲟⲩⲟϩ ⲁϥⲉⲣⲟⲩⲱⲓⲛⲓ ⲙⲡⲅⲉⲛⲟⲥ ⲛⲛⲓⲣⲱⲙⲓ ⲧⲉⲛⲧⲱⲃϩ ⲙⲙⲟⲕ Ⲡⲟⲥ ⲥⲱⲧⲉⲙ ⲉⲣⲟⲛ ⲟⲩⲟϩ ⲛⲁⲓ ⲛⲁⲛ.	يا من سر في آخر الأيام أن يولد من عذراء وأضاء على جنس البشر نسألك يا رب إستجب لنا وإرحمنا

(The priest turns and faces the couple.)

O You who attended the wedding of Cana of Galilee, bless this marriage as you blessed that marriage. We ask You O Lord to hear us and have mercy on us.	Ⲫⲏⲉⲧⲁϥⲣⲁⲟⲩⲱ ⲉⲡⲓϩⲟⲡ ϧⲉⲛ ⲧⲕⲁⲛⲁ ⲛⲧⲉ ϯⲅⲁⲗⲓⲗⲉⲁ ⲥⲙⲟⲩ ⲉⲡⲁⲓϫⲓⲛⲧⲟⲙⲓ ⲫⲁⲓ ⲕⲁⲧⲁ ⲫⲣⲏϯ ⲉⲧⲁⲕⲥⲙⲟⲩ ⲉⲡⲓϫⲓⲛⲧⲟⲙⲓ ⲉⲧⲉⲙⲙⲁⲩ ⲧⲉⲛⲧⲱⲃϩ ⲙⲙⲟⲕ Ⲡⲟⲥ ⲥⲱⲧⲉⲙ ⲉⲣⲟⲛ ⲟⲩⲟϩ ⲛⲁⲓ ⲛⲁⲛ.	يا من حضر في عرس قانا الجليل بارك هذا الزواج مثل ما باركت ذاك الزواج نتضرع إليك يا رب أن تسمعنا وترحمنا

A Textual History of the Coptic Wedding Rite

O You who transformed water into genuine wine by the authority of His divinity, bless Your two servants, and purify them with Your love for mankind. We ask You O Lord to hear us and have mercy on us.	Ⲫⲏⲉⲧⲁϥⲟⲩⲱⲧⲉⲃ ⲙⲡⲓⲙⲱⲟⲩ ⲉⲟⲩⲏⲣⲡ ⲙⲙⲏⲓ ϧⲉⲛ ⲡⲓⲉⲣϣⲓϣⲓ ⲛⲧⲉ ⲧⲉϥⲙⲉⲑⲛⲟⲩϯ ⲉⲕⲉⲥⲙⲟⲩ ⲉⲛⲉⲕⲉⲃⲓⲁⲓⲕ ϧⲉⲛ ⲟⲩⲙⲟⲩⲛ ⲉⲃⲟⲗ ⲟⲩⲟϩ ⲉⲕⲉⲧⲟⲩⲃⲱⲟⲩ ϧⲉⲛ ⲧⲉⲕⲙⲉⲧⲙⲁⲓⲣⲱⲙⲓ ⲧⲉⲛⲧⲱⲃϩ ⲙⲙⲟⲕ Ⲡⲟⲥ ⲥⲱⲧⲉⲙ ⲉⲣⲟⲛ ⲟⲩⲟϩ ⲛⲁⲓ ⲛⲁⲛ.	يا من حول الماء خمرا حقيقيا بسلطان لاهوته بارك عبديك وطهرهما بمحبتك للبشر نطلب إليك يا رب أن تستجب لنا وترحمنا
O You who attended the wedding of Cana of Galilee, and blessed that wedding, and transformed the water into genuine wine by the authority of His divinity, bless and guard this wedding of Your servants {GROOM} and {BRIDE}, in peace, harmony, love, and protection. We ask You O Lord to hear us and have mercy on us.	Ⲫⲏⲉⲧⲁϥϣⲱⲡⲓ ϧⲉⲛ ⲧⲕⲁⲛⲁ ⲛⲧⲉ ϯⲅⲁⲗⲓⲅⲗⲉⲁ ⲟⲩⲟϩ ⲁϥⲥⲙⲟⲩ ⲉⲡⲓϩⲟⲡ ⲙⲙⲁⲩ ⲟⲩⲟϩ ⲡⲓⲙⲱⲟⲩ ⲁϥⲟⲩⲟⲑⲃⲉϥ ⲉⲟⲩⲏⲣⲡ ⲙⲙⲏⲓ ϧⲉⲛ ⲡⲓⲉⲣϣⲓϣⲓ ⲛⲧⲉ ⲧⲉϥ ⲙⲉⲑⲛⲟⲩϯ ⲉⲕⲉⲥⲙⲟⲩ ⲟⲩⲟϩ ⲉⲕⲉⲉⲣⲥⲕⲉⲡⲁⲍⲓⲛ ⲙⲡⲁⲓϩⲟⲡ ⲫⲁⲓ ⲛⲧⲉ ⲛⲉⲕⲉⲃⲓⲁⲓⲕ ⲡⲁ (NIM) ⲛⲉⲙ ⲧⲁ (NIM) ϧⲉⲛ ⲟⲩϩⲓⲣⲏⲛⲏ ⲛⲉⲙ ⲟⲩⲙⲉⲧⲟⲩⲁⲓ ⲛⲉⲙ ⲟⲩⲁⲅⲁⲡⲏ ⲉⲕⲉⲣⲱⲓⲥ ⲉⲣⲱⲟⲩ ⲧⲉⲛⲧⲱⲃϩ ⲙⲙⲟⲕ Ⲡⲟⲥ ⲥⲱⲧⲉⲙ ⲉⲣⲟⲛ ⲟⲩⲟϩ ⲛⲁⲓ ⲛⲁⲛ.	يا من حل في عرس قانا الجليل وبارك ذاك العرس وحول الماء إلى خمر حقيقي بسلطان لاهوته بارك واستر هذا العرس الذي لعبديك (...) و (...) بسلامة وآلفة ومحبة وإحرسهما نطلب إليك يا رب أن تسمعنا وترحمنا

(The priest turns and faces the East.)

O You who are beneficent and compassionate, and full of goodness and affection, O Lord make us worthy to glorify	Ⲡⲓⲣⲉϥⲉⲣⲡⲉⲑⲛⲁⲛⲉϥ ⲟⲩⲟϩ ⲡⲓⲣⲉϥϣⲉⲛϩⲏⲧ ⲛⲁϣⲉ ⲧⲉⲕⲙⲉⲧⲁⲅⲁⲑⲟⲥ ⲛⲉⲙ ⲙⲉⲧϣⲁⲛⲑⲙⲁϧⲧ Ⲡⲟⲥ ⲁⲣⲓⲧⲉⲛ ⲛⲉⲙⲡϣⲁ	أيها المحسن الرؤوف الكثير الصلاح والتحنن يا رب إجعلنا أن نمجد صلاحك يا محب البشر نسألك يا رب أن تسمعنا وترحمنا

| Your goodness O Lover of mankind. We ask You O Lord to hear us and have mercy on us. | Ntentwoy ntekmetagathos pimairwmi tentwbh mmok Pos swtem epon oyoh nai nan. | |

Congregation:

| Lord Have Mercy
Lord Have Mercy
Lord Have Mercy | Kyrie eleyson
Kyrie eleyson
Kyrie eleyson | يا رب ارحم
يا رب ارحم
يا رب ارحم |

(The priest recites the three great litanies.)

Deacon:

| In the wisdom of God, let us attend. Lord have mercy. Lord have mercy. Truly | En sofia Theoy proscwmen. Kyrie eleyson Kyrie eleyson. ϧen oymethmhi | إنصتوا بحكمة الله يا رب إرحم يا رب إرحم بالحقيقة |

(Then the congregation says the Creed.)

The Matrimonial Prayers

Priest:

| Let us pray | ϢΛΗΛ | صلوا |

Deacon:

| Stand up for prayer | Epi proceyxh cta;hte | للصلاة قفوا |

A Textual History of the Coptic Wedding Rite

Priest:

| Peace be with all. | Ιρηνη παci | السلام لجميعكم |

Congregation:

| And with your spirit. | Κε τω πνευματι cογ | ولروحك أيضاً |

Priest *(facing East)*:

| O God who is eternal and everlasting, who has no beginning, whose wisdom has no limit, whose power has no end, who made man from the earth, and gave him a woman out of his side, and accommodated her for him as his helper fit for him, as it pleases Your Lordship and goodness, because "it is not good for a man to be alone." We ask You also now O our King to join Your two servants, {GROOM} and {BRIDE}, to be united to each other in one body, and to enter into the law of joy, and to abide in Your truthful teachings. Grant them a living fruit out of the womb so that they may rejoice in the birth of good children and have quiet and peaceful times. Prepare them for every | Ⲫϯ ⲫⲏⲉⲧϣⲟⲡ ⲫⲏⲉⲑⲙⲏⲛ ⲉⲃⲟⲗ ϣⲁ ⲉⲛⲉϩ ⲛⲁⲧⲁⲣⲭⲏ ⲫⲏⲉⲧⲉ ⲙⲙⲟⲛ ϣⲧⲟⲓ ⲉⲧⲉϥⲥⲟⲫⲓⲁ ⲟⲩⲟϩ ⲙⲙⲟⲛ ⲁⲩⲣⲏϫⲥ ⲛⲧⲉ ⲧⲉϥϫⲟⲙ ⲫⲏⲉⲧⲁϥⲑⲁⲙⲓⲟ ⲙⲡⲓⲣⲱⲙⲓ ⲉⲃⲟⲗϧⲉⲛ ⲡⲕⲁϩⲓ ⲁϥⲕⲱⲧ ⲛⲁϥ ⲉⲧⲉⲁϥⲧⲛⲁϥ ⲛⲟⲩⲥϩⲓⲙⲓ ⲉⲃⲟⲗϧⲉⲛ ⲡⲉϥⲥⲫⲓⲣ ⲁϥϩⲟⲧⲡⲥ ⲉⲟⲩⲃⲟⲏⲑⲟⲥ ⲕⲁⲧⲣⲟϥ. Ⲕⲁⲧⲁ ⲫⲣⲏϯ ⲉⲧⲁⲥⲣⲁⲛⲁ ⲛⲧⲉⲕⲙⲉⲧⲟⲥ ⲛⲉⲙ ⲧⲉⲕⲙⲉⲧⲁⲅⲁⲑⲟⲥ ϫⲉ ⲛⲁⲛⲉⲥ ⲁⲛ ⲛⲧⲉ ⲡⲓⲣⲱⲙⲓ ϣⲱⲡⲓ ⲙⲙⲁⲩⲁⲧϥ. Ⲛⲑⲟⲕ ⲟⲛ ϯⲛⲟⲩ ⲡⲉⲛⲛⲏⲃ ⲧⲉⲛϯϩⲟ ⲉⲣⲟⲕ ϩⲱⲧⲡ ⲛⲛⲉⲕⲉⲃⲓⲁⲓⲕ ⲡⲁ ⲛⲓⲙ ⲛⲉⲙ ⲧⲁ ⲛⲓⲙ ϫⲉϩⲁⲥ ⲉⲩⲉϩⲱⲧⲡ ⲉⲛⲟⲩⲉⲣⲏⲟⲩ ϧⲉⲛ ⲟⲩⲥⲁⲣϫ ⲛⲟⲩⲱⲧ ⲙⲁⲣⲟⲩⲓ ⲉϧⲟⲩⲛ ⲉⲫⲛⲟⲙⲟⲥ ⲙⲡⲟⲩⲛⲟϥ ⲙⲁⲣⲟⲩϣⲱⲡⲓ ϧⲉⲛ ϩⲁⲛⲥⲃⲱⲟⲩⲓ ⲉⲩⲉⲛϩⲟⲧ. | اللهُمَّ الأزلي الدائم إلى الأبد بغير إبتداء الذي لا حد لحكمته ولا إنتهاء لقوته الذي صنع الإنسان من الأرض وجعل له إمرأة نظيره من جنبه ووفقها له معينة نظيره كما يرضي ربوبيتك وصلاحك لأنه لا يحسن أن يكون الرجل وحده أنت الآن أيضاً يا ملكنا نسألك أن تصل عبديك (...) و (...) لكي يتصلا ببعضهما بعضا بجسد واحد وليدخلا إلى ناموس الفرح وليكونا في تعاليم صادقة هب لهما ثمرة محيية من البطن ليبتهجا بولادة البنين الحسنة والأزمنة الهادئة السالمة هيئهما في كل عمل صالح بالمسيح يسوع ربنا هذا الذي ينبغي لك معه مع الروح القدس المجد والكرامة والعز والسجود الآن وكل أوان وإلى دهر الدهور. آمين. |

good work through Christ Jesus our Lord. Through whom the glory, the honor, and the worship are due unto You, with Him and the Holy Spirit, now and at all times and unto the ages of all ages. Amen.	ⲁⲣⲓϩⲙⲟⲧ ⲛⲱⲟⲩ ⲛⲟⲩⲟⲩⲧⲁϩ ⲉϥⲟⲛϧ ⲉⲃⲟⲗϧⲉⲛ ⲑⲛⲉϫⲓ ⲉⲑⲣⲟⲩⲉⲣⲁⲡⲟⲗⲁⲩⲓⲛ ⲛⲟⲩⲙⲉⲧⲣⲉϥϫⲫⲉ ϣⲏⲣⲓ ⲉⲛⲁⲛⲉⲥ ⲛⲉⲙ ϩⲁⲛⲭⲣⲟⲩ ⲛϫⲁⲙⲏ ⲛϩⲓⲣⲏⲛⲓⲕⲟⲛ ⲥⲉⲃⲧⲱⲧⲟⲩ ϧⲉⲛ ϩⲱⲃ ⲛⲓⲃⲉⲛ ⲉⲑⲛⲁⲛⲉⲩ ϧⲉⲛ Ⲡⲭⲥ Ⲓⲏⲥ Ⲡⲉⲛⲟⲥ ⲫⲁⲓ ⲉⲧⲉ ⲉⲃⲟⲗϩⲓⲧⲟⲧϥ ⲉⲣⲉ ⲡⲓⲱⲟⲩ ⲛⲉⲙ ⲡⲓⲧⲁⲓⲟ ⲛⲉⲙ ⲡⲓⲁⲙⲁϩⲓ ⲛⲉⲙ ϯⲡⲣⲟⲥⲕⲩⲛⲏⲥⲓⲥ ⲉⲣⲡⲣⲉⲡⲓ ⲛⲁⲕ ⲛⲉⲙⲁϥ ⲛⲉⲙ ⲡⲓⲡⲛⲉⲩⲙⲁ ⲉⲑⲟⲩⲁⲃ ⲛⲣⲉϥⲧⲁⲛϧⲟ ⲟⲩⲟϩ ⲛⲟⲙⲟⲟⲩⲥⲓⲟⲥ ⲛⲉⲙⲁⲕ ϯⲛⲟⲩ ⲛⲉⲙ ⲛⲥⲏⲟⲩ ⲛⲓⲃⲉⲛ ⲛⲉⲙ ϣⲁ ⲉⲛⲉϩ ⲛⲧⲉ ⲛⲓⲉⲛⲉϩ ⲧⲏⲣⲟⲩ. ⲁⲙⲏⲛ.	

Congregation *(in the muḥayyar tune)*:

As David has said • in the book of the Psalms, • "The queen stood • at Your right hand O King."	Ⲕⲁⲧⲁ ⲫⲣⲏϯ ⲉⲧⲁϥϫⲟⲥ ⲛϫⲉ Ⲇⲁⲩⲓⲇ ϧⲉⲛ ⲡⲓⲯⲁⲗⲙⲟⲥ ϫⲉ ⲁⲥⲟϩⲓ ⲉⲣⲁⲧⲥ ⲛϫⲉ ϯⲟⲩⲣⲱ ⲥⲁⲟⲩⲓⲛⲁⲙ ⲙⲙⲟⲕ ⲡⲟⲩⲣⲟ	كما قال داود في المزمور قامت الملكة عن يمينك أيها الملك

Priest:

O Father our God who formed all nature; who formed man from earth, and made for him a helpmate from the rib You took from him, and	Ⲡⲟⲥ ⲡⲉⲛⲛⲟⲩϯ ⲫⲣⲉϥⲥⲱⲛⲧ ⲛⲧⲉ ⲫⲩⲥⲓⲥ ⲛⲓⲃⲉⲛ ⲫⲏⲉⲧⲁϥⲥⲱⲛⲧ ⲙⲡⲓⲣⲱⲙⲓ ⲉⲃⲟⲗϧⲉⲛ ⲡⲕⲁϩⲓ ⲟⲩⲟϩ ⲁⲕϩⲱⲧⲡ	أيها الآب إلهنا جابل كل الطبائع الذي جبل الإنسان من الأرض وأصلحت له معينة من الضلع الذي أخذته منه ووفقتهما لشركة الزواج

joined them together in the fellowship of marriage for life and the continuous growth of mankind, and told them, "Grow, multiply and fill the earth and have dominion over it." You also, O Good One and Lover of Mankind, bless the union of Your two servants {GROOM} and {BRIDE} who are united to each other according to Your will. Bless them and multiply them as You blessed our forefathers Abraham, Isaac and Jacob. Bless them as You have blessed Abraham and Sarah. Elevate them as You did Isaac and Rebecca. Multiply them as You multiplied Jacob and his offspring. Glorify them as You have glorified Joseph in Egypt. Grant them purity. Multiply them as Elkanah and Hannah, whom You blessed and to whom You granted Samuel, the faithful prophet. Make them worthy of the pure good tidings of the Archangel as You did with Zacharias and Elizabeth, to whom You granted the birth of John, the greatest among those born of women, who	ⲛⲁϥ ⲛⲟⲩⲃⲟⲏⲑⲟⲥ ⲉⲓⲧⲉⲛ ϯⲃⲏⲧ ⲉⲧⲁⲕⲉⲛⲥ ⲉⲃⲟⲗ ⲙⲙⲟϥ ⲟⲩⲟϩ ⲁⲕⲥⲟⲧⲡⲟⲩ ⲉⲟⲩⲕⲟⲓⲛⲱⲛⲓⲁ ⲛⲅⲁⲙⲟⲥ ϧⲉⲛ ⲟⲩϫⲓⲛⲱⲛϧ ⲛⲉⲙ ⲟⲩϫⲓⲛⲁⲓⲁⲓ ⲉⲑⲙⲏⲛ ϧⲉⲛ ⲡⲅⲉⲛⲟⲥ ⲛⲛⲓⲣⲱⲙⲓ. ⲟⲩⲟϩ ⲁⲕϫⲟⲥ ⲛⲱⲟⲩ ϫⲉ ⲁⲓⲁⲓ ⲟⲩⲟϩ ⲁϣⲁⲓ ⲙⲁϩ ⲡⲓⲕⲁϩⲓ ⲁⲣⲓⲟⲓⲥ ⲉⲣⲟϥ. ⲛⲑⲟⲕ ⲟⲛ ⲡⲓⲁⲅⲁⲑⲟⲥ ⲟⲩⲟϩ ⲙⲙⲁⲓⲣⲱⲙⲓ ⲥⲙⲟⲩ ⲉⲡϫⲓⲛϩⲱⲧⲡ ⲛⲧⲉ ⲛⲉⲕⲉⲃⲓⲁⲓⲕ ⲡⲁ ⲛⲓⲙ ⲛⲉⲙ ⲧⲁ ⲛⲓⲙ ⲛⲁⲓ ⲉⲧⲁⲩϩⲟⲧⲡⲟⲩ ⲉⲛⲟⲩⲉⲣⲟⲩ ⲕⲁⲧⲁ ⲫⲏⲉⲧⲉ ⲫⲱⲕ ⲛⲟⲩⲱϣ ⲥⲙⲟⲩ ⲉⲣⲱⲟⲩ ⲙⲁⲣⲟⲩⲁϣⲁⲓ ⲙⲫⲣⲏϯ ⲉⲧⲁⲕⲥⲙⲟⲩ ⲉⲛⲉⲛϣⲟⲣⲡ ⲛⲓⲟϯ ⲁⲃⲣⲁⲁⲙ ⲛⲉⲙ ⲓⲥⲁⲁⲕ ⲛⲉⲙ ⲓⲁⲕⲱⲃ ⲥⲙⲟⲩ ⲉⲣⲱⲟⲩ ⲙⲃⲣⲏϯ ⲛⲁⲃⲣⲁⲁⲙ ⲛⲉⲙ ⲥⲁⲣⲣⲁ ϭⲁⲥⲟⲩ ⲙⲫⲣⲏϯ ⲛⲓⲥⲁⲁⲕ ⲛⲉⲙ ⲓⲉⲣⲉⲃⲉⲕⲕⲁ. ⲙⲁⲣⲟⲩⲁϣⲁⲓ ⲙⲫⲣⲏϯ ⲉⲧⲁⲕⲉⲣⲉ ⲓⲁⲕⲱⲃ ⲁϣⲁⲓ ⲛⲉⲙ ⲡⲉϥϫⲣⲟϫ. ⲙⲁⲱⲟⲩ ⲛⲱⲟⲩ ⲙⲫⲣⲏϯ ⲉⲧⲁⲕϯⲱⲟⲩ ⲛⲓⲱⲥⲏⲫ ϧⲉⲛ ⲭⲏⲙⲓ. ⲉⲕⲉⲉⲣⲭⲁⲣⲓⲍⲉⲥⲑⲉ ⲛⲱⲟⲩ ⲙⲉⲡϥⲧⲟⲩⲃⲟ ⲉⲕⲉⲑⲣⲟⲩⲁϣⲁⲓ ⲙⲫⲣⲏϯ ⲛⲉⲗⲕⲁⲛⲁ ⲛⲉⲙ ⲁⲛⲛⲁ ⲉⲧⲁⲕⲥⲙⲟⲩ ⲉⲣⲱⲟⲩ ⲉⲁⲕⲉⲣϩⲙⲟⲧ ⲛⲱⲟⲩ	للحياة والنمو الدائم في جنس البشر وقلت لهما انميا واكثرا واملكا الأرض وتسلطا عليها أنت أيها الصالح محب البشر بارك بإتحاد عبديك (...) و (...) اللذين إتصلا ببعضهما بعضاً حسب إرادتك باركهما وليكثرا كما باركت آبائنا الأولين إبراهيم وإسحق ويعقوب باركهما كما باركت إبراهيم وسارة ارفعهما مثل إسحق ورفقة أكثرهما كما أكثرت يعقوب وزرعه ومجدهما كما مجدت يوسف بمصر هب لهما طهارة أكثرهما مثل ألقانة وحنة الذين باركتهما وأنعمت عليهما بصموئيل النبي الأمين إجعلهما أهلا لبشارة رئيس الملائكة الطاهرة مثل زكريا وأليصابات الذين أنعمت عليهما بولادة يوحنا المعمدان أعظم مواليد النساء الذي صار سابقاً قدام إبنك الوحيد الجنس وأنت أيضاً أيها السيد الرب بارك يواقيم وحنة وصنعت منهما التابوت العقلي والدة الإله مريم التي تجسد منها إبنك الوحيد وجاء إلى العالم وبارك عرس قانا الجليل بارك عبديك (...) و (...) اللذين اقترنا في هذه الساعة إنعم عليهما بالرخاء والحكمة وبركات الخلاص لكي يكونا بكل تقوى وكل عفاف متصلين بجسدهما وروحهما ويستحقا البركة التي من قبلك وتمجدا إسمك

138

became the forerunner before Your only begotten Son. You also, O Master Lord, blessed Joachim and Anna and made from them the rational ark, the Mother of God, Mary, of whom Your only begotten Son was incarnate and came into the world, and blessed the wedding of Cana of Galilee. Bless Your two servants {GROOM} and {BRIDE} who are united at this hour. Grant them prosperity, wisdom and salvation's blessing, that they may be in all godliness and all purity united in their bodies and souls, and be worthy of Your blessing and glorify Your holy name together with Your only-begotten Son and the Holy Spirit, now and at all times and unto the age of all ages. Amen.	ⲙ̅ⲡⲓⲡⲓⲥⲧⲟⲥ ⲥⲁⲙⲟⲩⲏⲗ ⲡⲓⲡⲣⲟⲫⲏⲧⲏⲥ ⲟⲩⲟϩ ⲉⲕⲉⲁⲓⲧⲟⲩ ⲛⲉⲙⲡϣⲁ ⲙ̅ⲡⲓϣⲉⲛⲛⲟⲩϥⲓ ⲙ̅ⲡⲉⲕⲁⲣⲭⲏⲁⲅⲅⲉⲗⲟⲥ ⲉⲑⲟⲩⲁⲃ. Ⲙ̅ⲫⲣⲏϯ ⲛ̅ⲍⲁⲭⲁⲣⲓⲁⲥ ⲛⲉⲙ ⲉⲗⲓⲥⲁⲃⲉⲧ ⲉⲧⲁⲕⲉⲣϩⲙⲟⲧ ⲛⲱⲟⲩ ⲙ̅ⲡⲓϫⲓⲛⲁⲫⲟ ⲙ̅ⲡⲓⲛⲓϣϯ ϧⲉⲛ ⲡⲓϫⲓⲛⲙⲓⲥⲓ ⲛ̅ⲧⲉ ⲛⲓϩⲓⲟⲙⲓ ⲟⲩⲁⲛⲛⲏⲥ ⲫⲁⲓ ⲉⲧⲁϥϣⲱⲡⲓ ⲙ̅ⲡⲓⲡⲣⲟⲇⲣⲟⲙⲟⲥ ϧⲁϫⲟϥ ⲙ̅ⲡⲉⲕⲙⲟⲛⲟⲅⲉⲛⲏⲥ ⲛ̅ϣⲏⲣⲓ. Ⲛⲑⲟⲕ ⲟⲛ ⲫⲛⲏⲃ Ⲡⲟⲥ ⲁⲕⲥⲙⲟⲩ ⲉⲓⲱⲁⲕⲓⲙ ⲛⲉⲙ ⲁⲛⲛⲁ ⲁⲕⲉⲣϩⲱⲃ ⲛ̅ϧⲏⲧⲟⲩ ⲛ̅ϯⲕⲩⲃⲱⲧⲟⲥ ⲛ̅ⲛⲟⲏⲣⲁ ϯⲑⲉⲟⲧⲟⲕⲟⲥ ⲙⲁⲣⲓⲁ ⲁϥϭⲓⲥⲁⲣⲝ ⲛ̅ϧⲏⲧⲥ ⲛ̅ϫⲉ ⲡⲉⲕⲙⲟⲛⲟⲅⲉⲛⲏⲥ ⲛ̅ϣⲏⲣⲓ ⲁϥⲓ ⲉⲡⲓⲕⲟⲥⲙⲟⲥ ⲁϥⲥⲙⲟⲩ ⲉⲡⲓϩⲟⲡ ⲛ̅ⲧⲉ ⲧⲕⲁⲛⲁ ⲛ̅ⲧⲉ ϯⲅⲁⲗⲓⲗⲉⲁ ⲥⲙⲟⲩ ⲉⲛⲉⲕⲉⲃⲓⲁⲓⲕ ⲡⲁ ⲛⲓⲙ ⲛⲉⲙ ⲧⲁ ⲛⲓⲙ ⲛⲁⲓ ⲉⲧⲁⲩⲙⲟⲩⲗϫ ϧⲉⲛ ⲧⲁⲓⲟⲩⲛⲟⲩ ⲑⲁⲓ. ⲁⲣⲓϩⲙⲟⲧ ⲛⲱⲟⲩ ⲛ̅ⲟⲩⲙⲉⲧϩⲉⲛⲟⲩϥⲓ ⲛⲉⲙ ⲟⲩⲙⲉⲧⲥⲁⲃⲉ ⲛⲉⲙ ϩⲁⲛⲥⲙⲟⲧ ⲛ̅ⲟⲩϫⲁⲓ ϩⲓⲛⲁ ⲛ̅ⲥⲉϣⲱⲡⲓ ϧⲉⲛ ⲟⲩⲙⲉⲧⲉⲩⲥⲉⲃⲏⲥ ⲛⲓⲃⲉⲛ ⲛⲉⲙ ⲙⲉⲧⲥⲉⲙⲛⲟⲥ ⲛⲓⲃⲉⲛ ⲉⲩϩⲱⲧⲡ ϧⲉⲛ ⲡⲟⲩⲥⲱⲙⲁ ⲛⲉⲙ ⲡⲟⲩⲡⲛⲉⲩⲙⲁ ⲉⲑⲣⲟⲩⲉⲣⲡⲉⲙⲡϣⲁ	القدس مع إبنك الوحيد والروح القدس الآن وكل أوان وإلى دهر الدهور آمين

A Textual History of the Coptic Wedding Rite

| | ⲙⲡⲓⲥⲙⲟⲩ ⲡⲓⲉⲃⲟⲗϩⲓⲧⲟⲧⲕ ⲛⲥⲉϯⲱⲟⲩ ⲙⲡⲉⲕⲣⲁⲛⲉⲑⲟⲩⲁⲃ ⲛⲉⲙ ⲡⲉⲕⲙⲟⲛⲟⲅⲉⲛⲏⲥ ⲛϣⲏⲣⲓ ⲛⲉⲙ ⲡⲓⲡⲛⲉⲩⲙⲁ ⲉⲑⲟⲩⲁⲃ ϯⲛⲟⲩ ⲛⲉⲙ ⲛⲥⲏⲟⲩ ⲛⲉⲃⲉⲛ ⲛⲉⲙ ϣⲁ ⲉⲛⲉϩ ⲁⲙⲏⲛ. | |

Congregation *(in the muḥayyar tune)*:

| Solomon has called you • in the Song of Songs, • "My sister and my spouse, • my true city Jerusalem." | Ⲥⲟⲗⲟⲙⲱⲛ ⲙⲟⲩϯ ⲉⲣⲟ ϧⲉⲛ ⲡⲓϫⲱ ⲛⲧⲉ ⲛⲓϫⲱ ϫⲉ ⲧⲁⲥⲱⲛⲓ ⲟⲩⲟϩ ⲧⲁϣⲫⲉⲣⲓ ⲧⲁⲡⲟⲗⲓⲥ ⲙⲙⲏⲓ Ⲓⲉⲣⲟⲩⲥⲁⲗⲏⲙ | سليمان داعك في نسيد الأنشاد أختي و خليلتي مدينتي الحقيقية أورشليم |

Priest *(facing the couple)*:

| O Lord, our God, the Great and Eternal, who brought life into existence out of nonexistence, and created the universe by Your Word, and formed man with Your pure hands in Your image and after Your likeness, and from one created the other, for You said that it is not good for man to be alone, so You caused sleep to fall upon Adam, so he slept, and You took a rib from his side and closed up its place with flesh instead of it. For this a man leaves his father and mother and | Ⲡⲟⲥ ⲡⲉⲛⲛⲟⲩϯ ⲡⲓⲛⲓϣϯ ⲡⲓϣⲁⲉⲛⲉϩ ⲫⲏⲉⲧⲁϥⲑⲣⲉ ⲡⲱⲛϩ ϣⲱⲡⲓ ⲉⲃⲟⲗ ϧⲉⲛ ⲫⲏ ⲉⲛⲁϥϣⲟⲡ ⲁⲛ ⲉⲁⲕⲉⲣⲭⲁⲣⲓⲍⲉⲥⲑⲉ ⲙⲡⲓϫⲓⲛϣⲱⲡⲓ ϩⲓⲧⲉⲛ ⲡⲉⲕⲥⲁϫⲓ ⲟⲩⲟϩ ⲡⲓⲣⲱⲙⲓ ⲛⲑⲟⲕ ⲁⲕⲉⲣⲡⲗⲁⲍⲓⲛ ⲙⲙⲟϥ ϩⲓⲧⲉⲛ ⲧⲉⲕϫⲓϫ ⲛⲁⲧⲑⲱⲗⲉⲃ ⲕⲁⲧⲁ ⲑⲉⲧⲉⲑⲱⲕ ⲛϩⲩⲕⲱⲛ ⲛⲉⲙ ⲕⲁⲧⲁ ⲡⲉⲕⲓⲛⲓ. Ⲉⲃⲟⲗϩⲓⲧⲉⲛ ⲡⲓⲟⲩⲁⲓ ⲁⲕⲧⲁϩⲉ ⲡⲓⲭⲉⲧ ⲉⲣⲁⲧϥ ⲉⲁⲕϫⲟⲥ ϫⲉ ⲛⲁⲛⲉⲥ ⲁⲛ ⲉⲑⲣⲉ ⲡⲓⲣⲱⲙⲓ ϣⲱⲡⲓ ⲙⲙⲁⲩⲁⲧϥ ⲟⲩⲟϩ ⲁⲕⲓⲛⲓ ⲛⲟⲩⲥⲣⲟⲙ ⲛϩⲓⲛⲓⲙ ⲉϫⲉⲛ ⲁⲇⲁⲙ ⲁϥⲉⲛⲕⲟⲧ ⲁⲕⲓⲛⲓ | أيها الرب إلهنا العظيم الأبدي الذي كونت الحياة مما لم يكن وخلقت الكون بكلمتك وجبلت الإنسان بيدك الطاهرة كصورتك ومثالك ومن الواحد أقمت الآخر إذ قلت أنه لا يحسن أن يكون الرجل وحده فأتيت بنعاس على آدم فرقد وأخرجت ضلعا من جنبه وملأت موضعها لحما عوضا عنها لهذا يترك الرجل أباه وأمه ويلتصق بامرأته ويكونان كلاهما جسدا واحدا وما جمعه الله لا يفرقه إنسان فيا من بارك إبراهيم مع سارة وإسحق مع |

cleaves to his wife, and they both become one body, and what God has joined together let no man put asunder. O You who blessed Abraham with Sarah, Isaac with Rebecca, and Jacob with Leah and Rachel, and purified all who were joined in blessing, now also O Master Lord, look upon Your servants {GROOM} and {BRIDE} his helpmate. Confirm their union, guard their bed in purity, cover them and their home with Your unconquerable right hand. Deliver them from all envy and intrigues. Preserve them in oneness, harmony and peace. Grant them joy and happiness to reveal unto You, O Living God, the fruit of life from the womb. Bless them, O God, as You blessed Abraham with Sarah, and Isaac with Rebecca, and Jacob with Leah and Rachel. As for the men and women who are here with us, bless them in the name of our Lord, our God, and our Savior Jesus Christ, through whom the glory is due unto You, with Him, and the Holy Spirit, now and	ⲛⲟⲩⲃⲏⲧ ⲉⲃⲟⲗ ϧⲉⲛ ⲡⲉϥⲥⲫⲓⲣ ⲁⲕⲙⲁϩ ⲡⲉⲥⲙⲁ ⲛⲥⲁⲣⲝ ⲛⲧⲉⲥϣⲉⲃⲓⲱ ϩⲓⲛⲁ ⲉⲑⲃⲉ ⲫⲁⲓ ⲉⲣⲉ ⲡⲓⲣⲱⲙⲓ ⲭⲁ ⲡⲉϥⲓⲱⲧ ⲛⲉⲙ ⲧⲉϥⲙⲁⲩ ⲛⲥⲱϥ ⲉϥⲉⲧⲟⲙϥ ⲉⲧⲉϥⲥϩⲓⲙⲓ ⲟⲩⲟϩ ⲉⲩⲉϣⲱⲡⲓ ⲙⲡⲥⲛⲁⲩ ⲛⲟⲩⲥⲁⲣⲝ ⲛⲟⲩⲱⲧ ⲫⲏⲉⲧ ⲁ ⲫϯ ⲧⲟⲙϥ ⲙⲡⲉⲛⲑⲣⲉ ⲫⲣⲱⲙⲓ ⲫⲟⲣϫϥ. ⲫⲏⲉⲧⲁϥⲥⲙⲟⲩ ⲛⲁⲃⲣⲁⲁⲙ ⲉϫⲉⲛ ⲥⲁⲣⲣⲁ ⲛⲉⲙ ⲓⲥⲁⲁⲕ ⲉϫⲉⲛ ⲓⲉⲣⲉⲃⲉⲕⲕⲁ ⲛⲉⲙ ⲓⲁⲕⲱⲃ ⲉϫⲉⲛ ⲉⲗⲓⲁ ⲛⲉⲙ ⲣⲁⲭⲏⲗ ⲟⲩⲟϩ ⲁⲕⲧⲟⲩⲃⲟ ⲛⲟⲩⲟⲛ ⲛⲓⲃⲉⲛ ⲉⲧⲁⲩⲙⲟⲩϫⲧ ϧⲉⲛ ⲟⲩⲥⲙⲟⲩ ⲛⲑⲟⲕ ⲟⲛ ϯⲛⲟⲩ ⲡⲉⲛⲛⲏⲃ Ⲡⲟⲥ ϫⲟⲩϣⲧ ⲉϩⲣⲏⲓ ⲉϫⲉⲛ ⲛⲉⲕⲉⲃⲓⲁⲓⲕ ⲡⲁ ⲛⲓⲙ ⲛⲉⲙ ⲧⲁ ⲛⲓⲙ ⲧⲉϥⲃⲟⲏⲑⲟⲥ ⲙⲁⲧⲁϫⲣⲉ ⲡⲟⲩϫⲓⲛϩⲱⲧⲡ ⲁⲣⲉϩ ⲉⲧⲟⲩϣⲁⲓ ⲉⲥⲧⲟⲩⲃⲏⲟⲩⲧ ⲁⲣⲓⲥⲕⲉⲡⲁⲍⲓⲛ ⲙⲙⲱⲟⲩ ⲛⲉⲙ ⲡⲟⲩⲏⲓ ϩⲓⲧⲉⲛ ⲧⲉⲕⲟⲩⲓⲛⲁⲙ ⲛⲁⲧϭⲣⲟ ⲉⲣⲟⲥ. Ⲛⲁϩⲙⲟⲩ ⲉⲃⲟⲗϩⲁ ⲫⲑⲟⲛⲟⲥ ⲛⲓⲃⲉⲛ ⲛⲉⲙ ⲉⲡⲓⲃⲟⲗⲏ ⲛⲓⲃⲉⲛ ⲣⲱⲓⲥ ⲉⲣⲱⲟⲩ ϧⲉⲛ ⲟⲩⲙⲉⲧϩⲏⲧ ⲛⲟⲩⲱⲧ ⲛⲉⲙ ⲟⲩϩⲓⲣⲏⲛⲏ ⲁⲣⲓⲭⲁⲣⲓⲍⲉⲥⲑⲉ ⲛⲱⲟⲩ ⲛⲟⲩⲑⲉⲗⲏⲗ ⲛⲉⲙ ⲟⲩⲣⲁϣⲓ ⲉⲑⲣⲟⲩⲟⲩⲱⲛϩ ⲛⲁⲕ ⲉⲃⲟⲗ ⲫϯ ⲉⲧⲟⲛϧ ⲛⲟⲕⲁⲣⲡⲟⲥ	رفقة ويعقوب في زواجه وطهرت كل الذين إجتمعوا بالبركة الآن أيضاً أيها السيد الرب إطلع على عبديك (...) و (...) معينته ثبت إتصالهما إحرس مضجعهما نقيا استرهما مع بيتهما بيمينك غير المغلوبة نجهما من كل حسد وكل مكيدة إحفظهما بإمتزاج واحد وسلام هب لهما فرحا وسرورا ليظهرا لك يا الله الحي ثمرة الحياة من البطن باركهما يا الله كما باركت إبراهيم مع سارة وإسحق مع رفقة ويعقوب في زواجه أما الرجال والنساء الذين ها هنا معنا فباركهم بإسم ربنا وإلهنا ومخلصنا يسوع المسيح هذا الذي من قبله يليق بك معه المجد مع الروح القدس الآن وكل أوان وإلى دهر الدهور آمين

at all times, and unto the age of all ages. Amen.	ⲉϥⲟⲛϩ ⲉⲃⲟⲗ ϧⲉⲛ ⲑⲛⲉⲭⲓ. Ⲥⲙⲟⲩ ⲉⲣⲱⲟⲩ ⲙ̅ⲫⲣⲏϯ ⲉⲧⲁⲕⲥⲙⲟⲩ ⲁⲃⲣⲁⲁⲙ ⲉϫⲉⲛ ⲥⲁⲣⲣⲁ ⲛⲉⲙ ⲓⲥⲁⲁⲕ ⲉϫⲉⲛ ⲓⲉⲣⲉⲃⲉⲕⲕⲁ ⲛⲉⲙ ⲓⲁⲕⲱⲃ ⲉϫⲉⲛ ⲉⲗⲓⲁ ⲛⲉⲙ ⲣⲁⲭⲏⲗ ⲛⲁⲓ ⲉⲧⲁⲩⲕⲱⲧ ⲙ̅ⲡⲏⲓ ⲙ̅ⲡⲓⲥⲣⲁⲏⲗ. Ⲟⲩⲟϩ ϧⲉⲛ ⲫⲣⲁⲛ ⲙ̅ⲡⲉⲛⲟⲥ Ⲓⲏⲥ Ⲡⲭⲥ ⲛⲏⲉⲧϧⲉⲛ ⲡⲁⲓ ⲙⲁ ⲛⲉⲙⲁⲛ ⲛⲓⲣⲱⲙⲓ ⲛⲉⲙ ⲛⲓϩⲓⲟⲙⲓ ⲥⲙⲟⲩ ⲉⲣⲱⲟⲩ ⲉⲃⲟⲗϩⲓⲧⲟⲧϥ ⲛ̅ⲑⲟϥ ⲡⲉⲛⲟⲥ ⲟⲩⲟϩ ⲡⲉⲛⲛⲟⲩϯ ⲟⲩⲟϩ ⲡⲉⲛⲥⲱⲧⲏⲣ Ⲓⲏⲥ Ⲡⲭⲥ ⲫⲁⲓ ⲉⲧⲉ ⲉⲃⲟⲗϩⲓⲧⲟⲧϥ ⲉⲣⲉ ⲡⲓⲱⲟⲩ ⲛⲉⲙ ⲡⲓⲧⲁⲓⲟ ⲛⲉⲙ ⲡⲓⲁⲙⲁϩⲓ ⲛⲉⲙ ϯⲡⲣⲟⲥⲕⲩⲛⲏⲥⲓⲥ ⲉⲣⲡⲣⲉⲡⲓ ⲛⲁⲕ ⲛⲉⲙⲁϥ ⲛⲉⲙ ⲡⲓⲡⲛⲉⲩⲙⲁ ⲉⲑⲟⲩⲁⲃ ⲛ̅ⲣⲉϥⲧⲁⲛϧⲟ ⲟⲩⲟϩ ⲛ̅ⲟⲙⲟⲟⲩⲥⲓⲟⲥ ⲛⲉⲙⲁⲕ ϯⲛⲟⲩ ⲛⲉⲙ ⲛ̅ⲥⲏⲟⲩ ⲛⲓⲃⲉⲛ ⲛⲉⲙ ϣⲁ ⲉⲛⲉϩ ⲛ̅ⲧⲉ ⲛⲓⲉⲛⲉϩ ⲧⲏⲣⲟⲩ. ⲁⲙⲏⲛ.	

Congregation (in the muḥayyar tune):

Do not forget the covenant • which You have made with our fathers • Abraham, Isaac, and Jacob • Israel Your saint.	Ⲙ̅ⲡⲉⲣⲉⲣⲡⲱⲃϣ ⲛ̅ϯⲇⲓⲁⲑⲏⲕⲏ ⲑⲏⲉⲧⲁⲕⲥⲉⲙⲛⲏⲧⲥ ⲛⲉⲙ ⲛⲉⲛⲓⲟϯ ⲁⲃⲣⲁⲁⲙ Ⲓⲥⲁⲁⲕ Ⲓⲁⲕⲱⲃ Ⲡⲓⲥⲣⲁⲏⲗ ⲡⲉⲑⲟⲩⲁⲃ ⲛ̅ⲧⲁⲕ	لا تنس العهد الذي قطعته مع آبائنا إبراهيم وإسحق ويعقوب إسرائيل قديسك

Deacon:

Bow your heads to the Lord	Ταc κεφαλαc γμων τω Κγριω κλιnατε	احنوا رؤوسكم للرب

Congregation:

Before You O Lord	Ενωπιων cογ Κγριε	أمامك يا رب

Priest *(facing East)*:

Listen, O Lord, to us, and hear us, we the unworthy sinners, and establish the union of Your two servants {GROOM} and {BRIDE} his helpmate. Deliver them from all evil and lengthen their lives with length of days, that they may live in meekness, calmness, endurance and submission, and keep them blameless and without offense. Enlighten their hearts and understanding so that they may always do Your will, for You are merciful, plenteous in mercy to all who cry out to You. And unto You we send up the glory, the honor, and the worship with Your good Father and the Holy Spirit, now and at all times and unto	Ρεκ πεκμαϣϫ Ποc ογοϩ cωτεμ ερον ανον ϧα νιρεϥερνοβι ογοϩ νατεμπϣα ματαϫρε πιϫινϩωτπ ντε νεκεβιαικ πα νιμ νεμ τα νιμ τεϥβοηθοc. Ναϩμογ εβολϩα πετϩωογ νιβεν μαρογερνεβαϩι ϧεν παϣαι ντε ϩανεϩοογ εγωνϧ ϧεν ογμετρεμραγϣ νεμ ογμετcεμνοc νεμ ϯϩγπομονη νεμ πϭνεϫωϥ εγοι ναταρικι νατϭροπ. αριογωινι ερωογ ϧεν νιβαλ ντε πογϩητ νεμ πογκαϯ επϫινιρι μπετεϩνακ νcηογ νιβεν νθοκ ογναητ γαρ ναϣε πεκναι νογον νιβεν ετωϣ εϩρηι ογβηκ τενογωρπ νακ επϣωι	أمل أذنك يا رب واسمعنا نحن الخطاة غير المستحقين وثبت إتصال عبديك (...) و (...) معينته نجهما من كل شر وليطل عمرها بكثرة الأيام وليعيشا بدعة وهدوء وإحتمال وخضوع وهما بلا لوم ولا عثرة أنر أعين قلبيهما وفهميهما ليصنعا إرادتك كل حين لأنك رحيم كثير الرحمة لكل الصارخين إليك ونرسل لك المجد والكرامة والسجود مع أبيك الصالح والروح القدس الآن وكل أوان وإلى دهر الدهور آمين

| the age of all ages. Amen. | ⲘⲠⲒⲰⲞⲨ ⲚⲈⲘ ⲠⲒⲦⲀⲒⲞ ⲚⲈⲘ ϮⲠⲢⲞⲤⲔⲎⲚⲎⲤⲒⲤ ϮⲚⲞⲨ ⲚⲈⲘ ⲚⲤⲎⲞⲨ ⲚⲒⲂⲈⲚ ⲚⲈⲘ ϢⲀ ⲈⲚⲈϨ ⲚⲦⲈ ⲚⲒⲈⲚⲈϨ ⲦⲎⲢⲞⲨ. ⲀⲘⲎⲚ. | |

Congregation *(in the muḥayyar tune)*:

| May God bless us, • and let us bless His holy name, • and may His praise continually be • always upon our mouths. | ⲈϥⲉⲤⲘⲞⲨ ⲈⲢⲞⲚ ⲚϪⲈ Ⲫϯ ⲦⲈⲚⲚⲀⲤⲘⲞⲨ ⲈⲠⲈϤⲢⲀⲚ ⲈⲐⲞⲨⲀⲂ ⲚⲤⲎⲞⲨ ⲚⲒⲂⲈⲚ ⲈⲢⲈ ⲠⲈϤⲤⲘⲞⲨ ⲚⲀϢⲰⲠⲒ ⲈϤⲘⲎⲚ ⲈⲂⲞⲖϦⲈⲚ ⲢⲰⲚ | يباركنا الله ولنبارك إسمه القدوس في كل حين تسبحته دائمة في أفواهنا |

Congregation *(in the Palm Sunday tune)*:

| Blessed is the Father and the Son • and the Holy Spirit • the perfect Trinity. • We worship him and glorify him. | Ϫⲉ ϥⲤⲘⲀⲢⲰⲞⲨⲦ ⲚϪⲈ ⲪⲒⲰⲦ ⲚⲈⲘ ⲠϢⲎⲢⲒ ⲚⲈⲘ ⲠⲒⲠⲚⲈⲨⲘⲀ ⲈⲐⲞⲨⲀⲂ ϮⲦⲢⲒⲀⲤ ⲈⲦϪⲎⲔ ⲈⲂⲞⲖ ⲦⲈⲚⲞⲨⲰϢⲦ ⲘⲘⲞⲤ ⲦⲈⲚϮⲰⲞⲨ ⲚⲀⲤ. | مبارك الآب و الابن و الروح القدس الثالوث الكامل نسبحه و نمجده |
| Lord Have Mercy Lord Have Mercy Lord Have Mercy | ⲔⲨⲢⲒⲈ ⲈⲖⲈⲎⲤⲞⲚ ⲔⲨⲢⲒⲈ ⲈⲖⲈⲎⲤⲞⲚ ⲔⲨⲢⲒⲈ ⲈⲖⲈⲎⲤⲞⲚ | يا رب ارحم يا رب ارحم يا رب ارحم |

Deacon:

| Let us beseech the Lord | Ⲧⲟⲩ Ⲕⲩⲣⲓⲟⲩ ⲆⲈⲎⲐⲰⲘⲈⲚ | من الرب نطلب |

The Prayer of the Oil

Priest:

O Master, Lord, God the Pantocrator, the Father of our Lord, God, and Savior Jesus Christ, who anointed out of the fruit of the rich olive tree priests, kings, and prophets.	Ⲫⲛⲏⲃ Ⲡⲟⲥ Ⲫϯ ⲡⲓⲡⲁⲛⲧⲟⲕⲣⲁⲧⲱⲣ Ⲫⲓⲱⲧ ⲙⲡⲉⲛⲟⲥ ⲟⲩⲟϩ ⲡⲉⲛⲛⲟⲩϯ ⲟⲩⲟϩ ⲡⲉⲛⲥⲱⲧⲏⲣ Ⲓⲏⲥ Ⲡⲭⲥ ⲫⲏⲉⲧⲉ ⲉⲃⲟⲗϩⲓⲧⲉⲛ ⲡⲓⲅⲉⲛⲛⲏⲙⲁ ⲛⲧⲉ ϯⲃⲱ ⲛϫⲱⲓⲧ ⲛⲛⲟⲧⲉⲙ ⲁⲕⲑⲱϩⲥ ⲛϩⲁⲛⲟⲩⲏⲃ ⲛⲉⲙ ϩⲁⲛⲟⲩⲣⲱⲟⲩ ⲛⲉⲙ ϩⲁⲛⲡⲣⲟⲫⲏⲧⲏⲥ.	أيها السيد الرب الإله ضابط الكل أبو ربنا وإلهنا ومخلصنا يسوع المسيح الذي من ثمرة شجرة الزيتون الدسم مسحت كهنة وملوكا وأنبياء
We ask and entreat You, O Good Lord, the Lover of Mankind, to bless this oil with blessings so that it becomes Oil to sanctify Your two servants {GROOM} and {BRIDE}. Amen A weapon of righteousness and justice. Amen An anointment of purity and incorruption. Amen Light and unfading beauty. Amen Joy, ornament, and true comfort. Amen Power, salvation, and victory over all the deeds of the adversary. Amen Renewal and salvation of their souls, bodies, and spirits. Amen	Ⲧⲉⲛϯϩⲟ ⲟⲩⲟϩ ⲧⲉⲛⲧⲱⲃϩ ⲙⲙⲟⲕ Ⲡⲟⲥ ⲡⲓⲙⲁⲓⲣⲱⲙⲓ ⲛⲁⲅⲁⲑⲟⲥ ϩⲟⲡⲱⲥ ϧⲉⲛ ⲟⲩⲥⲙⲟⲩ ⲛⲧⲉⲕⲥⲙⲟⲩ ⲉⲡⲁⲓⲛⲉϩ ⲫⲁⲓ ⲙⲁⲣⲉϥϣⲱⲡⲓ ⲛⲟⲩⲛⲉϩ ⲛⲁⲅⲓⲁⲥⲙⲟⲥ ⲛⲛⲉⲕⲉⲃⲓⲁⲓⲕ ⲡⲁ ⲛⲓⲙ ⲛⲉⲙ ⲧⲁⲛⲓⲙ ⲁⲙⲏⲛ ⲟⲩϩⲟⲡⲗⲟⲛ ⲛⲧⲉ ϯⲙⲉⲑⲙⲏⲓ ⲁⲙⲏⲛ ⲛⲉⲙ ϯⲇⲓⲕⲉⲟⲥⲩⲛⲏ ⲁⲙⲏⲛ ⲟⲩⲑⲱϩⲥ ⲛⲧⲉ ⲟⲩⲧⲟⲩⲃⲟ ⲛⲉⲙ ⲟⲩⲙⲉⲧⲁⲧⲧⲁⲕⲟ ⲁⲙⲏⲛ ⲟⲩ ⲟⲩⲱⲓⲛⲓ ⲛⲉⲙ ⲟⲩⲥⲁⲓ ⲛⲁⲑⲗⲱⲙ ⲁⲙⲏⲛ ⲉⲟⲩⲅⲉⲣⲟⲩⲟⲧ ⲛⲉⲙ ⲟⲩⲥⲟⲗⲥⲉⲗ ⲛⲧⲁⲫⲙⲏⲓ ⲁⲙⲏⲛ ⲉ ⲟⲩϫⲟⲙ ⲛⲉⲙ ⲟⲩϫⲁⲓ ⲛⲉⲙ ϭⲟⲣ ⲟⲩⲃⲉ ⲉⲛⲉⲣⲅⲓⲁ ⲛⲓⲃⲉⲛ ⲛⲧⲉ ⲡⲓⲁⲛⲧⲓⲕⲓⲙⲉⲛⲟⲥ ⲁⲙⲏⲛ ⲉ ⲟⲩⲙⲉⲧⲃⲉⲣⲓ ⲛⲉⲙ ⲟⲩⲥⲱⲧⲏⲣⲓⲁ ⲛⲧⲉ	نبتهل ونتضرع إليك أيها الرب محب البشر الصالح لكي تبارك هذا الزيت تبريكا ليكون زيتا لتقديس عبديك (...) و (...) آمين سلاح البر والعدل آمين مسحة الطهارة وعدم الفساد آمين نورا وجمالا لا يذبل آمين فرحا وزينة وعزاء حقيقيا آمين قوة وخلاصا وغلبة على كل أفعال المضاد آمين تجديدا وخلاصا لنفسيهما وجسديهما وروحيهما آمين غنى مع ثمرة الأفعال الحسنة آمين

Richness with the fruit of good deeds. Amen	ⲧⲟⲩⲯⲩⲭⲏ ⲛⲉⲙ ⲡⲟⲩⲥⲱⲙⲁ ⲛⲉⲙ ⲡⲟⲩⲡⲛⲉⲩⲙⲁ ⲁⲙⲏⲛ ⲉⲟⲩⲙⲉⲧⲣⲁⲙⲁⲟ ⲛⲉⲙ ⲟⲩⲧⲟⲩⲧⲁϩ ⲛⲧⲉ ϩⲁⲛϩⲃⲏⲟⲩⲓ ⲉⲛⲁⲛⲉⲩ ⲁⲙⲏⲛ	
Glory and honor to Your Holy Name with Your only-begotten Son and the Holy Spirit, the Giver of Life, who is of one essence with You now and forever and to the age of ages. Amen	ⲉⲟⲱⲟⲩ ⲛⲉⲙ ⲟⲩⲧⲁⲓⲟ ⲙⲡⲉⲕⲣⲁⲛ ⲉⲑⲟⲩⲁⲃ ⲛⲉⲙ ⲡⲓⲡⲛⲉⲩⲙⲁ ⲉⲑⲟⲩⲁⲃ ⲛⲣⲉϥⲧⲁⲛϧⲟ ⲟⲩⲟϩ ⲛⲟⲙⲟⲟⲩⲥⲓⲟⲥ ⲛⲉⲙⲁⲕ ϯⲛⲟⲩ ⲛⲉⲙ ⲛⲭⲟⲩ ⲛⲓⲃⲉⲛ ⲛⲉⲙ ϣⲁ ⲉⲛⲉϩ ⲛⲧⲉ ⲛⲓⲉⲛⲉϩ ⲧⲏⲣⲟⲩ. ⲁⲙⲏⲛ.	مجدا و اكراما لاسمك القدوس مع أبنك الوحيد الجنس و الروح القدس المحي المساوي معك الان و كل اوان و الى دهر الدهور أمين

Congregation *(said in the muḥayyar tune)*:

You have anointed my head with oil • and your cup intoxicated me	ⲁⲕⲑⲱϩⲥ ⲛⲧⲁⲁⲫⲉ ⲛⲟⲩⲛⲉϩ ⲟⲩⲟϩ ⲡⲉⲕⲁⲫⲟⲧ ⲉⲧⲑⲁϩⲓ ⲙⲫⲣⲏϯ ⲛⲟⲩⲁⲙⲁϩⲓ	دهنت بالزيت رأسي و كأسك اسكرتني مثل الصرف
Your mercy will seek me • all the days of my life	ⲡⲉⲕⲛⲁⲓ ⲉϥⲉϭⲟϫⲓ ⲛⲥⲱⲓ ⲛⲛⲓⲉϩⲟⲟⲩ ⲧⲏⲣⲟⲩ ⲛⲧⲉ ⲡⲁⲱⲛϧ	رحمتك و طيبك يطلباني كل ايام حياتي
All the nations of the earth bless me	ϩⲁⲛⲉⲑⲛⲟⲥ ⲧⲏⲣⲟⲩ ⲙⲡⲕⲁϩⲓ ⲥⲉⲉⲣⲙⲁⲕⲁⲣⲓⲍⲓⲛ ⲙⲙⲟⲓ	كل أمم الارض يغبطوني
All my people say may it be may it be	ⲡⲁⲗⲁⲟⲥ ⲧⲏⲣϥ ⲛⲁϫⲟⲥ ϫⲉ ⲉⲥⲉϣⲱⲡⲓ ⲉⲥⲉϣⲱⲡⲓ	و الشعب كانوا يقولون يكون يكون
You have increased in choice among my people	ⲁⲕϭⲓⲥⲓ ⲛⲟⲩⲥⲱⲧⲡ ϩⲓ ⲡⲁⲗⲁⲟⲥ	ارتفعت مختارا في شعبي

I found David my servant • so I anointed him with the holy oil. • My hand and my arm • shall strengthen him.	ⲁⲓϫⲓⲙⲓ ⲛⲇⲁⲩⲓⲇ ⲡⲁⲃⲱⲕ ⲁⲓⲑⲱϩⲥ ⲙⲙⲟϥ ϧⲉⲛ ⲡⲁⲛⲉϩ ⲉϥⲟⲩⲁⲃ ⲧⲁϫⲓϫ ⲟⲩⲟϩ ⲡⲁϣⲱⲃϣ ⲥⲉⲛⲁϯϫⲟⲙ ⲛⲁϥ	وجدت داود عبدي فدهنته بالدهن المقدس و ان يدي تساعده و ذراعي تعضده
The Lord said to His angel • so he lifted me from my father's sheep • and anointed me with the oil of his anointing.	ⲁ Ⲡϭⲟⲓⲥ ϫⲱ ⲙⲡⲉϥⲁⲅⲅⲉⲗⲟⲥ ⲁϥⲟⲗⲧ ⲉⲃⲟⲗ ϧⲉⲛ ⲛⲓⲉⲥⲱⲟⲩ ⲛⲧⲉ ⲡⲁⲓⲱⲧ ⲁϥⲑⲁϩⲥⲧ ϧⲉⲛ ⲫⲛⲉϩ ⲛⲧⲉ ⲡⲉϥⲑⲱϩⲥ	قال الرب لملاكه فاخذني من غنم أبي و دهني بدهن مسحته
My brothers are handsome and great.	Ⲛⲁⲥⲛⲏⲟⲩ ⲛⲁⲛⲉⲩ ⲟⲩⲟϩ ϩⲁⲛⲛⲓϣϯ ⲛⲉ	اخوتي حسان و هم الكبار

Priest *(said silently over the couple during the chanting of the preceeding verses)*:

O Lord, the God of hosts, whose mercies are countless, whose goodness is beyond comprehension, accept our supplications unto You. Guard Your two servants {GROOM} and {BRIDE}. Protect their unity. Keep their bed in purity. Fortify them by Your pure angels. Send upon us from Your prepared habitation a multitude of Your compassion. Disperse our many iniquities by Your goodness, and grant us also to be in the places of rest of Your saints in the heavenly	Ⲡⲟⲥ Ⲫϯ ⲛⲧⲉ ⲛⲓϫⲟⲙ ⲡⲓⲁⲧϭⲓⲏⲡⲓ ⲙⲙⲟϥ ϧⲉⲛ ⲛⲉϥⲙⲉⲧϣⲉⲛϩⲏⲧ ⲟⲩⲟϩ ⲛⲁⲧϣⲧⲁϩⲟϥ ϧⲉⲛ ⲧⲉϥⲙⲉⲧⲁⲅⲁⲑⲟⲥ ϣⲱⲡ ⲉⲣⲟⲕ ⲛⲛⲉⲛϯϩⲟ ⲁⲣⲓⲥⲕⲉⲡⲁⲍⲓⲛ ⲉϫⲉⲛ ⲛⲉⲕⲉⲃⲓⲁⲓⲕ ⲡⲁ ⲛⲓⲙ ⲛⲉⲙ ⲧⲁ ⲛⲓⲙ. Ⲣⲱⲓⲥ ⲉⲡⲟⲩϫⲓⲛϩⲱⲧⲡ ⲁⲡⲣⲉϩ ⲉⲧⲟⲩϣⲁⲓⲣⲓ ⲉⲥⲧⲟⲩⲃⲏⲟⲩⲧ. ⲁⲣⲓⲥⲟⲃⲧ ⲉⲣⲟⲛ ⲛⲉⲙⲱⲟⲩ ϩⲓⲧⲉⲛ ϩⲁⲛⲁⲅⲅⲉⲗⲟⲥ ⲉⲑⲟⲩⲁⲃ ⲟⲩⲱⲣⲡ ⲉϩⲣⲏⲓ ⲉϫⲱⲛ ⲉⲃⲟⲗϧⲉⲛ ⲡⲉⲕⲙⲁⲛϣⲱⲡⲓ ⲉⲧⲥⲉⲃⲧⲱⲧ ⲙⲡⲁϣⲁⲓ ⲛⲧⲉ ⲛⲉⲕⲙⲉⲧϣⲉⲛϩⲏⲧ ϫⲱⲣ	أيها الرب إله القوات الذي لا تحصى مراحمه غير المدرك في صلاحه إقبل إليك تضرعنا استر على عبديك (...) و (...) واحرس إتصالهما وإحفظ مضجعهما نقيا حصنهما بملائكتك الأطهار وأرسل علينا من مسكنك المستعد كثرة رأفاتك بدد زلاتنا الكثيرة بصلاحك وإنعم علينا أيضا أن نكون في أماكن راحة قديسيك في ملكوت السموات بإبنك الوحيد يسوع المسيح ربنا هذا الذي يليق بك المجد والإكرام والعزة والسجود تليق بك معه مع الروح القدس المحيي

kingdom, through Your only-begotten Son Jesus Christ our Lord. Through whom the glory, the honor, the dominion, and the worship are due unto You, with Him, and the Holy Spirit, the Giver of Life, who is of one essence with You, now and at all times, and unto the age of all ages. Amen.	ⲉⲃⲟⲗ ⲙⲡⲁϣⲁⲓ ⲛⲧⲉ ⲛⲉⲛⲡⲁⲣⲁⲡⲧⲱⲙⲁ ϩⲓⲧⲉⲛ ⲧⲉⲕⲙⲉⲧⲁⲅⲁⲑⲟⲥ ⲟⲩⲟϩ ⲉⲕⲉⲉⲣϩⲙⲟⲧ ⲛⲁⲛ ⲟⲛ ⲉⲑⲣⲉⲛϣⲱⲡⲓ ϧⲉⲛ ⲛⲓⲙⲁⲛⲉⲙⲧⲟⲛ ⲛⲧⲉ ⲛⲏⲉⲑⲟⲩⲁⲃ ⲛⲧⲁⲕ ⲛϩⲣⲏⲓ ϧⲉⲛ ⲑⲙⲉⲧⲟⲩⲣⲟ ⲛⲛⲓⲫⲏⲟⲩⲓ ϩⲓⲧⲉⲛ ⲡⲉⲕⲙⲟⲛⲟⲅⲉⲛⲏⲥ ⲛϣⲏⲣⲓ Ⲓⲏⲥ Ⲡⲭⲥ ⲡⲉⲛϬⲟⲓⲥ ⲫⲁⲓ ⲉⲧⲉ ⲉⲃⲟⲗϩⲓⲧⲟⲧϥ ⲉⲣⲉ ⲡⲓⲱⲟⲩ ⲛⲉⲙ ⲡⲓⲧⲁⲓⲟ ⲛⲉⲙ ⲡⲓⲁⲙⲁϩⲓ ⲛⲉⲙ ϯⲡⲣⲟⲥⲕⲩⲛⲏⲥⲓⲥ ⲉⲣⲡⲣⲉⲡⲓ ⲛⲁⲕ ⲛⲉⲙⲁϥ ⲛⲉⲙ ⲡⲓⲡⲛⲉⲩⲙⲁ ⲉⲑⲟⲩⲁⲃ ⲛⲣⲉϥⲧⲁⲛϧⲟ ⲟⲩⲟϩ ⲛⲟⲙⲟⲟⲩⲥⲓⲟⲥ ⲛⲉⲙⲁⲕ ϯⲛⲟⲩ ⲛⲉⲙ ⲛⲥⲏⲟⲩ ⲛⲓⲃⲉⲛ ⲛⲉⲙ ϣⲁ ⲉⲛⲉϩ ⲛⲧⲉ ⲛⲓⲉⲛⲉϩ ⲧⲏⲣⲟⲩ. ⲁⲙⲏⲛ.	المساوي لك الآن وكل أوان وإلى دهر الدهور آمين

The Prayer of the Crowns

Priest:

O Holy God, who crowned the saints with unfading crowns, and reconciled the heavenly and earthly and united them; O You our Master, now also bless these crowns which we prepared to be set upon Your two servants to be for them:	Ⲫϯ ⲫⲏⲉⲑⲟⲩⲁⲃ ⲫⲏⲉⲧⲁϥϯ ⲭⲗⲟⲙ ⲉϫⲉⲛ ⲛⲏⲉⲑⲟⲩⲁⲃ ⲛⲧⲁϥ ϧⲉⲛ ϩⲁⲛⲭⲗⲟⲙ ⲛⲁⲑⲗⲱⲙ ⲟⲩⲟϩ ⲁϥϩⲱⲧⲡ ⲛⲛⲁⲧⲫⲉ ⲛⲉⲙ ⲛⲁ ⲡⲕⲁϩⲓ ϧⲉⲛ ⲟⲩⲙⲉⲧⲟⲩⲁⲓ ⲛⲑⲟⲕ ⲟⲛ ϯⲛⲟⲩ ⲡⲉⲛⲛⲏⲃ ⲥⲙⲟⲩ ⲉⲛⲁⲓ ⲭⲗⲟⲙ ⲉⲧⲁⲛⲥⲉⲃⲧⲱⲧⲟⲩ ⲉⲑⲣⲉⲛⲧⲏⲓⲧⲟⲩ ⲉϫⲉⲛ	يا الله القدوس الذي كلل قديسيه بأكاليل لا تذبل وصالح السمائيين مع الأرضيين ووحدهما أنت أيضا الآن يا سيدنا بارك هذه الأكاليل التي هيأناها لنضعها على عبديك لتكون لهما أكاليل مجد وكرامة آمين أكاليل بركة وخلاص آمين

- Crowns of glory and honor. Amen.
- Crowns of blessing and salvation. Amen.
- Crowns of joy and happiness. Amen.
- Crowns of jubilation and delight. Amen.
- Crowns of virtue and justice. Amen.
- Crowns of wisdom and understanding hearts. Amen.
- Crowns of comfort and confirmation. Amen.

Grant Your two servants, who shall wear them, the angel of peace and the bond of love. Deliver them from all evil thoughts and vile desires. Deliver them from every weight of cunning and from every devilish hardship. Let your mercy be upon them. Hear the voice of their supplication. Set your fear in their hearts. Manage their lives without delay unto old age. Make them rejoice by beholding the sons and daughters whom they will beget. Make them useful in Your one, holy, catholic, and apostolic Church. Confirm them in the Orthodox faith to the end. Lead them in the

ⲛⲉⲕⲉⲃⲓⲁⲓⲕ. Ⲙⲁⲣⲟⲩϣⲱⲡⲓ ⲛⲱⲟⲩ ⲛⲟⲩⲭⲗⲟⲙ ⲛⲱⲟⲩ ⲛⲉⲙ ⲟⲩⲧⲁⲓⲟ ⲁⲙⲏⲛ
ⲟⲩⲭⲗⲟⲙ ⲛⲧⲉ ⲟⲩⲥⲙⲟⲩ ⲛⲉⲙ ⲟⲩ ⲟⲩϫⲁⲓ ⲁⲙⲏⲛ
ⲟⲩⲭⲗⲟⲙ ⲛⲧⲉ ⲟⲩⲣⲁϣⲓ ⲛⲉⲙ ⲟⲩϯⲙⲁϯ ⲁⲙⲏⲛ
ⲟⲩⲭⲗⲟⲙ ⲛⲧⲉ ⲡⲑⲉⲗⲏⲗ ⲛⲉⲙ ⲡⲟⲩⲛⲟϥ ⲁⲙⲏⲛ
ⲟⲩⲭⲗⲟⲙ ⲛⲧⲉ ϯⲁⲣⲉⲧⲏ ⲛⲉⲙ ϯⲇⲓⲕⲉⲟⲥⲩⲛⲏ ⲁⲙⲏⲛ
ⲟⲩⲭⲗⲟⲙ ⲛⲥⲟⲫⲓⲁ ⲛⲉⲙ ⲙⲉⲧⲣⲉⲙⲛϩⲏⲧ ⲁⲙⲏⲛ
ⲟⲩⲭⲗⲟⲙ ⲛⲛⲟⲙϯ ⲛⲉⲙ ⲟⲩⲧⲁϫⲣⲟ ⲁⲙⲏⲛ
ⲁⲣⲓⲭⲁⲣⲓⲍⲉⲥⲑⲉ ⲛⲛⲉⲕⲉⲃⲓⲁⲓⲕ ⲉⲑⲛⲁⲉⲣⲫⲟⲣⲓⲛ ⲙⲙⲱⲟⲩ ⲛⲟⲩⲁⲅⲅⲉⲗⲟⲥ ⲛⲧⲉ ϯϩⲓⲣⲏⲛⲏ ⲛⲉⲙ ⲫⲙⲟⲩⲣ ⲛⲧⲉ ϯⲁⲅⲁⲡⲏ ⲙⲁⲧⲟⲩϫⲱⲟⲩ ⲉⲃⲟⲗϩⲁ ⲙⲉⲩⲓ ⲛⲓⲃⲉⲛ ⲛϭⲗⲟϥ ⲛⲉⲙ ⲟⲩⲉⲡⲓⲑⲩⲙⲓⲁ ⲉⲥϫⲁⲓⲱⲟⲩ. Ⲟⲩⲟϩ ⲥⲟⲧⲟⲩ ⲉⲃⲟⲗϩⲁ ⲃⲁⲣⲟⲥ ⲛⲓⲃⲉⲛ ⲙⲡⲟⲛⲏⲣⲟⲛ ⲛⲉⲙ ⲉⲡⲏⲣⲁ ⲛⲓⲃⲉⲛ ⲛⲇⲓⲁⲃⲟⲗⲓⲕⲟⲛ. Ⲙⲁⲣⲉϥϣⲱⲡⲓ ⲛϫⲉ ⲡⲉⲕⲛⲁⲓ ⲉϩⲣⲏⲓ ⲉϫⲱⲟⲩ ⲥⲱⲧⲉⲙ ⲉⲡϩⲣⲱⲟⲩ ⲛⲧⲉ ⲡⲟⲩⲧⲱⲃϩ ϩⲓⲟⲩⲓ ⲛⲧⲉⲕϩⲟϯ ⲉϩⲣⲏⲓ ⲉⲡⲟⲩϩⲏⲧ ⲁⲣⲓϩⲉⲙⲓ ⲙⲡⲟⲩϫⲓⲛⲱⲛϩ ⲉⲩⲟⲓ ⲛⲁⲧⲉⲣϧⲁⲉ ϣⲁ ⲉϩⲣⲏⲓ ⲉⲟⲩⲙⲉⲧϩⲉⲗⲗⲟ ⲉⲕⲉⲑⲣⲟⲩⲟⲩⲛⲟϥ ϧⲉⲛ ⲡϫⲓⲛⲛⲁⲩ ⲛⲧⲉ ϩⲁⲛϣⲏⲣⲓ

أكاليل فرح ومسرة آمين
أكاليل تهليل وبهجة آمين
أكاليل فضيلة وعدل آمين
أكاليل حكمة وفهم قلب آمين
أكاليل عزاء وثبات آمين

هب لعبديك اللذين يلبسانها ملاك السلامة ورباط المحبة وأنقذهما من كل فكر قبيح وشهوة رديئة ونجهما من كل ثقل الخبث ومن كل محنة شيطانية ولتكن رحمتك عليهما إستمع صوت طلبتهما إطرح مخافتك في قلبيهما دبر حياتهما بغير تأخير إلى حد الشيخوخة إجعلهما يفرحان بنظر البنين والبنات الذين يلدانهما إئت بهم نافعين في كنيستك الواحدة المقدسة الجامعة الرسولية ثابتين في الإيمان الأرثوذكسي إلى الإنقضاء دبرها في سبيل برك بمسرة أبيك الصالح والروح القدس الآن وكل أوان وإلى دهر الدهور أمين

A Textual History of the Coptic Wedding Rite

way of Your righteousness through the pleasure of Your good Father and the Holy Spirit, now and forever and unto the end. Amen.	ⲛⲉⲙ ϩⲁⲛϣⲉⲣⲓ ⲟⲩⲟϩ ⲛⲏⲉⲧⲟⲩⲛⲁⲫⲱⲟⲩ ⲉⲕⲉⲉⲛⲟⲩ ⲉⲃⲟⲗ ⲉⲩⲉⲣϣⲁⲩ ϧⲉⲛ ⲧⲉⲕⲟⲩⲓ ⲙⲙⲁⲩⲁⲧⲥ ⲛⲕⲁⲑⲟⲗⲓⲕⲏ ⲛⲁⲡⲟⲥⲧⲟⲗⲓⲕⲏ ⲛⲉⲕⲕⲗⲏⲥⲓⲁ ⲉⲑⲟⲩⲁⲃ ⲉⲩⲧⲁϩⲣⲏⲟⲩⲧ ϧⲉⲛ ⲡⲓⲛⲁϩϯ ⲛⲟⲣⲑⲟⲇⲟⲍⲟⲥ ϣⲁ ⲉⲃⲟⲗ. ⲉⲕⲉⲉⲣϩⲉⲙⲓ ⲙⲙⲱⲟⲩ ϧⲉⲛ ⲫⲙⲱⲓⲧ ⲛⲧⲉ ϯⲙⲉⲑⲙⲏⲓ ϩⲓⲧⲉⲛ ⲡϯⲙⲁϯ ⲙⲡⲉⲕⲓⲱⲧ ⲛⲁⲅⲁⲑⲟⲥ ⲛⲉⲙ ⲡⲓⲡⲛⲉⲩⲙⲁ ⲉⲑⲟⲩⲁⲃ ϯⲛⲟⲩ ⲛⲉⲙ ⲛⲥⲏⲟⲩ ⲛⲓⲃⲉⲛ ⲛⲉⲙ ϣⲁ ⲉⲛⲉϩ ⲛⲧⲉ ⲛⲓⲉⲛⲉϩ ⲧⲏⲣⲟⲩ. ⲁⲙⲏⲛ.	

(The priest puts the crowns on the heads of the couple while saying:)

Place, O Lord, upon Your two servants crowns of unvanquished grace. Amen. Crowns of elevated and everlasting glory. Amen Crowns of unopposed and unattacked good faith and bless all their actions. Amen For You, Christ our God, are the giver of all good things, and glory and honor are due to You with Your good Father, and Your Holy Spirit, the Giver of Life who is of	ⲉⲕⲉⲭⲱ Ⲡⲟⲥ ⲉϫⲉⲛ ⲛⲉⲕⲉⲃⲓⲁⲓⲕ ⲛⲟⲩⲭⲗⲟⲙ ⲛⲧⲉ ⲟⲩϩⲙⲟⲧ ⲛⲁⲧϭⲣⲟ ⲉⲣⲟϥ ⲟⲩⲭⲗⲟⲙ ⲛⲧⲉ ⲟⲩⲱⲟⲩ ⲉϥϭⲟⲥⲓ ⲟⲩ ⲉⲛⲁϣⲱϥ ⲟⲩⲭⲗⲟⲙ ⲛⲧⲉ ⲟⲩⲛⲁϩϯ ⲉⲛⲁⲛⲉϥ ⲟⲩⲟϩ ⲉⲕⲉⲥⲙⲟⲩ ⲟⲩϩ ⲛⲁⲧⲃⲱⲧⲥ ⲟⲩⲃⲏϥ ⲟⲩⲟϩ ⲉⲕⲉⲥⲙⲟⲩ ⲉⲛⲟⲩϩⲃⲏⲟⲩⲓ ⲧⲏⲣⲟⲩ. Ⲇⲉ ⲛⲑⲟⲕ ⲡⲉ ⲡⲓⲣⲉϥϯ ⲛⲛⲓⲁⲅⲁⲑⲟⲛ ⲧⲏⲣⲟⲩ Ⲡⲭⲥ ⲡⲉⲛⲛⲟⲩϯ ⲉⲣⲉ ⲡⲓⲱⲟⲩ ⲛⲉⲙ ⲡⲓⲧⲁⲓⲟ ⲉⲣⲡⲣⲉⲡⲓ ⲛⲁⲕ ⲛⲉⲙ ⲡⲉⲕⲓⲱⲧ ⲛⲁⲅⲁⲑⲟⲥ ⲛⲉⲙ	ضع يا رب على عبديك أكاليل النعمة غير المغلوبة آمين أكاليل مجد مرتفع وغير فان آمين أكاليل أمانة حسنة غير مضادة ولا محاربة وبارك جميع أعمالهما آمين لأنك أنت المعطي سائر الخيرات أيها المسيح إلهنا ويليق بك المجد والإكرام مع أبيك الصالح وروحك القدس المحيي المساوي لك الآن وكل أوان وإلى دهر الدهور أمين

one essence with You now and forever and unto the age of all ages. Amen	ⲡⲉⲕⲡⲛⲉⲩⲙⲁ ⲉⲑⲟⲩⲁⲃ ⲛⲣⲉϥⲧⲁⲛϧⲟ ⲟⲩⲟϩ ⲛⲟⲙⲟⲟⲩⲥⲓⲟⲥ ⲛⲉⲙⲁⲕ ϯⲛⲟⲩ ⲛⲉⲙ ⲛⲥⲏⲟⲩ ⲛⲓⲃⲉⲛ ⲛⲉⲙ ϣⲁ ⲉⲛⲉϩ ⲛⲧⲉ ⲛⲓⲉⲛⲉϩ ⲧⲏⲣⲟⲩ. ⲁⲙⲏⲛ.	

(The priest cries aloud saying these three blessings. With each one, he makes the sign of the cross over the couple's heads. The congregation responds to each one with Amen.)

"You crowned him with glory and honor." (Ps. 8:5)	ⲇⲟⲝⲏ ⲕⲉ ⲧⲓⲙⲏ ⲉⲥⲧⲉⲫⲁⲛⲱⲥⲁⲥ ⲁⲩⲧⲟⲛ	بالمجد و الكرامة توجته
The Father blesses.	Ο ⲡⲁⲧⲏⲣ ⲉⲩⲗⲟⲅⲉⲓ	الآب يبارك
The Son crowns.	Ο ⲩⲓⲟⲥ ⲥⲧⲉⲫⲁⲛⲉⲓ	الابن يكلل
The Holy Spirit surrounds and perfects.	Το ⲁⲅⲓⲟ ⲡⲛⲉⲩⲙⲁ ⲡⲁⲣⲁⲅⲓⲅⲛⲉⲧⲁⲓ ⲕⲉ ⲧⲉⲗⲉⲓ	الروح القدس يشمل و يتمم

Congregation:

Worthy, Worthy, Worthy are you O bridegroom and your helpmate	ⲁⲝⲓⲟⲥ ⲁⲝⲓⲟⲥ ⲁⲝⲓⲟⲥ ⲡⲓⲡⲁⲧϣⲉⲗⲉⲧ ⲛⲉⲙ ⲧⲉⲕⲃⲟⲏⲑⲟⲥ	مستحق مستحق مستحق أيها العريس و معينتك
You received grace and blessing through our Lord Jesus Christ.	ⲁⲕϭⲓ ⲧⲭⲁⲣⲓⲥ ⲕⲉ ⲉⲩⲗⲟⲅⲓⲧⲟⲥ ϩⲓⲧⲉⲛ ⲡⲉⲛϭⲟⲓⲥ Ⲓⲏⲥ Ⲡⲭⲥ	أنت قابلت النعمة و البركة من ربنا يسوع المسيح
You received a perfect crown full of freedom.	ⲁⲕϭⲓ ⲥⲧⲉⲫⲁⲛⲟⲥ ⲛⲧⲉⲗⲓⲟⲥ ⲉⲑⲙⲉϩ ⲛⲉⲗⲉⲩⲑⲉⲣⲟⲥ	أنت قابلت اكليل كامل مملوء حرية

A Textual History of the Coptic Wedding Rite

| You received the beautiful promise O bridegroom and your helpmate. | ⲁⲕϭⲓ ⲛ̀ϯⲉⲡⲁⲅⲅⲉⲗⲓⲁ ⲉⲑⲛⲉⲥⲟⲥ ⲱ ⲡⲓⲛⲩⲙⲫⲓⲟⲥ ⲛⲉⲙ ⲧⲉⲕⲃⲱⲏⲑⲟⲥ | أنت قابلت الموعد الحسن أيها العريس و معينتك |

The Verses of Blessing for the Groom

(The priest says these verses in the Axios tune. If he does not know the tune, he may delegate the deacons to chant these verses. In both cases, the priest makes the sign of the cross over the groom with each verse. Then he does the same for the bride while saying verses for her.)

He who blessed • our father Adam and Noah • and Abraham and Moses • in the land of Midian • is blessing you O the bridegroom and your helpmate.	Ⲫⲏⲉⲧⲁϥ ⲥⲙⲟⲩ ⲙ̀ⲡⲉⲛⲓⲱⲧ ⲁⲇⲁⲙ ⲛⲉⲙ Ⲛⲱⲏ ⲛⲉⲙ Ⲁⲃⲣⲁⲁⲙ ⲛⲉⲙ Ⲙⲱⲩⲥⲏⲥ ϧⲉⲛ ⲡⲕⲁϩⲓ ⲙ̀Ⲙⲁⲇⲓⲁⲛ ⲉϥⲥⲙⲟⲩ ⲉⲣⲟⲕ ⲱ ⲡⲓⲡⲁⲧϣⲉⲗⲉⲧ ⲛⲉⲙ ⲧⲉⲕⲃⲟⲏⲑⲟⲥ	الذى بارك ابينا ادم و حوى ابراهيم و موسى قى ارض مدين يباركك ايها العريس و معينتك
He who blessed • our father Isaac the beloved • and Abel the first righteous • and Solomon and his father David • is blessing you O the bridegroom and your helpmate.	Ⲫⲏⲉⲧⲁϥⲥⲙⲟⲩ ⲙ̀ⲡⲉⲛⲓⲱⲧ Ⲓⲥⲥⲁⲕ ⲡⲓⲙⲉⲛⲣⲓⲧ ⲛⲉⲙ Ⲉⲃⲉⲗ ⲡⲓⲑⲙⲏⲓ ⲛ̀ϩⲟⲩⲓⲧ ⲛⲉⲙ Ⲥⲟⲗⲟⲙⲱⲛ ⲛⲉⲙ ⲡⲉϥⲓⲱⲧ Ⲇⲁⲩⲓⲇ ⲉϥⲥⲙⲟⲩ ⲉⲣⲟⲕ ⲱ ⲡⲓⲡⲁⲧϣⲉⲗⲉⲧ ⲛⲉⲙ ⲧⲉⲕⲃⲟⲏⲑⲟⲥ	الذى بارك أسحق الحبيب و بارك هابيل الصديق الأول و سليمن و ابيه داود يباركك ايها العريس و معينتك
He who blessed • our father Jacob • and Esau • and the righteous Job • is blessing you O the bridegroom and your helpmate.	Ⲫⲏⲉⲧⲁϥⲥⲙⲟⲩ ⲙ̀ⲡⲉⲛⲓⲱⲧ Ⲓⲁⲕⲱⲃ ⲛⲉⲙ Ⲏⲥⲁⲩ ⲛⲉⲙ ⲡⲓⲑⲙⲏⲓ Ⲓⲱⲃ ⲉϥⲥⲙⲟⲩ ⲉⲣⲟⲕ ⲱ ⲡⲓⲡⲁⲧϣⲉⲗⲉⲧ ⲛⲉⲙ ⲧⲉⲕⲃⲟⲏⲑⲟⲥ	الذى بارك ابينا يعقوب وعيسو و البار ايوب يباركك ايها العريس و معينتك

The Verses of Blessing for the Bride

May He who blessed • our father Abraham with Sarah • by the tree • of Mamre • now also bless this union.	Ⲫⲏⲉⲧⲁϥⲥⲙⲟⲩ ⲙⲡⲉⲛⲓⲱⲧ ⲁⲃⲣⲁⲁⲙ ⲛⲉⲙ Ⲥⲁⲣⲣⲁ ϧⲁⲧⲉⲛ ⲡⲓϣϣⲏⲛ ⲛⲧⲉ Ⲙⲁⲙⲣⲏ ϯⲛⲟⲩ ⲟⲛ ⲥⲙⲟⲩ ⲉⲡⲁⲓϫⲓⲛⲧⲟⲙⲓ ⲫⲁⲓ	الذى بارك لأبينا أبراهيم في ساره على شجرة ممرا الآن بارك هذا الاتصال
May He who blessed • Isaac with Rebecca • now also bless this union.	Ⲫⲏⲉⲧⲁϥⲥⲙⲟⲩ ⲛⲒⲥⲁⲁⲕ ⲛⲉⲙ Ⲓⲉⲣⲉⲃⲉⲕⲭⲁ ϯⲛⲟⲩ ⲟⲛ ⲥⲙⲟⲩ ⲉⲡⲁⲓϫⲓⲛⲧⲟⲙⲓ ⲫⲁⲓ	الذى بارك اسحق و رفقا الآن بارك هذا الاتصال
May He who blessed • our father Jacob • with Leah and Rachel • who built the house of Israel • now also bless this union.	Ⲫⲏⲉⲧⲁϥⲥⲙⲟⲩ ⲙⲡⲉⲛⲓⲱⲧ Ⲓⲁⲕⲱⲃ ⲉϫⲉⲛ Ⲉⲗⲓⲁ ⲛⲉⲙ Ⲣⲁⲭⲏⲗ ⲛⲏⲉⲧⲁⲩⲕⲱⲧ ⲉⲡⲏⲓ ⲙⲡⲒⲥⲣⲁⲏⲗ ϯⲛⲟⲩ ⲟⲛ ⲥⲙⲟⲩ ⲉⲡⲁⲓϫⲓⲛⲧⲟⲙⲓ ⲫⲁⲓ.	الذى بارك لأبينا يعقوب في اليا و راحيل الثاني بنين بيت أسرائيل الآن بارك هذا الاتصال
May He who blessed • Joseph with Asenath • and Zacharias with Elizabeth • and Joachim and Anna the blessed • now also bless this union.	Ⲫⲏⲉⲧⲁϥⲥⲙⲟⲩ ⲛⲒⲟⲩⲥⲏϥ ⲛⲉⲙ Ⲁⲥⲏⲛⲛⲁⲑ ⲛⲉⲙ Ⲍⲁⲭⲁⲣⲓⲁⲥ ⲉϫⲉⲛ Ⲉⲗⲓⲥⲁⲃⲉⲧ ⲛⲉⲙ Ⲓⲱⲁⲕⲓⲙ ⲛⲉⲙ Ⲁⲛⲛⲁ ⲉⲧⲥⲙⲁⲙⲁⲧ ϯⲛⲟⲩ ⲟⲛ ⲥⲙⲟⲩ ⲉⲡⲁⲓϫⲓⲛⲧⲟⲙⲓ ⲫⲁⲓ.	الذى بارك يوسف و اسنات و زكريا و اليصابات و يواقيم و حنه المباركة الآن بارك هذا الاتصال

(If desired, they may also add these verses.)

He who blessed • Michael and Gabriel • and Raphael and Suriel • and the four incorporeal creatures • and the twenty four presbyters • and the Cherubim • and the Seraphim • and the heavenly orders • is	Ⲫⲏⲉⲧⲁϥⲥⲙⲟⲩ ⲙⲘⲓⲭⲁⲏⲗ ⲛⲉⲙ Ⲅⲁⲃⲣⲓⲏⲗ ⲛⲉⲙ Ⲣⲁⲫⲁⲏⲗ ⲛⲉⲙ Ⲥⲟⲩⲣⲓⲏⲗ ⲛⲉⲙ ⲡⲓϥⲧⲟⲩ ⲛⲍⲱⲟⲛ ⲛⲁⲥⲱⲙⲁⲧⲟⲥ ⲛⲉⲙ ⲡⲓϫⲟⲩⲧ ϥⲧⲟⲩ ⲙⲡⲣⲉⲥⲃⲩⲧⲉⲣⲟⲥ ⲛⲉⲙ ⲛⲓⲬⲉⲣⲟⲩⲃⲓⲙ ⲛⲉⲙ ⲛⲓⲤⲉⲣⲁⲫⲓⲙ ⲛⲉⲙ	الذى بارك ميخائيل و غبريال و رافائيل و سوريال و الاربع الحيوانات الغير المتجسدين و الاربع و العشرين قسيس و الشاروبيم و السيرافيم يباركك أيها العريس و معينتك

A Textual History of the Coptic Wedding Rite

blessing you O the bridegroom and his helpmate.	ⲛⲓⲧⲁⲅⲙⲁ ⲛⲉⲡⲟⲩⲣⲁⲛⲓⲟⲛ ⲉϥⲥⲙⲟⲩ ⲉⲣⲟⲕ ⲱ ⲡⲓⲡⲁⲧϣⲉⲗⲉⲧ ⲛⲉⲙ ⲧⲉⲕⲃⲟⲏⲑⲟⲥ.	
He who blessed • my lords and fathers • the Apostles, Peter and our teacher Paul, • and the rest of the disciples, • and my lord the prince George, • and Theodore the general, and Theodore Anatolius, • and Philopater Mercurius, • and Abba Mina, and Abba Victor, • and Claudius, and all the choir of the martyrs • is blessing you O the bridegroom and his helpmate.	Ⲫⲏⲉⲧⲁϥⲥⲙⲟⲩ ⲛⲛⲁϭⲟⲓⲥ ⲛⲓⲱϯ ⲛⲁⲡⲟⲥⲧⲟⲗⲟⲥ ⲉⲧⲉ Ⲡⲉⲧⲣⲟⲥ ⲛⲉⲙ ⲡⲉⲛⲥⲁϧ Ⲡⲁⲩⲗⲟⲥ ⲛⲉⲙ ⲡⲥⲉⲡⲓ ⲛⲧⲉ ⲛⲓⲙⲁⲑⲏⲧⲏⲥ ⲛⲉⲙ ⲡⲁϭⲟⲓⲥ ⲡⲟⲩⲣⲟ Ⲅⲉⲱⲣⲅⲓⲟⲥ ⲛⲉⲙ Ⲑⲉⲟⲇⲟⲣⲟⲥ ⲡⲓⲥⲧⲣⲁⲧⲓⲗⲁⲧⲏⲥ ⲛⲉⲙ Ⲑⲉⲟⲇⲟⲣⲟⲥ ⲡⲓⲁⲛⲁⲧⲟⲗⲉⲟⲥ ⲛⲉⲙ Ⲫⲓⲗⲟⲡⲁⲧⲏⲣ Ⲙⲉⲣⲕⲟⲩⲣⲓⲟⲥ ⲛⲉⲙ ⲁⲡⲁ Ⲙⲏⲛⲁ ⲛⲉⲙ ⲁⲡⲁ Ⲃⲓⲕⲧⲱⲣ ⲛⲉⲙ Ⲕⲗⲁⲩⲇⲓⲟⲥ ⲛⲉⲙ ⲡⲭⲱⲣⲟⲥ ⲧⲏⲣϥ ⲛⲧⲉ ⲛⲓⲙⲁⲣⲧⲩⲣⲟⲥ ⲉϥⲥⲙⲟⲩ ⲉⲣⲟⲕ ⲱ ⲡⲓⲡⲁⲧϣⲉⲗⲉⲧ ⲛⲉⲙ ⲧⲉⲕⲃⲟⲏⲑⲟⲥ.	الذي بارك أبائي الرسل بطرس و معلمنا بولس و باقي التلميذ وسيدي الملك جرجس و تدرس المشرقي و فيلوباتير مركوريوس و أبا مينا و أبا بقطر و اكلاديوس و جميع صفوف الشهداء يباركك أيها العريس و معينتك

(If desired, they may also add these verses.)

O You who who blessed • the wedding at Cana of Galilee, • also bless this crowning • through the intercessions of the Archangel Michael • and the prayers of our Lady Mary (and the saint of the church)	أيها الذي بارك عرس قانا الجليل بارك أيضا هذا الاكليل بشفاعة رئيس الملائكة ميخائيل و بصلاة سيدتنا مريم و (يذكر اسم شفيع الكنيسة)
O You who blessed • His servant Abraham • and gave the law to Moses the prophet • bless this couple with Your Holy Name • through the	أيها الذي بارك عبده ابراهيم و أعطى الناموس لموسى الكليم بارك العروسين باسمك العظيم بصلاة سيدتنا مريم و (يذكر اسم شفيع الكنيسة)

prayers of • our Lady Mary (and the saint of the church)	
May He who blessed • the five loaves, and from them • fed thousands and myriads, • and raised Lazarus from among the dead, • bless you O bridegroom, and bless you O bride • through the prayers • of our Lady Mary (and the saint of the church)	الذي بارك في الخمس خبزات و أشبع منها ألوف مع ربوات و أقام لعازر من الأموات يبارك عليك أيها العريس و يبارك عليك أيتها العروس بصلاة سيدتنا مريم و (يذكر اسم شفيع الكنيسة)
O You who saved Jonah • from the belly of the whale, • and raised Lazarus from the dead, • make them children of the Kingdom • through the prayers of • our Lady Mary (and the saint of the church)	أيها الذي خلص يونان من بطن الحوت و أقام لعازر من الموت اجعلهما من أبناء الملكوت بصلاة سيدتنا مريم و (يذكر اسم شفيع الكنيسة)
O You who healed • His servant Job, • and reunited Joseph with his father Jacob, • write their names in the Book of Life • through the prayers of • our Lady Mary (and the saint of the church)	أيها الذي شفى عبده أيوب و جمع يوسف على أبيه يعقوب أجعل اسميهما في سفر الحياة مكتوب بصلاة سيدتنا مريم و (يذكر اسم شفيع الكنيسة)
May He who accepted • the penitent in His mercy, • and gave the authority • to His priests, • grant you grace • through the prayers of our Lady Mary (and the saint of the church)	الذي قبل التائب برحمته و أعطى السلطان لكهنته يديم عليكما نعمته بصلاة سيدتنا مريم و (يذكر اسم شفيع الكنيسة)
O You who spoke • with Moses on Mount Tabor • and healed the blind man • and illuminated him, • make their days • glad and joyful • through the prayers of • our Lady Mary (and the saint of the church)	أيها الذي كلم موسى فوق جبل الطور و شفى الأعمى و أوهب له النور اجعل أيامهم في هناء و سرور بصلاة سيدتنا مريم و (يذكر اسم شفيع الكنيسة)

(The congregation concludes with this last verse.)

A crown of gold, • a crown of silver, • a crown of precious stone. • Alleluia, Alleluia, • Alleluia glory be to our God.	Ⲟⲩⲭⲗⲟⲙ ⲛⲛⲟⲩⲃ ⲟⲩⲭⲗⲟⲙ ⲛϩⲁⲧ ⲟⲩⲭⲗⲟⲙ ⲛⲱⲛⲓ ⲙⲙⲁⲣⲅⲁⲣⲓⲧⲏⲥ ⲁⲗⲗⲏⲗⲟⲩⲓⲁ ⲁⲗⲗⲏⲗⲟⲩⲓⲁ ⲕⲉ ⲁⲗⲗⲏⲗⲟⲩⲓⲁ ⲡⲓⲱⲟⲩ ⲫⲁ ⲡⲉⲛⲛⲟⲩϯ ⲡⲉ.	اكليل ذهب و اكليل فضة و اكليل جوهري ألليلويا ألليلويا ألليلويا المجد لالهنا

The Doxology of the Crowns

Unfading crowns • the Lord has placed • upon the bridegroom • of Jesus Christ	ϩⲁⲛⲭⲗⲟⲙ ⲛⲁⲧⲗⲟⲙ ⲁϥⲧⲏⲓⲧⲟⲩ ⲛϫⲉ Ⲡϭⲟⲓⲥ ⲉϫⲉⲛ ⲡⲓⲡⲁⲧϣⲉⲗⲉⲧ ⲛⲧⲉ Ⲓⲏⲥⲟⲩⲥ Ⲡⲓⲭⲣⲓⲥⲧⲟⲥ	أكاليل غير مضمحلة منحمها الرب لهذا العريس الذي ليسوع المسيح
Illuminate, Illuminate • O bridegroom • and your true bride • who is in the prepared place	ϭⲓⲟⲩⲱⲓⲛⲓ ϭⲓⲟⲩⲱⲓⲛⲓ ⲱ ⲡⲓⲡⲁⲧϣⲉⲗⲉⲧ ⲛⲉⲙ ⲧⲉⲕϣⲉⲗⲉⲧ ⲙⲙⲏⲓ ⲉⲧϧⲉⲛ ⲡⲓⲙⲁ ⲉⲧⲥⲉⲃⲧⲱⲧ	استضيء استضيء أيها العريس مع عروستك الحقيقية التي في موضعك المتعد
Take unto you joy • and the gift of God • which Christ our God • has given you	ϭⲓ ⲛⲁⲕ ⲛⲟⲩⲣⲁϣⲓ ⲛⲉⲙ ϯⲇⲱⲣⲉⲁ ⲛⲧⲉ Ⲫⲛⲟⲩϯ ⲉⲧⲁϥⲧⲏⲓⲧⲟⲩ ⲛⲁⲕ ⲛϫⲉ Ⲡⲓⲭⲣⲓⲥⲧⲟⲥ ⲡⲉⲛⲛⲟⲩϯ	اقبل الفرح و موهبة الله التي أعطاها لك المسيح الهنا
Go with joy • to your bridal chamber • that is decorated • in various ways	Ⲙⲁϣⲉⲛⲁⲕ ϧⲉⲛ ⲟⲩⲣⲁϣⲓ ⲉⲡⲉⲕⲙⲁⲛϣⲉⲗⲉⲧ ⲉⲧⲥⲉⲗⲥⲱⲗ ⲉⲃⲟⲗ ϧⲉⲛ ⲟⲩⲑⲟ ⲛⲣⲏϯ	أمض بفرح الى خدرك المزين بكل نوع

The Commandments

Priest *(facing East)*:

Glory to God, who exists before all ages, the beginning, the indescribable, the One who remains after the passing of creation, the compassionate, the	المجد لله الدائم قبل كل الدهور الاول الغير الموصوف و الأخر بعد فناء الخلائق الرؤوف خالق الخلق بقدرته المنعم عليهم برحمته العظيم الربوبية المنفرد بالوحدانية

creator of creation with His power, who grants it His lordship with His great mercy, who alone is unique, the creator of the heavenlies with His high power and supreme wisdom, the ancient, the Being, whose being has no beginning, whose lordship has no end, whose greatness the tongues fail to express, the knowledge of whom the minds receded to know, the mighty, to whom the mighty submit, the greatly majestic, whose majesty and dignity the kings fear, who hears every voice and gives life to all souls after death, to him be the praise. The originator of the first and the last through the mystery of His lordship and the one who rewards the good with His abundant grace, who answers the call of those among His loyal servants who cry out to Him, the good prize-giver, the vast forgiver, the harsh punisher, the tolerant of offenses, the preventer of disasters, the forgiver of transgressions, the giver of good things, the bestower of blessings, who is not preceded by an age or time, who is not preceded by a century or epoch, whose mercy inundated all creation, whose compassion and beneficence surrounded all the righteous and faithful, who has no likeness or partner in any thing, nor equal nor comparison, who is above all characterization, who is exalted in the highest heaven, who is thanked among the gods, who is praised for His graces, by whom the good is completed and blessings and grace are renewed, to Him be the glory and to His virtues be the praise, the lover of unity and confirmation in sound

خالق السماويين بقدرته العالية و حكمته السامية القديم الدائم الذي ليس لقدمه ابتداء و لا لربوبيته انتهاء الذي كلت الالسن عن تعبير عظمته و انحسرت العقول عن كنه معرفته الجبار الذي خضعت له الجبابرة العزيز العظيم الذي ذلت و خشعت لعزه و جلاله الملوك المتظافرة سامع كل صوت و محي الأنفس بعد الموت له السبح مبدع الاولين و الاخرين بسر ربوبيته و موفق الصالحين بوفير نعمته مجيب دعوة الداعين من عباده المخلصين الحسن التجاوز الواسع المغفرة الشديد العقاب المقبل من العثرات الواقي من البليات الغافر السيئات المعطي الخيرات المنزل البركات الذي لم يتقدمه دهر و لا زمان و لم يسبقه عصر و لا أوان الذي رحمته قد غمرت كل الخلائق و رأفته و احساناته قد شملت كل العباد و ذوي الحقائق الذي ليس له في جميع الاشياء شكل و لا نظير و لا مثل و لا قرين جل و تنزه عن الصفات و تعالى في أعلا السموات المشكور على ألائه المحمود على نعمائه الذي به تتمم الصالحات و تتجدد النعم و البركات له المجد و لأفضاله الحمد محب الأتلاف و الثبوت على المناهج القويمة بغير انحراف ناظم الأسباب الفريدة و مقرب الانساب البعيدة مطلق الحلال و مؤيده و محذر عن الحرام و مبعده معطي أفضل ما أراده من الغيب المكنون فسبحانه المقدس من الشاروبيم و الممجد من السيرافيم و المهلل و المرتل من مراتب السماويين و الارضيين الذي تباركه أنفس و أرواح النبيين و المرسلين و الابرار و الصالحين مع المقرين بقدرة ربوبيته و الساجدين لاسمه و لقوة لاهوته له نسجد و اياه نمجد و به نعترف الذي له السلطان و اللاهوت و العظمة و الجبروت و الآن و كل أوان و الى دهر الداهرين و أبد الابدين أمين

principles without deviation, the organizer of the unique causes, who brings distant relations closer, who releases and supports the permissible, who warns against and keeps away the forbidden, who grants virtuous requests, who acquiesces to beautiful desires. His works were beheld by eyes, His prophets and apostles were sent to reveal the hidden things. His holy praise is by the Cherubim. He is glorified by the Seraphim. The heavenly and earthly ranks sing and chant to Him. The souls and spirits of the prophets, apostles, the righteous, and the just bless Him. They repeatedly speak of the power of His lordship. They worship His name and the power of His divinity. We worship Him and glorify Him. We confess Him to whom belongs glory, divinity, greatness, and might now and ever and unto the age of ages Amen.	

Congregation *(in the muḥayyar tune)*:

My peace which I have taken from my Father • I leave with you both now and forever	Ταϩιρηνη ανοκ ⲑⲉⲧⲁⲓϭⲓⲧⲥ ϩⲓⲧⲉⲛ ⲡⲁⲓⲱⲧ ⲁⲛⲟⲕ ϯⲭⲱ ⲙⲙⲟⲥ ⲛⲉⲙⲱⲧⲉⲛ ⲓⲥϫⲉⲛ ϯⲛⲟⲩ ⲛⲉⲙ ϣⲁ ⲉⲛⲉϩ	سلامي أنا الذي أخذته من أبي أتركه لكم من الآن و الى الأبد
O King of peace, grant us Your peace, • confirm Your peace on us and forgive us our sins	Ⲡⲟⲩⲣⲟ ⲛⲧⲉ ϯϩⲓⲣⲏⲛⲏ ⲙⲟⲓ ⲛⲁⲛ ⲛⲧⲉⲕϩⲓⲣⲏⲛⲏ ⲥⲉⲙⲛⲓ ⲛⲁⲛ ⲛⲧⲉⲕϩⲓⲣⲏⲛⲏ ⲭⲁ ⲛⲉⲛⲛⲟⲃⲓ ⲛⲁⲛ ⲉⲃⲟⲗ	يا ملك السلام أعطنا سلامك قرر لنا سلامك و اغفر لنا خطايانا

Priest *(facing the couple)*:

May the peace of our Lord, God, and Savior, Jesus Christ, which He has given to His pure disciples in the Upper Room of Zion, be with you both. May it always stay with you and dwell in your house. May the Lord grant you a long and prosperous life together, for this great joy that He has sanctioned for you. And may God protect you my son with His mighty arm and establish the Orthodox faith in you. May He bring all your efforts to a good and successful end through His great power and benevolence. Know that God the Pantocrator, after creating everything, looked at His creation and saw that it was good. Then He said, "Let us make man in Our image after Our likeness." God, blessed be His name, has no parallel or counterpart, but what He said meant that man has three attributes: reason, speech, and spirit. So, God created Adam and made him priest, prophet, and king. He said in the Torah, through Moses, after creating Adam, "It is not good that the man should be alone. I will make a helpmate for him", for God so loved and cared for Adam. And the Lord God caused a deep sleep to fall upon Adam, and he slept. And He took one of his ribs, and closed up the flesh instead thereof, and made it a woman, and brought her unto the man, and he called her Eve. When Adam woke up and looked at the woman, he liked her and said, "This is now bone of my bones and flesh of my flesh." Woman was created from man's rib so that she may belong to him and be submissive	سلام سيدنا و الهنا و مخلصنا يسوع المسيح الذي أعطاه لتلاميذه الاطهار في علية صهيون يكون معكما و حالا عليكما و في منازلكما و يرزقكما العمر الطويل و العيش الرغيد و الحياة المهناة لاجل هذا الفرح العظيم الذي وفقه الله لكما و أنت أيها الأخ حفظك الله بيمينه و ثبتك على الدين الصحيح و الايمان المستقيم الصريح و هوجلت قدرته بفضله يجعل عاقبة أموركما الى خير و توفيق اعلم أن الله تعالى ذكره لما أكمل سائر خلائقه نظر ما خلقه فرأه حسنا جدا فقال و هو أعز قائل لنخلق انسانا على صورتنا كمثالنا و الله جل اسمه ليس له شبه و لا مثال و انما أشار بقوله هذا أن الانسان ثلاث خواص أعني ذا عقل و نطق و روح فخلق آدم و جعله كاهنا و نبيا و ملكا و قال في التوراة على لسان موسى النبي لما خلق آدم لا يجب ان يكون آدم وحده عناية به و محبة له بل نخلق له معينا يؤنسه قالتمي على آدم سباتا فرقد و اخذ من جنبه الايمن ضلعا و جعل عوضه لحما و خلق من ذلك الضلع امرأة و سماها حواء فلما انتبه آدم من نومه و نظر الى حواء أنس اليها و قال هذه الآن عضو من أعضائي و لحم من لحمي و انما خلقت المرأة من ضلع الرجل لتكون تحت حوزه و أمره و يكون هو أيضا حنونا عليها و شفوقا بها و لا يهملها و لا ترتفع هى أيضا عليه بل تكون مطيعة له و ليكونا كلاهما متفقين بالعقل و المحبة و الرأي السديد و لا ينفرد أحدهما برأي دون صاحبه لتكون ذريتهما صالحة مباركة و قد أحل الله الزيجة الروحانية في العهدين و أكد ذلك بما شهد به الانجيل الطاهر اذ قال يدع الرجل أباه و أمه و يلصق بامرأته و قال أيضا في الانجيل المقدس ما أزوجه الله لا يفرقه الانسان و قال داود النبي في المزمور طوبى للانسان الذي

A Textual History of the Coptic Wedding Rite

to him, while he too may be gentile and kind to her and not neglect her. She may not redeem herself above him, but should be obedient to him. They should both be in harmony through good reasoning and love. Neither of them should make a decision separately without consulting the other. In this way, their offspring may be blessed. God has sanctioned marriage in both the Old and New Testaments. He further confirmed that in the Holy Gospel saying, "Therefore shall a man leave his father and mother, and shall cleave unto his wife, and they shall be one flesh." He also said, "What God has joined together, let no man separate." Also David the Psalmist said, "Blessed is every one that fears the Lord, your wife shall be as a fruitful vine by the sides of your house, your children like olive plants around your table, this shall the Lord bless, and you shall see good all the days of your life." Also St. Paul the Apostle said, "Wives, submit yourselves unto your own husbands, as unto the Lord." He also commanded men to love their wives saying, "Husbands, love your wives, even as Christ also loved the church, and gave Himself for her."	يخاف من الرب فان زوجته تكون مثل الكرمة المخصبة التى تزهر حول مسكنه و تكون أولاده كاغصان الزيتون بين يديه و على مائدته ذلك الذي يباركه الله و يرى الخيرات طول أيام حياته و قال بولس الرسول أيها النساء اخضعن لازواجكن مثل خضوعكن للرب جل اسمه و قد أمر أيضا بمحبة الرجل لزوجته مثل محبة سيدنا يسوع المسيح لكنيسته و ابد له نفسه دونها

Congregation *(in the muḥayyar tune)*:

| This is the time of blessing, this is the time of chosen incense, • this is the time for us to praise our Savior the Lover of mankind | Ⲫⲛⲁⲩ ⲙⲡⲓⲥⲙⲟⲩ ⲡⲉ ⲫⲁⲓ Ⲫⲛⲁⲩ ⲙⲡⲓⲥⲑⲟⲓⲛⲟⲩϥⲓ ⲉⲧⲥⲱⲧⲡ. Ⲫⲛⲁⲩ ⲧⲉⲛϩⲟⲥ ⲉⲡⲉⲛⲥⲱⲧⲏⲣ ⲡⲓⲙⲁⲓⲣⲱⲙⲓ ⲛⲁⲅⲁⲑⲟⲥ | هذا وقت البركة و هذا وقت البخور المختار هذا الوقت الذي فيه نسبح مخلصنا محب البشر الصالح |

The incense is Mary, the incense is the one to whom she gave birth, • the incense is the One in her womb. He forgives us our sins.	Ⲟⲩⲑⲟⲓⲛⲟⲩϥⲓ ⲡⲉ Ⲙⲁⲣⲓⲁ Ⲟⲩⲑⲟⲓⲛⲟⲩϥⲓ ⲁⲥⲙⲓⲥⲓ ⲙⲙⲟϥ Ⲟⲩⲑⲟⲓⲛⲟⲩϥⲓ ⲉⲧϧⲉⲛ ⲧⲉⲥⲛⲉϫⲓ ϣⲁϥⲭⲁ ⲛⲉⲛⲛⲟⲃⲓ ⲛⲁⲛ ⲉⲃⲟⲗ	البخور مريم البخور هي ولدته البخور هو الذي في بطنها و يغفر لنا خطايانا
Jesus is incense. Come let us worship Him. • When we keep His commandments, He forgives us our sins.	Ⲟⲩⲑⲟⲓⲛⲟⲩϥⲓ ⲡⲉ Ⲓⲏⲥⲟⲩⲥ. ⲁⲙⲱⲓⲛⲓ ⲙⲁⲣⲉⲛⲟⲩⲱϣⲧ ⲙⲙⲟϥ ⲁⲛϣⲁⲛⲁⲣⲉϩ ⲉⲛⲉϥⲉⲛⲧⲟⲗⲏ ϣⲁϥⲭⲁ ⲛⲉⲛⲛⲟⲃⲓ ⲛⲁⲛ ⲉⲃⲟⲗ	البخور هو يسوع هلم نسجد له اذا حفظنا وصاياه فيغفر لنا خطايانا
The Cherubim worship Him, the Seraphim glorify Him • crying out and saying, "Holy Holy	Ⲛⲓⲭⲉⲣⲟⲩⲃⲓⲙ ⲥⲉⲟⲩⲱϣⲧ ⲙⲙⲟϥ ⲛⲓⲤⲉⲣⲁⲫⲓⲙ ⲥⲉϯⲱⲟⲩ ⲛⲁϥ ⲉⲩⲱϣ ⲉⲃⲟⲗ ⲉⲩϫⲱ ⲙⲙⲟⲥ ϫⲉ ⲭⲟⲩⲁⲃ ⲟⲩⲟϩ ⲭⲟⲩⲁⲃ	الشاروبيم يسجدون له و السيرافيم يمجدونه سارخين قائلين قدوس قدوس
Holy are You O Lord among the thousands. • You are honored by the myriads.	Ⲭⲟⲩⲁⲃ Ⲡϭⲟⲓⲥ ϧⲉⲛ ⲛⲓⲁⲛⲁⲛϣⲟ ⲕⲧⲁⲓⲏⲟⲩⲧ ϧⲉⲛ ⲛⲓⲁⲛⲁⲛⲉⲃⲁ	قدوس أنت يا رب الألوف مكرم بالربوات
You are incense O my savior for • You came and saved us. Have mercy on us.	Ⲛⲑⲟⲕ ⲟⲩⲑⲟⲓⲛⲟⲩϥⲓ ⲡⲉ ⲡⲁⲥⲱⲧⲏⲣ ϫⲉ ⲁⲕⲓ ⲁⲕⲥⲱϯ ⲙⲙⲟⲛ ⲛⲁⲓ ⲛⲁⲛ	أنت بخور يا مخلصي لأنك أتيت و خلصتنا

A Textual History of the Coptic Wedding Rite

Priest:

Now since you have been present at this blessed time before the sanctuary of the Lord of Hosts and His holy altar and this Orthodox gathering, you have been joined by this blessed marriage and holy crowning. According to this rite and this law, so also the rest of the fathers, the believers, took one wife in purity and cleanliness for the sake of descendants and childbearing. So, you should know each other's rights and submit yourselves to one another, and let each of you be faithful to the other according to our teacher Paul the Apostle, "The wife does not have authority over her own body, but her husband does. And likewise the husband does not have authority over his own body, but the wife does."	والآن قد حضرتما في هذه الساعة المباركة قدام هيكل رب الصباؤوت ومذبحه المقدس في هذا المحفل الأرثوذكسي وجمعتكما هذه الزيجة المباركة والإكليل المقدس فعلى هذا الرسم وهذه الشريعة هكذا إتخذ سائر الآباء المؤمنون إمرأة واحدة بطهر ونقاوة لطلب الذرية وإيجاد الخلف فيجب عليكما أن يعرف بعضكما حق بعض ويخضع كل منكما لصاحبه وليكن كل منكما أمينا نحو الآخر كقول معلمنا بولس الرسول ليس للمرأة تسلط على جسدها بل للرجل وكذلك الرجل أيضا ليس له تسلط على جسده بل للمرأة

My blessed son {GROOM}, who is supported by the grace of the Holy Spirit, you are required to receive your wife at this blessed hour with a clear conscience, a pure soul, and a full heart. Excel in doing all that is good for her. Have compassion on her and always hasten to do that which will gladden her heart. Today, you are responsible for her instead of her parents. You have both been crowned with the heavenly crowning and the spiritual marriage. The grace of God has settled upon you. When you accept what has been commanded of you, the Lord will take your hand, increase your livelihood, grant you blessed children by whom God will delight your eyes, grant you a long age and prosperous life, and prosper your outcome in this life and the hereafter.	يجب عليك أيها الإبن المبارك (...) المؤيد بنعمة الروح القدس أن تتسلم زوجتك (...) في هذه الساعة المباركة بنية خالصة ونفس طاهرة وقلب سليم وتجتهد فيما يعود لصالحها وتكون حنونا عليها وتسرع إلى ما يسر قلبها فأنت اليوم المسئول عنها من بعد والديها وقد تكللتما بالإكليل السمائي والزيجة الروحانية وحلت عليكما نعمة الله ومتى قبلت ما أوصيت به أخذ الرب بيدك وأوسع في رزقك ويرزقك أولادا مباركين يقر الله بهم عينيك ويمنحك العمر الطويل والعيش الرغد ويحسن لك العاقبة في الدنيا والآخرة

Congregation *(in the muḥayyar tune)*:

Listen O daughter and see and lend your ear. Forget your people and your father's house. • For the king has desired your beauty, for he alone is your lord.	Cωτεμ ταϣερι αναυ ρεκ πεμαϣϫ αριπωβϣ μπελαοc νεμ πηι τηρϥ ντε πειωτ. ϫε α πιουρο ερεπιθυμιν επεcαι ϫε ουηι νθοϥ πε πεбоιс.	أسمعي يا ابنتي و انظري و ميلي اذنك و انسي شعبك و بيت أبيك لأن الملك قد اشتهى حسنك لأنه وحده ربك
All the glory of the daughter is within, her clothing is wrought with gold.	Πωου τηρϥ ντϣερι μπουρο νεcεβων εcϫολϩ ϧεν ϩανϣτατ νιεβ ννουβ.	كل مجد ابنة الملك من داخل مشتملة بأنواع كثيرا

A Textual History of the Coptic Wedding Rite

Alleluia, Alleluia, • Alleluia Glory be to our God.	ⲁⲗⲗⲏⲗⲟⲩⲓⲁ ⲁⲗⲗⲏⲗⲟⲩⲓⲁ ⲕⲉ ⲁⲗⲗⲏⲗⲟⲩⲓⲁ ⲡⲓⲱⲟⲩ ⲫⲁ ⲡⲉⲛⲛⲟⲩϯ ⲡⲉ.	هلليلويا هلليلويا هلليلويا المجد لالهنا

Priest:

And you, blessed daughter, and happy bride, {BRIDE}, you have heard what was commanded of your husband. So you are required to honor and respect him. Do not act against his opinion, but increase your obedience to him many times over what was commanded. For today you are alone with him and he is responsible for you instead of your parents. So you must receive him with joy and cheer. Do not frown in his face. Do not neglect any of his rights upon you, and fear God in all matters with him because God commanded you to submit to him and ordered you to obey him as your parents. So be with him as our mother Sarah was obedient to our father Abraham, and used to address him "my lord." Thus God looked upon her obedience to him, blessed her, gave her Isaac in her old age, and made her offspring as the stars of heaven and the sand on the seashore. As you listen to what we commanded you to do, the Lord will take your hand, increase your livelihood, and blessings will descend upon your home, and He will grant you blessed children by whom God will delight your eyes.	وأنتِ أيتها الإبنة المباركة والعروس السعيدة (...) قد سمعتي ما أوصي به زوجك فيجب عليك أن تكرميه وتهابيه ولا تخالفي رأيه بل زيدي في طاعته على ما أوصي به أضعافا فقد صرت اليوم منفردة معه وهو المسئول عنك بعد والديك فيجب عليك أن تقابليه بالبشاشة والترحاب ولا تضجري في وجهه ولا تضيعي شيئا من حقوقه عليك وتتقي الله في سائر أمورك معه لأن الله تعالى أوصاك بالخضوع له وأمرك بطاعته بعد والديك فكوني معه كما كانت أمنا سارة مطيعة لأبينا إبراهيم وكانت تخاطبه يا سيدي فنظر الله إلى طاعتها و بارك عليها وأعطاها إسحق بعد الكبر وجعل نسلها مثل نجوم السماء والرمل الذي على شاطئ البحر فإذا سمعتي ما أوصيناك به واتبعتي جميع الأوامر أخذ الرب بيدك ووسع في رزقك وحلت البركات في منزلك ورزقك أولادا مباركين يقر الله بهم عينيك
May the Lord bless you my brother and bless your wife as He blessed Noah and his wife when they left the	كذلك يباركك الرب أيها الأخ ويبارك زوجتك كما بارك نوح وزوجته عند خروجهما من السفينة وعمر الأرض

ark and populated the earth with their seed and as He blessed Abraham with Sarah, and Isaac with Rebecca, and Jacob with Leah and Rachel. May the blessing of the Lord, to His name be the honor, at the wedding of Cana of Galilee, settle upon you and your home, unify you in harmony, create spiritual love in your hearts, sustain your livelihood, fill your house, and grant you a long age and happy life with blessed children. We ask Him to accept from us the prayers of this blessed crowning, reward us with the eternal for the temporal, the heavenly for the earthly, and forgive us our sins, iniquities, and transgressions, and keep away from us the traps and cunning of the devil, the evil enemy. May He keep the rest of the brethren who attended with us, with His protective right hand, all the days of their lives and fill their homes, and keep away from them the temptations of the enemy and grant them heavenly joy free from trouble. Through the intercession of the Lady of us all and the pride of our race, the Lady the pure virgin, the honored mother of salvation, who is preferred over all mankind, the pure St. Mary, and the honored chosen martyr St. Mark the evangelist and apostle, and all the righteous martyrs and holy saints. Amen.

من ذريتهما وكما بارك لإبراهيم في سارة ولإسحق في رفقة وليعقوب في زواجه

وبركة الرب جل إسمه الحالة في عرس قانا الجليل تحل عليكما وفي منزلكما وتوفق بينكما وتجعل المحبة الروحانية في قلوبكما وتديم أرزاقكما وتعمر منزلكما وتمنحكما العمر الطويل والحياة الهنيئة مع الأولاد المباركين

وإياه نسأل أن يتقبل منا صلوات هذا الإكليل المبارك ويعوضنا عن الفانيات بالباقيات وعن الأرضيات بالسمائيات ويغفر لنا خطايانا وذنوبنا وزلاتنا ويكفينا مكائد ومكاره العدو الشيطان الشرير

ويحفظ كافة الإخوة الحاضرين معنا بيمينه الحصين كل أيام حياتهم ويعمر منازلهم ويكفيهم تجارب العدو ويعطيهم الفرح السمائي الذي لا يشو به كدر بشفاعة سيدتنا كلنا وفخر جنسنا السيدة العذراء الطاهرة والدة الخلاص الزكية المفضلة على سائر جنس البشر القديسة مريم النقية والشهيد المكرم المختار مرقس الإنجيلي الرسول وكافة الشهداء الأبرار والقديسين الأطهار آمين

The Conclusion

(The congregation says Our Father while the priest says the first two absolutions. The priest goes to the couple and says the Absolution of the Son with his hands placed crosswise over their heads and joining

their heads together. After the Absolution of the Son, the congregation chants the following concluding canon:)

Rejoice O shining bride, the mother of One who enlightens; • Rejoice she who accepted the Word who dwelt in her womb	Ⲭⲉⲣⲉ ϯϣⲉⲗⲉⲧ ⲉⲧⲉⲣⲟⲩⲱⲓⲛⲓ ⲑⲙⲁⲩ ⲙ̅ⲡⲓⲣⲉϥⲉⲣⲟⲩⲱⲓⲛⲓ ⲭⲉⲣⲉ ⲑⲏⲉⲧϣⲱⲡ ⲉⲣⲟⲥ ⲙ̅ⲡⲓⲥⲁϫⲓ ⲫⲏⲉⲧϣⲟⲡ ϧⲉⲛ ⲧⲉⲥⲛⲉϫⲓ	السلام للعروس المضيئة أم الذي ينير السلام للتي قبلت اليها الكلمة الكائن في أحشاها
Rejoice she who is honored more than the Cherubim; • Rejoice she who gave birth to the Savior of our souls	Ⲭⲉⲣⲉ ⲑⲏⲉⲧⲧⲁⲓⲏⲟⲩⲧ ⲉϩⲟⲧⲉ ⲛⲓⲭⲉⲣⲟⲩⲃⲓⲙ ⲭⲉⲣⲉ ⲑⲏⲉⲧⲁⲥⲙⲓⲥⲓ ⲙ̅ⲡⲥⲱⲧⲏⲣ ⲛ̅ⲧⲉ ⲛⲉⲛⲯⲩⲭⲏ	السلام للتي هي أكرم من الشاروبيم السلام للتي ولدت لنا مخلص أنفسنا
Glory be to the Father and the Son and the Holy Spirit	Ⲇⲟⲝⲁ Ⲡⲁⲧⲣⲓ ⲕⲉ Ⲩⲓⲱ ⲕⲉ ⲁⲅⲓⲱ Ⲡⲛⲉⲩⲙⲁⲧⲓ	المجد للآب و الابن و الروح القدس
Now and forever and unto the age of all ages. Amen.	Ⲕⲉ ⲛⲩⲛ ⲕⲉ ⲁⲓ ⲕⲉ ⲓⲥ ⲧⲟⲩⲥ ⲉⲱⲛⲁⲥ ⲧⲱⲛ ⲉⲱⲛⲱⲛ ⲁⲙⲏⲛ	الآن و كل أوان و الى دهر الدهور آمين
We cry out and say O our Lord Jesus Christ	Ⲧⲉⲛⲱϣ ⲉⲃⲟⲗ ⲉⲛϫⲱ ⲙ̅ⲙⲟⲥ ϫⲉ ⲱ Ⲡⲉⲛϭⲟⲓⲥ Ⲓⲏⲥⲟⲩⲥ Ⲡⲓⲭⲣⲓⲥⲧⲟⲥ	نصرخ قائلين يا ربنا يسوع المسيح
Bless the air of heaven, bless the waters of the rivers, bless the plants and the herbs and may Your mercy and Your peace be a fortress to Your people.	Ⲥⲙⲟⲩ ⲉⲛⲓⲁⲏⲣ ⲛ̅ⲧⲉ ⲧ̅ⲫⲉ ⲥⲙⲟⲩ ⲛ̅ⲛⲓⲙⲱⲟⲩ ⲙ̅ⲫⲓⲁⲣⲟ ⲥⲙⲟⲩ ⲛ̅ⲛⲓⲥⲓϯ ⲛⲉⲙ ⲛⲓⲙ ⲙⲁⲣⲉ ⲡⲉⲕⲛⲁⲓ ⲛⲉⲙ ⲧⲉⲕϩⲓⲣⲏⲛⲏ ⲟⲓ ⲛ̅ⲥⲟⲃⲧ ⲙ̅ⲡⲉⲕⲗⲁⲟⲥ	بارك اهوية السماء بارك مياه النهر بارك الزروع و العشب و لتكن رحمتك و سلامك حصنا لشعبك
Save us and have mercy on us. Lord have mercy, Lord have mercy, Lord bless us, Amen. Bless me, Bless me, Behold	Ⲥⲱϯ ⲙ̅ⲙⲟⲛ ⲟⲩⲟϩ ⲛⲁⲓ ⲛⲁⲛ. Ⲕⲩⲣⲓⲉ ⲉⲗⲉⲏⲥⲟⲛ Ⲕⲩⲣⲓⲉ ⲉⲗⲉⲏⲥⲟⲛ Ⲕⲩⲣⲓⲉ ⲉⲩⲗⲟⲅⲏⲥⲟⲛ ⲁⲙⲏⲛ. Ⲥⲙⲟⲩ	خلصنا و ارحمنا يا رب ارحم يا رب ارحم يا رب بارك آمين باركني باركني ها مطانية اغفر لي قل البركة

the repentance, Give the blessing.	ⲉⲣⲟⲓ ⲥⲙⲟⲩ ⲉⲣⲟⲓ ⲓⲥ ϯⲙⲉⲧⲁⲛⲟⲓⲁ ⲭⲱ ⲛⲏⲓ ⲉⲃⲟⲗ ⲭⲱ ⲙⲡⲓⲥⲙⲟⲩ	

Priest:

May God have compassion upon us, bless us, manifest His face upon us, and have mercy upon us. O Lord, save Your people, bless Your inheritance, shepherd them, and raise them up forever. Exalt the horn of Christians through the power of the life-giving Cross	Ⲫϯ ⲉϥⲉϣⲉⲛϩⲏⲧ ϧⲁⲣⲟⲛ ⲉϥⲉⲥⲙⲟⲩ ⲉⲣⲟⲛ ⲉϥⲉⲟⲩⲱⲛϩ ⲙⲡⲉϥϩⲟ ⲉϩⲣⲏⲓ ⲉϫⲱⲛ ⲟⲩⲟϩ ⲉϥⲉⲛⲁⲓ ⲛⲁⲛ. Ⲡ϶ⲟⲓⲥ ⲛⲟϩⲉⲙ ⲙⲡⲉⲕⲗⲁⲟⲥ ⲥⲙⲟⲩ ⲉⲧⲉⲕⲕⲗⲏⲣⲟⲛⲟⲙⲓⲁ ⲁⲙⲟⲛⲓ ⲙⲙⲱⲟⲩ ϭⲁⲥⲟⲩ ϣⲁ ⲉⲛⲉϩ. ϭⲓⲥⲓ ⲙⲡⲧⲁⲡ ⲛⲛⲓⲭⲣⲓⲥⲧⲓⲁⲛⲟⲥ ϩⲓⲧⲉⲛ ⲧϫⲟⲙ ⲙⲡⲓⲥⲧⲁⲩⲣⲟⲥ ⲛⲣⲉϥⲧⲁⲛϧⲟ	الله يترأف علينا ويباركنا ويظهر وجهه علينا ويرحمنا يا رب خلص شعبك بارك ميراثك إرعهم وإرفعهم إلى الأبد إرفع شأن المسيحيين بقوة الصليب المحيي
and through the supplications and prayers which our Lady, the Lady of us all, the holy Theotokos, Saint Mary, makes for us.	ϩⲓⲧⲉⲛ ⲛⲓϩⲟ ⲛⲉⲙ ⲛⲉⲛⲧⲱⲃϩ ⲉⲧⲉⲥⲓⲣⲓ ⲙⲙⲱⲟⲩ ϩⲁⲣⲟⲛ ⲛⲥⲟⲩ ⲛⲓⲃⲉⲛ ⲛϫⲉ ⲧⲉⲛϭⲟⲓⲥ ⲛⲛⲏⲃ ⲧⲏⲣⲉⲛ ϯⲑⲉⲟⲧⲟⲕⲟⲥ ⲉⲑⲟⲩⲁⲃ ϯⲁⲅⲓⲁ Ⲙⲁⲣⲓⲁ	بالسؤالات والطلبات التي تصنعها عناكل حين سيدتنا وملكتنا كلنا والدة الإله القديسة الطاهرة مريم
and the three great holy luminaries Michael, Gabriel, and Raphael;	ⲛⲉⲙ ⲡⲓϣⲟⲙⲧ ⲛⲛⲓϣϯ ⲛⲣⲉϥⲉⲣⲟⲩⲱⲓⲛⲓ ⲉⲑⲟⲩⲁⲃ Ⲙⲓⲭⲁⲏⲗ ⲛⲉⲙ Ⲅⲁⲃⲣⲓⲏⲗ ⲛⲉⲙ Ⲣⲁⲫⲁⲏⲗ	والثلاثة العظماء المنيرون الأطهار ميخائيل وغبريال و رافائيل
the four incorporeal creatures; the twenty-four priests; all the heavenly orders;	ⲛⲉⲙ ⲡⲓϥⲧⲟⲩ ⲛⲍⲱⲟⲛ ⲛⲁⲥⲱⲙⲁⲧⲟⲥ ⲛⲉⲙ ⲡⲓϫⲱⲧ ϥⲧⲟⲩ ⲙⲡⲣⲉⲥⲃⲩⲧⲉⲣⲟⲥ ⲛⲉⲙ ⲛⲓⲧⲁⲅⲙⲁ ⲧⲏⲣⲟⲩ ⲛⲉⲡⲟⲩⲣⲁⲛⲓⲟⲛ	والأربعة الحيوانات غير المتجسدين والأربعة والعشرون قسيسا وكل الطغمات السمائية

Saint John the Baptist; the hundred and forty-four thousand; my masters and fathers the apostles; the three holy youths; Saint Stephen;	Νεμ πιαγιος Ιωαννης πιρεϥⲧⲱⲙⲥ ⲛⲉⲙ ⲡⲓϣⲉ ϩⲙⲉ ϥⲧⲟⲩ ⲛϣⲟ ⲛⲉⲙ ⲛⲁϭⲟⲓⲥ ⲛⲓⲟϯ ⲛⲁⲡⲟⲥⲧⲟⲗⲟⲥ ⲛⲉⲙ ⲡⲓϣⲟⲙⲧ ⲛⲁⲗⲟⲩ ⲛⲁⲅⲓⲟⲥ ⲛⲉⲙ ⲡⲓⲁⲅⲓⲟⲥ Ⲥⲧⲉⲫⲁⲛⲟⲥ	والقديس يوحنا المعمدان والمائة والأربعة والأربعين ألفا وسادتي الآباء الرسل والثلاثة فتية القديسين والقديس إستفانوس
the beholder-of-God, Saint Mark the Evangelist, the apostle and martyr;	Νεμ πιθεωριμος ⲛⲉⲩⲁⲅⲅⲉⲗⲓⲥⲧⲏⲥ Ⲙⲁⲣⲕⲟⲥ ⲡⲓⲁⲡⲟⲥⲧⲟⲗⲟⲥ ⲉⲑⲟⲩⲁⲃ ⲟⲩⲟϩ ⲙⲙⲁⲣⲧⲩⲣⲟⲥ	وناظر الإله الإنجيلي مرقس الرسول القديس والشهيد
Saint George; Saint Theodore; Philopater Mercurius; Saint Abba Mina; and the whole choir of the martyrs;	Νεμ πιαγιος Ⲅⲉⲱⲣⲅⲓⲟⲥ ⲛⲉⲙ ⲡⲓⲁⲅⲓⲟⲥ Ⲑⲉⲟⲇⲱⲣⲟⲥ ⲛⲉⲙ Ⲫⲓⲗⲟⲡⲁⲧⲏⲣ Ⲙⲉⲣⲕⲟⲩⲣⲓⲟⲥ ⲛⲉⲙ ⲡⲓⲁⲅⲓⲟⲥ ⲁⲡⲁ Ⲙⲏⲛⲁ ⲛⲉⲙ ⲡⲭⲟⲣⲟⲥ ⲧⲏⲣϥ ⲛⲧⲉ ⲛⲓⲙⲁⲣⲧⲩⲣⲟⲥ	والقديس جرجس والقديس تادرس وفيلوباتير مرقوريوس والقديس أبا مينا وكل مصاف الشهداء
our righteous father, the great Abba Anthony; the righteous Abba Paul; the three saints Abba Macarii;	Νεμ πενιωτ ⲛⲇⲓⲕⲉⲟⲥ ⲡⲓⲛⲓϣϯ ⲁⲃⲃⲁ Ⲁⲛⲧⲱⲛⲓⲟⲥ ⲛⲉⲙ ⲡⲓⲑⲙⲏⲓ ⲁⲃⲃⲁ Ⲡⲁⲩⲗⲉ ⲛⲉⲙ ⲡⲓϣⲟⲙⲧ ⲉⲑⲟⲩⲁⲃ ⲁⲃⲃⲁ Ⲙⲁⲕⲁⲣⲓ	وأبونا الصديق العظيم الأنبا أنطونيوس والبار أنبا بولا والثلاثة أنبا مقارات القديسون
our father Abba John; our father Abba Pishoi; our father Abba Paul of Tammoh; our Roman fathers Maximus and Dometius; our father Abba Moses; the Forty-nine Martyrs;	Νεμ πενιωτ ⲁⲃⲃⲁ Ⲓⲱⲁⲛⲛⲏ ⲛⲉⲙ ⲡⲉⲛⲓⲱⲧ ⲁⲃⲃⲁ Ⲡⲓϣⲱⲓ ⲛⲉⲙ ⲡⲉⲛⲓⲱⲧ ⲁⲃⲃⲁ Ⲡⲁⲩⲗⲉ ⲡⲓⲣⲉⲙⲧⲁⲙⲙⲟϩ ⲛⲉⲙ ⲛⲉⲛⲓⲟϯ ⲛⲣⲱⲙⲉⲟⲥ Ⲙⲁⲍⲓⲙⲟⲥ ⲛⲉⲙ Ⲇⲟⲙⲉⲧⲓⲟⲥ ⲛⲉⲙ ⲡⲉⲛⲓⲱⲧ ⲁⲃⲃⲁ Ⲙⲟⲩⲥⲏ ⲛⲉⲙ ⲡⲓϥⲙⲉ ⲯⲓⲧ ⲙⲙⲁⲣⲧⲩⲣⲟⲥ	وأبونا أنبا يوحنا وأبونا أنبا بيشوي وأبونا أنبا بولا الطموهي وأبانا الروميان مكسيموس ودوماديوس وأبونا انبا موسى والتسعة والأربعون شهيدا

the whole choir of the cross-bearers; the just; the righteous; all the wise virgins; the angel of this blessed day	Νεμ πχορος τηρϥ ντε νιςταυροφορος νεμ νιθμηι νεμ νιδικεος νεμ νιςαβευ τηρου μπαρθενος νεμ παγγελος ντε παιεϩοου	وكل مصاف لباس الصليب والأبرار والصديقون وجميع العذارى الحكيمات وملاك هذا اليوم المبارك
(The patron saint of the church is mentioned, followed by the saint(s) of the day.)		يذكر اسم صاحب الكنيسة ثم قديس اليوم
and the blessing of the holy Theotokos, first and last.	Νεμ πιςμου ντθεοτοκος εθουαβ ϯαγια Μαρια νϣορπ νεμ ϧαε	وبركة والدة الإله القديسة الطاهرة مريم أولا وآخرا
On Sunday, add: and the blessing of the Lord's Day of our good Savior.	Νεμ πιςμου ντκυριακη ντε πενςωτηρ ναγαθος	أن كان يوم الأحد يقول وبركة يوم الأحد الذي لمخلصنا الصالح
May their holy blessing, their grace, their power, their gift, their love, and their help rest upon us all forever. Amen.	Ερε πουςμου εθουαβ νεμ πουϩμοτ νεμ τουϫομ νεμ τουχαρις νεμ τουαγαπη νεμ τουβοηθια ϣωπι νεμαν τηρεν ϣα ενεϩ αμην	بركتهم المقدسة ونعمتهم وقوتهم وهبتهم ومحبتهم ومعونتهم تكون معنا كلنا إلى الأبد آمين
O Christ our God	Πιχριςτος Πεννουϯ	أيها المسيح إلهنا

People:

Amen. So be it.	αμην εςεϣωπι	آمين يكون

A Textual History of the Coptic Wedding Rite

Priest:

O King of peace, grant us Your peace, establish for us Your peace, and forgive us our sins. For Yours is the power, the glory, the blessing, and the might, forever. Amen.	Ⲡⲟⲩⲣⲟ ⲛⲧⲉ ϯⲥⲓⲣⲏⲛⲏ ⲙⲟⲓ ⲛⲁⲛ ⲛⲧⲉⲕϩⲓⲣⲏⲛⲏ ⲥⲉⲙⲛⲓ ⲛⲁⲛ ⲛⲧⲉⲕϩⲓⲣⲏⲛⲏ ⲭⲁ ⲛⲉⲛⲛⲟⲃⲓ ⲛⲁⲛ ⲉⲃⲟⲗ ϫⲉ ⲑⲱⲕ ⲧⲉ ϯϫⲟⲙ ⲛⲉⲙ ⲡⲓⲱⲟⲩ ⲛⲉⲙ ⲡⲓⲥⲙⲟⲩ ⲛⲉⲙ ⲡⲓⲁⲙⲁϩⲓ ϣⲁ ⲉⲛⲉϩ ⲁⲙⲏⲛ	يا ملك السلام أعطينا سلامك قرر لنا سلامك وإغفر لنا خطايانا لأن لك القوة والمجد والبركة والعزة إلى الأبد آمين
Make us worthy to pray thankfully:	ⲁⲣⲓⲧⲉⲛ ⲛⲉⲙⲡϣⲁ ⲛϫⲟⲥ ϧⲉⲛ ⲟⲩ ϣⲉⲡϩⲙⲟⲧ	اجعلنا مستحقين ان نقول بكل شكر

Congregation:

Our Father who art in heaven, hallowed be Thy name. Thy kingdom come. Thy will be done, on earth as it is in heaven. Give us this day our daily bread; and forgive us our trespasses, as we forgive those who trespass against us; and lead us not into temptation, but deliver us from the evil one. In Christ Jesus our Lord, for Thine is the kingdom and the power and the glory forever. Amen.	ϫⲉ ⲡⲉⲛⲓⲱⲧ ⲉⲧϧⲉⲛ ⲛⲓⲫⲏⲟⲩⲓ ⲙⲁⲣⲉϥⲧⲟⲩⲃⲟ ⲛϫⲉ ⲡⲉⲕⲣⲁⲛ ⲙⲁⲣⲉⲥⲓ ⲛϫⲉ ⲧⲉⲕⲙⲉⲧⲟⲩⲣⲟ ⲡⲉⲧⲉϩⲛⲁⲕ ⲙⲁⲣⲉϥϣⲱⲡⲓ ⲙⲫⲣⲏϯ ϧⲉⲛ ⲧⲫⲉ ⲛⲉⲙ ϩⲓϫⲉⲛ ⲡⲓⲕⲁϩⲓ ⲡⲉⲛⲱⲓⲕ ⲛⲧⲉ ⲣⲁⲥϯ ⲙⲏⲓϥ ⲛⲁⲛ ⲙⲫⲟⲟⲩ ⲟⲩⲟϩ ⲭⲁ ⲛⲏⲉⲧⲉⲣⲟⲛ ⲛⲁⲛ ⲉⲃⲟⲗ ⲙⲫⲣⲏϯ ϩⲱⲛ ⲛⲧⲉⲛⲭⲱ ⲉⲃⲟⲗ ⲛⲛⲏⲉⲧⲉ ⲟⲩⲟⲛ ⲛⲧⲁⲛ ⲉⲣⲱⲟⲩ ⲟⲩⲟϩ ⲙⲡⲉⲣⲉⲛⲧⲉⲛ ⲉϧⲟⲩⲛ ⲉⲡⲓⲣⲁⲥⲙⲟⲥ ⲁⲗⲗⲁ ⲛⲁϩⲙⲉⲛ ⲉⲃⲟⲗϩⲁ ⲡⲓⲡⲉⲧϩⲱⲟⲩ ϧⲉⲛ Ⲡⲭⲥ Ⲓⲏⲥ ⲡⲉⲛϭⲟⲓⲥ ϫⲉ ⲑⲱⲕ ⲧⲉ ϯⲙⲉⲧⲟⲩⲣⲟ ⲛⲉⲙ ϯϫⲟⲙ ⲛⲉⲙ ⲡⲓⲱⲟⲩ ϣⲁ ⲉⲛⲉϩ ⲁⲙⲏⲛ	أبانا الذي في السموات ليتقدس إسمك ليأت ملكوتك لتكن مشيئتك كما في السماء كذلك على الأرض خبزنا كفافنا أعطنا اليوم وأغفر لنا ذنوبنا كما نغفر نحن أيضا للمذنبين إلينا ولا تدخلنا في تجربة لكن نجنا من الشرير بالمسيح يسوع ربنا لأن لك الملك والقوة والمجد إلى الأبد آمين

Priest:

The love of God the Father; the grace of the only-begotten Son, our Lord, God, and Savior Jesus Christ; and the communion and gift of the Holy Spirit be with you all.	Ⲏ ⲁⲅⲁⲡⲏ ⲧⲟⲩ Ⲑⲉⲟⲩ ⲕⲉ Ⲡⲁⲧⲣⲟⲥ ⲕⲉ ⲏ ⲭⲁⲣⲓⲥ ⲧⲟⲩ ⲙⲟⲛⲟⲅⲉⲛⲟⲩⲥ Ⲩⲟⲩ ⲕⲩⲣⲓⲟⲩ ⲇⲉ ⲕⲉ Ⲑⲉⲟⲩ ⲕⲉ ⲥⲱⲧⲏⲣⲟⲥ ⲏⲙⲱⲛ Ⲓⲏⲥⲟⲩ Ⲭⲣⲓⲥⲧⲟⲩ ⲕⲉ ⲏ ⲕⲟⲓⲛⲱⲛⲓⲁ ⲕⲉ ⲏ ⲇⲱⲣⲉⲁ ⲧⲟⲩ ⲁⲅⲓⲟⲩ Ⲡⲛⲉⲩⲙⲁⲧⲟⲥ ⲓⲏ ⲙⲉⲧⲁ ⲡⲁⲛⲧⲱⲛ ⲩⲙⲱⲛ	محبة الله الآب ونعمة الإبن الوحيد ربنا وإلهنا وملكنا ومخلصنا يسوع المسيح وشركة وموهبة الروح القدس تكون مع جميعكم
Whoever desires to go, go in peace. The peace of the Lord be with you all.	Ⲙⲁϣⲉⲛⲱⲧⲉⲛ ϧⲉⲛ ⲟⲩϩⲓⲣⲏⲛⲏ Ⲡϭⲟⲓⲥ ⲛⲉⲙⲱⲧⲉⲛ	من أراد ان يمض فليمض بسلام سلام الرب مع جميعكم

Congregation:

And with your spirit.	Ⲕⲉ ⲧⲱ ⲡⲛⲉⲩⲙⲁⲧⲓ ⲥⲟⲩ	مع روحك أيضاً

(The priest bids the bride to take a seat in the nave while they begin the liturgy. If the groom belongs to the minor orders of the deaconate, he may vest and serve in the sanctuary. Otherwise, he may stand on the men's side with his party. The liturgy begins with the prayers of the third and sixth hours from the horologion followed by the Prothesis.)

Liturgy

Pauline Epistle
(Ephesians 4:1-7)

Reader:

I, therefore, the prisoner of the Lord, beseech you to walk worthy of the calling with which you were called, with all lowliness and gentleness, with longsuffering, bearing with one another in love, endeavoring to keep the unity of the Spirit in the bond of peace. *There is one body and one Spirit, just as you were called in one hope of your calling; one Lord, one faith, one baptism; one God and Father of all, who is above all, and through all, and in you all. But to each one of us grace was given according to the measure of Christ's gift.*	ϮϮϩο ογΝ ερωτεΝ ανοκ πετcωΝϩ ϧεΝ Ποc εμοϣι κατα πεμπϣα ντε πιθωϩεμ ϕη εταγθαϩεμ θηΝογ εροϥ ϧεΝ θεβιο Νϩητ ΝιβεΝ Νεμ ογμετρεμραγϣ Νεμ ογμετρεϥωογΝϩητ ερετενεραναχεcθε ΝΝετενερηογ ϧεΝ ογαγαπη ερετενιηc εαρεϩ εϮμετογαι ντε πιπΝεγμα ϧεΝ πιμογρ εταϩκ εβολ ντε ϮϩιρηΝη ογcωμα Νογωτ νεμ ογπΝεγμα Νογωτ κατα ϕρηϮ εϥαγθαϩεμ θηΝογ εροϥ ϧεΝ ογϩελπιc Νογωτ ντε πετενθωϩεμ ογϬοιc Νογωτ ογΝαϩϮ Νογωτ ογωμc Νογωτ. Ογαι πε ΦϮ ϕιωτ ντε ογον νιβεν ϕηετχη ϩιχεν ογον νιβεν ογοϩ εβολϩιτεν ογον νιβεν ογοϩ Νϩρηι ϧεν ογον νιβεν. Πιογαι δε πιογαι μμον αγϮ ναϥ Νογϩμοτ κατα πϣι νϮδωρεα ντε Πχc.	في ضوء هذا أسألكم أنا الأسير من أجل الرب أن تَسلكوا كما يليق بالدعوة التي تلقّيتموها من الله أظهروا في كل ظرف تواضعا ووداعة وصبرا محتملين بعضكم بعضا في المحبة لا تبخلوا بأي جهد للمحافظة على الوحدة التي يصنعها الروح بالسلام الذي يربطكم معا إذ يوجد جسد واحد وروح واحد كما دعيتم أيضا في رجاء واحد عندما دعيتم يوجد ربٌ واحد وإيمان واحد ومعمودية واحدة يوجد إله واحد وآب واحد للكل وهو سيد الكل ويستخدم الكل وهو في الكل وقد أعطيت لكل واحد منا موهبة بالمقياس الذي يشاؤه المسيح

Meena Abdou

Catholic Epistle

(1 Peter 3:1-9)

Reader:

Wives, likewise, be submissive to your own husbands, that even if some do not obey the word, they, without a word, may be won by the conduct of their wives, when they observe your chaste conduct accompanied by fear. Do not let your adornment be merely outward—arranging the hair, wearing gold, or putting on fine apparel—rather let it be the hidden person of the heart, with the incorruptible beauty of a gentle and quiet spirit, which is very precious in the sight of God. For in this manner, in former times, the holy women who trusted in God also adorned themselves, being submissive to their own husbands, as Sarah obeyed Abraham, calling him lord, whose daughters you are if you do good and are not afraid with any terror. Husbands, likewise, dwell with them with understanding, giving honor to the wife, as to the weaker vessel, and as	Ⲡⲁⲓⲣⲏϯ ⲅⲁⲣ ⲛⲟⲩⲥⲏⲟⲩ ⲡⲉ ⲛⲛⲓϩⲓⲟⲙⲓ ⲉⲑⲟⲩⲁⲃ ⲉⲧⲉⲣϩⲉⲗⲡⲓⲥ ⲙⲫϯ ⲛⲁⲩⲥⲟⲗⲥⲉⲗ ⲙⲙⲱⲟⲩ ⲉⲩϭⲛⲟⲛⲇⲱⲟⲩ ⲛⲛⲟⲩϩⲁⲓ ⲙⲫⲣⲏϯ ⲛⲥⲁⲣⲣⲁ ⲉⲥⲥⲱⲧⲉⲙ ⲛⲥⲁ ⲁⲃⲣⲁⲁⲙ ⲉⲥⲙⲟⲩϯ ⲉⲣⲟⲥ ϫⲉ ⲡⲁϭⲟⲓⲥ. Ⲑⲏⲉⲧⲁⲣⲉⲧⲉⲛ ⲉⲣϣⲉⲣⲓ ⲛⲁⲥ ⲉⲣⲉⲧⲉⲛⲓⲣⲓ ⲙⲡⲓⲡⲉⲑⲛⲁⲛⲉϥ ⲟⲩⲟϩ ⲛⲧⲉⲧⲉⲛⲉⲣϩⲟϯ ⲁⲛ ϧⲁ ⲧϩⲏ ⲛⲍⲗⲓ ⲛϩⲟϯ. Ⲡⲁⲓⲣⲏϯ ⲟⲛ ⲛⲓⲕⲉⲣⲱⲙⲓ ⲉⲣⲉⲧⲉⲛϣⲟⲡ ⲛⲉⲙⲱⲟⲩ ⲉⲣⲉⲧⲉⲛⲉⲙⲓ ϫⲉ ⲟⲩⲥⲕⲉⲩⲟⲥ ⲛⲁⲥⲑⲉⲛⲏⲥ ⲡⲉ ⲛⲓϩⲓⲟⲙⲓ ⲉⲣⲉⲧⲉⲛϯⲧⲁⲓⲟ ⲛⲱⲟⲩ ϩⲱⲥ ⲉⲩⲟⲓ ⲛϣⲫⲏⲣ ⲛⲕⲗⲏⲣⲟⲛⲟⲙⲟⲥ ⲛⲧⲉ ⲡⲓϩⲙⲟⲧ ⲛⲧⲉ ⲡⲱⲛϧ ϫⲉⲛ ⲟⲩⲑⲟ ⲛⲣⲏϯ ϫⲉ ϩⲓⲛⲁ ⲛⲛⲉⲧⲉⲛⲧⲁϩⲛⲟ ϧⲉⲛ ⲛⲉⲧⲉⲛⲡⲣⲟⲥⲉⲩⲭⲏ. Ⲡϫⲱⲕ ⲇⲉ ⲉⲣⲉⲧⲉⲛⲟⲓ ⲛⲟⲩⲙⲉⲩⲓ ⲛⲟⲩⲱⲧ ⲧⲏⲣⲟⲩ ⲉⲣⲉⲧⲉⲛⲟⲓ ⲛϣⲫⲏⲣ ⲛϭⲓϩⲓⲥⲓ ⲟⲩⲟϩ ⲉⲣⲉⲧⲉⲛⲟⲓ ⲙⲙⲁⲓⲥⲟⲛ ⲛϣⲁⲛⲑⲙⲁϧⲧ ⲉⲣⲉⲧⲉⲛⲑⲉⲃⲓⲏⲟⲩⲧ ⲛⲧⲉⲧⲉⲛϯ ⲛⲟⲩⲡⲉⲧϩⲱⲟⲩ ⲁⲛ ϧⲁ ⲟⲩ ⲡⲉⲧϩⲱⲟⲩ ⲟⲩⲇⲉ ⲟⲩϩⲱⲟⲩϣ ϧⲁ ⲟⲩϩⲱⲟⲩϣ ⲡⲉⲧⲟⲩⲃⲏϥ ⲇⲉ	وأنتن أيتها الزوجات اخضعن أيضا لأزواجكن فحتى الذين يرفضون أن يطيعوا رسالة الله يربحون من خلال سلوك زوجاتهم دون أن يتكلمنَ فَهم سيلاحظون سلوككن الطاهر التقي لا ينبغي أن يعتمد جمالكن على أشياء خارجية كالتصفيف المتكلف للشعر والتزين بالذهب وارتداء الملابس الفاخرة بل ينبغي أن ينبع جمالكن من القلب فيكون جمال الروح الوديعة المسالمة الذي لا يذبل وهو جمال لا يقدر بثمن عند الله هكذا تجملت النساء المقدسات في الماضي فكن يثقن بالله ويخضعنَ لأزواجهن وهكذا كانت سارة تطيع إبراهيم وتناديه سيدي وأنتن بناتها شريطة أن تفعلن الصواب غير خائفات شيئا وأنتم أيضا أيها الأزواج عاملوا زوجاتكم بتفهم لأنهن الجنس الأضعف فأكرموهن كشريكات لكم في نوال نعمة الحياة الجديدة افعلوا هذا لئلا تعاق صلواتكم وأخيرا عيشوا جميعا منسجمي الفكر يتفهم بعضكم بعضا ويحب بعضكم بعضا كإخوة شفوقين ومتواضعين لا

being heirs together of the grace of life, that your prayers may not be hindered. Finally, all of you be of one mind, having compassion for one another; love as brothers, be tenderhearted, be courteous; not returning evil for evil or reviling for reviling, but on the contrary blessing, knowing that you were called to this, that you may inherit a blessing.	ⲉⲣⲉⲧⲉⲛⲥⲙⲟⲩ ⲇⲉ ⲉⲧⲁⲩⲑⲁϩⲉⲙ ⲑⲏⲛⲟⲩ ⲉⲡⲁⲓϩⲱⲃ ϩⲓⲛⲁ ⲛⲧⲉⲧⲉⲛⲉⲣⲕⲗⲏⲣⲟⲛⲟⲙⲓⲛ ⲙⲡⲓⲥⲙⲟⲩ	تردوا على الإساءة بمثلها أو على الإهانة بمثلها بل اطلبوا بركة الله لمن يسيئ إليكم لأنكم تعلمون أن الله دعاكم لكي تنالوا بركة

Meena Abdou

Acts of the Apostles

(Acts 4:32-35)

Now the multitude of those who believed were of one heart and one soul; neither did anyone say that any of the things he possessed was his own, but they had all things in common. And with great power the apostles gave witness to the resurrection of the Lord Jesus. And great grace was upon them all. Nor was there anyone among them who lacked; for all who were possessors of lands or houses sold them, and brought the proceeds of the things that were sold, and laid them at the apostles' feet; and they distributed to each as anyone had need.	Ⲛⲓⲙⲏϣ ⲇⲉ ⲉⲧⲁⲩⲛⲁϩϯ ⲛⲁⲩⲟⲓ ⲛⲟⲩϩⲏⲧ ⲛⲟⲩⲱⲧ ⲟⲩⲟϩ ⲙⲙⲟⲛϩⲗⲓ ⲉϥϫⲱ ⲙⲙⲟⲥ ⲉⲟⲩⲉⲛⲭⲁⲓ ⲛⲧⲉ ⲛⲉϥϩⲩⲡⲁⲣⲭⲟⲛⲧⲁ ϫⲉ ⲫⲱⲓ ⲡⲉ ⲁⲗⲗⲁ ⲛⲁⲣⲉ ϩⲱⲃ ⲛⲓⲃⲉⲛ ϣⲟⲡ ⲛⲱⲟⲩ ϧⲉⲛ ⲟⲩⲙⲉⲧϣⲫⲏⲣ. Ⲟⲩⲟϩ ⲛϩⲣⲏⲓ ϧⲉⲛ ⲟⲩⲛⲓϣϯ ⲛϫⲟⲙ ⲛⲁⲣⲉ ⲛⲓⲁⲡⲟⲥⲧⲟⲗⲟⲥ ⲛⲁϯ ⲛϯⲙⲉⲧⲙⲉⲑⲣⲉ ϧⲁ ⲧⲁⲛⲁⲥⲧⲁⲥⲓⲥ ⲛⲒⲏⲥ Ⲡⲭⲥ Ⲡϭⲟⲓⲥ ⲟⲩⲛⲓϣϯ ⲇⲉ ⲛϩⲙⲟⲧ ⲁϥϣⲱⲡ ϩⲓϫⲱⲟⲩ ⲧⲏⲣⲟⲩ. Ⲛⲉ ⲙⲙⲟⲛ ⲡⲉⲧⲉⲣⲭⲣⲓⲁ ⲅⲁⲣ ⲛϩⲏⲧⲟⲩ ⲡⲉ ⲛⲏ ⲅⲁⲣ ⲉⲧⲉ ⲟⲩⲟⲛⲧⲟⲩ ⲓⲟϩⲓ ⲓⲉ ⲏⲓ ⲙⲙⲁⲩ ⲛⲁⲩϯ ⲙⲙⲱⲟⲩ ⲉⲃⲟⲗ ⲉⲩⲓⲛⲓ ⲛⲛⲓⲧⲓⲙⲏ ⲛⲧⲉ ⲛⲏⲉⲧⲁⲩⲧⲏⲓⲧⲟⲩ ⲉⲃⲟⲗ ⲛⲁⲩⲭⲱ ⲙⲙⲱⲟⲩ ϩⲁⲣⲁⲧⲟⲩ ⲛⲛⲓⲁⲡⲟⲥⲧⲟⲗⲟⲥ. Ⲛⲁⲩϯ ⲇⲉ ⲙⲫⲟⲩⲁⲓ ⲫⲟⲩⲁⲓ ⲕⲁⲧⲁ ⲡⲉⲧⲁϥⲉⲣⲭⲣⲓⲁ ⲙⲙⲟϥ.	وكان المؤمنون جميعا متّحدين في القَلب والنفس ولم يكن أحد يقول إن شيئا من ممتلكاته لَه بل كانوا يَتَشاركونَ في كل شيء يملكونه وكان الرسل يشهدونَ بقوة عظيمة عن قيامة الرب يسوعَ وكانت بركة عظيمة مِنَ الله عليهم جميعا ولم يكن أحد منهم محتاجا فكل الذينَ كانَ لديهم حقول أو بيوت كانوا يبيعونها ويسلمون ثمنها إلى الرسل فيوزع المال على الجميع حسب احتياج كل واحد

The Hymn of the Wedding at Cana of Galilee

(This hymn may be said after the reading of the Synaxarium except during the Holy 50 Days, in which the hymns of the Feast of the Resurrection are said.)

A Textual History of the Coptic Wedding Rite

All the villages of Jericho, the Mount of Olives and Jerusalem, come see this great wonder, that was made in the wedding of Cana of Galilee.	Ⲛⲓⲭⲱⲣⲁ ⲧⲏⲣⲟⲩ ⲛⲧⲉ Ⲓⲉⲣⲓⲭⲱ ⲛⲉⲙ ⲡⲧⲱⲟⲩ ⲛⲧⲉ ⲛⲓϫⲱⲓⲧ ⲛⲉⲙ Ⲓⲉⲣⲟⲩⲥⲁⲗⲏⲙ ⲁⲙⲱⲓⲛⲓ ⲁⲛⲁⲩ ⲉⲧⲁⲓⲛⲓϣϯ ⲛϣⲫⲏⲣⲓ ⲑⲏⲉⲧⲁⲥϣⲱⲡⲓ ϧⲉⲛ ⲡϩⲟⲡ ⲛⲧⲕⲁⲛⲁ ⲛⲧⲉ ϯⲅⲁⲗⲓⲗⲉⲁ	يا كل كور أريحا وجبل الزيتون وأورشليم تعالوا انظروا هذه الأعجوبة العظيمة التي صارت في عرس قانا الجليل
This is the first miracle • that our good Savior performed • before His Disciples • that they believed in Him to be the Christ.	Ⲫⲁⲓ ⲡⲉ ⲡⲓϩⲟⲩⲓⲧ ⲙⲙⲏⲛⲓ ⲉⲧ ⲁ Ⲡⲉⲛⲥⲱⲧⲏⲣ ⲛⲁⲅⲁⲑⲟⲥ ⲁⲓϥ ⲙⲡⲉⲙⲑⲟ ⲛⲛⲉϥⲙⲁⲑⲏⲧⲏⲥ ⲁⲩⲛⲁϩϯ ⲉⲣⲟϥ ϫⲉ Ⲡⲓⲭⲣⲓⲥⲧⲟⲥ	هذه هي الآية الأولى التي صنعها مخلصنا الصالح أمام تلاميذه وآمنوا به أنه المسيح
Jesus of Nazareth • blessed the water and it became wine. • No one has seen such wonder • since Adam till today.	Ⲓⲏⲥⲟⲩⲥ Ⲡⲓⲣⲉⲙⲛⲁⲍⲁⲣⲉⲑ ⲁϥⲥⲙⲟⲩ ⲉⲛⲓⲙⲱⲟⲩ ⲁϥⲁⲓⲧⲟⲩ ⲛⲏⲣⲡ ⲙⲡⲉϩⲓⲗ ⲛⲁⲩ ⲉⲟⲩϣⲫⲏⲣⲓ ⲉⲥⲟⲛⲓ ⲛⲑⲁⲓ ⲓⲥϫⲉⲛ ⲁⲇⲁⲙ ϣⲁ ⲉϧⲟⲩⲛ ⲛⲫⲟⲟⲩ	يسوع الناصري بارك المياه فصيرها خمرا ما نظر أحد أعجوبة مثل هذه منذ آدم إلى اليوم
Six jars of water • You changed into chosen wine • with Your great glory • at the wedding of Cana of Galilee.	Ⲥⲟⲟⲩ ⲛϩⲩⲇⲣⲓⲁ ⲙⲙⲱⲟⲩ ⲟⲩⲏⲣⲡ ⲉϥⲥⲱⲧⲡ ⲁⲕⲟⲩⲱⲧⲉⲃ ⲙⲙⲱⲟⲩ ⲉⲃⲟⲗϩⲉⲛ ⲡⲉⲕⲛⲓϣϯ ⲛⲱⲟⲩ ϧⲉⲛ ⲡϩⲟⲡ ⲛⲧⲕⲁⲛⲁ ⲛⲧⲉ ϯⲅⲁⲗⲓⲗⲉⲁ	ستة أجران ماء حولتها إلى خمر مختار من قبل مجدك العظيم في عرس قانا الجليل
Jesus Christ the same yesterday, • today, and forever, • in one hypostasis. • We worship and glorify Him.	Ⲓⲏⲥⲟⲩⲥ Ⲡⲓⲭⲣⲓⲥⲧⲟⲥ ⲛⲥⲁϥ ⲛⲉⲙ ⲫⲟⲟⲩ ⲛⲑⲟϥ ⲛⲑⲟϥ ⲡⲉ ⲛⲉⲙ ϣⲁ ⲉⲛⲉϩ ϧⲉⲛ ⲟⲩϩⲩⲡⲟⲥⲧⲁⲥⲓⲥ ⲛⲟⲩⲱⲧ ⲧⲉⲛⲟⲩⲱϣⲧ ⲙⲙⲟϥ ⲧⲉⲛϯⲱⲟⲩ ⲛⲁϥ	يسوع المسيح هو هو أمس واليوم وإلى الأبد بأقنوم واحد نسجد له ونمجده

Intercede on our behalf, • O the Lady of us all the Theotokos, • Mary the Mother of our Savior, • that He may forgive us our sins.	ⲁⲣⲓⲡⲣⲉⲥⲃⲉⲩⲓⲛ ⲉϩⲣⲏⲓ ⲁϫⲱⲛ ⲱ ⲧⲉⲛϬⲟⲓⲥ ⲛⲛⲏⲃ ⲧⲏⲣⲉⲛ ϯⲑⲉⲟⲧⲟⲕⲟⲥ Ⲙⲁⲣⲓⲁ ⲑⲙⲁⲩ ⲙⲡⲉⲛⲥⲱⲧⲏⲣ ⲛⲧⲉϥⲭⲁ ⲛⲉⲛⲛⲟⲃⲓ ⲛⲁⲛ ⲉⲃⲟⲗ	اشفعي فينا يا سيدتنا كلنا السيدة والدة الإله مريم أم مخلصنا ليغفر لنا خطايانا

The Psalm

(Psalm 21:1-2)

The king shall have joy in Your strength, O LORD • and in Your salvation how greatly shall he rejoice! • You have given him his heart's desire • and have not withheld the request of his lips.	Ⲡϭⲟⲓⲥ ϧⲉⲛ ⲧⲉⲕϫⲟⲙ ⲉϥⲉⲟⲩⲛⲟϥ ⲙⲙⲟϥ ⲛϫⲉ ⲡⲓⲟⲩⲣⲟ ⲉϥⲉⲑⲉⲗⲏⲗ ⲙⲙⲟϥ ⲉⲙⲁϣⲱ ⲉϫⲉⲛ ⲡⲉⲕⲛⲟϩⲉⲙ. ϯⲉⲡⲓⲑⲩⲙⲓⲁ ⲛⲧⲉ ⲧⲉϥⲯⲩⲭⲏ ⲁⲕⲧⲏⲓⲥ ⲛⲁϥ ⲟⲩⲟϩ ⲡⲧⲱⲃϩ ⲛⲧⲉ ⲛⲉϥⲥⲫⲟⲧⲟⲩ ⲙⲡⲉⲕϣⲟⲛϩϥ ⲙⲙⲟϥ.	يفرح الملك بقوتك يا الله يتهج كثيرا بخلاصك أعطيته مشتهى قلبه ولم تحرمه من مطلب شفتيه

The Gospel

(John 2:1-11)

On the third day there was a wedding in Cana of Galilee, and the mother of Jesus was there. Now both Jesus and His disciples were invited to the wedding. And when they ran out of wine, the mother of Jesus said to Him, "They have no wine." Jesus said to her, "Woman, what does your concern have to do with Me? My	Ⲟⲩⲟϩ ⲛϩⲣⲏⲓ ϧⲉⲛ ⲡⲓⲉϩⲟⲟⲩ ⲙⲙⲁϩϣⲟⲙⲧ ⲟⲩⲟⲡ ⲁϥϣⲱⲡⲓ ϧⲉⲛ ⲧⲕⲁⲛⲁ ⲛⲧⲉ ϯⲅⲁⲗⲓⲗⲉⲁ ⲟⲩⲟϩ ⲛⲁⲣⲉ ⲑⲙⲁⲩ ⲛⲒⲏⲥ ⲙⲙⲁⲩ ⲁⲩⲑⲁϩⲉⲙ ⲡⲕⲉⲒⲏⲥ ⲇⲉ ⲛⲉⲙ ⲛⲉϥⲙⲁⲑⲏⲧⲏⲥ ⲉⲡⲓϩⲟⲡ ⲟⲩⲟϩ ⲉⲧⲁϥⲙⲟⲩⲛⲕ ⲛϫⲉ ⲡⲓⲏⲣⲡ ⲡⲉϫⲉ ⲑⲙⲁⲩ ⲛⲒⲏⲥ ⲛⲁϥ ϫⲉ ⲙⲙⲟⲛⲧⲟⲩ ⲏⲣⲡ ⲙⲙⲁⲩ ⲟⲩⲟϩ ⲡⲉϫⲉ Ⲓⲏⲥ ⲛⲁⲥ ϫⲉ	وفي اليوم الثالث أقيم عرس في بلدة قانا في إقليم الجليل وكانت أم يسوع هناك وقد دعي أيضا يسوع وتلاميذه إلى العرس وعندما فرغت الخمر قالت أم يسوع له ليس لهم خمر فقال لها يسوع لماذا تأتين إلي يا أمي لم يحن الوقت لأبدأ عملي بعد أما أمه فقالَت للخدام افعلوا كل ما يقوله لكم

hour has not yet come." His mother said to the servants, "Whatever He says to you, do it." Now there were set there six waterpots of stone, according to the manner of purification of the Jews, containing twenty or thirty gallons apiece. Jesus said to them, "Fill the waterpots with water." And they filled them up to the brim. And He said to them, "Draw some out now, and take it to the master of the feast." And they took it. When the master of the feast had tasted the water that was made wine, and did not know where it came from (but the servants who had drawn the water knew), the master of the feast called the bridegroom. And he said to him, "Every man at the beginning sets out the good wine, and when the guests have well drunk, then the inferior. You have kept the good wine until now!" This beginning of signs Jesus did in Cana of Galilee, and manifested His glory; and His disciples believed in Him.	ⲁϩⲟ ⲛⲉⲙⲏⲓ ϩⲱⲓ ϯⲥϩⲓⲙⲓ ⲙⲡⲁⲧⲉⲥⲓ ⲛϫⲉ ⲧⲁⲟⲩⲛⲟⲩ. ⲡⲉϫⲉ ⲧⲉϥⲙⲁⲩ ⲇⲉ ⲛⲛⲓⲇⲓⲁⲕⲱⲛ ϫⲉ ⲫⲉⲧⲉⲧⲉϥⲛⲁϫⲟϥ ⲛⲱⲧⲉⲛ ⲁⲣⲓⲧϥ. ⲛⲁϥⲭⲏ ⲇⲉ ⲙⲙⲁⲩ ⲡⲉ ⲛϫⲉ ⲥⲟⲟⲩ ⲛϩⲩⲇⲣⲓⲁ ⲛⲱⲛⲓ ⲕⲁⲧⲁ ⲡⲧⲟⲩⲃⲟ ⲛⲧⲉ ⲛⲓⲓⲟⲩⲇⲁⲓ ⲉⲩⲱⲗⲓ ⲙⲙⲉⲧⲣⲓⲧⲏⲥ ⲥⲛⲁⲩ ⲓⲉ ϣⲟⲙⲧ ⲉⲑⲟⲩⲓ. ⲡⲉϫⲉ Ⲓⲏⲥ ⲛⲱⲟⲩ ⲇⲉ ⲙⲟϩ ⲛⲛⲓϩⲩⲇⲣⲓⲁ ⲙⲙⲱⲟⲩ ⲟⲩⲟϩ ⲁⲩⲙⲁϩⲟⲩ ϣⲁ ⲉⲡϣⲱⲓ. ⲡⲉϫⲁϥ ⲛⲱⲟⲩ ϫⲉ ⲟⲩⲱⲧϩ ϯⲛⲟⲩ ⲟⲩⲟϩ ⲁⲛⲓⲟⲩⲓ ⲙⲡⲓⲁⲣⲭⲏⲧⲣⲓⲕⲗⲓⲛⲟⲥ ⲛⲑⲱⲟⲩ ⲇⲉ ⲁⲩⲓⲛⲓ. ϩⲱⲥⲧⲉ ⲉⲧⲁϥϫⲉⲙϯⲡⲓ ⲙⲡⲓⲙⲱⲟⲩ ⲛϫⲉ ⲡⲓⲁⲣⲭⲏⲧⲣⲓⲕⲗⲓⲛⲟⲥ ⲉⲁϥⲉⲣⲏⲣⲡ ⲟⲩⲟϩ ⲛⲁϥⲉⲙⲓ ⲁⲛ ϫⲉ ⲟⲩ ⲉⲃⲟⲗ ⲑⲱⲛ ⲡⲉ. ⲛⲓⲇⲓⲁⲕⲱⲛ ⲇⲉ ⲛⲁⲩⲉⲙⲓ ⲛⲏⲉⲧⲁⲩⲙⲁϩⲟⲩ ⲡⲓⲙⲱⲟⲩ. ⲁ ⲡⲓⲁⲣⲭⲏⲧⲣⲓⲕⲗⲓⲛⲟⲥ ⲙⲟⲩϯ ⲉⲡⲓⲡⲁⲧϣⲉⲗⲉⲧ ⲡⲉϫⲁϥ ⲛⲁϥ ϫⲉ ⲣⲱⲙⲓ ⲛⲓⲃⲉⲛ ⲉϣⲁⲩⲭⲱ ⲙⲡⲓⲏⲣⲡ ⲉⲑⲛⲁⲛⲉϥ ⲛϣⲟⲣⲡ ⲟⲩⲟϩ ⲉϣⲱⲡ ⲁⲩϣⲁⲛⲑⲓϧⲓ ϣⲁⲩⲉⲛ ⲫⲏⲉⲧⲥⲃⲟⲕ ⲉⲣⲟϥ. ⲛⲑⲟⲕ ⲇⲉ ⲁⲕⲁⲣⲉϩ ⲉⲡⲓⲏⲣⲡ ⲉⲑⲛⲁⲛⲉϥ ϣⲁ ϯⲛⲟⲩ. ⲫⲁⲓ ⲡⲉ ⲡⲓϩⲟⲩⲓⲧ ⲙⲙⲏⲓⲛⲓ ⲉⲧⲁϥⲁⲓϥ ⲛϫⲉ Ⲓⲏⲥ ϧⲉⲛ ⲧⲕⲁⲛⲁ ⲛⲧⲉ ϯⲅⲁⲗⲓⲗⲉⲁ	وكانت هناك ستة أحواض حجرية للماء يستخدمها اليهود للاغتسال وفقا لطقوسهم وكان كل حوض منها يتسع لثمانين أو لمئة وعشرين لترا فقال يسوع للخدام املأوا الأحواض بالماء فملأوها إلى حافتها ثم قال لهم والآن اغرفوا منها وقدموا لرئيس الحفل ففعلوا ذلك فذاق رئيس الحفل الماء الذي تحول إلى خمر ولَم يكن يعلَم من أين جاء الخمر لكن الخدامَ الذين غرفوا الماء كانوا يعلمون فاستَدعى العريس وقال له في العادة يقدم الناس الخمر الجيد أولا وبعد أن يسكر الضيوف يقدمون الخمر الأقل جودة لكنك أبقيت الخمر الجيد إلَى الآن كانت هذه أولى المعجزات التي صنعها يسوع وقد صنعها في بلدة قانا في إقليم الجليل فأظهر يسوع مجده وآمن به تلاميذه

	ⲟⲩⲟϩ ⲁϥⲟⲩⲱⲛϩ ⲙⲡⲉϥⲱⲟⲩ ⲉⲃⲟⲗ ⲟⲩⲟϩ ⲁⲩⲛⲁϩϯ ⲉⲣⲟⲙ ⲛϫⲉ ⲛⲉϥⲙⲁⲑⲏⲧⲏⲥ.	

Gospel Response

Six jars of water • You have changed into chosen wine • with great glory • at the wedding at Cana of Galilee.	Ⲥⲟⲟⲩ ⲛϩⲩⲇⲣⲓⲁ ⲙⲙⲱⲟⲩ ⲉⲟⲩⲏⲣⲡ ⲉϥⲥⲱⲧⲡ ⲁⲕⲟⲩⲱⲧⲉⲃ ⲙⲙⲱⲟⲩ ⲉⲃⲟⲗϩⲓⲧⲉⲛ ⲡⲉⲕⲛⲓϣϯ ⲛⲱⲟⲩ ϧⲉⲛ ⲡϩⲟⲡ ⲛⲧⲕⲁⲛⲁ ⲛⲧⲉ ϯⲅⲁⲗⲓⲗⲉⲁ	ستة أجران ماء حولها الى خمر مختار بمجده العظيم فى عرس قانا الجليل

Communion Hymn

(This melody may be sung after Psalm 150 during the distribution of the Eucharist. Its tune will depend on the liturgical season. It will either be the annual or the festal tune. The English is my own attempt at translating the poetic Arabic.)

Today is a wedding feast, today is worthy of song and praise for the one Savior, the Lord of the honorable.	اليوم بالاكليل عيد اليوم لاق به النشيد و الحمد للفادي الوحيد مولى المكارم الجسام
Today began with good news, and was strengthened with glee, singing and congratulating the offspring of the honorable.	اليوم بالبشر بدا و بلبل الأنس شدا مرتلا مغردا مهنئا نسل الكرام
By it the day of happiness was honored, by it the ink wells drained, by it faces smiled, by it perfection was suddenly achieved	أكرم به يوم السرور به صفت كأس الحبور به تبسمت الثغور به زها بدر التمام

It is a cheerful day in which the bridegroom transfigured, with his bride the precious offspring, sparkling with smiles.	أهلا به يوما أنيس يوما تجلى فيه العريس و عروسه النسل النفيس متلألئين بابتسام
Today happiness spread forth and bliss radiated out and was manifested when our bride and groom, the honorable offspring, were esteemed by the award.	اليوم قد عم الفرح و سنا الهناء قد وضح لما تجمل بالمنح عريسنا نسل الكرام
The clouds of honor rained down with the placement of the crown of grace. Happiness was achieved through the covenant and good fortune led to fulfillment of desires.	هطلت سحائب الكرم بوضع اكليل النعم و السعد بالتوفيق تم و الحظ قد بلغ المرام
The crowning of {GROOM} and {BRIDE} was done by the right hand and holiness was made boastful. Virtue was granted from the Creator, the Giver of great awards.	تكليل (..) زها باليمين و القدس ازدهى و الفضل من باري النهى الواهب المنح العظيم
The Spirit of the Most High sanctified him and crowned him with the crown of our God. He blessed him and his bride and united them in peace.	روح العلي قدسه تاج الهنا البسه باركه و عروسه و أقرنهما بالسلام
O our Lord, the granter of guidance, O bestower of good things, continue the bliss for your servants, protecting them at all times.	يا ربنا مولى الهدى يا مانحا أسمى العطا أدم لعبيدك الهناء في كل وقت باعتصام
You are the One who blessed the wedding at Cana of Galilee. Grant them beautiful offspring O Lord with good harmony.	أنت المبارك للتحليل و العرس في قانا الجليل امنحهما النسل الجميل يا رب مع حسن الوئام
Preserve them in unity and let them achieve their goals. Guide them on the right path and gift them a happy ending.	احفظهما بالاتحاد و امنحهما أقصى المراد وفقهما الى الرشاد و هبهما حسن الختام

Exit Hymn

(After the liturgy, the bride and groom are processed out of the church to the following hymn.)

Rejoice O Mary the queen, • the young unaging vine • that no farmer had ploughed • and on which was found the spring of life.	Ⲭⲉⲣⲉ Ⲙⲁⲣⲓⲁ ϯⲟⲩⲣⲱ ϯⲃⲱ ⲛⲁⲗⲟⲗⲓ ⲛⲁⲧⲉⲣϭⲉⲗⲗⲱ ⲑⲏⲉⲧⲉ ⲙⲡⲉⲟⲩⲱⲓ ⲉⲣⲟⲩⲱⲓ ⲉⲣⲟⲥ ⲁⲩϫⲉⲙ ⲡⲓⲥⲙⲁϩ ⲛⲧⲉ ⲡⲱⲛϧ ⲛϧⲏⲧⲥ	السلام لمريم الملكة الكرمة غير الشائخة التي لم يفَلحها فلاح ووجد فيها عنقود الحياة
The Son of God truly • incarnated from the Virgin. • She gave birth to Him and He saved us • and forgave us our sins.	Ⲡϣⲏⲣⲓ ⲙⲫϯ ϧⲉⲛ ⲟⲩⲙⲉⲑⲙⲏⲓ ⲁϥϭⲓⲥⲁⲣϫ ϧⲉⲛ ϯⲡⲁⲣⲑⲉⲛⲟⲥ ⲁⲥⲙⲓⲥⲓ ⲙⲙⲟϥ ⲁϥⲥⲱϯ ⲙⲙⲟⲛ ⲁϥⲭⲁ ⲛⲉⲛⲛⲟⲃⲓ ⲛⲁⲛ ⲉⲃⲟⲗ	إبن الله بالحقيقة تجسد من العذراء ولدته وخلصنا وغفر لنا خطايانا
You found grace, O bride. • Many proclaimed your honor, • because the Word of God • came and incarnated from you.	Ⲁⲣⲉϫⲉⲙ ⲟⲩϩⲙⲟⲧ ⲱ ⲧⲁⲓϣⲉⲗⲉⲧ ϩⲁⲛⲙⲏϣ ⲁⲩⲥⲁϫⲓ ⲉⲡⲉⲧⲁⲓⲟ ϫⲉ ⲁ ⲡⲓⲗⲟⲅⲟⲥ ⲛⲧⲉ ⲫⲓⲱⲧ ⲁϥϭⲓⲥⲁⲣϫ ⲉⲃⲟⲗⲛϧⲏϯ	وجدت نعمة يا أيتها العروس كثيرون نطقوا بكرامتك لأن كلمة الآب أتى وتجسد منك
Which woman on earth • became the mother of God except you? • For you are an earthly woman • who became the mother of the Creator.	Ⲛⲓⲙ ⲛⲥϩⲓⲙⲓ ⲉⲧϩⲓϫⲉⲛ ⲡⲓⲕⲁϩⲓ ⲁⲥⲉⲣⲙⲁⲩ ⲙⲫϯ ⲉⲃⲏⲗ ⲉⲣⲟ ϫⲉ ⲛⲑⲟ ⲟⲩⲥϩⲓⲙⲓ ⲛⲣⲉⲙⲛⲕⲁϩⲓ ⲁⲣⲉⲉⲣⲙⲁⲩ ⲙⲡⲓⲣⲉⲥⲱⲛⲧ	أية إمرأة على الأرض صارت أما لله سواك لأنك إمرأة أرضية صرت أما للباري
Many women received honor • and won the kingdom • but they could not attain such honor as yours, • O the best of all women.	Ⲁⲟⲩⲙⲏϣ ⲛⲥϩⲓⲙⲓ ϭⲓⲧⲁⲓⲟ ⲁⲩϣⲁϣⲛⲓ ⲉϯⲙⲉⲧⲟⲩⲣⲟ ⲁⲗⲗⲁ ⲙⲡⲟⲩϣϥⲟϩ ⲉⲡⲉⲧⲁⲓⲟ ⲑⲏⲉⲑⲛⲉⲥⲱⲥ ϧⲉⲛ ⲛⲓϩⲓⲟⲙⲓ	نساء كثيرات نلن كرامات وفزن بالملكوت لكن لم يبلغن كرامتك أيتها الحسنة في النساء

For You are the high tower • in which they found the jewel • that is Emmanuel • who came and stayed in your womb.	Ⲛⲑⲟ ⲅⲁⲣ ⲡⲉ ⲡⲓⲡⲩⲣⲅⲟⲥ ⲉⲧϭⲟⲥⲓ ⲉⲧⲁⲩϫⲉⲙ ⲡⲓⲁⲛⲁⲙⲏⲓ ⲛϧⲏⲧϥ ⲉⲧⲉ ⲫⲁⲓ ⲡⲉ Ⲉⲙⲙⲁⲛⲟⲩⲏⲗ ⲉⲧⲁϥⲓ ⲁϥϣⲱⲡⲓ ϧⲉⲛ ⲧⲉⲛⲉϫⲓ	أنت هي البرج العالي الذي وجدوا فيه الجوهر أي عمانوئيل الذي أتى وحل في بطنك
Let us honor the Virginity • of the bride who is without evil, • the pure, the wholly sacred, • the mother of God, Mary.	Ⲙⲁⲣⲉⲛⲧⲁⲓⲟ ⲛⲧⲡⲁⲣⲑⲉⲛⲓⲁ ⲛϯϣⲉⲗⲉⲧ ⲛⲁⲧⲕⲁⲕⲓⲁ ϯⲕⲁⲑⲁⲣⲟⲥ ⲙⲡⲁⲛⲁⲅⲓⲁ ϯⲑⲉⲟⲧⲟⲕⲟⲥ Ⲙⲁⲣⲓⲁ	فلنكرم بتولية العروس التي بغير شر النقية الكلية القداسة والدة الإله مريم
You rose higher than heaven, • and you are more honored than earth • and all the creatures on it, • for you became the mother of the Creator.	Ⲁⲣⲉϭⲓⲥⲓ ⲉϩⲟⲧⲉ ⲧⲫⲉ ⲧⲉⲧⲁⲓⲏⲟⲩⲧ ⲉϩⲟⲧⲉ ⲡⲕⲁϩⲓ ⲛⲉⲙ ⲥⲱⲛⲧ ⲛⲓⲃⲉⲛ ⲉⲧⲉ ⲛϧⲏⲧϥ ϫⲉ ⲁⲣⲉⲉⲣⲙⲁⲩ ⲙⲡⲓⲣⲉϥⲥⲱⲛⲧ	إرتفعت أكثر من السماء وأنت أكرم من الأرض وكل المخلوقات التي فيها لأنك صرت أما للخالق
You are truly • the pure bridal chamber • of Christ the Groom • according to the prophetic sayings.	Ⲛⲑⲟ ⲅⲁⲣ ⲁⲗⲏⲑⲱⲥ ⲡⲓⲙⲁⲛϣⲉⲗⲉⲧ ⲛⲕⲁⲑⲁⲣⲟⲥ ⲛⲧⲉ Ⲡⲓⲭⲣⲓⲥⲧⲟⲥ ⲡⲓⲛⲩⲙⲫⲓⲟⲥ ⲕⲁⲧⲁ ⲛⲓⲥⲙⲏ ⲙⲡⲣⲟⲫⲏⲧⲓⲕⲟⲛ	أنت بالحقيقة الخدر النقي الذي للمسيح الختن كالأصوات النبوية
Intercede for us, • O lady of us all, the Theotokos, • Mary the mother of Jesus Christ, • that He may forgive us our sins.	Ⲁⲣⲓⲡⲣⲉⲥⲃⲉⲩⲓⲛ ⲉϩⲣⲏⲓ ⲉϫⲱⲛ ⲱ ⲧⲉⲛϭⲟⲓⲥ ⲛⲛⲏⲃ ⲧⲏⲣⲉⲛ ϯⲑⲉⲟⲧⲟⲕⲟⲥ Ⲙⲁⲣⲓⲁ ⲑⲙⲁⲩ ⲛⲒⲏⲥⲟⲩⲥ Ⲡⲓⲭⲣⲓⲥⲧⲟⲥ ⲛⲧⲉϥⲭⲁ ⲛⲉⲛⲛⲟⲃⲓ ⲛⲁⲛ ⲉⲃⲟⲗ	إشفعي فينا يا سيدتنا كلنا السيدة مريم والدة الإله أم يسوع المسيح ليغفر لنا خطايانا

CHAPTER 7

Conclusion

This study traced the history of the Coptic wedding rite through historical sources. It showed that major changes occurred in the rite, particularly in the nineteenth and twentieth centuries. These changes along with the current high degree of customization in modern practice make it difficult to know what the full original rite actually was. Some of the changes are not compatible with how the rite was described in the source material. The various Arabic and English translations produced in the twentieth century did not include everything from the original rite, but rather reflected the contemporary practice. The study showed that almost the entire first half of the rite along with the subsequent liturgy has been abandoned, along with a few hymns. The tunes for the hymns that remain have changed and some Coptic responses have been replaced by newer Arabic ones. The main contribution of this book is to present an argument for returning to the original rite with practical considerations. To facilitate that, a reconstruction of the full text of the original rite was compiled all together in one place in Coptic, English, and Arabic, including directions for priests and deacons as well as for musical tunes. It is intended to be ready for use or as a base starter for personalized wedding booklets. The main differences between my reconstruction and the current practice are that I restore the full set of prayers that I have called the Vesting of the Groom, including the processional hymns "Blessed is he who comes" and "Come see this bride," I restore the use of the broad white cloth over the heads, I remove the Hymn of the Holy Spirit and the Arabic commandment responses, and I restore the original Coptic commandment responses with their tunes along with the concluding canon. Finally, I prescribe that the wedding be conducted after Matins and followed by a liturgy. It is my hope that future generations of youth will be inspired to conduct their weddings consistent with the traditions of our Coptic Orthodox Church. I hope this book inspires scholars and clergy to raise awareness for this issue and ultimately for the original practice to be restored by the Holy Synod.

Bibliography

Articles

Atiya, Aziz Suryal. *Claremont Coptic Encyclopedia,* s.v. "Ibn Kabar." Claremont, 1991. https://ccdl.claremont.edu/digital/collection/cce/id/1049

Atiya, Aziz Suryal. *Claremont Coptic Encyclopedia,* s.v. "Gabriel V." Claremont, 1991. https://ccdl.claremont.edu/digital/collection/cce/id/876

Atiya, Aziz Suryal. *Claremont Coptic Encyclopedia,* s.v. "Philuthawus Ibrahim al-Baghdadi." Claremont, 1991. https://ccdl.claremont.edu/digital/collection/cce/id/1574

Books

Al-Maqari, Athanasius. *al-Dubla wa al-Iklīl [The Ring and the Crown].* Cairo: MD Graphics, 2005.

Evetts, B.T.A., trans. *The Rites of the Coptic Church: The Order of Baptism and The Order of Matrimony according to the use of the Coptic Church.* London: Ballanyne, Hanson & Co, 1888.

Hanna, Fr. Markos. *The Coptic Offices for the Coptic Orthodox Church: Part 2 Holy Matrimony & Second Matrimony 4th edition.* Los Angeles: self-published, 2004.

Ibrahim, Hegumen Philotheos. *Rutbat al-Iklīl al-Jalīl [The Dignified Rank of Crowning].* Cairo: al-Watan, 1888.

Mikhail, Albair Gamal. *al-Asās fī khidmat al-Shammās [The Essentials in the Deacon's Service] 3rd Edition.* Shubra, Egypt: Shikolani, 2013.

Secretariat of the Holy Synod. *The Decisions of the Holy Synod during the reign of His Holiness Pope Shenouda III 3rd Edition*. Cairo: Coptic Orthodox Cultural Center, 2011.

Woolley, Reginald Maxwell, trans. *Coptic Offices*. London: Society for Promoting Christian Knowledge, 1930.

Manuscripts

'Abdallah, Alfonso, trans. *L'ordinamento liturgico di Gabriele V: 88° Patriarca Copto (1409-1427)*. Cairo: SOC Aegyptiaca, 1962.

Gabriel V. *Kitāb tartīb*. Manuscript. Bibliothèque nationale de France. Département des Manuscrits. Arabe 98. https://gallica.bnf.fr/ark:/12148/btv1b11000385k/f15.item.r=COPTE (accessed July 3, 2021).

Salama, Salama, ed. *Miṣbāḥ al-ẓulmah fī Īḍāḥ al-khidmah: by Shams al-Ri'āsah Abū al-Barakāt Ibn Kabar [The Lamp That Enlightens the Darkness in Clarifying the Service]*. Cairo: Maktabat Al-Karūz, 1971.

Shams al-Ri'āsah Abū al-Barakāt Ibn Kabar. *Miṣbāḥ al-ẓulmah fī Īḍāḥ al-khidmah*. Manuscript. Bibliothèque nationale de France. Département des Manuscrits. Arabe 203. https://gallica.bnf.fr/ark:/12148/btv1b110048384/f225.item.r=ARABE%204 (accessed July 3, 2021).

Appendix A
Translation of Ibn Kabar

Section 1

The legal crowning and the ecclesiastical contract: the first marriage is contracted in the church. Incense is raised along with its associated prayers followed by the full crowning prayers. None of the rite is done in a house. The weddings that take place in houses are merely agreements and not contract signings. Therefore, it is right to consider those weddings null. Weddings are not to be officiated by those of the rank of deacon. As for the second marriage, it does not have the blessing of crowning, unless one of the couple is a virgin, in which case the contract is contracted. But if not, then a prayer of forgiveness is said for one or both of them. A third marriage is allowed and its rite follows that of the second marriage. There is no more marriage beyond that allowed by the Christian law.

The preparation of the contract of properties and the crowning should include a public announcement. It is in the holy law that a crowning should not happen in secret but in the presence of many. A marriage contract cannot happen except by the presence of a priest officiating its rite and offering a liturgy at the time of crowning through which the couple is united and becomes one body, as God said to Him be the glory. And without that, the marital union cannot happen, for the prayer is that which absolves the women for the men and the men for the women.

Section 2

It is the custom of the Egyptians that the Godparents bring a tray containing an oblation bread, a cross, rings, some sugar, two crowns made from either silver, gold, or green jewels. The groom stands in front of the sanctuary. The priest says the Thanksgiving Prayer and raises incense. Psalm 50 is said. The Pauline Epistle from 1 Corinthians is read in Coptic and Arabic. It begins with "With one mind." The Psalm begins with, "Mercy and truth." The Gospel is read from John beginning with, "In the beginning was the Word." The three great litanies are said followed by the holy creed. Then these two prayers: "O Master and Philanthropic One" and "O God who created." The third prayer, "We thank You O Master Lord" is a prayer of thanks. Then Our Father is said followed by the Absolution of the Son with the cross placed on the groom's head. Then they say Lord Have Mercy. Then they bring the wedding outfit. It is better for it to be white. A prayer beginning with "O Lord Jesus Christ our God" is said over it. Then the priest puts it on the groom along with his clerical hat and girds the groom's waist with a belt while the chanters sing "Come see this bride" in the tune of the cross. This psali to the Lady is the order of a monk of the Monastery of St. Macarius from the cell of Kedrān. The letters of his name are the first letters of its verses. It is sung with candles. They process the groom outside the area of the sanctuary where the crowning will happen. Then they sing the concluding canon of the contract.

Section 3

The prayer of the wedding and crowning after the contract: the bride and groom stand together in front of the door of the sanctuary with a broad white cloth draped over their heads. The priest says the Thanksgiving Prayer and raises incense followed by Psalm 50. The Pauline is read from Ephesians 5 beginning with, "Wives submit" until "long life on the earth." The Psalm is, "Which is like a bridegroom" and the Gospel from Matthew beginning with "When Jesus finished these words" until "let not man tear asunder." After the Gospel finishes, the people sing the response.

Section 4

The priest recites the supplications facing the West towards the couple. After each supplication, the people say Amen. The supplications may then be translated. It is better to say them in Arabic, with only three or four of them in Coptic. Then they pray the three great litanies followed by the Creed. Then this prayer is said for the groom, "O Lord God the Pantocrator" then "O God who is who exists forever", then "Our God the creator" then "O Lord our God the Great". The deacon says, "Bow your heads to the Lord." Then the priest turns toward the East and says this prayer of submission beginning with "Lend your ear".

At its conclusion, the priest takes the container of the holy oil, that is the oil of gladness, and prays over it thusly, "O Master Lord God the Pantocrator" then he anoints the foreheads of the couple and both sides of their hands saying "O Lord God of powers". The people sing these verses, "You have anointed my head with oil..., All the people of the earth bless me..., You are exalted among my people..., The Lord said to His angels..., He lifted me and anointed me with the oil of his anointing..., Blessed is the Father"

Then the priest takes the crowns in his hands and says a prayer over them beginning with "O God the Holy". At its conclusion he says these Greek verses with his hand on the groom's head, "With Honor glorify this crown O Father, Bless O Son, Crown and perfect O Holy Spirit." The people sing Axios three times. The priest sings "May He who blessed our father Adam and Noah". The people sing this song in its entirety in the Morning Doxology tune, "Unfading crowns..., Illuminate, Illuminate..., Receive joy..., Go with joy." The priest puts his hand on the couple and says this prayer, "Place O Lord on Your servants". The people say Our Father. The priest says the Absolution of the Son followed by the commandment to the groom beginning with "Glory to God." The people say, "My peace which I have taken". The priest continues with "May the peace of our Lord God Jesus Christ" and after he says "in this blessed time" the people sing, "This is the time of blessing". The priest continues and after he says "in this world and the next" the people sing "Listen O daughter". The priest continues and when he finishes the commandments the people say Lord Have Mercy followed by this concluding canon, "Rejoice O shining bride". And when the groom enters the sanctuary for the liturgy they sing "For blessed."

Section 5

The divine liturgy is prayed during which these readings are read which are specific to the wedding: Ephesians beginning with "I ask you as a prisoner", The Catholic Epistle from 1 Peter beginning with "Likewise in the days of old", the Acts beginning with "As for those who believed." The Psalm begins with, "O Lord in your power." The Gospel is from John beginning with "In that day" and ending with "and his disciples believed in Him." The duties of the wedding of virgins is complete. Glory to the Father of lights.

Appendix B
Translation of Pope Gabriel

Section 1

It is customary to have the wedding after the midnight praise. The groom attends Matins along with his family, friends, and guests. The priests and deacons of the church whom he invited meet him at the church doors with candles and cymbals. If any of them knows the hymn of the groom, let him say it. It is "Blessed is he who comes according to the order of angels. Alleluia 3x." They shall say it while standing at the doors of the church until its end. They begin with "Christ the Logos of the Father" in the tune of the cross until they reach the place of contracting the properties. And if nobody knows the hymn, then they say "Galilee of the Nations."

Then they leave and meet the bride also at the door of the church with candles and cymbals singing "Rejoice O Mary" from "You are called" until she enters the house of women. Then they enter the chorus. The priest uncovers his head and wears the sticharion and the omophorion. If he chooses, he may wear the phelonion. Likewise the deacon vests with the sticharion and omophorion. If the Patriarch is in attendance, then he is the one who officiates the ceremony. They process him from his room with candles until they reach the chorus. A tray is placed on the lectionary containing the groom's vestment, the cincture, the white cloth, the cross, the ring, and incense. The patriarch uncovers his head as usual. If the groom made for him a phelonion, then he vests with that. He removes the phelonion with which he left his room and wears the groom's phelonion.

He begins with the Thanksgiving Prayer. He raises incense with the Pauline Litany while the deacons chant Lord Have Mercy in the long tune and after it "We worship", "Rejoice O church", "Through the intercessions", "Through the prayers" for the Patriarch, and they finish with "That we may praise." The priests offer incense to the patriarch as usual. Then they say Lord Have Mercy, Alleluia, Glory be to You, Our Father, and Psalm 50. The incense of the Pauline is raised. The Pauline Epistle is read in Coptic while the priest performs the Pauline incense circuit. Then the Pauline is read in Arabic. The Trisagion is said. The Patriarch says the Litany of the Gospel. If it is the season of the Holy 50 Days, the psalm is "Mercy and Truth embraced each other. Righteousness and peace received each other. Truth shone froth from the Earth. Righteousness sought after the Heavens." Alleluia. Afterwards, the priest reads the Gospel in Coptic and a deacon interprets it in Arabic. The following response is said in the tune of the Cross: "Rejoice O bridal chamber adorned in various ways which is for the true bridegroom who united humanity." If the Patriarch is in attendance, they add, "Likewise we magnify you" but if not they proceed to "Intercede on our behalf" for the Virgin and after that, "Blessed is the Father".

Section 2

Then they say the three great litanies which are for peace, fathers, and congregations, followed by the Creed. They say Lord Have Mercy three times. The priest says Peace be to all then says the first litany fully in Coptic. They respond in the tune of "This is the time of blessing" with "Christ the Logos" and "Blessed is the Father." They say Lord Have Mercy three times. The priest says Peace be to all then says the second litany in Coptic. They respond with "As you gave your holy apostles" followed by "Blessed is the Father" and Lord Have Mercy three times. The priest says Peace be to all then says the third litany in Coptic. They respond with "My peace which I took" followed by "Blessed is the Father" and Lord Have Mercy three times. Then the priest says Peace be to all.

The fourth prayer is a prayer of thanksgiving. After it they say Our Father then the priest says "Yes O Lord." If the Patriarch attends, he says "You O Lord" and the Absolution of the Son. He raises the cross over the groom's head until the absolution finishes. He then removes the cross and they say Lord Have Mercy 43 times. Then the priest says Peace be to all. The godparent loosens the vestment and the patriarch or priest prays over it with its litany. He vests the groom with it and ties it with the cincture around the groom's waist. He covers the groom's head with the broad white cloth. He gives the groom the ring in his right hand. If the patriarch attends, then during the vesting of the groom, they sing in the tune of the cross, "The spiritual raiment… Pray to the Lord for the patriarch…You received the grace of Moses" until its end. The patriarch dons his clerical cap and reads the blessing. He blesses the groom then retires to rest while they begin singing this hymn. They depart with candles and cymbals to the house of crowning. If the patriarch is not attending, then "The spiritual raiment" is not said but rather they say "Come see this bride" and nothing else.

Section 3

When the priest enters the house of crowning, he takes the bride by herself to where the groom is seated. He commands the groom to put the ring upon which he contracted the crowning on her right ring finger. If she extends her hand and accepts the cross of the contract, then it is a sign that she is willing to take the groom to be her husband. Then the priest hands the bride to the groom and commands the godmother to present them to the masses. The bride stands at the right of the groom and they both cover their heads with the single broad white cloth. That is a testimony to those present of their union with each other. The white cloth is a manifestation of pure righteous union. This is the hymn sung during this time. It is a hymn to the true bride, the Theotokos: "Come see this bride adorned for the lamb. She is clothed in great glory, said the son of thunder. John the son of Zebedee cries out and says, This bride shines more brightly than the morning star. This is the new Zion, the city of our God, wherein is the gladness of all the saints. Blessed is the Father."

Section 4

If the patriarch chooses, he may put the phelonion on the priest who will perform the crowning. That is his prerogative and it is an honor to the groom. The priest starts with the Thanksgiving Prayer. He raises incense with the litany of the Pauline while they sing the Hymn of the Censer (Taishouri) followed by "We worship" followed by one more spoon of incense. The Pauline Epistle is read in Coptic then translated into Arabic. During that time the priest processes around the house of crowning with the incense. After the Pauline, the Trisagion is said followed by "Glory be to the Father" and the Litany of the Gospel. This Psalm is said, "Which is like a bridegroom..." and it is followed by the short annual Alleluia response. "Stand up" is said. The priest reads the gospel in Coptic and the serving deacon translates it in Arabic. This response is said in Adam tune, "Those whom the Holy Spirit attuned..We worship"

Section 5

Then they say Lord Have Mercy three times. The priest says the first three supplications in Coptic facing East. Then he says them again in Arabic from the beginning until he reaches the part where he says, "bless this marriage" after which he turns and faces West from here on. Whenever he says the name of the bride and groom, he signs them with the sign of the cross. They continue until he reaches, "O the compassionate." He says, "O the beneficent the great in mercy" facing East. They say Lord Have Mercy three times. Then he says the three great litanies: peace, fathers, congregations. Then they say the Creed.

They say Lord Have Mercy three times. The priest says, "Peace be to all" followed by the first prayer in Coptic facing East. If time permits, they say the following in the tune of "This is the time of blessing", "As David said in the psalm, 'The queen stood at the right hand of the king. Blessed is the Father." They say Lord Have Mercy three times. The second litany is said in Coptic followed by this verse in the same tune, "Solomon has called you in the Song of Songs My sister and my spouse my true city Jerusalem." They say Lord Have Mercy three times. The priest says the third prayer facing the West either in Coptic or Arabic. They respond with, "Do not forget the covenant...Blessed is the Father." They say Lord Have Mercy three times. The deacon says, "Bow your heads to the Lord." They respond with, "And with your spirit." The priest says the prayer of submission facing East. They respond in the same tune as before with, "May God bless us and let us bless...Blessed is the Father."

Section 6

They say Lord Have Mercy three times. The deacon says, "Let us pray to the Lord." They respond, "Lord Have Mercy." The priest prays over the oil containers. At the end of the prayer, he anoints the groom and bride while the people sing, "You have anointed" as previously explained. While they sing "You have anointed.", the priest rushes through the prayer after the anointing. Then he prays over the crowns. When they finish "You have anointed" he places the crowns over the heads of the groom and bride. This is what they say during the anointing, "You have anointed my head with oil and your cup intoxicated me. Your mercy shall seek me all the says of my life. All the peoples of the earth bless me. All the people say, may it be, may it be. Blessed is the Father."

Section 7

When the prayer of the crowns finishes, the priest puts the crown on the groom's head and says, "Glory and honor and a crown. The Father blesses. The Son crowns. The Holy Spirit perfects and completes. Worthy (3x) is the groom and his helpmate." The translation of this is, "You have crowned him with glory and honor. The Father blesses. The Son crowns. The Holy Spirit perfects and completes." They respond with Worthy three times in the same tune previously explained. Then the priest says these verses according to the custom of the Hanging Church and the majority of the other churches, "You received grace.. You received perfect crowns." Then one of the priests says these while they respond after each one with Worthy, "May He who blessed our father Adam..., May He who blessed Isaac..., May He who blessed our father Jacob..." Then he places the crown on the bride's head and says, "May He who blessed Abraham..., May He who blessed Isaac..., May He who blessed Jacob..., May He who blessed Michael..., May He who blessed our fathers the Apostles..., A crown of gold a crown of silver a crown of precious stone Alleluia Alleluia & Alleluia Glory be to our God." During that he says the prayer after the crowning to the Lord. When Worthy is finished, they say this with its tune, "Unfading crowns..., Illuminate Illuminate." They say Our Father and the priest says, "Yes O Lord" followed by "You O Lord" and the Absolution of the Son with the cross over the heads of the groom and bride and his hands placed crosswise as our father Jacob Israel blessed the sons of Joseph. After the Absolution of the Son, he says the commandment facing East until he finished with saying "unto the ages of ages, Amen." They say with the cymbals in its special tune, "My peace I give you" followed by "O King of Peace." The priest says, "The peace of our Lord Jesus Christ..." towards the West. Then he delivers the bride to the groom and commands him saying, "This is the time of blessing."

The priest says to the groom, "It behooves you O beloved brother, and blessed son..." until "may it be good to you in this world and the next." They respond saying, "Listen O daughter...All the glory of the king...Alleluia (3x) Glory be to our God." The priest says, "And you blessed and glad daughter" until the end of the commandment. They respond with Amen. The priest lifts the cross and they say Lord Have Mercy 43 times. They sing the canon of "Rejoice O groom" during which the priest says the blessing over the heads of the couple as in the case of the Absolution of the Son with his hands crosswise. Then he blesses the bride and bids her to sit and rest. Then he gives the groom the cross in his hand and stands him in the East. Then, holding candles, they sing before him, "Blessed is he who comes" and "Galilee of the Nations" while processing into the church until they reach the sanctuary.

Section 8

Then they begin the service of the Divine Liturgy whether the Patriarch is in attendance or not. If the groom is a deacon, and is prepared, he serves in the sanctuary and carries the chalice. The gospel response of the liturgy is the response of the Feast of Cana of Galilee, "Six jars of water.." When the liturgy concludes, they process the bride first to the doors of the church with "Rejoice O Mary". They have the groom stand at the door of the chorus and sing before him the him of "Blessed is he who comes" and after it "May God bless us" and if time permits, "Galilee of the Nations", until the doors of the church. After that, they return to their home in peace. May the Lord make it a blessed hour for them.

APPENDIX C

Translation of the Holy Synod's Decree

Building on the assignment of the Holy Synod in its previous session a detailed study of the Rite of the 'aqd al-amlāk and its relation with the Rite of Crowning and the Engagement Prayer in our Coptic Church, and with the comparison with similar rites in the Eastern Orthodox churches as the most ancient apostolic churches closest to us, and after researching the ancient rite of weddings in the Coptic manuscripts and the ancient Greek rite which continues with the two languages, Greek and Arabic, the following was revealed:

- The rite called 'aqd al-amlāk is more accurately translated 'arbūn of the marriage. It comes from the Greek word Arrabwna which is Aryb in Coptic. It is considered the engagement according to the ancient interpretation of our heritage.

- The inherited prayers of the 'arbūn of the marriage in the Greek Church do not include a reading of the Pauline epistle nor a Gospel reading, but fundamentally focus on the blessing of the two rings and their exchange and donning by the couple along with some other prayers like the 'arbūn of the wedding.

The committee orders that the rite of crowning be preceded by the rite of 'arbūn including the signing of the rings, the prayer of thanks, the special supplication for the 'arbūn, the prayer blessing the vestment, the hymn of the spiritual raiment, the putting on of the rings by the hand of priest and not by the couple themselves. Then the rite of crowning begins with the reading of the Pauline from Ephesians.

This is the order of the 'arbūn of the wedding ('aqd al-amlāk) and the holy crowning:

1. The three introductory signings: In the name of our God and Savior Jesus Christ…

2. The Thanksgiving Prayer followed by verses of the cymbals including the special verse for weddings

3. The prayer for the 'arbūn O God who created man with His hands (full text)

4. The prayer for the vestment O Master Lord Jesus Christ followed by Tiestoly

5. TiShouri, Tenouosht

6. Pauline Epistle from Ephesians

7. Continue the rite of crowning until reaching And now since you attended this Orthodox gathering (full text).

8. Continue the rite of crowning as usual

Appendix D

A Comparison Table of all the Versions of the Rite

Part 1 – The Vesting of the Groom

Ibn Kabar	Pope Gabriel	Heg Philotheos
	Groom enters with Eflogimenos	
	Bride enters side building with Shere ne Maria	
		Declarations
Thanksgiving Prayer	Thanksgiving Prayer	Thanksgiving Prayer
	Verses of Cymbals	
	Kyrie Eleison, Alleluia, Doxasi, Our Father	
Psalm 50	Psalm 50	
	Taishouri	Taishouri
	Pauline Incense	Pauline Incense

A Textual History of the Coptic Wedding Rite

Ibn Kabar	Pope Gabriel	Heg Philotheos
Pauline	Pauline	Pauline
	Trisagion	Trisagion
Gospel	Gospel	Gospel
	Gospel Response	Gospel Response
3 Great Litanies	3 Great Litanies	3 Great Litanies
Creed	Creed	Creed
	Kyrie Eleison 3x	
	Peace be to all	
O master and philanthropic one	O master and philanthropic one	O God who created
	Christ the Logos	Christ the Logos
	Je Efesmarouot	Je Efesmarouot
	Kyrie Eleison 3x	
	Peace be to all	
O God who created	O God who created	O master and philanthropic one
	As you have given	As you have given
	Je Efesmarouot	Je Efesmarouot

Ibn Kabar	Pope Gabriel	Heg Philotheos
	Kyrie Eleison 3x	
	Peace be to all	
O master lord god	O master lord god	O master lord god
	My peace which I have taken	My peace which I have taken
	Je Efesmarouot	Je Efesmarouot
	Kyrie Eleison 3x	
	Peace be to all	
We thank you o master lord	We thank you o master lord	We thank you o master lord
		May God bless us
		Je Efesmarouot
Our Father	Our Father	Our Father
Absolution of the Son (cross on groom's head)	Absolution of the Son (cross on groom's head)	Absolution of the Son (cross on groom's head)
Kyrie Eleison	Kyrie Eleison 43 times	Kyrie Eleison 3 times
	Peace be to all	
O Lord Jesus Christ	O Lord Jesus Christ	O Lord Jesus Christ

A Textual History of the Coptic Wedding Rite

Ibn Kabar	Pope Gabriel	Heg Philotheos
	Tiestoly 1 verse (if patriarch present) Pray to the Lord (patriarch) You received the grace of Moses in the concluding canon tune	Tiestoly 5 verses
Come see this bride in the same tune as Tiestoly	Come see this bride	

Part 2 – The Crowning

Ibn Kabar	Pope Gabriel	Heg Philotheos	Fr. Marcos	Albair Mikhail
Couple stand in front of sanctuary with white cloth over their heads	Couple stand in front of sanctuary with white cloth over their heads		Couple stand on the South side with nothing over their heads	Couple stand on the South side with white veil over their hands
Thanksgiving Prayer	Thanksgiving Prayer	Thanksgiving Prayer	Thanksgiving Prayer	Thanksgiving Prayer
Psalm 50				
	Taishouri	Tishouri	Taishouri	Taishouri
Pauline	Pauline	Pauline	Pauline	Pauline
			Piepnevma	Piepnevma

Ibn Kabar	Pope Gabriel	Heg Philotheos	Fr. Marcos	Albair Mikhail
	Trisagion	Trisagion	Trisagion	Trisagion
Gospel	Gospel	Gospel	Gospel	Gospel
Nai etafhotpou	Nai etafhotpou	Nai etafhotpou	Nai etafhotpou	Nai etafhotpou
	Tenouosht			
	Kyrie Eleison 3x			Kyrie Eleison 3x
	First 3 supplications facing East			
Supplications facing West	Next few supplications facing West	Supplications	Supplications	Supplications
	Remaining supplications facing East			
	Kyrie Eleison 3x			
		Christ the Logos	Christ the Logos	Christ the Logos
			Je Efesmarouot	Je Efesmarouot

A Textual History of the Coptic Wedding Rite

Ibn Kabar	Pope Gabriel	Heg Philotheos	Fr. Marcos	Albair Mikhail
				Kyrie Eleison 3x
3 Great Litanies	3 Great Litanies	3 Great Litanies	3 Great Litanies	3 Great Litanies
Creed	Creed	Creed	Creed	Creed
	Kyrie Eleison 3x			
	Peace be to all			
1st Mat Prayer	1st Mat Prayer	1st Mat Prayer	1st Mat Prayer	1st Mat Prayer
	As David said	As David said	As you have given	As you have given
	Je Efesmarouot	The door of the East	The door of the East	The door of the East
	Kyrie Eleison 3x			Kyrie Eleison 3x
	Peace be to all			
2nd Mat Prayer	2nd Mat Prayer	2nd Mat Prayer	2nd Mat Prayer	2nd Mat Prayer

Ibn Kabar	Pope Gabriel	Heg Philotheos	Fr. Marcos	Albair Mikhail
		My peace which I have taken	My peace which I have taken	My peace which I have taken
		All the kings of the earth		Je Efesmarouot
	Solomon called you	Solomon called you		
			Je Efesmarouot	
	Kyrie Eleison 3x			Kyrie Eleison 3x
3rd Mat Prayer	3rd Mat Prayer	3rd Mat Prayer	3rd Mat Prayer	3rd Mat Prayer
	Do not forget	Do not forget	Do not forget	Do not forget
		O the angel	O the angel	O the angel
		You're brighter than the sun		
	Je Efesmarouot		Je Efesmarouot	Je Efesmarouot
	Kyrie Eleison 3x			Kyrie Eleison 3x

A Textual History of the Coptic Wedding Rite

Ibn Kabar	Pope Gabriel	Heg Philotheos	Fr. Marcos	Albair Mikhail
	Bow heads to the Lord			
	And with your spirit			
Submission Prayer	Submission Prayer	Submission Prayer	Submission Prayer	Submission Prayer
	May God bless us	May God bless us	May God bless us	May God bless us
	Je Efesmarouot	Je Efesmarouot	Je Efesmarouot	Je Efesmarouot
	Kyrie Eleison 3x			Kyrie Eleison 3x
	Let us pray to the Lord			
	Lord Have Mercy			
Oil Prayer	Oil Prayer	Oil Prayer	Oil Prayer	Oil Prayer
		May this oil destroy demons	May this oil destroy demons	May this oil destroy demons
		Je Efesmarouot	Je Efesmarouot	Je Efesmarouot

Ibn Kabar	Pope Gabriel	Heg Philotheos	Fr. Marcos	Albair Mikhail
You have anointed 5 verses	You have anointed 2 verses	You have anointed 5 verses	You have anointed 1 verse	You have anointed 1 verse
		Je Efesmarouot	Je Efesmarouot	Je Efesmarouot
				Kyrie Eleison 3x
Crowns Prayer	Crowns Prayer	Crowns Prayer	Crowns Prayer	Crowns Prayer
			Deacon: Place the crowns O priest of Emmanuel	Deacon: Place the crowns O priest of Emmanuel
				Axios
		Priest: Place O Lord on your servants	Priest: Place O Lord on your servants	Priest: Place O Lord on your servants
		White cloth placed over heads		
Crown them O Father	Crown them O Father	Crown them O Father	Crown them O Father	Crown them O Father
			Khen Efran	Khen Efran

A Textual History of the Coptic Wedding Rite

Ibn Kabar	Pope Gabriel	Heg Philotheos	Fr. Marcos	Albair Mikhail
Axios	Axios	Axios	Axios	Axios
	You received verses			You received verses Slightly different from Pope Gabriel's
Fietaf verses	Fietaf verses			Fietaf verses
	Oueklom nnoub			
	Al, Al, ke Al. Pioou fa pennouti pe			
Haneklom	Haneklom 2 verses	Haneklom 4 verses	Haneklom 4 verses	Haneklom 4 verses
Priest: Place O Lord on your servants	silently			
Our Father	Our Father	Our Father	Our Father	
Absolution	Absolutions with hands over couple	Absolutions with hands over couple	Absolutions	
		Fietaf verses	Fietaf verses	
Glory to God	Glory to God	Glory to God		

Ibn Kabar	Pope Gabriel	Heg Philotheos	Fr. Marcos	Albair Mikhail
		Nisherobim	Nisherobim	Nisherobim
		Ekouab	Ekouab	Ekouab
My peace which I have taken	My peace which I have taken			
	O King of Peace			
The peace of our master	The peace of our master	The peace of our master	The peace of our master	The peace of our master
			You have been crowned	
			Kyrie Eleison 3x	
		My peace which I have taken		
Efnav empismou	Efnav empismou			
		And now since you have attended	And now since you have attended	And now since you have attended

A Textual History of the Coptic Wedding Rite

Ibn Kabar	Pope Gabriel	Heg Philotheos	Fr. Marcos	Albair Mikhail
			Receive O bridegroom	Receive O bridegroom
			Kyrie Eleison 3x	Kyrie Eleison 3x
		O King of Peace		
It behooves you	It behooves you	It behooves you	It behooves you	It behooves you
Sotem tasheri	Sotem tasheri	Sotem tasheri		
	Epou tirf em empouro			
	Alleluia, Alleluia, ke Alleluia. Pioou fa pennouti pe			
		Sotem o tishelet	Listen O bride	Listen O bride
			Kyrie Eleison 3x	Kyrie Eleison 3x
And you blessed daughter	And you blessed daughter	And you blessed daughter	And you blessed daughter	And you blessed daughter

Ibn Kabar	Pope Gabriel	Heg Philotheos	Fr. Marcos	Albair Mikhail
			A pure marriage	A pure marriage
			Kyrie Eleison 3x	Kyrie Eleison 3x
		O King of Peace		
		Likewise May God bless both of you	Likewise May God bless both of you	Likewise May God bless both of you
				You have been crowned
		Efnav empismou 1 verse		
		And unto Him we ask	And unto Him we ask	And unto Him we ask
Kyrie Eleison	Kyrie Eleison 43x	Kyrie Eleison 1x		
		Our Father	Our Father	Our Father
			Absolution	Absolution
Concluding Canon	Concluding Canon	Concluding Canon	Concluding Canon	Concluding Canon

APPENDIX E
A Wedding Sermon by Hegumen Philotheos Ibrahim

This is a sermon written by Hegumen Philotheos Ibrahim that may be said during the wedding or during the post-wedding liturgy. The English translation is my own.

If during the wedding, after the readings, the supplications, and the crowning, or during the removal of the crowns, it is desired to give a sermon and nobody present is able to give a sermon of their own creation, then this sermon may be said. It is specific to marriage and is composed by the weak Hegumen Philotheos.	اذا أريد وقت الاكليل بعد نهاية الفصول المقدسة و الطلبات و وضع الأكاليل على رؤوس العرسان أو وقت التجلسة تلاوة خطبة أخرى علاوة على ما هو مقرر في الترتيب و لم يكن خطيب يلقي من ذاته خطبة خصوصية فلتنقل هذه الخطبة المختصة الاكليل و هي من قلم الحقير الاغومانس فيلوثاؤس
Glory to He who betrothed His mysterious Church as a pure virgin bride to the joys of eternal life, establishing in His kingdom brilliant happiness, and appointed her companionship in superb standing. Her memory is exceeded above all creation by the blood of the Only-Begotten Word, the Creator, Who acquitted her from her burden through His crucifixion, Who freed her from her imprisonment, Who crowns her with a crown of grace bejeweled with the pearl of His illuminating faith, Who dignifies her years with the lamp of judgement, Who makes her glisten	مجدا لمن خطب بيعته السرية كعروس عذراء طاهرة لافراح الحياة الابدية في ملكوته مقر السعادة الباهرة و عين صداقها قيمة فائقة يعلو خطرها شأن الكائنات بأسرها دم الوحيد الكلمة المتجسدة الخالقة من برها بصلبه من وزرها و حررها من أسرها مكللا اياها بتاج النعم مرصعا بلألئ ايمانه الانور مجللا سناها بنبراس الحكم ساطعا بفرائد فرائض دينه الازهر متحفها باسرار شرعه حرز الكمال الامين منقفها بارشاد انجيله كنز الهدى للمقتدين مروفقا عرسها بمواكب أعاجيبه المدهشة و آياته الغراء و معجزاته الخارقة مطربا أسماعها بنغمات ناموسه المنعسة مبشرا لها بجناته الخالدة الرائقة الى أن

with the unique duties of His blossoming religion, Who surrounds her with the mysteries of His law, Who protects the faithful perfection, Who educates her by the guidance of His Gospel, the treasure of direction for His followers, Who accompanies her wedding with processions of His astonishing wonders, His honorable sayings, and His marvelous miracles, Who fills her ears with the melodious tunes of His invigorating law, Who preaches to her about His magnificent everlasting paradise until she arrives at the celebration of the blessed glory, surrounded by the signs of hope that are associated with the beauty of Heavenly love, in a wedding procession to the vast residence of the King, that she may enjoy the sight of her most holy Bridegroom, the object of her faith and the result of her hope, Who appears in His incarnate form, the point of return of her happiness and the target of her drawing near. There the shouts of joy and cheer ring against her ears, before which the Heavenly shake with joy and glorification. To the bride Come, hurry, inherit the kingdom prepared before the ages. Take pleasure in what no eye has seen nor an ear heard nor description defined. To Him be the thanks for what He bestowed upon us from the greatness of His favor and the instruments of direction and for what He prepared for us from the honors of His mercies and the pride of His generosity.	تبلغ باحتفال المجد الطوباوى محفوفة بأعلام الرجاء مقرونة بجمال الحب السماوى مزفوفة لمقام الملك الواسع الارجاء لتحفظي بمرأى عريسها الاقدس غاية أمانيها و نهاية آمالها مساهدا بهيئة لتأنس الانفس نقطة دائرة سعادتها وكمال اقبالها و هنا لك يطرق أسماعها هتاف البهجة والحبور يهتز له العلوين فرحا و تمجيدا هيا رئي ملكا أعد قبل الدهور تمتعي بما لم تره عين و لم تسمع به أذن و لم يكن وصفه محدودا له الحمد على ما تكرم به علينا من عظائم المنن و وسائل الهدى و ما أعده الينا من كرائم المراحم و نفاخر الندى
O eminent lords, children of the true faith, members of the noble Church, the first among the shining honorable, our day today is a joyous day. Its	أيها السادة الاجلاء أبناء الامانة الحقة أعضاء البيعة النبلا أولو المكارم المشرفة أن يومنا هذا يوم سعيد

aroma is fragranced with the expression of grace. It is granted the breezes of the New Testament. On it flow the rains of prosperity from the heaven of wisdom. For those who live through it, it is a day of blessing from the Master the Savior. It shines with the pleasure of our God. It is a day prepared for a joyous festival and glad celebration for the union of a branch of goodness with a twig of righteousness bearing the honorable fruit of purity and faithfulness according to the religious texts that testify to the dignity of the Sacrament of Matrimony. Its announcement is summed by the esteem of spiritual fathers, first in piety and holiness, and completed by the shining of exalted faces of glory and leadership. It is glamoured by the tunes of the chanters and deacons, the righteous servants of the mysteries of the Most High, who sound in our ears holy poems that depict in our minds the praises of the angels of glory and honor, and Biblical verses that discipline lazy attitudes, and apostolic voices that guide elders and youth. All are with peaceful hearts that boast in the glistening lights, and with lips fragrant with beautiful prayers, and sincere connections circumscribed by the rests of the supplication for the pouring down of the exalted majesty, caught in the heavy rain of the downpour of blessing and virtues from the honor of the great Divine presence that it may come upon this amiable bridegroom and his favorable bride, {{Groom}} the precious virgin and {{Bride}} the safeguarded virgin.

تعطرت أرائحه بعبيرا النعمة وهبت عليه نسمات العهد الجديد و تدفقت فيه غيوث المين من سماء الحكمة يوم تمين محياه بمنن السيد الفادي و تلألأ بدرسناه بانبساط الهنا الفوادي يوم أعد لمهرجان الافراح و احتفال السرور باقتران غصن الصلاح قرع التقا المبرور بثمرة الطهارة و الامانة كريمة الشرف الاثيل طبقا لنصوص الديانة الشاهدة بسمو سر الاكليل فناديه بمجمل بتشريف أباء روحيين أولى ورع و قداسة م مكمل باشراق وجوه معظمين ذوى مج ورئاسة و مرونق بنغمات المرتلين و السمامسة خلدمي أسرار العلي باستقامة المطر بين الاسماع بأناشيد مقدسة ترسم في الاذهان تسابيح ملائكة المجد و الكرامة و آيات الانجيلية تذكي فتور الالباب و أصوات رسولية ترشد الكهول و الشباب و الكل بأفئدة تسليمه تزهو على الاضواء الساطعة و أفواه معطرة بأدعية و سيمه و توسلات مخلصة متتابعه باسطون واحات الابتهال نحو جود العزة العليا مستمطرين وابل اليمن و الافضال من كرم الحضرة الالهية العظمى لتحل على ذاتي العريس الانيس و عروسته الميمونة (فلان) البكر النفيس و (فلانة) البتول المصونة

The chanters respond saying Amen three times	يجاوب المرتلون قائلين آمين ثلاث مرات
O noble son, accept the gift of your Master with a cheerful chest. Receive her with praise and great thanks, joyous thought, and a happy face. Consider the sacrament of lawful marriage as an honorable rank and status, wondrous in comparison, as explained by the honorable passage in the apostolic text clarifying this precious analogy, "For the husband is the head of the wife as Christ is the head of the Church" (Eph 5:23). Notice this amazing measurement and consider its honor. Keep this pure mystery. Magnify it. Honor it. Remember, the crowns with which the bride and groom were crowned are indicators of the preservation of their virginity, symbols of their adherence to the principles of the faith, their virtuous proper conduct, and their sublime excellence. So receive O noble one this grace with feelings of appreciation and thanks for the majesty of He who granted us his delightful mysteries and furnished us with the path of happiness and glory. Know that the groom was called the head of his bride, and that the two become one flesh, that he may whisper unto her with his wisdom, and act with her in the position of a distinguished administrator. For the woman was created from the rib of man that his desire may be affectionate toward her, knowing that he is united with her. The way to achieve that desire is to take care of her affairs until the end. So take pleasure O beloved with your bride, with foresight and principle, and plan	فتقبل أيها الابن النبيل آلاء سيدك بصدر منشرح و قابلها بحمد و شكر جليل و فكر بهيج و وجه فرح و اعتبر أن سر الزواج الشرعي شريف القدر و القيمة عجيب في التمثيل الوضعي بحسب الآية الكريمة اذ أعلن النص الرسولي عنع مصرحا بهذه المماثلة النفيسة لان الرجل هو رأس المرأة كما أن المسيح هو رأس الكنيسة فلاحظ هذا القياس الفاخر و اعتبر شرفه و حافظ على هذا السر الطاهر و عززه و شرفه و اذكر ان الإكليل الذي تتوج به العرسان انما هو عنوان حفظ البكورية و دلالة الاعتصام بقواعد الايمان، و التصرف بالآداب الفاضلة و المزايا السنية فتلق أيها النجيب هذه المنة بشعائر الثناء و الحمد لعزة من أتحفنا بأسراره الحسنى و مهد لنا سبيل السعادة و المجد و اعلم ان العريس ما دعى رأسا لعروسته و انهما يكونان كجسد واحد الا لأن يسوقها بحكمته و يستسير معها سير المدبر الماجد على أن المرأة ما جبلت من ضلع الرجل الا ليكون عطوفا بها للغاية علما بأن اتحاده وإياها متصل و ماسبيله الا الرأفة بشأنها للنهاية فسر أيها العزيز مع عروستك بفطنة و سياسة و تدبر معها بحكمتك تدبير أولي النهى و الرئاسة أعن معها بشؤونها الاعتناء الجميل عين اعتنائك بنفسك و اذكر أن النساء أناء ضئيل فعاملها بحملك و أنسك أغرس في جنانها قواعد الدين و شرائط الايمان المسيحي القويم أسس في ذهنها صفات الكاملات و حل سجاياها بالذوق السليم تصرف معها تصريف الكملاء فانها مشاركتك في حالتي الفقر و الغنى و كن في اكرامها حكيما فضلا فتنال معها غاية المنا و اعلم انها موعودة مثلك اذا سارت سيرة حميدة بان تحظى بالنعيم معك و تحيا الحياة السعيدة (آمين)

with her in your wisdom a plan from beginning to end as the leader. Pay attention to her needs with beautiful care. Prioritize the attention yourself. Remember that women are meager vessels so treat her with patience and amiability. Implant within her the foundations of our religion and the details of the sound Christian faith. Establish in her mind the characteristics of the perfect and respond to her attitude with gentle manners. Cooperate with her, for she is your companion in poverty and wealth. Be wise and virtuous in honoring her so that you may attain with her the goal of life. Know that, like you, she is obligated, having chosen the thankful path of living joyfully with you. May you both live a happy life. Amen.

And you O chaste daughter, she of the righteous origins, the blessed and honored fruit, she of the splendid measure, congratulations for the grace of your eminent Savior with whose splendor you enjoyed. Consider the blessing of the sacrament of matrimony through which you were crowned. Remember that woman was created for man to be his helpmate and assistant, looking after him in all things, being gracious to him forever and ever. Take note of the history of the perfect chaste women, and how they acted with their husbands in obedience and submission, distinguishing themselves in their ways and appearance. So be continually with your virtuous groom in love, agreeableness, meekness, good judgement, perfect courtesy, and respect with love and obedience. Take

و أنت أيتها الابنة العفيفة ذات الاصول الزكية الثمرة المباركة الشريفة ذات المزايا البهية تهني بنعمة فاديك الجليل التي تحليتي ببهائها و اعتبري بركة سر الإكليل التي توجتي بسنائها واذكري أن المرأة ما جبلت من جانب الانسان الا لتكون له عضدا و ساعدا قائمة بصوالحه في كل شأن مشفقة عليه دائما أبدا لاحظي تاريخ النساء العفيفات الكاملات كيف كن مع أزواجهن طائعات خاضعات مصافيات في سرهن و ظاهرهن فكوني دائما مع عريسك الفاضل بحب و أنس و وداعة و تدين و تهذب كامل و احترام بمحبة و طاعة لاحظي شؤونه ببصيرة سلمية حافظي على حقوقه محافظة مستديمة تذكري التعليم الرسولي الذي ينير القلب لتخضع النساء لرجالهن كما للرب و اعلمي ان هذا الخضوع المقصود لا يتم الا بالضمير النقي و الحب السليم المحمود و الود الخالص التقي خضوعا بنشاط و سرور مقرونا بيسر

note of his affairs with a sound vision. Preserve his rights continually. Recall the apostolic teaching that illuminates the heart, "Wives, submit to your husbands, as to the Lord" (Eph 5:22). Know that this intended submission is not accomplished except with a pure conscience, praiseworthy perfect love, completely godly friendliness, active cheery submission coupled with good behavior, and righteous true judgement in both private and public. Be confident that acting in these ways will take you to goodness and excellence, and let you attain the eminent victory and happiness upon its realization. Amen.	حسن و تدين حقيقي مبرور في السر و العلن و ثقي ان سلوك هذا السبيل سيكون موصلا للخير و التوفيق مبلغا للفوز الجليل بسعادة الحالة على التحقيق (آمين)
Know O beloved couple that when you become one and unite, and walk in the ways of righteousness and goodness, you will reap what you sow from the inheritance of abundance, you will overflow with blessings, you will rejoice with grace, you will have a multitude of the best characteristics among the greatest of the nations, you will win what the divine revelation promised the godly man, "Your wife shall be like a vine in the doors of your house, your children like olive branches all around your table" (Ps 128:3). Amen.	و اعلما أيها العزيزان انكما اذا تحاببتما و تألفتما و سلكتما طرق السداد و الصلاح ستحصدان مما غرستما ثمرات الخير و الفلاح و تغمران بالبركات و تتنتعان بالنعم و تنعتان بحسن الصفات بين أكبر الأمم و تفوزان بما وعد به الوحي الرجل التقي هكذا امرأتك تكون مثل كرمة مخصبة في جانب بيتك و بنوك مثل غروس الزيتون حول مائدتك (آمين)
And behold, we send up the greatest supplication to our Lord and Creator, and beseech our Savior and Life-Giver, that He may complete our joy with the granting of happiness and perfection, and that He grant you that which you desire from the hoped-for beneficence, and grant you the beautiful excellence, and a long happy life, that He may pour upon you	و ها نحن نرفع أكف الضراعة لمولانا و بارينا و نبسط راحات التوسل لفادينا و محيينا ان يتمم فرحكما بانبساط الهناء و الكمال و يبلغكما مرادكما من الخيرات غاية الآمال و يمنحكما التوفيق الجميل و العمر الهنى المديد و يصب عليكما الرزق المبارك الجزيل و الاسم الصالح السعيد و يزرع في قلبكما محبة سليمة متبادلة و مودة مستديمة كاملة و لتكونا كشجرة مثمرة المزايا زاهية

overflowing blessed sustenance, a good happy name, and may he instill in your hearts requited sound love, and perfect continuous affection. May you both be like a fruitful tree gleaming with fortunate descendants, growing in politeness and good qualities, protected by His well-guarded oversight. May He shield you from all envy and division and guard you from adversity and tribulation. May He keep you in quiet and orderliness encompassed by companionship and abundance. May He bless you as He blessed the first fathers and confirm you in the true faith, walking in the path of godliness and victory, inheriting the exalted joy.	بنسل ميمون نام بالأداب و حسن السجايا محروس برعايته مصون و ليقيكما بفضله من كل حسد و انقسام و يصنكما من المحن و الآفات و يدمكما في هدؤ و انتظام محفوفين بالرفاهة و الخيرات و يبارككما كما بارك الآباء الأولين و يثبتكما في روض الامانة الحقة سالكين في التقوى سبيل الفائزين مؤهلين للسعادة الفائقة
O God, as You blessed and sanctified the Wedding at Cana of Galilee, bless and sanctify O Master the contract/marriage of this eminent crowning. And keep for us the leadership and continued peace of our holy father, our eldest shepherd, our great father the patriarch. And keep the rest of the ranks of entrusted priests, and the blessed children of the Church. O God, honor us with the joyful victory with happiness in Your eternal kingdom, for Yours is the glory with the Good Father and the Holy Spirit, One God, Eternal and Immortal. Amen.	اللهم كما باركت و قدست عرس قانا الجليل بارك و قدس أيها السيد عقد هذا الاكليل الجليل و احفظ لنا رئاسة و دوام سلامة غبطة سيدنا الطوباني راعينا الاكبار الأب البطريرك المعظم و أدم بقاء مصاف الكهنة المؤتمنين و حضرات أبناء البيعة المباركين تكرم اللهم علينا بالفوز السعيد بالفرح في ملكوتك الابدي لك المجد مع الآب الصالح و الروح القدس الاله الواحد الازلي السرمدي آمين